Vintage Life

ENCYCLOPEDIA
OF
INSPIRATION

UPPERCASE

TEXTILES BY MELANIE HILL, SUITCASE PHOTO BY FRENCH GENERAL

UPPERCASE PUBLISHING INC
201B – 908, 17TH AVENUE SW
CALGARY, ALBERTA, CANADA T2T 0A3

©2019 UPPERCASE
PUBLISHING INC

This book may not be reproduced
in any manner without written
permission, except for review
purposes. You are welcome to
share photos of this book
in your life on Instagram:
#encyclopediaofinspiration
#uppercasevintagelife
@uppercasemag

All art copyright belongs to
the artists and photographers.

WRITING
& DESIGN
JANINE
VANGOOL

COPYEDITING
CORREY
BALDWIN

PRINTED IN CANADA BY THE PROLIFIC GROUP

AESTHETICS, OBSESSIONS
and ARTISTIC PURSUITS

Vintage Life

Living in the Past

encyclopediaofinspiration.com
uppercasemagazine.com

ARTWORK BY AMY DUNCAN

VINTAGE LIFE

Contents

INTRODUCTION

In one way or another, most of my creative endeavours are influenced by a love of old things. A personal obsession with typewriters led to researching and writing a book on the subject. An appreciation of vintage textiles? I published a book entitled *Feed Sacks*. Vintage typography and gorgeous old graphics? You'll find that in *Ephemera*.

The people profiled within the pages of *Vintage Life* have immersed themselves in the aesthetics, technologies and trends of bygone eras. Vintage sellers, collectors, decorators, stylists, writers, musicians, artists, designers and other creative old souls. And in the same way that they collect vintage artifacts, clothing and furniture, I collect inspiration from these items, not to furnish a home, style a photo or decorate a retail shop, but rather to populate the pages of books.

Publishing an Encyclopedia of Inspiration is a throwback to another era, to a time when the news was on paper and print materials were sources of knowledge and entertainment—rather than the digital devices now consuming our attention.

Jenine Vangol

STYLE

The White Pepper Vintage
Christina Gerstner 8

Cartolina
Fiona Richards
& Doug Jones 18

Long Hill Carriage
Annie & Chris Stanford 28

The Crafty Squirrel
Morgan Wills 38

Lara Rossignol 50

Pauliina Pitkänen 58

French General
Kaari Meng & Jon Zabala 68

The Linen Garden
Vicky Trainor 78

Magpie Ethel
Laurie Romanaggi 86

Junk Bonanza
Ki Nassauer 96

Squirrel Vintage Shop
Ruth Rosenfield 106

Vintage Rose Girl
Eliza Schneider-Green 116

Bésame Cosmetics
Gabriela Hernandez 130

No Accounting for Taste
Jessica Parker 138

Patti Blau 146

Sydney Crabaugh 156

This Victorian Life
Sarah & Gabriel Chrisman.. 166

Stepback
Robin Muxlow
& Chris Switzer 174

Artistry Engraving
Philip Gattuso 182

Theatre of Dreams
Wendy Addison 190

Tinsel Trading
Marcia Ceppos 200

Donna Flower Vintage 206

Stitched and Found
Hannah Kelly 214

The Floyd Country Store
Dylan Locke
& Heather Krantz 222

A. Goodwin Signwriting
Amy Goodwin 228

ARTISTS, MAKERS, CREATORS

Vintage Bead Jewellery
Kateri Morton 238

Tin Patchwork
Kim Fox 242

New Old Books
Gina Johnson 246

Cherished China
Paige Smith 250

Curated Collections
Deborah Humphries 256

Artistic Artifacts
Nancy Callahan 260

Collages of the Past
Amy Duncan 264

Upcycled Accessories
Chrissy Smith 270

Analogue Photography
Colleen Rauscher 274

Wet Plate Photography
Rainika Photographik 278

VINTAGE LIFE

Contents

Textile Allsorts
Melanie Hill 284

Ephemeral Artwork
Nell Nordlie 290

Renewed Bowls
Julie Wons. 296

Dish Watching
Chanel Martineau. 300

Shadow Boxes
Jessica Jewett. 302

Handkerchief Vases
Andrea Christie. 306

Toys as Sculpture
Chris Theiss 310

Imagination at Play
Claudia Verhelst 314

Non-Traditional Books
Margaret Suchland. 318

Nostalgic Knits
Antonia Sullivan. 322

Layers of Memory
Sara Sandler 326

Sheets of Style
Thouraya Battye 330

Threads of Ideas
Camille Esposito 334

Floral Doilies
Lori Siebert 338

Found Photos
Clare Etheridge. 342

Paper Searches
Sydney Rose 346

Collaged Quilts
Shari Seltzer 350

Watchful Sources
Lisa Wine. 354

Monoprinted
Undergarments
Rose Deler. 358

New Art History
Cabaret Typographie. 364

Rubber Stamps
Ilene Kalish 368

OBJECT OBSESSIONS

Bakelite Bangles
Nancy Gary Ward 372

Cameras
Eileen Schramm. 374

Poster Stamps
Niko Courtelis 376

Postage Stamps
Laura Capp
& Esméralda Jönsson 378

Shop Class Art
Kristin Bickal 382

Chocolate Box Bindings
Sharon Pattison 384

Old Books
Lori Siebert 386

Vintage Clothing
Kiki Stash 388

Crochet Hangers
Kerrie More 390

Crochet Potholders
Nancy Myers 392

Dachshunds!
Joanna Jerome 394

Anthropomorphic Egg Cups
Sandy Machado 396

Enamelware & Tinware
Sher Hackwell 400

Greetings & Gift Wrap
Lisa Andrade 402

Handkerchiefs
Barb Brown 404

Sewing Stuff
Erika Mulvenna. 408

Picnic Tins
Susan Borgen 412

Stout Jugs & Creamers
Cynthia Boyd 414

Pottery, Plates & More
Emily Thompson 416

Street Nameplates
George Wright 422

Sewing Ducks
Nancy Johnston 424

Souvenir Plates
Snowden Flood 426

Tatting Shuttles
Dorothy A. Cochran 428

Tea Towels
Cindy Funk 430

Tiny Toy Televisions
Jane Housham 434

Santas
Jean Cameron 436

Aprons
Carolyn Terry 438

Pyrex
Jacqueline Goring. 442

Millinery Florals & Birds
Katie Baker 444

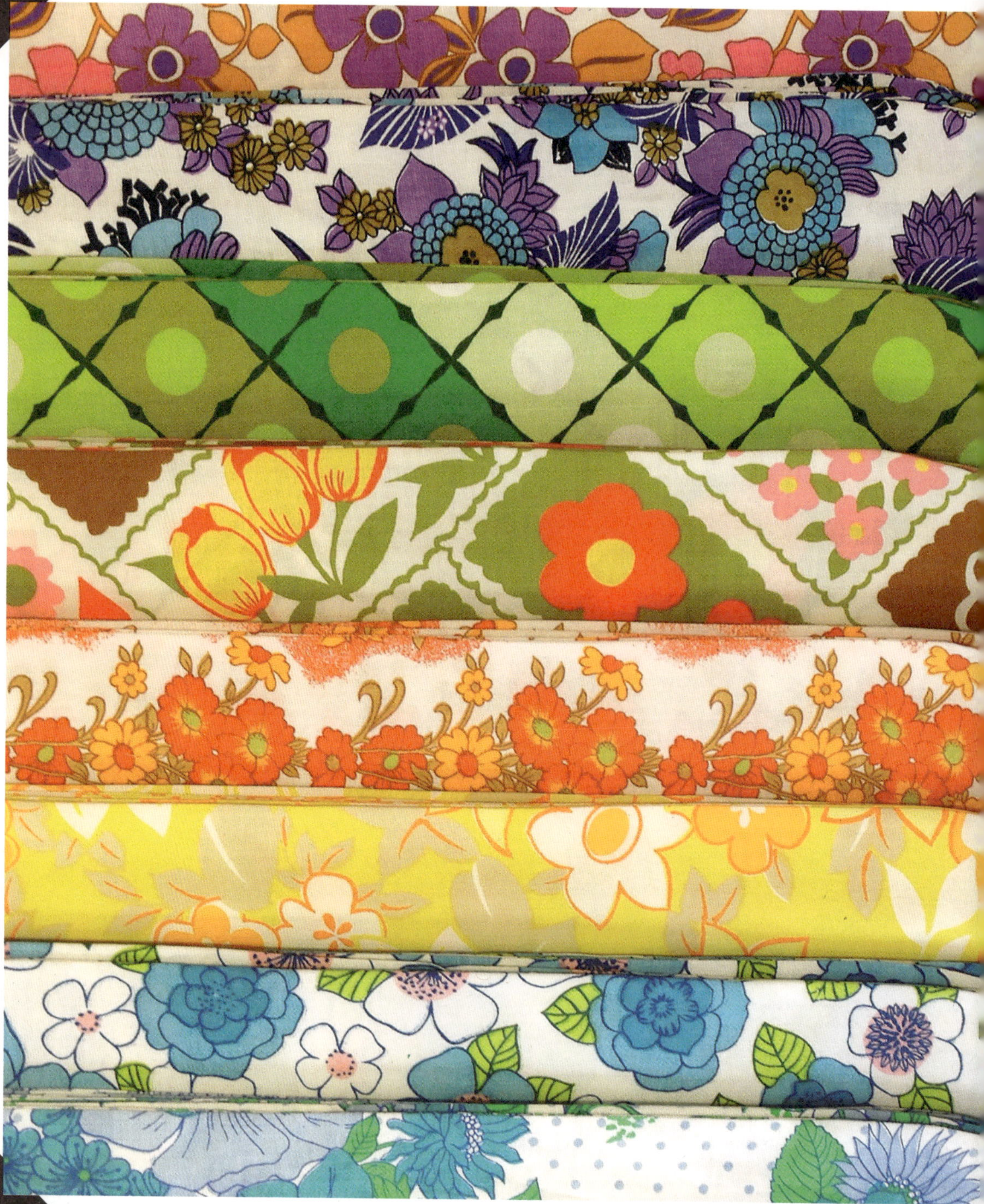

Style

PHOTO BY MORGAN WILLS

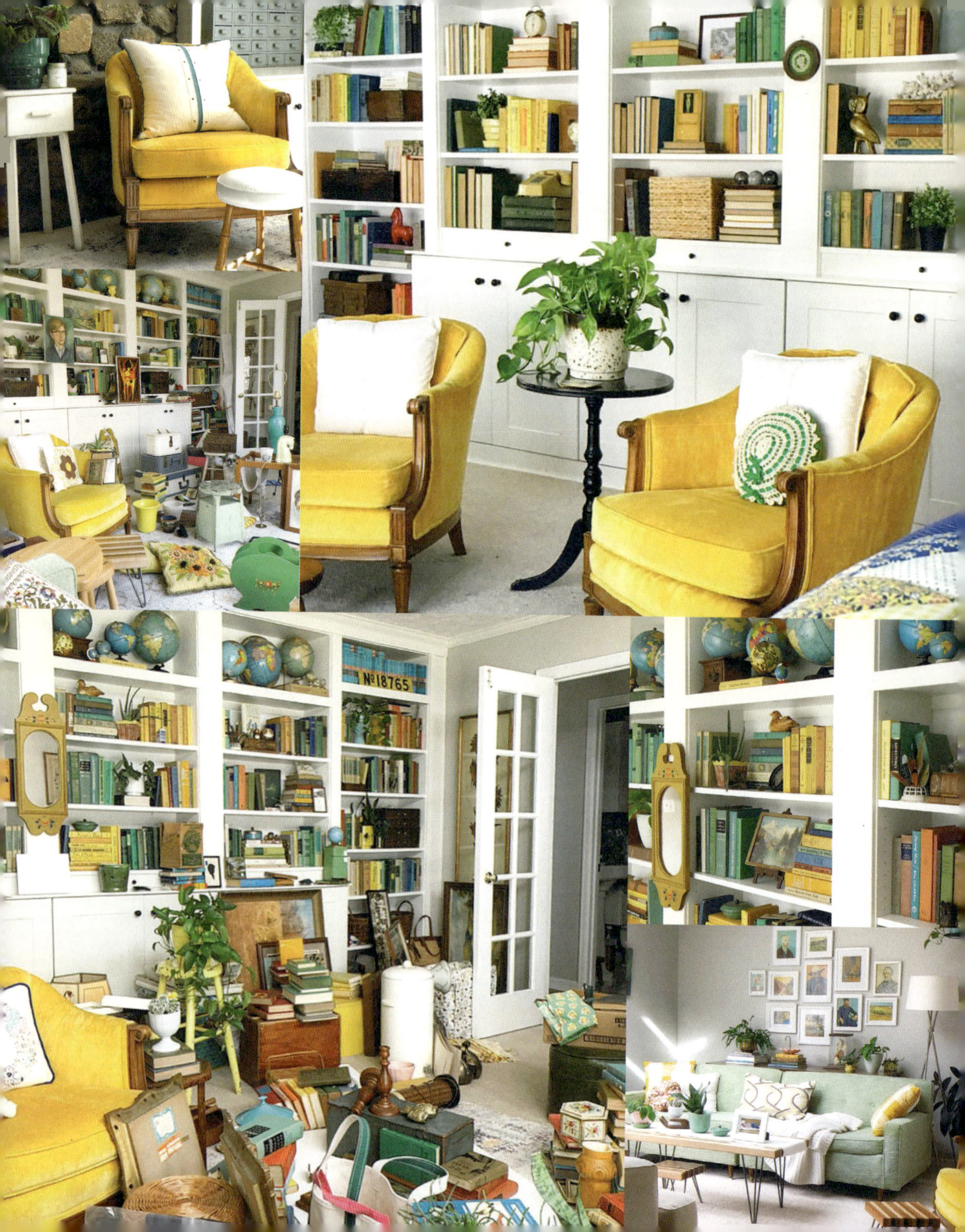
Nº18765

VINTAGE SELLER

The White Pepper Vintage

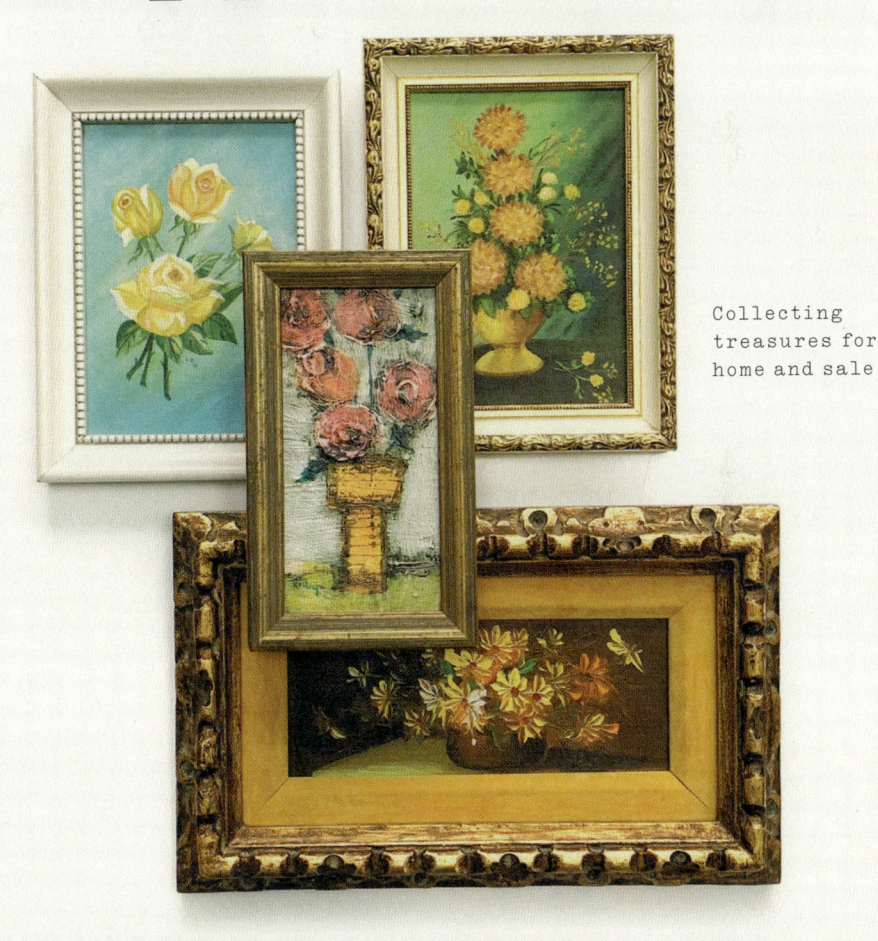

Collecting
treasures for
home and sale

CHRISTINA GERSTNER

"For me, yellow is one of the more cheerful and invigorating colours. It tends to lift my spirits and encourage contentedness. I like to pair it with white or subdued shades of blue and green in order to let it really stand out."

When Christina Gerstner of Forest, Virginia, became a mother, she also became something else. "I'm a former Montessori school teacher, turned professional treasure hunter," she explains. "For as long as I can remember, I have loved all things vintage, especially items from the '40s and '60s. When my son Orion was born, I became a stay-at-home mom and found myself with extra time on my hands. I needed a hobby, and I had a surplus of unused vintage items, so I started selling on Etsy."

She never expected that buying and selling vintage would evolve into a 40-hour-a-week job, but thanks to her keen eye and photography skills, her shop took off in a matter of months. "By the time Orion was school age, I didn't even consider returning to teaching but chose instead to work for myself and remain fully dedicated to the hunt. Now here we are, seven years later, and most of my time is spent thrifting and reselling."

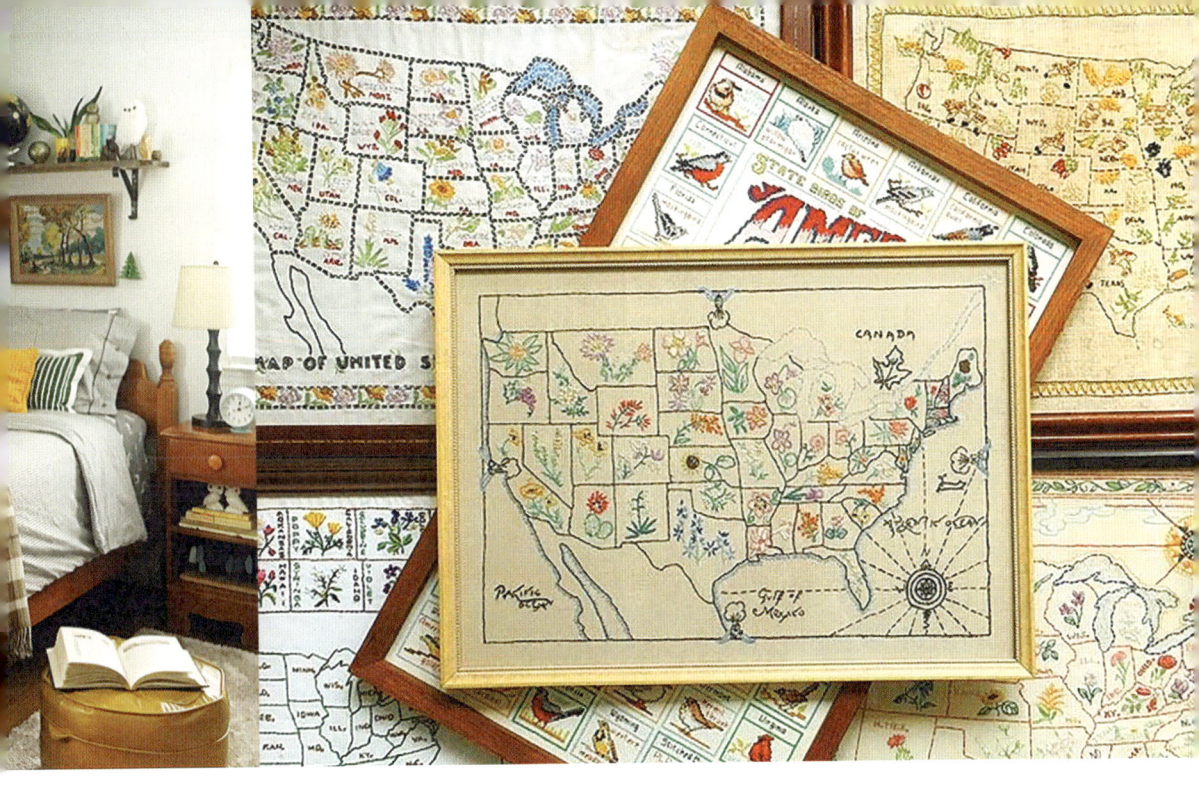

The conveniences of modern technology and social media have played a large part in the success of The White Pepper Vintage. On Instagram, she posts appealing images of her vintage hauls being sorted in her living room, giving customers a tantalizing peek into what will be for sale next. "It has enabled me to become a seller and a sharer of my passions," she says. "Being able to showcase my collections via social media has allowed me to connect with like-minded individuals and meet up with folks who understand my love for vintage without any explanation."

"Vintage living has become my hobby and my profession. I'm fortunate to have been able to turn a passion into a job that I enjoy. I love hunting for old treasures and sharing them with others. The only downside to loving it so much is that I end up keeping more than I should!" ❖

WHITE PEPPER VINTAGE 11

VINTAGE LIFE

"Collecting is my passion. Whether it be vintage nature books (anything related to birds, flowers and trees), colourful vintage pottery, hand-embroidered maps or vintage art, I am there for it. It's always so exciting to find what I've been hunting for and add it to my collection."

WHITE PEPPER VINTAGE

SMALL TREASURES

I have found so many wonderful treasures over the years, but the one that I love most is a vintage oil painting that I found when my husband and I were on a trip to France. We spent the day roaming the aisles and stalls of Paris' Les Puces de Saint-Ouen and it's not an exaggeration to say that wanted to buy it all. There were stacks upon stacks of antique paintings, small bric-a-brac, vintage jewellery and so much beautiful furniture. I only had a small amount of space in my suitcase, though, so I had to be choosy. I found several small items but had my heart set on finding an original painting to remember the trip by. Near the end of the day, I had almost given up hope, but at the last minute I wandered over to a table near the entrance and saw a small floral painting leaning against a wall. It wasn't exactly what I was looking for, but the size was right so I haggled a bit and ended up leaving with an original French painting for 10 euro. At the time, I was underwhelmed by its simplicity, but I've come to adore it because of the memories attached.

MUSIC APPRECIATION

It was the music of the 1960s that first attracted me about 20 years ago. Then it was the fashion of the '40s and '60s, and as I got older it was the history of the past that intrigued me. I studied the decades through historical film fiction and became enamoured with the style, the furniture and the home decor. The idea of living during a simpler time appealed to me. I understand now that life was more difficult in many ways, but I still have an idealized idea of life during the years of my grandparents' youth and young adulthood.

LOVE IT ALL (FOR A WHILE)

The temptation to keep almost everything I find is strong, but in recent months I've been trying to part with items that I just don't have space for or I'm not truly in love with. I'll live with something for a while, showcasing it in my living room for Instagram photos or Etsy listings. I've learned that I should only keep what inspires delight. Take my collection of vintage tea towels, for example. They are useful, they are beautiful and I enjoy hunting for them more than other things. They have a way of making an everyday task feel more joyful, so I scoop them up whenever possible. Thankfully, most lovers of vintage have no reservations when it comes to buying previously used items, so when I tire of one, it's time to pass it along to its next owner.

```
"I'm drawn to simple,
useful items that
make everyday
tasks less mundane:
vintage Ball jars
with floral lids,
colourful floral
shelf liner and 1950s
office supplies."
```

VINTAGE LIFE

thewhitepeppervintage.com
@thewhitepeppervintage

17

HOLDEN MANUFACTURING COMPANY
OTTAWA, Canada
PARIS
PLEASE DO NOT OPEN BOXES

RETAIL & HOSPITALITY

Cartolina

A former hotel from 1892 flourishes with heritage hospitality

FIONA RICHARDS *and* **DOUG JONES**

"Customers love all the vintage pieces. They create a great atmosphere for shopping."

For three decades, Fiona Richards and Doug Jones have shared a creative life together—and an entrepreneurial spirit. "We have been self-employed for most of those years," says Fiona. "Doug is a professional illustrator, working for all the major American magazines and newspaper, such as the *New York Times, Wall Street Journal, Rolling Stone*. I am a self-taught designer and illustrator. We don't have kids but we do have a 12-year-old wholesale greeting card line and a 5-year-old retail store!"

Located in a small historic ski town on the edge of Kootenay Lake in southeast British Columbia, their businesses are housed in a building dating back to 1892. "Our retail store was originally the Tremont Hotel mercantile and served the miners and prospectors with supplies for their hard-working lives," says Fiona. "Nelson was a booming silver mining town in the 1890s and you can't live in Nelson without being influenced in some way by its history."

With their love of heritage architecture and keen attention to detail, the couple renovated the building back to its roots in hospitality. "Our flagship retail store, Cartolina, and wholesale business occupy the entire main floor of the building, and we have renovated the original hotel rooms upstairs into a luxury vacation rental called the Tremont Loft. Our retail store has become a destination for locals and tourists looking for unique gifts in a beautiful, historic atmosphere."

Their home is heritage as well, a renovated 1900s stone cottage on Kootenay Lake. "The property was once known as Killarney-on-the-Lake and belonged

CREATIVITY INSPIRED BY THE PAST

Because Doug and I are both drawn to vintage imagery it pops up in our work. Doug's art is inspired by illustration from the 1890s through to the 1930s and he has become well-known for this style. Cartolina Cards are designed using a digital collage technique, a layering of vintage images. Most of the imagery for the card collection came from years and years of collecting ephemera from around the world— an obsession for me that started when I was young in Scotland. This style has been what has set us apart in the stationery industry for many years.

to Fred Hume, who built the famous Hume Hotel in Nelson and was Nelson's sixth mayor," explains Fiona. "It was his summer home and is located directly across the water from downtown Nelson. It's a beautiful, historic property and we feel honoured to live here. There's not much left of the original house, but the gardens are spectacular."

"Having lived here now for 25 years, the 1890s have permeated our blood and we are always drawn to design details from that era." ❋

WOODS
CANADA
Cut
FLOWER
$1.0
OPEN
Cartolina
BAKER
ANTIQUE
FRESH
CUT
FARMHO
FRESH
COFFEE
FARMER'S MARKET

WESTERN CANADIAN HISTORY

In Western Canada, it does seem like the most influential decade in architecture and design was 1890 to 1900. When you roadtrip around British Columbia, every small town has remnants of the 1890s. Many small towns have museums and if you take the time to check out the photographs of these towns in the 1890s, it's as if the whole of the province was having a building boom.

1890s architecture and design details in Western Canada are interesting because the original developer had often come from a big city, like San Francisco or Chicago, and attempted to build "big city glamour" but could only use local materials available to him such as cedar or fir. So the resulting vernacular style was a slightly rustic version of the popular Victorian styles in the city. This rustic 1890s style is very specific to this area of Canada—and we love it!

FIXTURES & FURNITURE

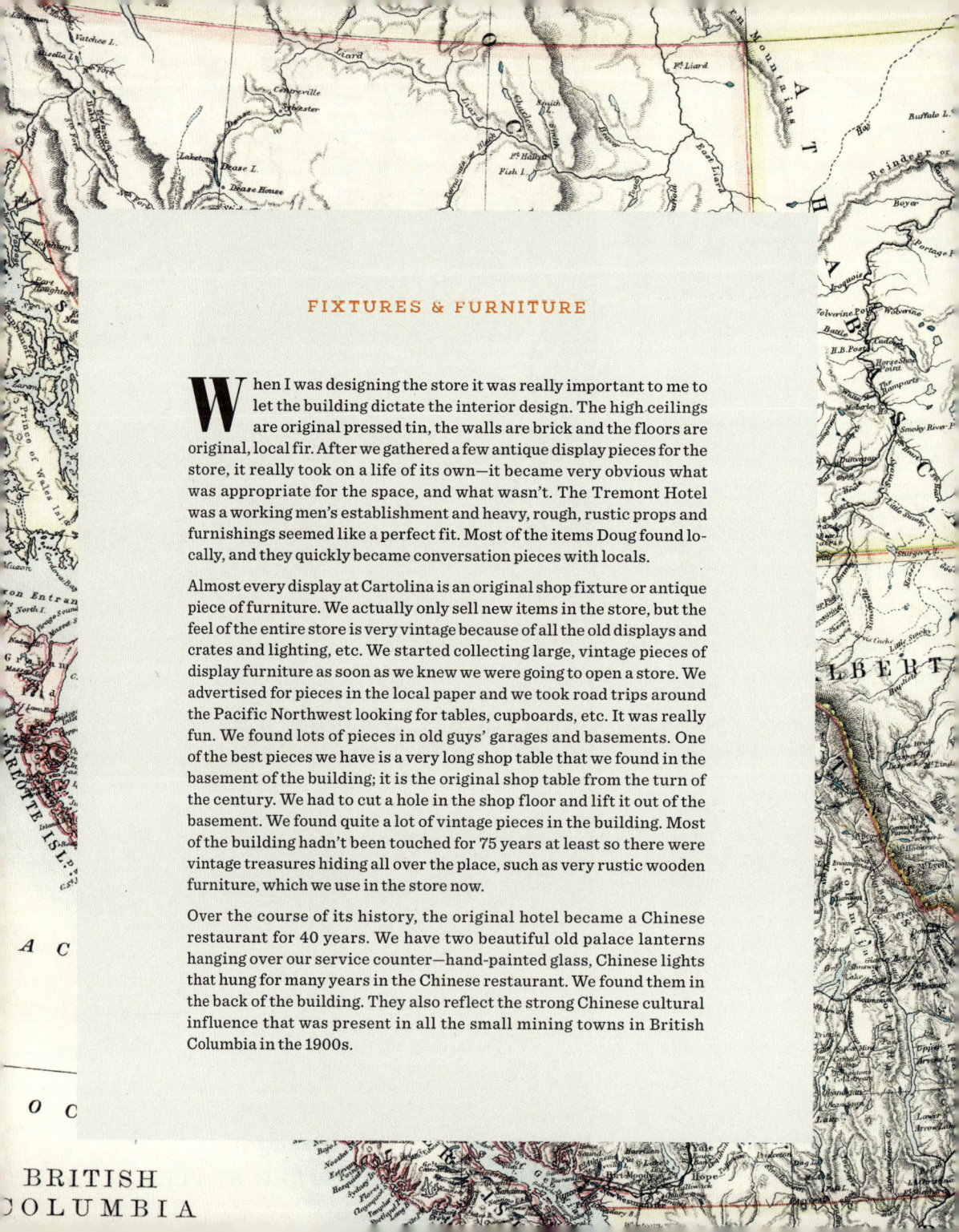

When I was designing the store it was really important to me to let the building dictate the interior design. The high ceilings are original pressed tin, the walls are brick and the floors are original, local fir. After we gathered a few antique display pieces for the store, it really took on a life of its own—it became very obvious what was appropriate for the space, and what wasn't. The Tremont Hotel was a working men's establishment and heavy, rough, rustic props and furnishings seemed like a perfect fit. Most of the items Doug found locally, and they quickly became conversation pieces with locals.

Almost every display at Cartolina is an original shop fixture or antique piece of furniture. We actually only sell new items in the store, but the feel of the entire store is very vintage because of all the old displays and crates and lighting, etc. We started collecting large, vintage pieces of display furniture as soon as we knew we were going to open a store. We advertised for pieces in the local paper and we took road trips around the Pacific Northwest looking for tables, cupboards, etc. It was really fun. We found lots of pieces in old guys' garages and basements. One of the best pieces we have is a very long shop table that we found in the basement of the building; it is the original shop table from the turn of the century. We had to cut a hole in the shop floor and lift it out of the basement. We found quite a lot of vintage pieces in the building. Most of the building hadn't been touched for 75 years at least so there were vintage treasures hiding all over the place, such as very rustic wooden furniture, which we use in the store now.

Over the course of its history, the original hotel became a Chinese restaurant for 40 years. We have two beautiful old palace lanterns hanging over our service counter—hand-painted glass, Chinese lights that hung for many years in the Chinese restaurant. We found them in the back of the building. They also reflect the strong Chinese cultural influence that was present in all the small mining towns in British Columbia in the 1900s.

Tremont

BLACKBERRIES
OREGON
BOYSENBERRIES
Rosemary
CAN
FORMULARY
THE MACHINE
YOU WILL EVENTUALLY BUY
UNDERWOOD TYPEWRITER Co. Inc.
NEW YORK, U.S.A.

cartolina.com
@fionacartolina

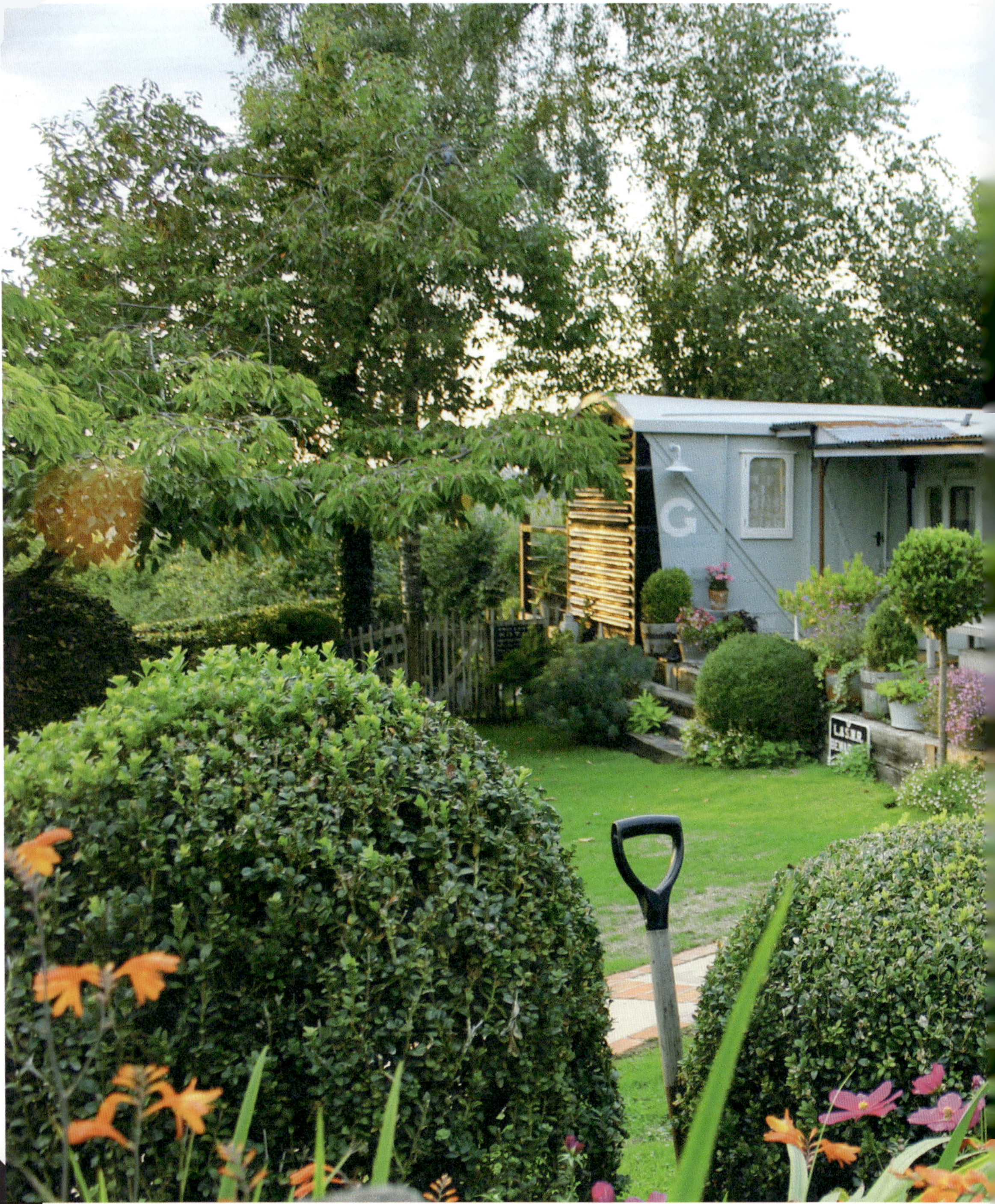
G

GARDENING & HOSPITALITY

Long Hill Carriage

ANNIE *and* CHRIS STANFORD

"As an artist and illustrator, most of my time is spent in the studio (with my two dogs), painting large botanical pieces and researching, writing and illustrating my second book on the history of useful plants and their stories. I am passionate about all things botanical and on a dry sunny day will happily, but guiltily, desert my studio for the garden!"

After many moves and four children, Annie and Chris Stanford settled in the idyllic English countryside. "My naval husband and I eventually put down roots, far from the sea, in a tiny hilltop village in rural Somerset," Annie says. "Here, we set up a small business—a holiday let based in a Victorian railway carriage nestled in the lower part of our garden."

"Our 1882 Victorian Great Western railway carriage is the only kind left in the world. Its defining and most idiosyncratic feature is its raised 'birdcage,' which allowed the guard to look up and down the train through the glazed windows." Decommissioned in 1927, it was home for a family in North Devon until 2001. Had Annie and Chris not discovered the carriage in a field years later, the old structure might have been headed for a bonfire. "We spent the next two years renovating it, scraping and painting, and, with the help of a master craftsman, repairing and preserving much of the carriage's woodwork and fittings."

"After an arduous journey on the back of a lorry, it was swung over the hedge with the help of an enormous crane and positioned to sit serenely in the lower part of our garden, overlooking the spectacular pastoral landscape of Somerset's Blackmore Vale—made famous by the novelist Thomas Hardy." After using the light-filled carriage as an office and summerhouse for several years, they decided it should be enjoyed by a larger audience and the idea of a holiday let was born.

To accommodate guests, they needed to add a bedroom and bathroom. This time, rather than tromping through fields, a quick search on eBay led to a 1952 fruit and vegetable wagon waiting to be restored. "The wagon had enjoyed an equally varied afterlife as an archery store in Shakespeare's birthplace at Stratford-upon-Avon. Nurtured and coaxed into the present, these two examples of British railway history, now in their third reincarnation, make a unique, comfortable and quirky base for a restful and tranquil escape from the pressures of modern life." ❋

VINTAGE-INSPIRED LIFE

For a start, my interest in vintage has provided an opportunity to unlock and indulge my enduring passion for collecting. There are no set parameters or rules. You can combine and display items from different eras, construct imaginative and unexpected juxtapositions and narratives, and create your own original and unique style, driven by your personal interests and preferences. Rescuing unloved, discarded and outmoded objects—whether manufactured or handmade, decorative or functional—and giving them a new life is infinitely satisfying (and often cheaper than buying new). One person's junk is, after all, another person's treasure! For instance, in our garden, a push mower from the 1950s, seized with rust, sits gracefully and beautifully beneath a tree. To me, the effects of time—deterioration, fading, decay—often seem to add profoundly to an object's emotional, visual and sensory appeal.

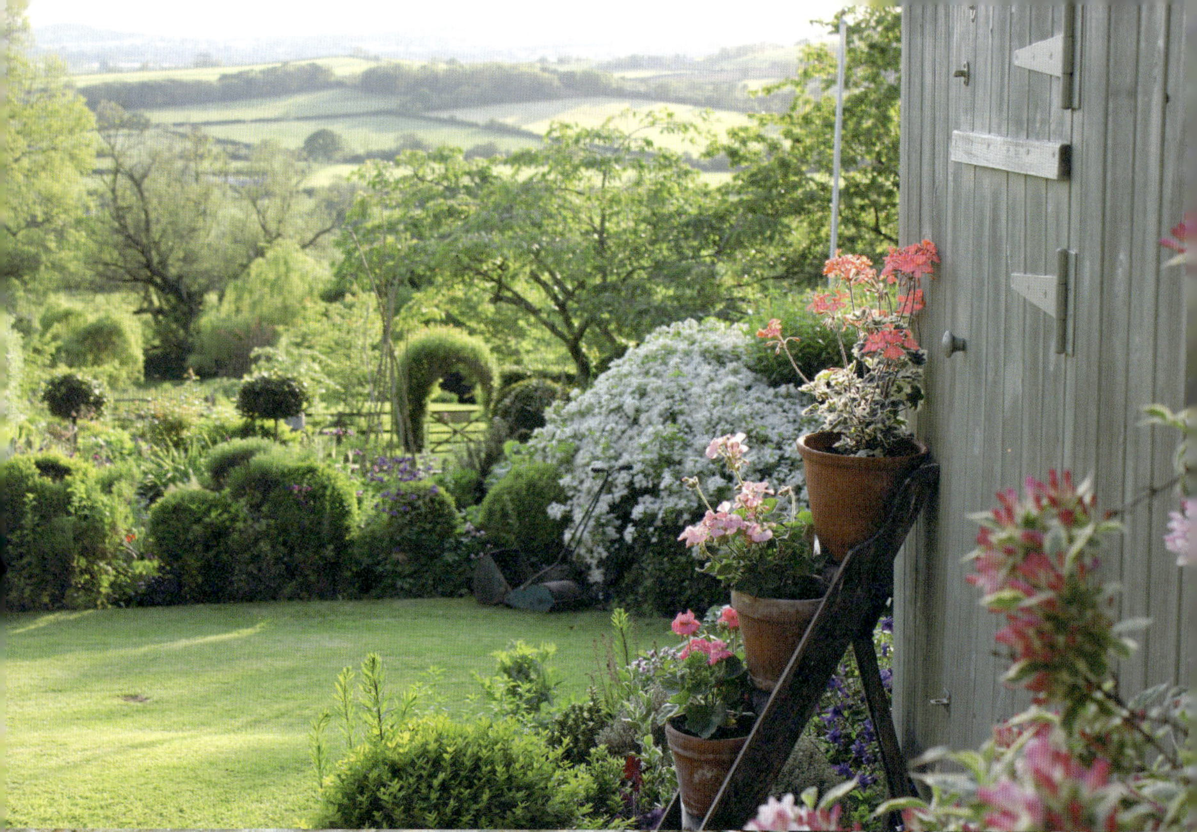

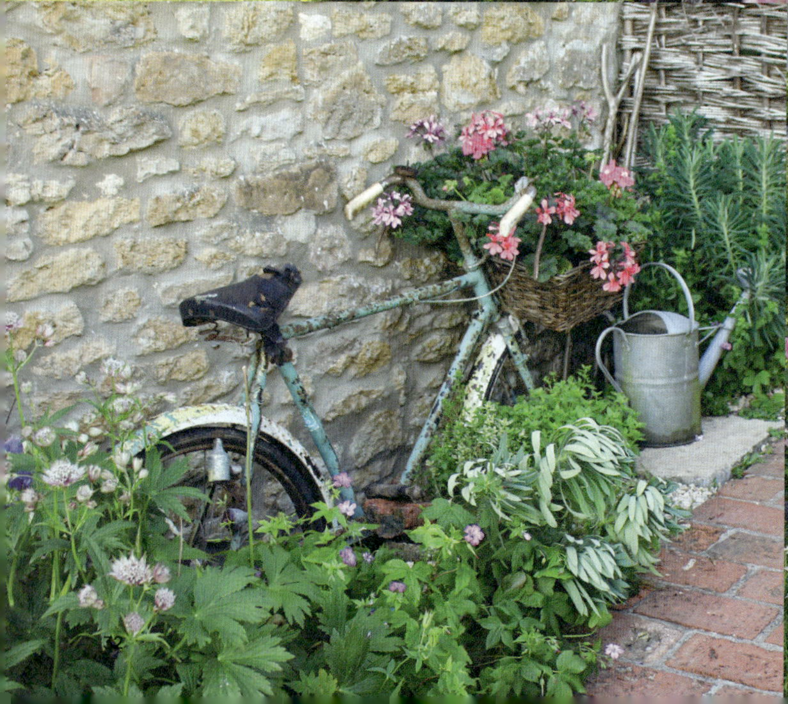

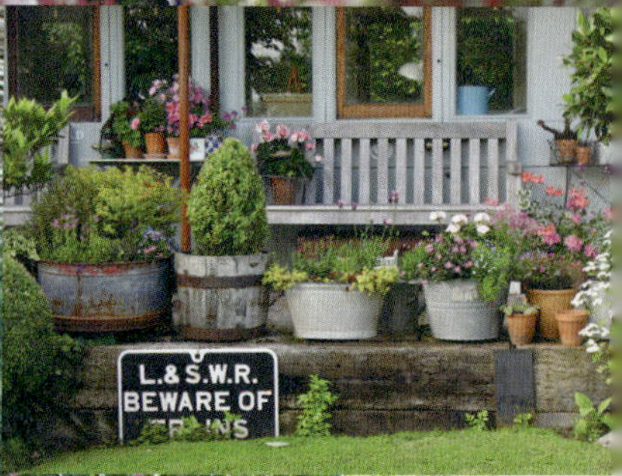
L.& S.W.R.
BEWARE OF

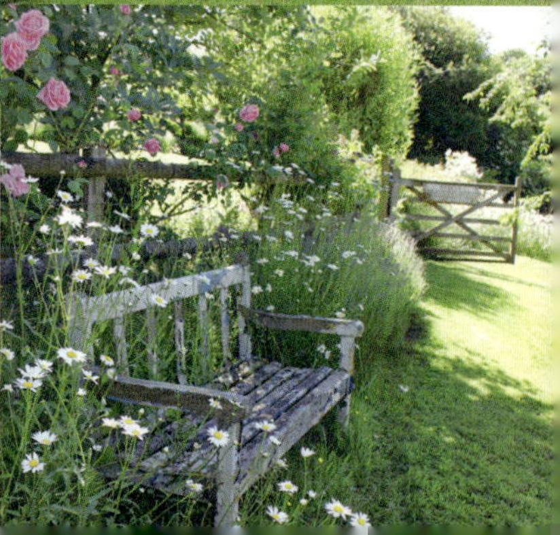

GARDEN DESIGN AND STYLE

The large garden is designed, or rather has evolved, to sit comfortably and happily with the 350-year-old stone cottage at its centre. Packed with a profusion of colourful flowers and shrubs, the informal design harks back to cottage gardens of the past, associated not only with the gently pastoral and nostalgic, but also the functional. My love of vintage is very much in evidence in the garden. Admiring of—and sympathetic to—the discarded, marginal and overlooked, I have rescued, reused and recycled many objects and artifacts, from the two Victorian shepherd's huts to smaller items like tin baths, animal feeding troughs, buckets, old sinks and broken wheelbarrows, all now used as containers for plants. Chairs, now too wobbly to use, make perfect stands for pots of plants, whilst a rickety wooden step ladder is used to display old-fashioned pelargoniums. The wicker basket of a bicycle that has seen better days boasts a profusion of bright pansies. Elsewhere, there are weather-worn terracotta pots, rusted galvanized metal buckets, moss-encrusted stone basins and old French metal garden tables, resplendent with peeling paint: the patina of time is very much part of their charm. A large water tank, studded with metal rivets, is home to an explosion of brilliantly hued dahlias, whilst an old cast iron stove provides space for trailing strawberry plants. Beautiful, useful, often detached from their original function and given a new lease of life, these vintage objects add decorative interest, character and individuality to the cottage garden.

"Another keen interest is collecting found objects—pebbles, seedpods in their diverse forms, tufts of lichen, fragments of sea-worn wood, and the broken shards of pottery and china recovered from the seashore and every time I dig in the garden."

LONG HILL CARRIAGE

STYLE AND SENSIBILITY

The lynchpin of Long Hill Carriage is its vintage style and sensibility. Although the carriage is Victorian, a rigid approach to historical accuracy and "authenticity" was never a priority, and we decided to pursue a broadly mid-century palette of primary colours, along with objects from the same era (which, for me, exert a powerful appeal). Rescued and recontextualized, textiles are an easy way to bring vintage style into a home. Larger pieces have been made into curtains, cushions and tablecloths; smaller scraps are simply framed and hung. The variety of patterns used in the carriage are unified by their vivid colour scheme, and the abundance of 1950s barkcloth introduces a wonderful textural quality. Railwayana (of course) makes an appearance in the form of old toys, guard's lamps and vintage signage. Stacks of old books are for guests to enjoy, meals are eaten off a mixture of colourful vintage china, and old tins once containing baby milk, chocolates and brass polish provide a riot of colour and visual interest. Milk bottles from the 1980s line a shelf in the little kitchen, their diverse slogans advertising anything from toothpaste to orange juice, whilst vintage cookery books not only provide a decorative and historically interesting addition to the kitchen but give inspiration to visiting cooks keen to embrace the recipes of bygone times! Metal factory trolleys, still sporting their original blue paint and once used to carry tools, provide useful storage space. Redolent with historical and often powerfully nostalgic associations, vintage objects can be repurposed in different ways and creatively reinterpreted for our age. Collecting these humble everyday items is a labour of love, often taking time, thought and effort. It is, of course, also terribly addictive!

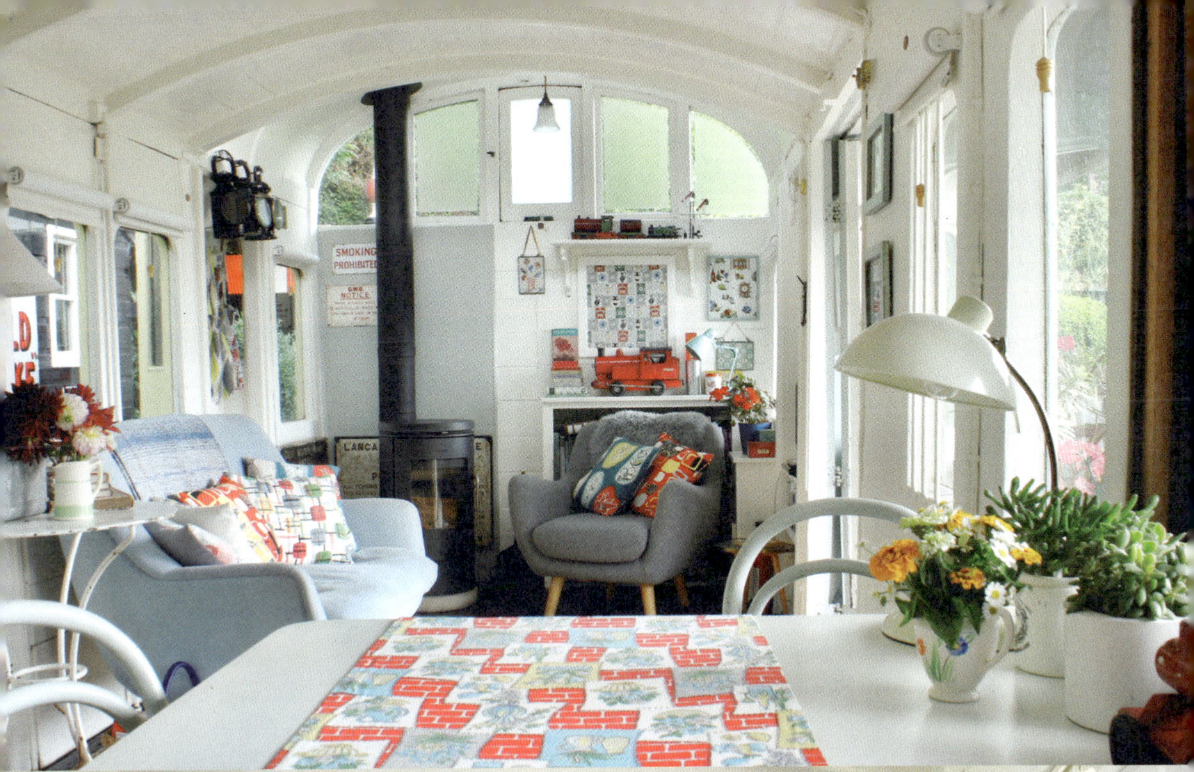
SMOKING
PROHIBITED

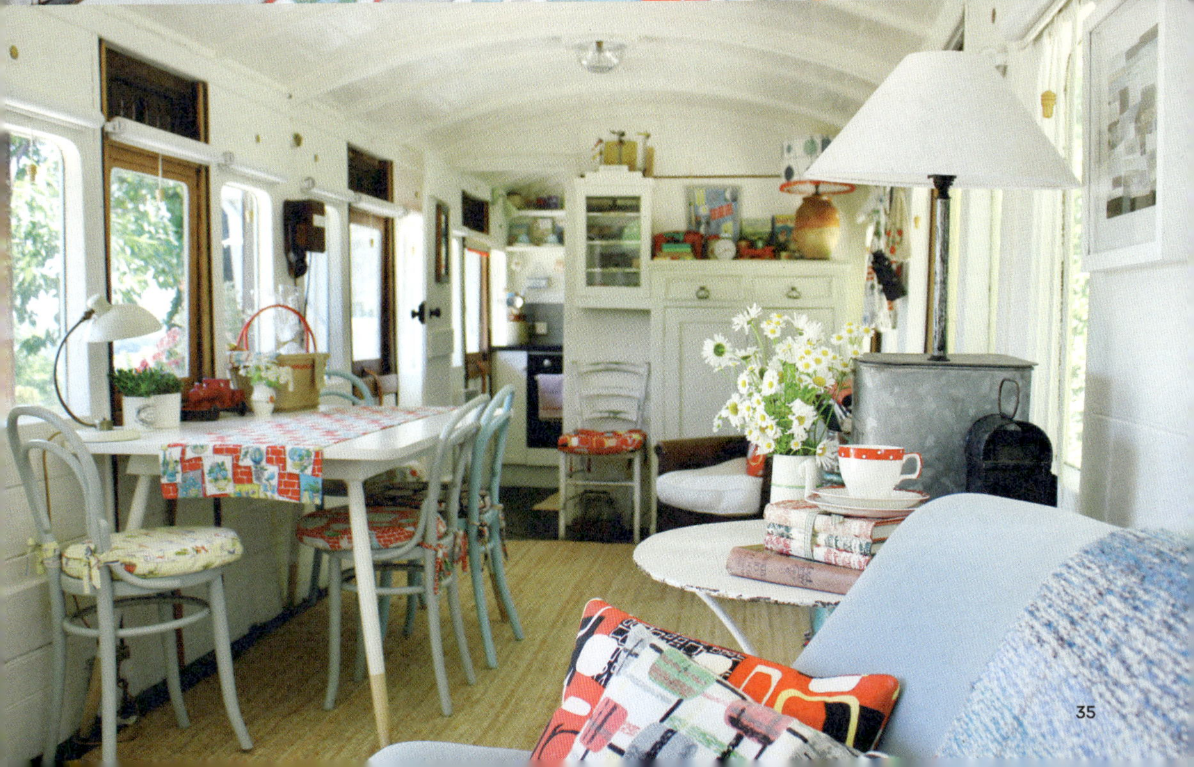

A PASSION FOR TEXTILES

I have been collecting vintage and antique textiles for many years. Around the cottage are stacks of old-fashioned feather-filled eiderdowns (worthy of the Princess and the Pea), antique quilts piled high, mountains of old French plain linen sheets, faded patchworks, Chinese embroideries inherited from my grandmother, samplers painstakingly sewn by young and old (one dating from 1733 and rescued from an aunt's attic), faded florals, and baskets and bowls filled to overflowing with snippets of old materials. In the carriage, mid-century barkcloths abound, and the striking geometric patterns of Lucienne Day and Jacqueline Groag are given pride of place.

In my studio, too, shelves groan beneath piles of colourful vintage fabrics, exquisitely embroidered tablecloths from the 1930s and '40s (hand-stitched with a seasonal variety of cottage garden flowers, and further embellished with an edging of lace), vintage aprons fashioned from stylized culinary designs, and padded clothes hangers, made from leftover scraps. I also collect tiny doll clothes, stitched by hand from pastel-coloured satins and delicate sprigged cottons. Many items in my collection are "perfectly imperfect," that is, damaged, patched, faded and worn, and often all the more appealing for it. Stains, holes and darns are, after all, part of their unique and diverse histories. In fact, the more they show their maker's hand and the tangible patina of age, the more I seem to love them!

longhillcarriage.co.uk
@longhillcarriage

The Crafty Squirrel
OPEN
NOW OPEN
Bullwinkle
WHEELS
Snow White and Rose Red
Tammy
We Help Daddy
Happy Birthday
HOW BIG
THE COLOUR KITTENS
SYLKO
FAST COLOUR
Vintage Charm Pack

RETAIL CRAFT

The Crafty Squirrel

An Australian emporium of vintage goodness

MORGAN WILLS

"I think my love of vintage has a lot to do with an attraction to the design aesthetic of bygone eras, in particular the colours, patterns, illustrations and designs. One of my favourite dream scenarios is to be able to travel back in time so I could go shopping. Sounds silly, I know, but I'd love to go back to a haberdashery shop, or a book or toy store, or even just the supermarket to see all the lovely vintage goodies I collect and love in their original settings."

Morgan Wills grew up with the desire to make things. "I had a shoebox (more a treasure chest) that I would fill with countless items I'd found, squirreled away to use in creating one craft project or another, like dollhouse furniture, sewn textile items and fun projects from children's craft books. I was then, and am now, a self-confessed bowerbird."

This tendency to collect and create has served her well over the years as proprietress of The Crafty Squirrel, an emporium of colour, pattern and vintage appeal. It is nestled in a former corner store dating back to the mid-1880s, located in Ballarat in the central highlands of Australia, about 120 kilometres west of Melbourne. "I am a creative designer and crafter who enjoys using predominantly repurposed and upcycled materials in my work," she explains, "I am passionate about craft, colour and treasure hunting. My products often have a nostalgic vintage-inspired element to them, and as a collector by nature, I love to seek out sweet gems from yesteryear and mix both old and new in my studio shop."

Morgan loves upcycling, thinking of ways that she can reuse vintage and secondhand materials that she has collected in her travels. "I have been designing and making different things for a long time, and over the years I have made many different products out of all sorts of recycled textiles like sheets, tea towels, tablecloths, handkerchiefs, woolen sweaters, fabrics, doilies, feed sacks, haberdashery, books and ephemera. I've been working particularly with old woolen jumpers for many years now—refashioning them into scarves, blankets, babushka dolls, jewellery, needlebooks and all sorts of DIY craft kits."

"The first product in my range that I ever made to sell was my Cast Offs scarves. Way back in 2004 I was playing around with some felted woolen jumpers that I had, and I made one for my husband. He was chuffed and wore it all through the winter. When I was pregnant with our daughter Kitty, I made her a baby cot blanket using a similar idea. One thing led to another and before I knew it, I was collecting old woolen jumpers here, there and everywhere!" Making for her family led to making for craft fairs, and then for wholesale

Simplicity
PATTERN BOOK
Simplicity
Simplicity
PATTERN BOOK
Special
MARKING POWDER
WHITE
ANIMAL
Knitwear
No 3
9d
Patons
OOK 933

accounts and finally to opening The Crafty Squirrel storefront in 2011.

"I think the thing that I love the most is that I get to create something new out of something discarded. Often the vintage textiles I buy have a hole in them or something else that makes them a bit daggy, or the colour or pattern is not in fashion at the moment. It doesn't matter to me, I just wash them and cut around the blemish. I only see the potential, the good bits I can still use. When I combine these materials to create my various products, they are all one of a kind. I like that I can make certain items over and over again, with no two ever being exactly the same. What I find in my travels dictates what I make."

Travel is indeed incorporated into her business: "For the last three years I have also run craft and vintage tours of Japan—taking small groups of women to all my favourite craft stores and flea and antique markets twice a year." ✽

"One of my absolute treasures, though, is an original 1955 Butterick shop counter pattern book filled with the current fashions of the time. I just love looking at those dresses. The thing is, I know that I could probably jump on the computer and google or pinterest my way through any number of vintage fashion patterns or craft inspirations, but there is nothing quite like the smell and feel of old magazines and books, and marking a page that you want to come back to again."

APRONS

"My great-grandmother always wore a pretty apron over her dress and had a fabulous collection of souvenir tea towels and linens, tea spoons, tea cups and all sorts of cute ceramic animals in a special china cabinet. I loved visiting her house and looking through her collected treasures.

As a teenager I discovered thrift stores (we call them op shops in Australia), and with this, cute vintage dresses from the 1950s and '60s, and clothes I could dye or modify and make my own."

Over the years I have amassed quite the textile collection and in particular vintage aprons (I own around 400), which I began to buy to repurpose the fabric into something else but then realized that there were so many different ones— each of its own homemade design, including styles and manufactured brands (the Australian Taniwha label is one of my favourites). Many people now know me for my vintage apron collection because over the years in the shop I have worn many of my aprons as I work. Each Friday for over 200 weeks, I celebrated my "vintage apron of the day" through my social media, sharing a little story about its provenance. This generated lots of apron love in return (and lots of apron gifts). This also led me to start up (with a fellow apron enthusiast) the world's first Apron Festival. Now six years later, the Ballarat Apron Festival runs once a year and stitches together a love of sewing, baking, crafting and nostalgia in celebrating all things apron. I also captured the attention of a shopping centre in Hong Kong who invited me in 2017 to curate an exhibition of my own vintage apron collection for Mother's Day. I was flown over by the organizers as an honored guest to launch the show. I was so proud to give my collection its moment in the spotlight.

OLD-FASHIONED SERVICE

I use a 1940s national cash register that dings when you open it and an old-fashioned ledger book to track my sales. It works for me and definitely suits the vibe of my store—however, the flip side of it is that I then have to hop on to my computer to update my inventory and webstore. Other stores would just have a computer-based system from the get-go and manage sales and inventory together as the customer makes a purchase, but I just can't imagine having a laptop or iPad on my counter—it would look so out of place.

I always play music from the 1930s to '60s in the store, too, to set the scene. The Andrews Sisters, Billie Holiday and Frank Sinatra are a few favs. Visitors have been known to sing along whilst shopping, which is always fun. Occasionally customers ask me if I feel as though I was born in the wrong era and I have to say that I don't, but I do have fun and certainly enjoy the best of both worlds. I am also dedicated to old-fashioned service with a smile (and a bit of a chat)—a quality I feel is sometimes lacking in other stores.

45

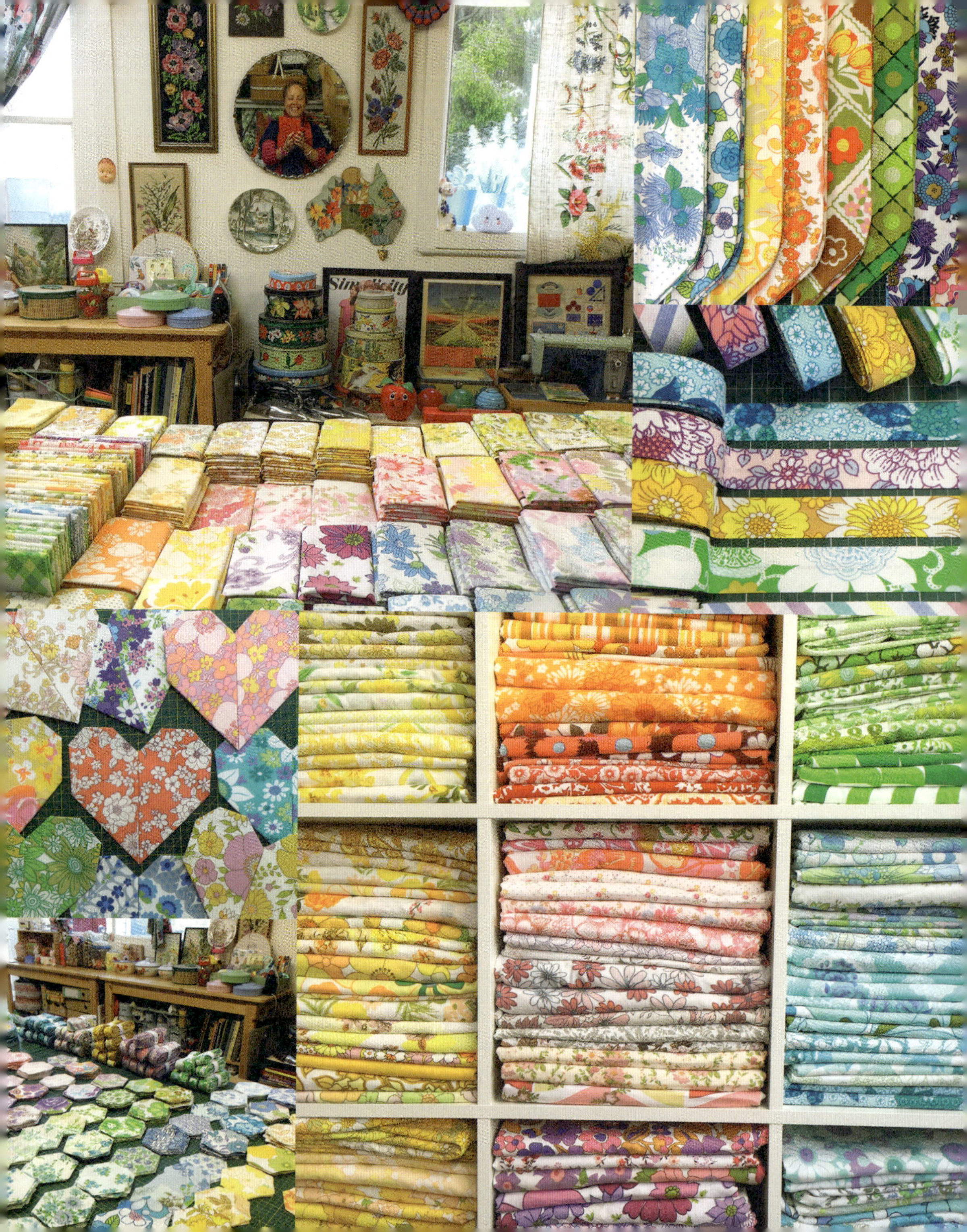

"I find real beauty in vintage objects that others may overlook in their desire to always have the latest and newest things."

SHEETS

Over the years whilst collecting materials from here, there and everywhere, I discovered vintage sheets from the '60s and '70s. It was the floral patterns and colours that particularly caught my eye, and let's face it, I was a child of the '70s, so I have a good dose of nostalgia associated with them. As I collected, I kept stacking them up in the corner of my studio knowing that one day they would become a new product, and in 2014 I started to use them when I produced my "Cute as a Button" range of cushions, pincushions and rattles, and then as time went on, vintage-inspired quilts (and the kits to make them) and women's clothing (dresses, tops and scarves), plus fabric-covered notebooks, pincushions and DIY kits to make your own cushions.

A SQUIRRELLY SCHEDULE

Our home is located next door and the whole property is interconnected. Each week I spend three days in my studio (the old horse stables) and office (behind the shop); my time is largely spent designing and making, working through my never-ending to-do list, planning my crafty tours of Japan, and packing and sending orders from my online shop. On Thursday, Friday and Saturday you'll find me behind the shop counter, where I love to meet like-minded crafty visitors from all over the world.

HANDKERCHIEF ORIGAMI

A couple of years ago, I came across about 300 vintage handkerchiefs that had been collected from all over the world by the women of one family from the 1930s on. I jumped at the chance to purchase them and have had a fabulous time turning them into miniature dresses (origami style) to frame as finished artworks alongside a collage of vintage illustrations and ephemera. My interest in making and crafting is diverse in terms of technique. One of my favourite creations was a series of upholstered stools I made using vintage tablecloths. Much of my work uses reclaimed textiles like vintage tea towels, which I make into cushions and bags, but I also love paper and paper crafting, using vintage golden books and other children's books to make cards, bookmarks, DIY envelope and gift tag kits and more.

When I travel to Japan (a couple of times a year), I always keep a look out for vintage goodies at the flea and antique markets (particularly kokeshi dolls and sewing-related items) that I can bring back and sell in the store. When I do, they never last long!

"My heart, however, loves to remember those who went before us, how they did everything by hand, and I am continually in awe of the quality with which they made and produced everyday products."

48 VINTAGE LIFE

thecraftysquirrel.com.au
@thecraftysquirrel

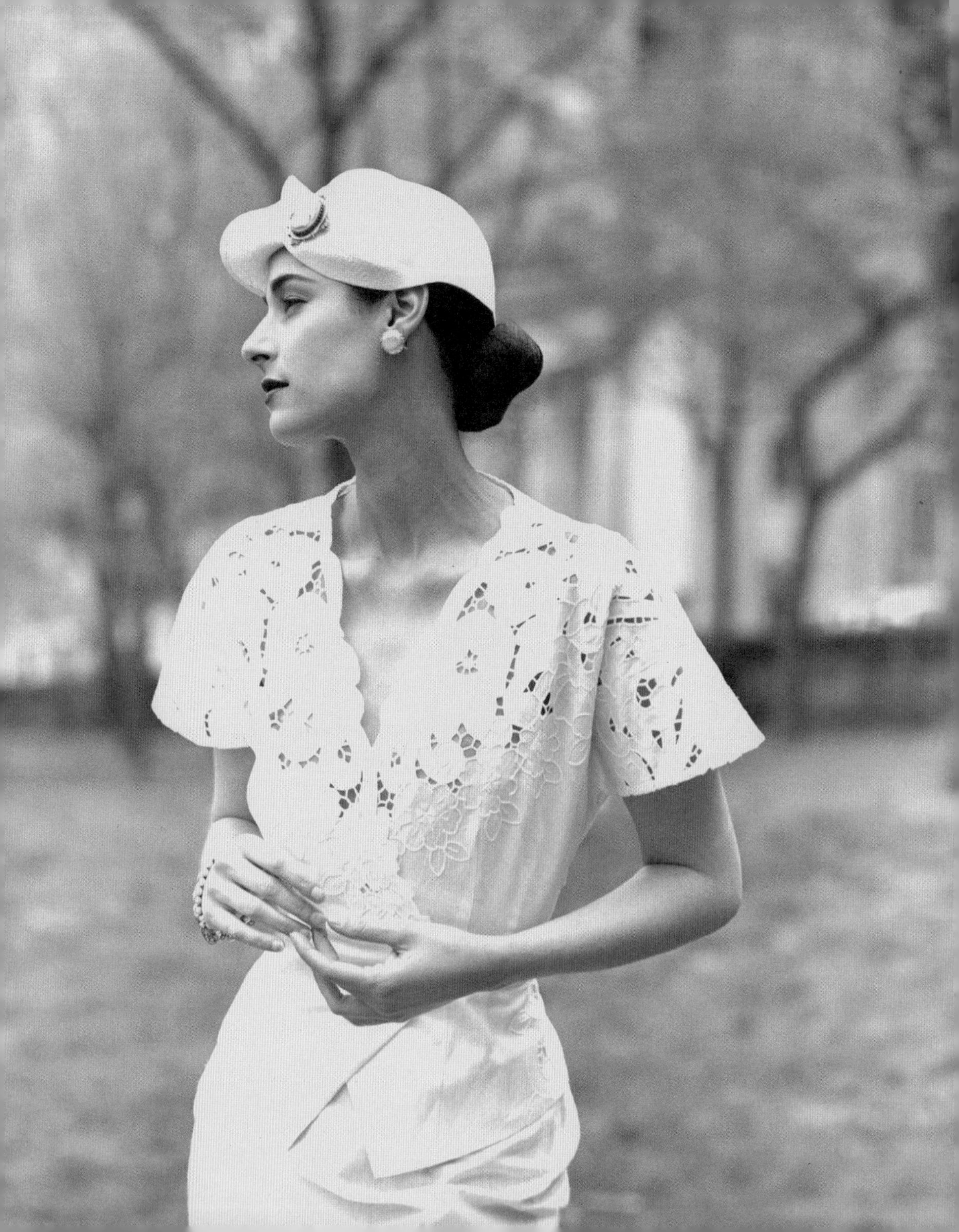

PHOTOGRAPHY

Lara Rossignol

Stylish photography
with a sophisticated vintage vibe

Lara Rossignol has been a professional photographer for over 30 years, shooting celebrity portraits, fashion and lifestyle. Her photographs often have a vintage vibe, through the styling of the models' clothes, hair and makeup, but also through Lara's composition, colour palette and photographic mood. "My use of vintage is not always so obvious, it may just be a barkcloth curtain used as a backdrop or slight touches to the styling. In this way, vintage adds more of a twist to a modern image, rather than recreating a full time warp."

Life and career have taken her many places. "My work has appeared in hundreds of magazines and I've shot numerous retail and advertising campaigns. I've navigated between Los Angeles, New York and the South East, landing most recently in South Carolina just outside Greenville. My recent move back to the South reflects a decision to make a move based more on what was good for my soul rather than my career. I am still doing commercial work but also more personal projects and teaching."

VINTAGE LIFE

In addition to photography, she collects and resells vintage items through her Etsy shop, Fresh Pie Vintage. "Though I like many different periods, I'm particularly drawn to the innovation of mid-century modern design," she says. Customers will find vintage kitsch and collectibles but also photography equipment like a 1950s Ricohflex in its original leather case, a Polaroid OneStep Flash camera from the 1980s or a Falcon Miniature 127 film camera from the 1930s with a bakelite body.

"I love history and like knowing there is a story behind the objects I collect—even if I don't know exactly what that story is. At a very young age, I preferred old black-and-white movies to new. I remember pouring over my mother's collection of books she had as a child and pestering her with questions. I would try to imagine her as a child reading them."

"I think this is where it started. This fascination with history inspires my work and where and how I live. I need an environment that is rich in design, colour and style to motivate me." ✽

"I went through a major downsizing before my last move. I began to feel weighed down by stuff. So I had my own estate sale and also gave away quite a bit. You really learn through the purging process what is important to you."

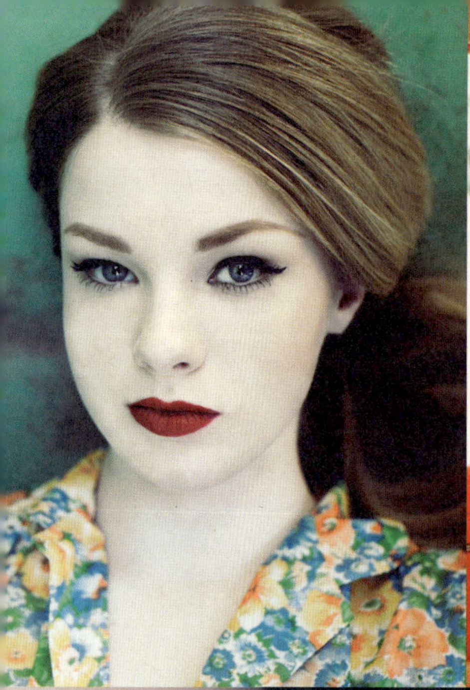
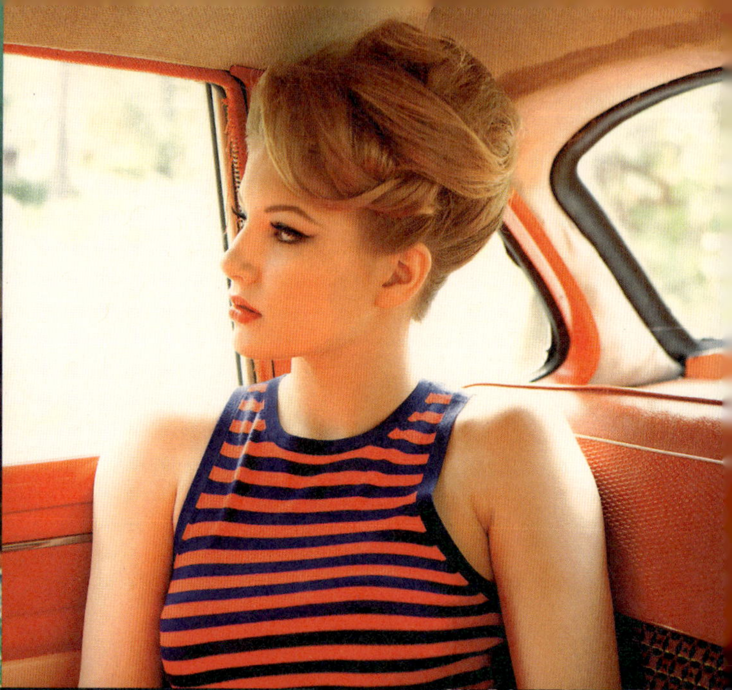
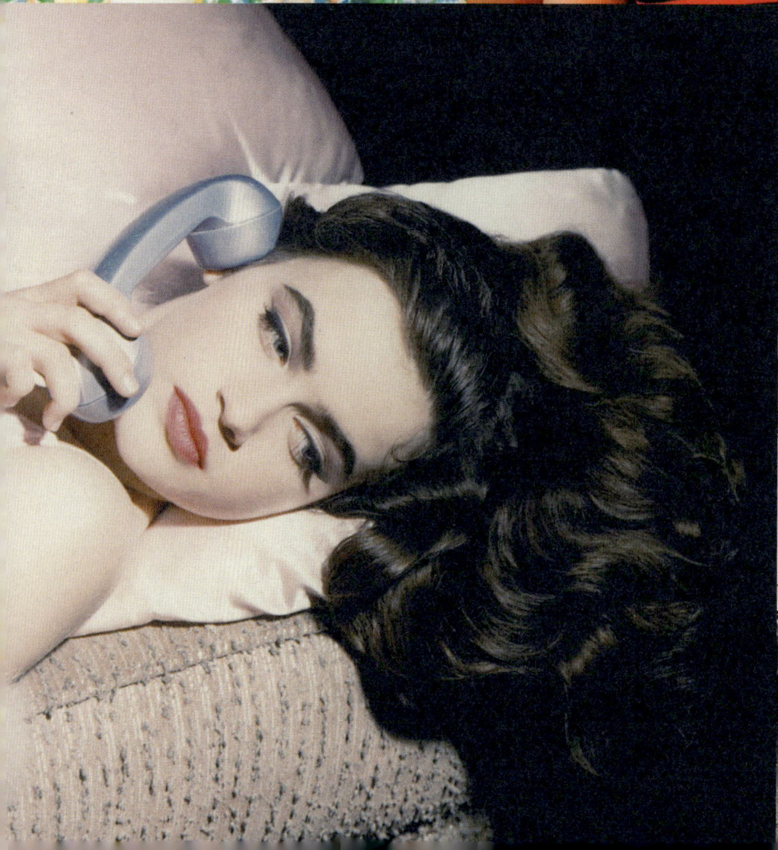
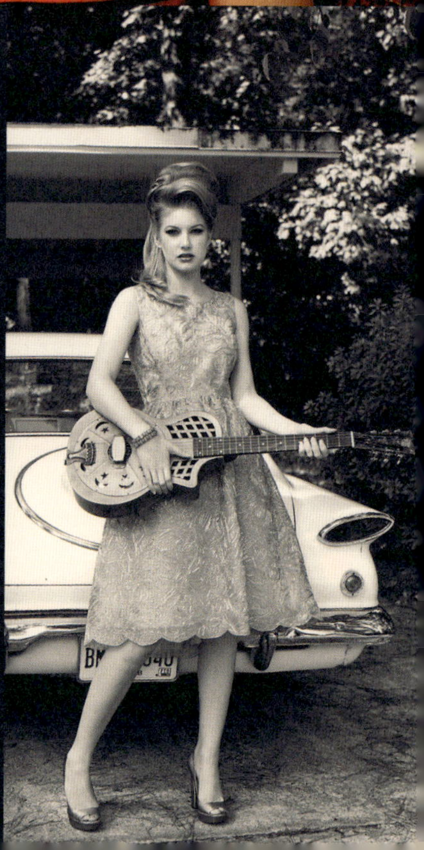

"I love good design, be it old or new. I am not a purist; sometimes a true vintage item is just not practical. When I last lived in LA, I was the proud owner of a SMEG fridge. It made the best of vintage style with modern function."

INSPIRATION IN A SONG

I still love old movies, which often inspire, as do music, books and the world around me. I'm always looking, always hunting for ideas. It is not really a conscious thing, just part of how my mind works. I was listening to a lot of vintage country music and watching old clips on YouTube when I came up with the idea to do a Dolly Parton-inspired fashion shoot for *Rue* magazine.

STYLING SHOOTS

A good creative team is often necessary to achieve certain goals and I have been lucky to have found great people to work with. I have also styled quite a few of my smaller shoots. I think part of my strength as a photographer is having a good eye for styling.

When I work with stylists, including hair and makeup artists, it's important to be able to convey your vision to them. Pinterest is a very good tool for this. We will talk before the shoot and then I will create a "secret" board for that shoot, which they can also contribute to. I like working with people who bring a lot of their own creativity and ideas to a project. I may have one person doing clothing and one doing sets and props, and then the hair and makeup person or team, so good communication is key.

When it is just me, I keep it simple. I get a lot of my backdrops at fabric stores and I will pick up props and accessories thrifting or at Target or from my own collections. Also a basic hair and makeup kit is crucial. A little powder, blotting tissues, a comb, bobby pins and clothespins for loose garments can save the day. A successful shoot is all about good preparation.

lararossignol.com
@lararossignolfoto

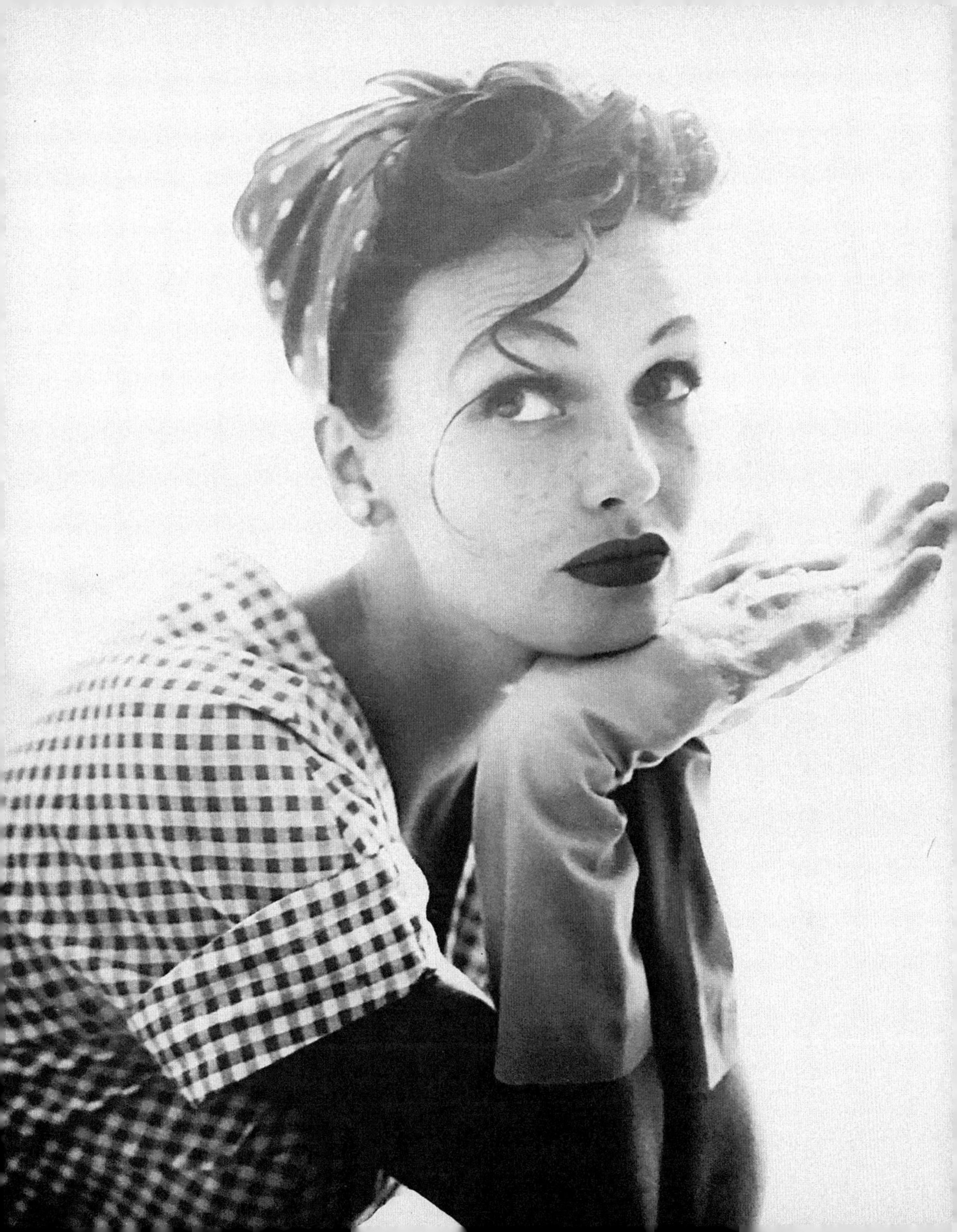

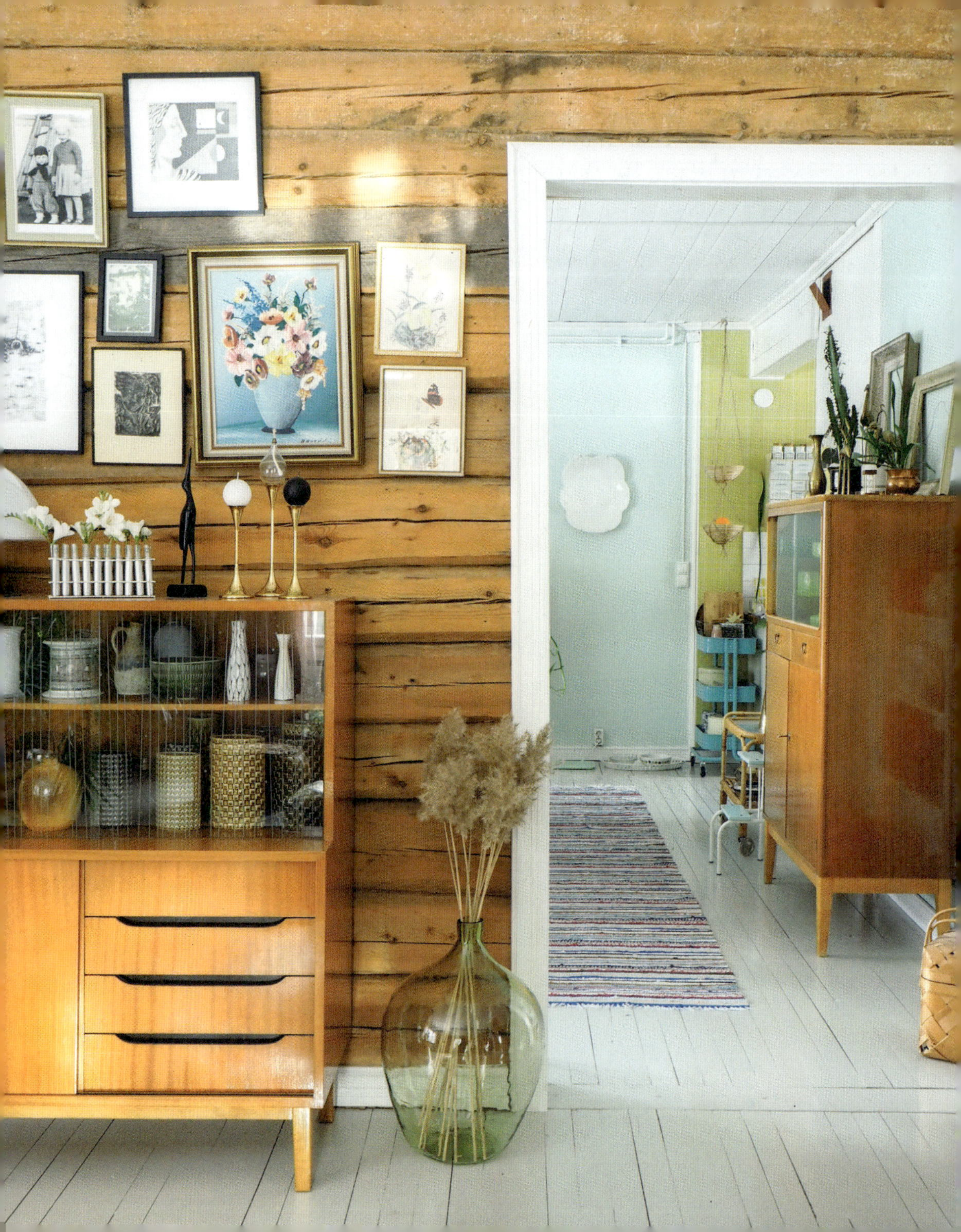

VINTAGE DECOR

Pauliina Pitkänen

Vintage style at home in Finland

Pauliina Pitkänen may live in a small town in western Finland, but her home is open to the world. In fact, she has nearly eight times as many followers on her Instagram account, @vintageinteriorxx, than the population of Harjavalta, which has around 7,000 people.

Her home was built in 1948. "Because we are living in an old house, I think vintage items fit perfectly in our home," she says. "Vintage is a perfect match." The home is bright and airy, with colourful rag rug accents and plenty of plants. There are also a couple of cats. Perhaps part of the popularity of Pauliina's Instagram feed is owed to a handsome grey cat named Kaapo and its unique perch: a wooden TV cabinet, minus the television, in which the box interior is prettily wallpapered.

"I think many have found my account just because of this cat TV," posted Pauliina when the account reached 50,000. "Our Kaapo has charmed quite a many of you there on the other side of the screen."

60 VINTAGE LIFE

Kaapo is indeed quite the poser and offers a bit of a story from one Instagram photo to another.

Decorating her home and posting pictures is a hobby for Pauliina, as is the interior design blog that she writes: "I want to share inspiration to others."

She says her charming home is "like a puzzle." Each piece of furniture, vignette of objects or small jungle of plants fits together so well. "There are different ways of how I bring things into my home," she explains. "Sometimes I go to a thrift store and see something nice and I just buy it." Other times, she has a vision of something specific and goes on the hunt for just the right thing.

"I love to recycle and I think most old furniture is better quality than new. I also like to think of the history behind these old things. I like that I can find different kinds of things from a thrift store and create an interior piece by piece." ❖

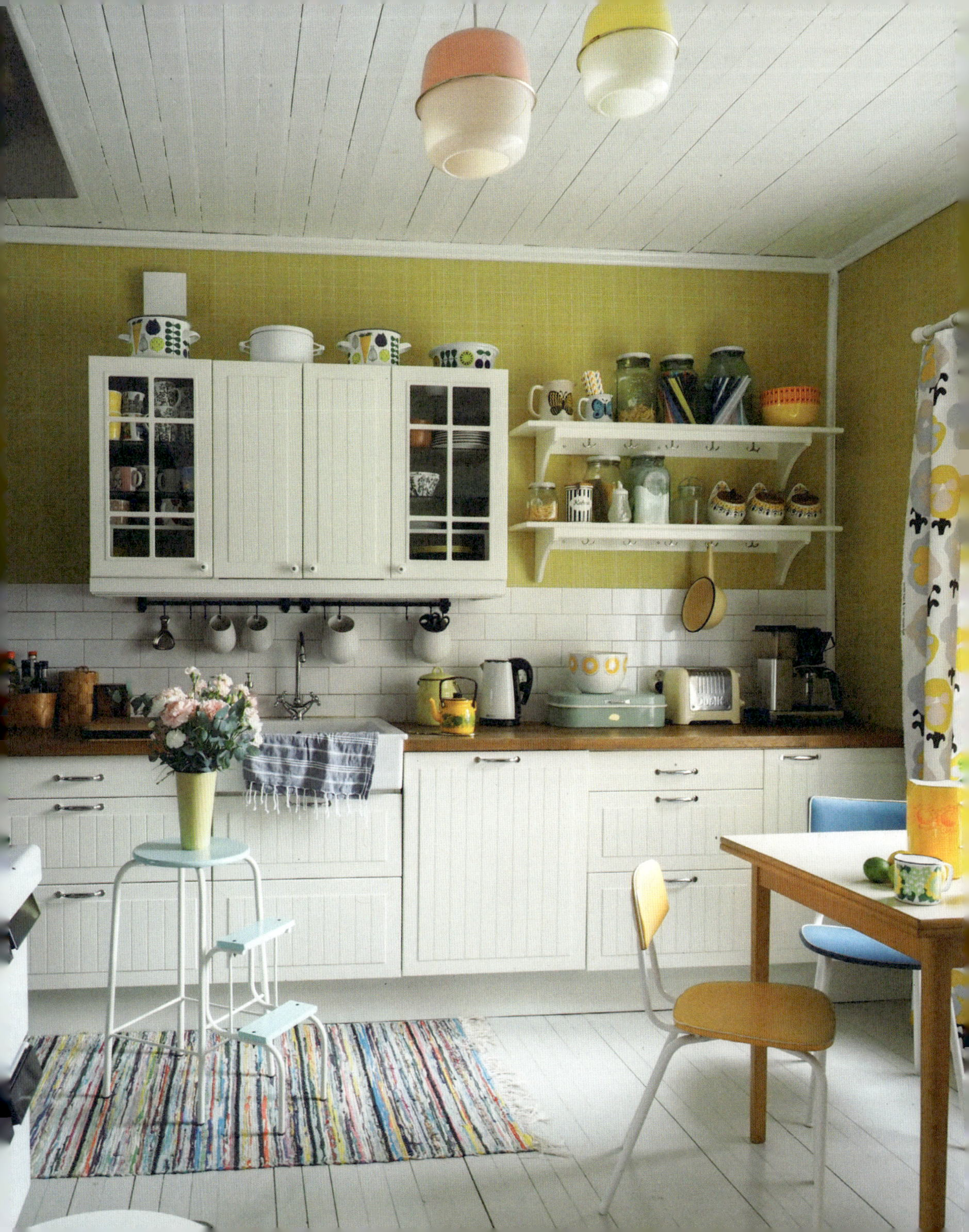

"I love the Finnish porcelain factory Arabia's products from the '50s and '60s—especially old coffee cups. I have almost 150 different cups in my collection."

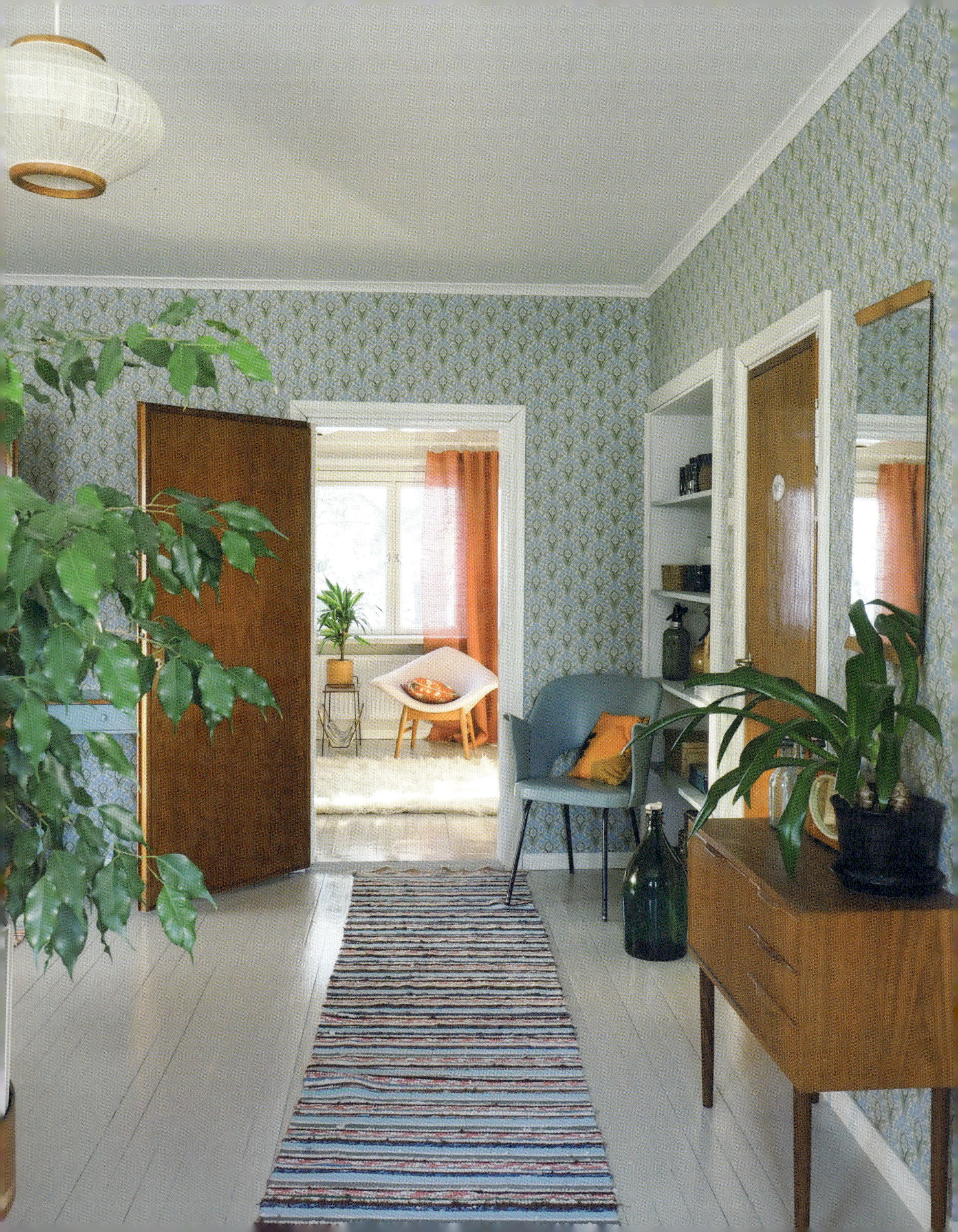

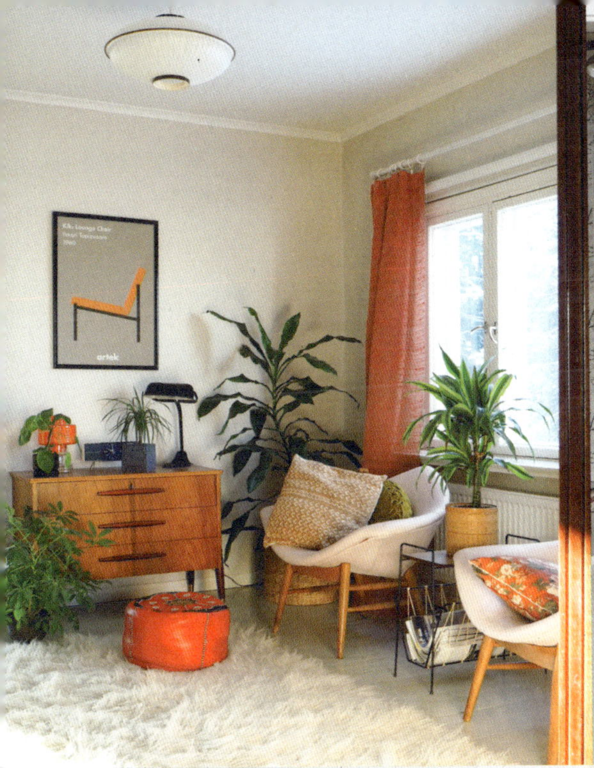
artek
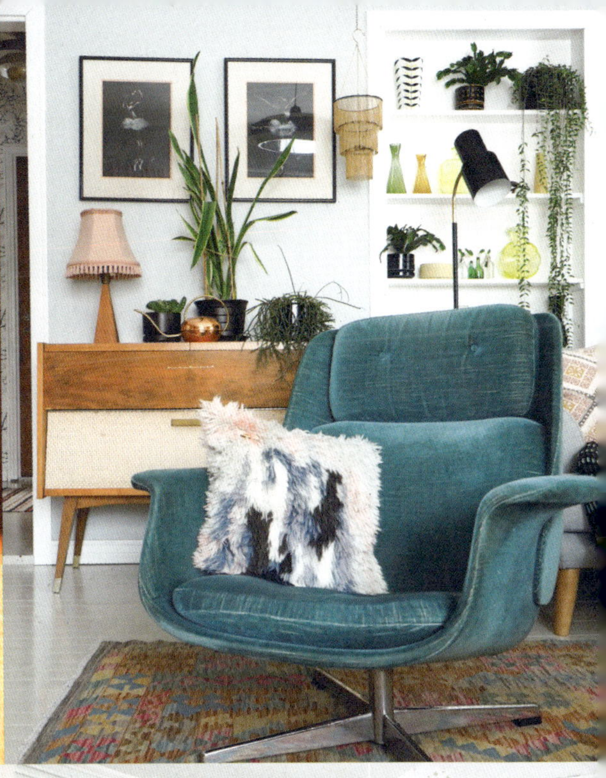
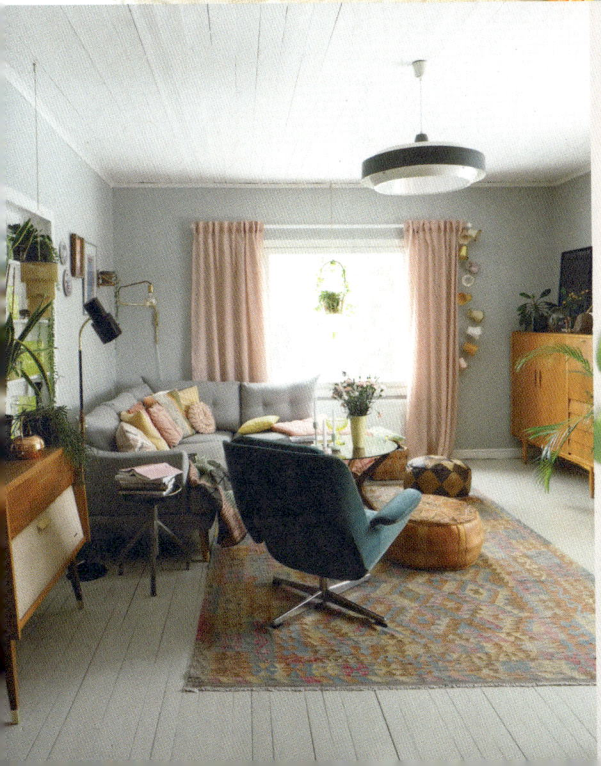
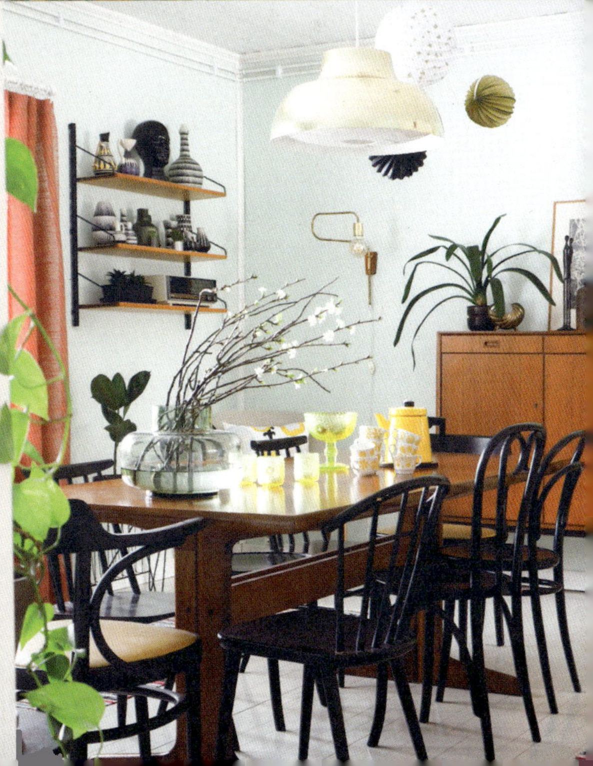

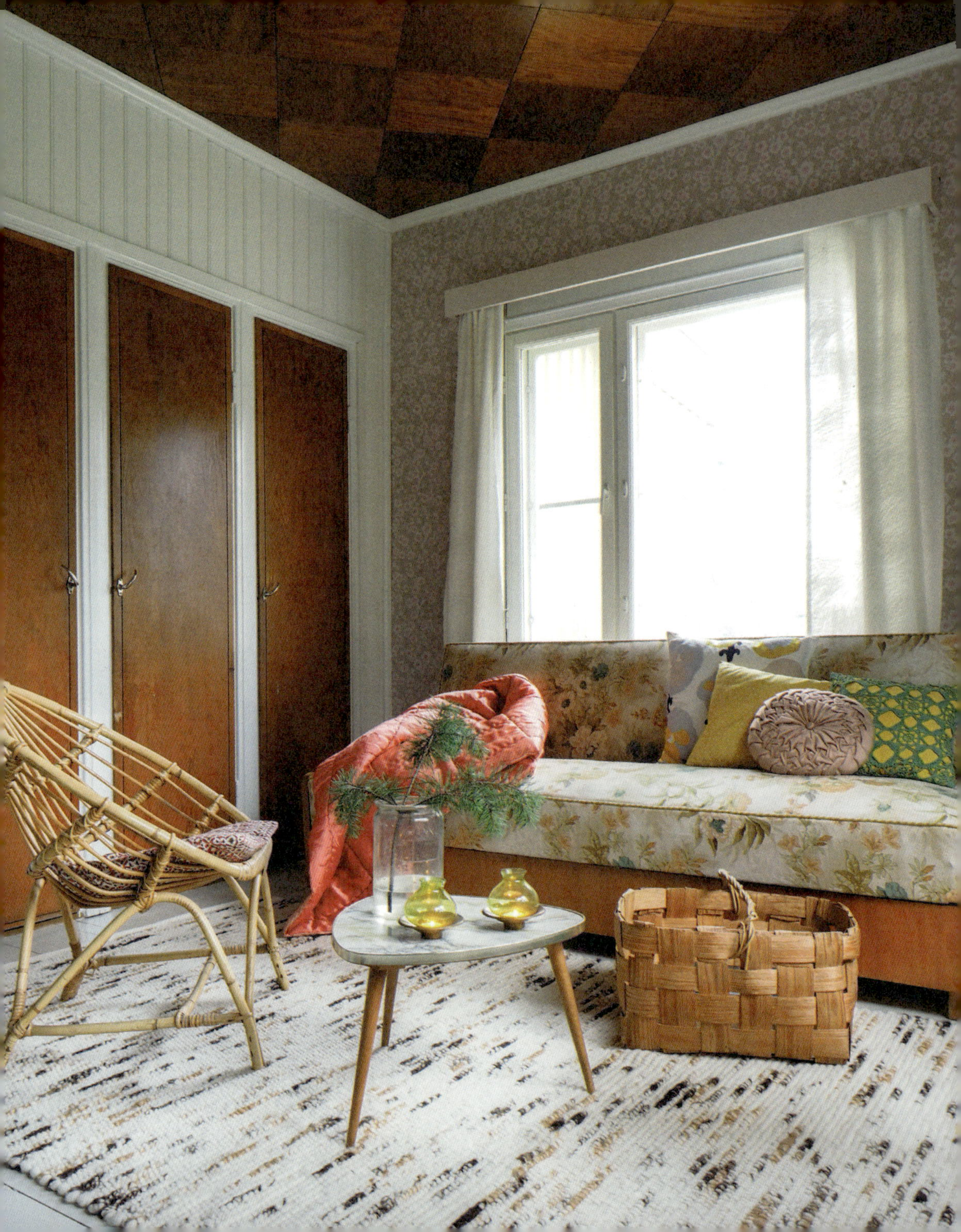

keltainenkahvipannu.blogspot.com
@vintageinteriorxx

French General
French General
French General
French General
French General

French General

Bonjour Bonjour

RETAIL & RETREATS

French General

Creating products and experiences
inspired by France's brocantes

KAARI MENG and **JON ZABALA**

Growing up, Kaari Meng never imagined the life she has now. "I actually thought I would have to dress up, go to an office every day and actually try to fit in," she says. "I never knew you could create something in your mind and then make it come true." With studies in political science, Kaari assumed she would work in Washington, DC. "But an urgent need for a hat pin (due to a boat ride in Central Park) led me to a life of design." She discovered the appealing world of handmade jewellery and started making her own.

Her husband, Jon Zabala, is Basque. During a fateful sojourn in his native Spain, Kaari realized that France was literally just 10 minutes from San Sebastián. "I was in the car and headed to Toulouse. I spent the whole day at the flea market in the blazing sun and met a woman named Antonia who convinced me that French textiles would change my life—and I would sleep better under a linen sheet! Both happened."

Later, on a trip to France to celebrate her mother's 60th birthday, Kaari had an epiphany. "I woke up to

"I love walking into an antique shop, museum, old house or hotel and learning about the past—the smells, the chips, the repairs—it's all there for the taking."

the name—French General—and it seemed to encompass a challenge and a chance to do different things under one name: travel, buy old French linen sheets, craft and follow my heart." She and Jon opened a retail store on Crosby Street, New York City, in 1999. "It was almost like a museum," she recalls, "but everything was for sale. I had never been in a store like French General before and I liked that it was strange but familiar at the same time."

"When I opened French General in New York my dad wondered how we would ever pay the rent selling notions—I told him I thought it would work. We weren't just selling notions, we were selling a vintage way of life. Stepping into French General is like stepping into your (great) grandmother's favourite general store."

French General has evolved over the years; it is now located on the near-east side of Los Angeles. "Besides being open for retail two days a week, we offer workshops on hand-stitching, indigo dyeing, jewellery making, paper crafts, embroidery, weaving and anything else that we fall in love with."

"My life and business mix pretty well," says Kaari. "My husband, JZ, and I work together to design fabric for Moda and Fabricut as well as to create kits for our shop and workshops. Life is hectic when you work with your husband, but we each do what we are good at and keep the business moving forward. If I have one foot in the past, I have the other foot firmly planted in the future. I am always working on ideas for what's next. Collecting antique textiles led me to Moda and Fabricut—and turning my old French scraps into fabric collections for quilters and home interiors." ❋

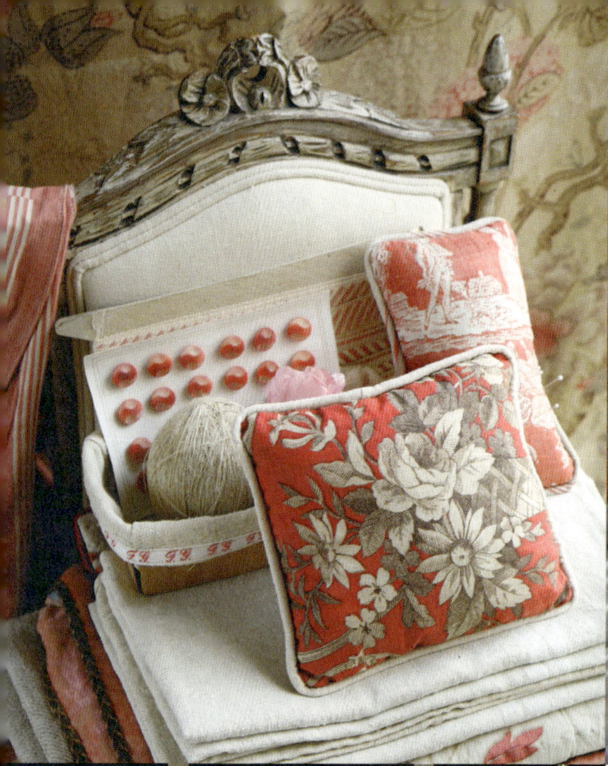

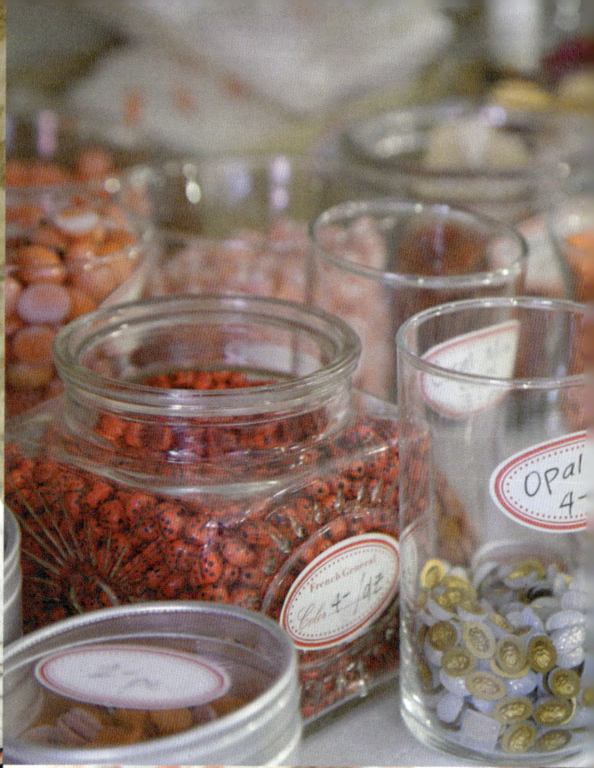
Opal

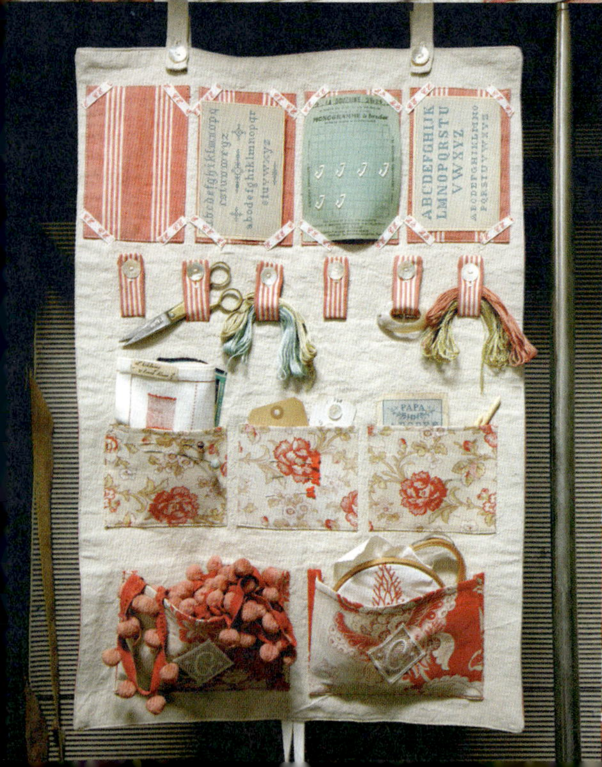

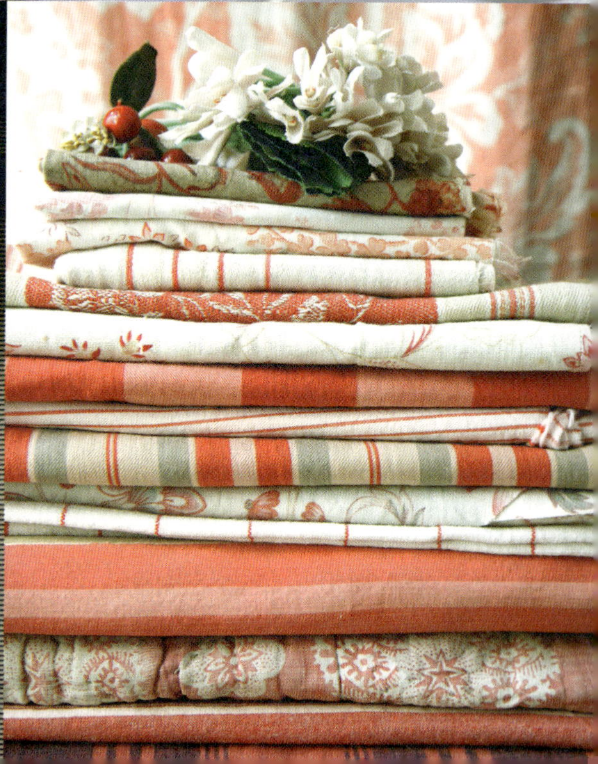

"Everything I collect I use as inspiration for something soon to be—whether it's an old quilt, a woven basket, seaside paintings or tiny bits of striped cloth."

FRENCH ROMANCE

I am crazy in love with antique French fabric—the smell, the hand, the faded colours, the repairs—all create a sense of history and stories in my head of how life was lived in the past. I first found fabrics when I was digging in an old French antique shop on Broome Street in Manhattan.

The shop owner sat at his desk the whole time so I would wander around to study the old, damaged pieces that were stored in the basement. There was a door slightly ajar and I pushed it open and what to my wandering eyes did appear but row after row of metal shelving filled with stacks of old fabric. I spent three hours picking out a small pile—common old cloth, really, with beautiful faded flowers—as if the fabric had been around for hundreds of years, but still in perfect shape.

The owner looked at every piece and added up my bill. When I heard the amount I almost fell over! I told him I would have to go home to think about it. The next day I returned with borrowed money and bought the cloth, and he said, "You have bought with your heart, you will never be sorry." That was it—I was hooked.

FRENCH GENERAL

THE PULL OF THE PAST

I was drawn to the textiles from France and in turn fell in love with France and what life looked like years and years ago. I love thinking about the homes in the 18th century. What were the interiors like? How were textiles used in the home? How were they made and repaired? What kind of fibres have held up over the past 200 years—what survives? I am drawn to the old fibres and how they were used. I learned the difference between hemp, nettle, thistle and linen, and how these fibrous plants could be spun and woven into material that can actually breathe. There is nothing better than sleeping under a fine old linen sheet—it will keep you cool in the summer and warm in the winter. Old linen torchons (kitchen towels) will last a lifetime or two with good care.

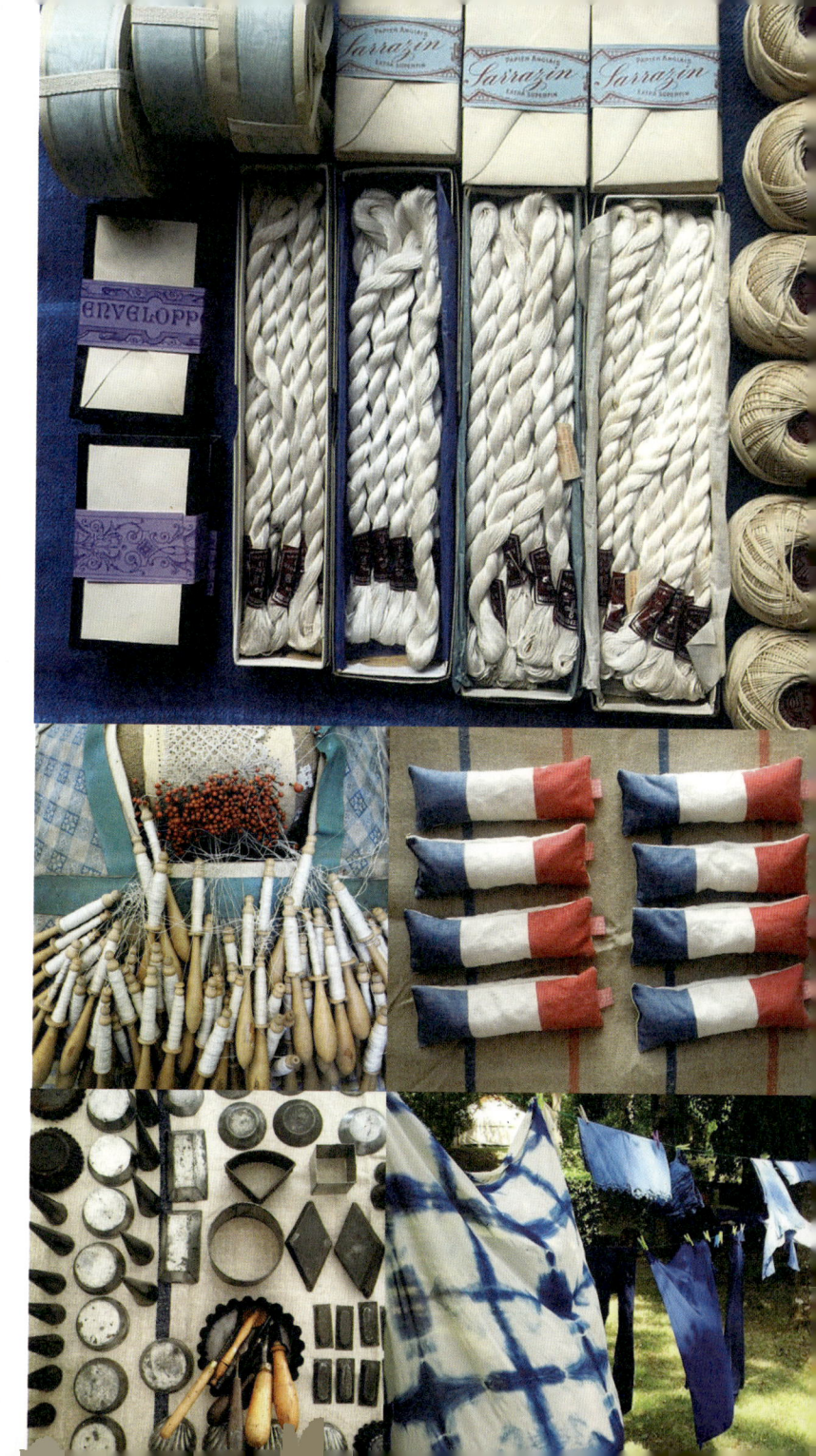

74   VINTAGE LIFE

NAVAJO RUGS

We live with vintage Navajo rugs strewn over the floors of our 1930 Spanish home in Los Angeles. We return every year to the Navajo Nation to pick up a new rug or two and work on a little idea called the Navajo Quilt Project. We collect and deliver fabric to the senior centres across the Navajo Nation so that the grandmothers have fabric and supplies to continue creating. The quilts can hopefully be traded or passed on to family members for warmth. The Navajo Nation represents living history, and like with France I feel the pull to return year after year.

I love walking on the rugs barefoot—knowing they have been woven by some of the finest weavers in the world and walked on for over a hundred years. Friends wonder why I don't hang them on the wall, so as not to cause any damage, but rugs are made for walking on and so on the floor they stay!

FRANCE GETAWAY RETREATS

Our France Getaway retreats started over 10 years ago as a way for us to share our love of France. We invite women to spend a week in the south of France with us every summer and learn about a rural lifestyle that includes visits to the brocantes, farmer's markets and local artisans. Our days are filled with creativity and inspiration as we spend time in the studio slow stitching or dyeing old linen sheets in a woad vat.

Our chef Charlotte fills us with local French fare and serves wine from the vineyards, all while teaching us about the seasons in France and what to look for at the local markets.

Over the years, we have met so many wonderful women from all over the world. We gather together for one short week, but in that week you learn about a whole lifetime—and that people love digging through the brocantes to find that perfect vintage treasure!

frenchgeneral.com
@frenchgeneral

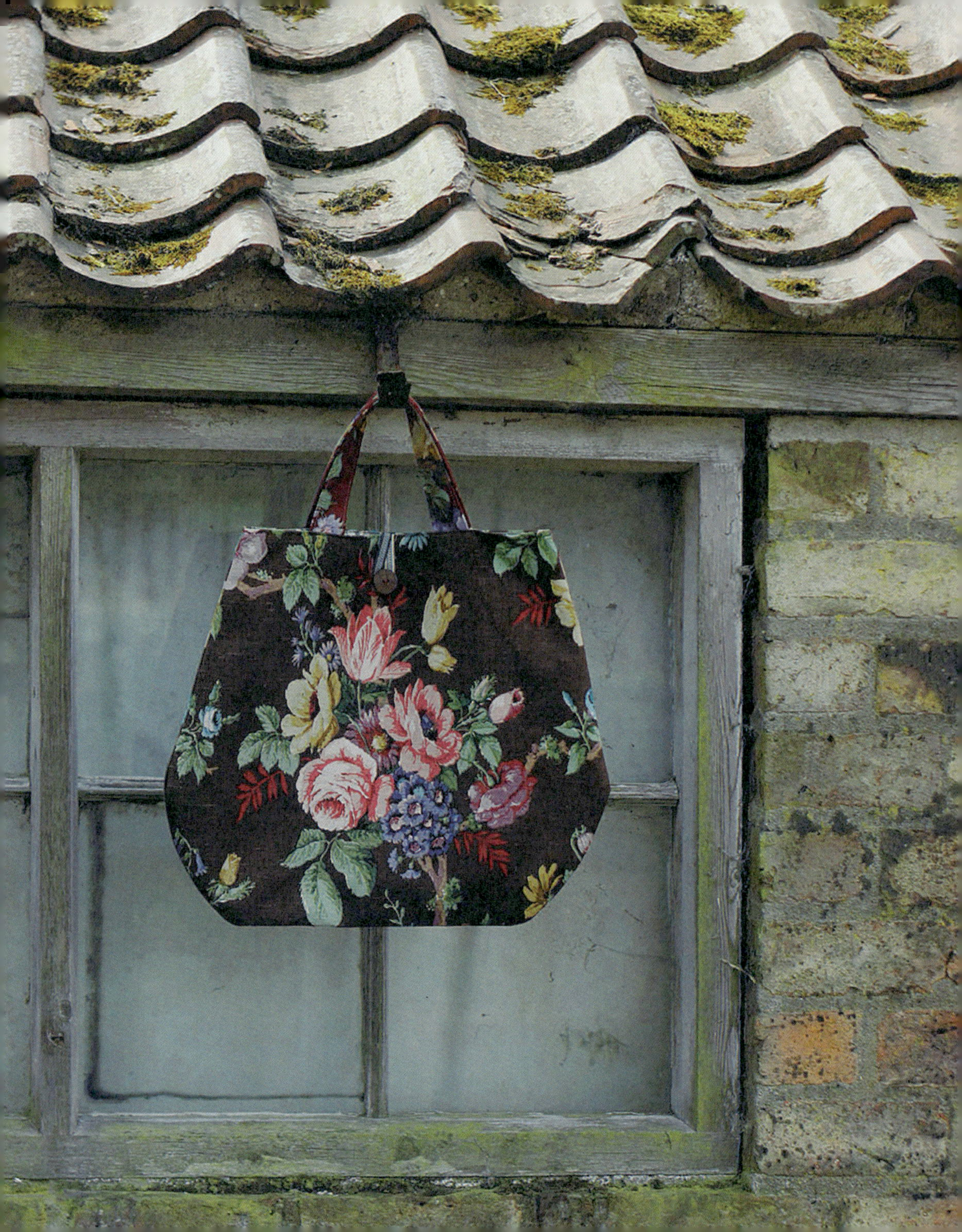

UPCYCLED STYLE

The Linen Garden

Beautiful
reinvention for
beloved textiles

VICKY TRAINOR

HEAD OF A GIRL

Do you remember when childhood was wide open, and time and space was yours to fill? It was devoid of iPads and technology, except perhaps our favourite television show that we had to make a point of watching specifically when it aired. "Being a child in the 1970s, well before this digital world, I had plenty of time to fill," recalls Vicky Trainor. "I was always encouraged, from a young age, to be interested in *something*, and this ignited my passion for collecting. I was never bored. I learned about the positioning of countries by collecting stamps and locating them on the globe. I adored collecting flowers during family walks and enjoyed, even more, identifying them and then pressing them."

"Since as early as I remember my time has been filled with the simple acts of drawing, making, creating, arranging and collecting. This time has been a true investment, as I have seamlessly taken each act through to adulthood and collated them all together to form my 'profession.' I don't think there is a single definitive word that can describe my day-to-day job, but all I know is that I am very much aware of how lucky I am to have formed a role that makes me happy. Each day is never the same."

On weekends, Vicky would get lost in a colourful world of paints and felt tips, collage and fabrics. "I was a young maker who didn't realize at the time that her passion for pattern and drawing would develop into studying textile design at university," she says.

Now, from her home in North Yorkshire in the United Kingdom, Vicky has taken her love of designing and collecting, and translated it to an online department store of "the decorative old and used" that

"I have a little obsession to try and get others to live with beautiful old textiles by lining their walls with long panels and lengths of printed linens like wallpaper, or purchasing a small and old textile sampler to simply pin to the wall like a painting. This can look stunning in a more modern interior."

THE LINEN GARDEN

OBJECTS OF HISTORY

Vintage items hold history: the wear of wood on the arm of a chair from many a sitting, the softening of linen that only time and endless laundering can deliver are all beautiful characteristics that cannot be found in modern manufacture. The pleasure in collecting flowers from the garden and then placing them in an old vase, imagining all the mothers and grandmothers and daughters and sons who have done just the same over the decades. The conversations, the dramas, the purpose and the social changes that that small, functional object has witnessed; how I wish each product would arrive with a diary of owners.

she calls The Linen Garden—"although there's far more than linen that settles here," she admits. "I mainly sell vintage and antique wares from the 1940s and older, however I am also interested in the inspiration of the Arts and Crafts movement in the design of fabrics during the 1970s, so the occasional delights from this period sneak onto the shelves at times."

Vicky makes products from personal paintings and drawings that also marry with vintage printed linens and cottons. "I try to recycle, reinvent, remake and mend where I can," she explains. "I love the challenge of repurposing items and turning them into 'the new,' and these kinds of projects arrive on the shelves of the store, too. The store is a wonderfully eclectic mix of varied design periods that I feel have a current voice in today's interiors world." ❋

HOME STUDIO

My studio is part of my home. Products that are available in the store tend to blend through to the house on plate rails, on shelves, on walls and in cupboards. If I purchase a piece that I personally love, I will live with it in my home first for a month or a year or beyond until I am ready to sell it to a new owner and let the decorative plate or length of linen continue its journey.

The decorative content and layers of objects collected inspire my personal work and collections too. I may purchase an old Victorian cup that could inspire a card design or an old cushion whose edging or finish inspires techniques for seaming or fringing.

"My most-prized vintage possession is my very loyal Bernina Minimatic sewing machine. It was made in 1967 (just two years older than myself). I purchased it when I was in my 20s and it has sewn thousands of miles over the decades, and wherever I have lived or worked it has just quite happily settled into a corner. My dad has just recently mended the electrics for me so it can continue (fingers crossed) for another decade, or two."

OLD LINENS AND TEXTILES

I love discovering old linens and textiles, and the excitement of finding a design that I have yet to own and never seen before is an absolute delight. The design content of older textiles is always exquisite, from the figurative details to the seductive colour palettes, and the quality of the linen is particularly special.

The old processes of block printing and screen printing by hand forces the design through to the reverse. This result is what I find the most appealing, and I very often prefer the gentler reverse of a print to use in my work rather than the "right" side.

thelinengarden.com
@thelinengarden

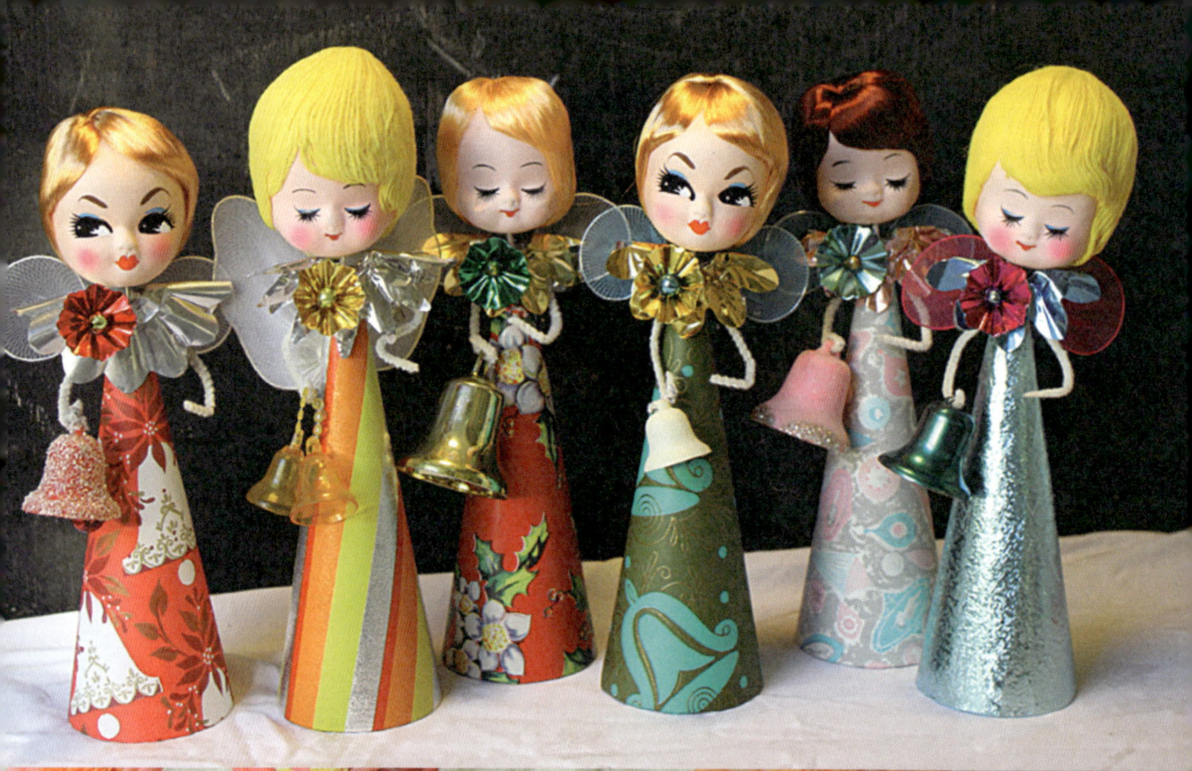
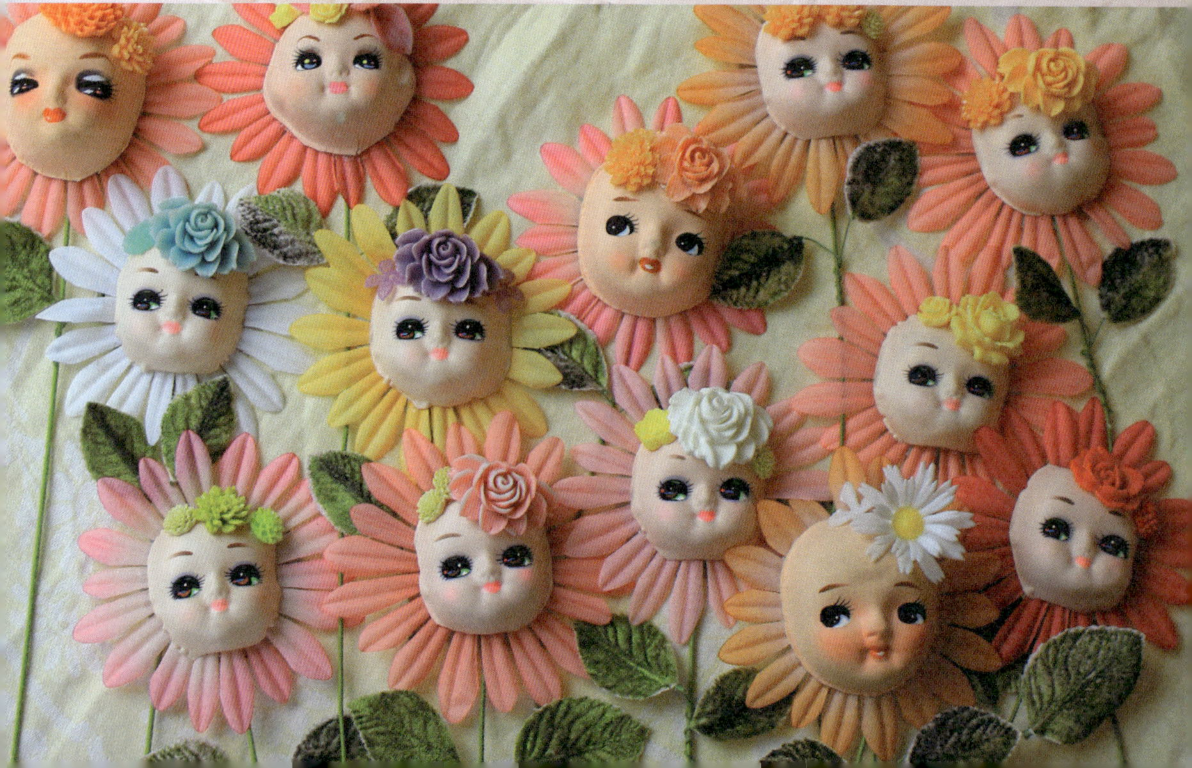

COLLECTIONS & CRAFT

Magpie Ethel

A year-round passion for holiday celebrations

LAURIE ROMANAGGI

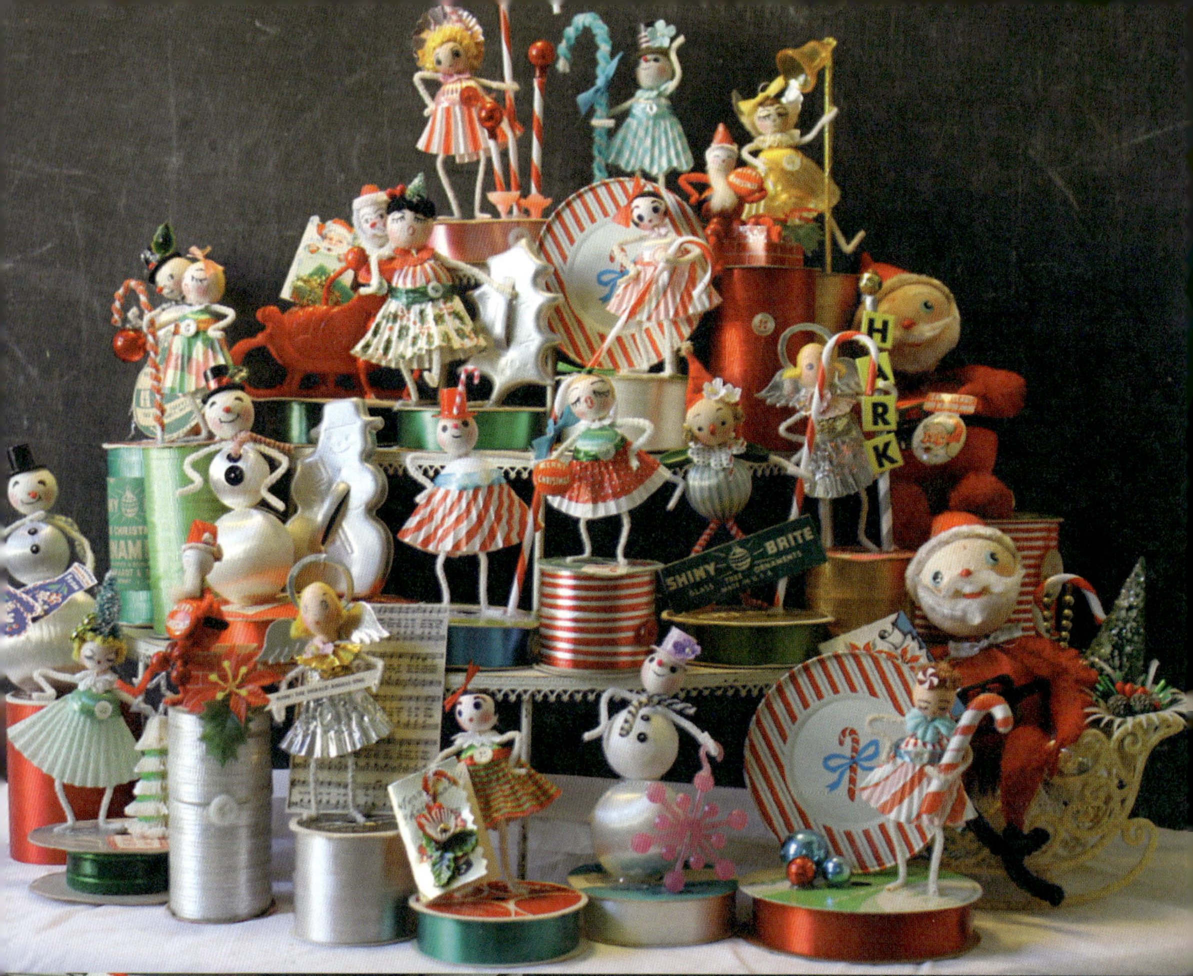
HARK
SHINY BRITE

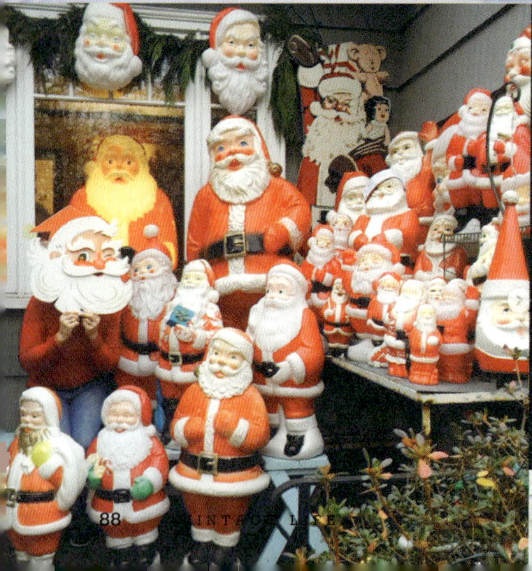

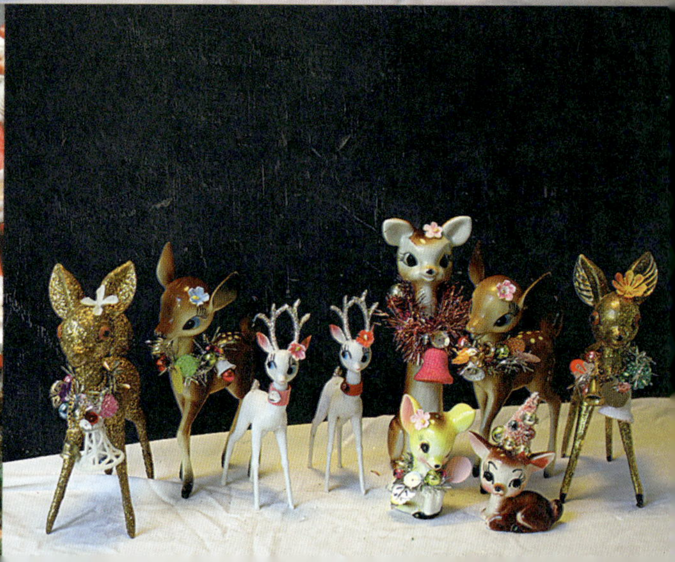

Laurie Romanaggi has an ongoing love affair with old stuff. "My passion is vintage holiday," she says. "I decorate for the majority of holidays with vintage finds. Not in a small way where I display a couple of things, but in a 'bring out the bins and make it over the top' way." In fact, her front window wonderland display is a neighbourhood event. "At Christmas, I am known as the Santa house, and there is a reason for that! I have about 40 blow mould Santas that decorate my front porch."

Laurie had a rather nomadic childhood, never living in a house longer than three years. "My dad worked for an international construction company," she explains. "While it was fun to travel and live in a multitude of places, it also made me want to establish some roots and stay put. Portland, Oregon, is now that home."

She has been married for 30 years, and her two kids are now grown. "I was lucky to be a stay-at-home mom. As my kids grew older I became more and more involved in the world of vintage. I started with a blog,

A PARTIAL LIST OF COLLECTIONS

Vintage child birthday invites, dentures/false teeth, mothball tins (one particular type), old chalk boxes, vintage swim caps, coloured wood mop or broom handles, old cake decorations, old Santa visit photos, children's barrettes, Santa blow moulds, bubble wands, baby rattles with faces, plastic outdoor swans, jingle bells on original cards, honeycomb balls, vintage wrapping paper, vintage dice, vintage fish, coloured dish drainers, valentine card boxes, vintage beach towels, ceramic turkeys, storks, plastic doilies, metal paint tins. The list goes on and on... I like to collect!

Daffodils

GIANT HYACINTHS

CROCUS

Come in and get ALL the FACTS

fresh tasty SNACKS 10¢

local craft shows and eventually two Etsy shops." In one shop, Magpie Ethel, Laurie sells whimsical, crafted creatures and decorations using vintage materials and found objects. Her second shop, E is for Ethel, is a place to resell her estate sale finds.

"My business would not be what it is today without the Internet," she says. "I started out connecting with other vintage-loving souls via my blog in 2007. Part of my vintage love has been sharing that with others who love it too. My blog and Instagram have led me to a whole tribe of people who think like I do and enjoy the same thing. I have friends in many countries and across the USA and have had the pleasure to meet many of them, all because of the Internet and the love of vintage."

Laurie is happy to call herself "the keeper of the family hand-me-downs." She takes on this responsibility from her own family's heirlooms but also acquires the artifacts of strangers, objects respectfully purchased at estate sales and flea markets. "I enjoy these treasures and all the stories that come with them." ❈

SHEER EXUBERANCE

I truly get excited when I find something to add to my collections, decorate my house with or craft with. It's truly a "junkers high." I also enjoy trying to figure out how to display something in an interesting and unexpected manner. I rotate collections in and out quite a bit (especially since they are holiday related). I occasionally let go of a collection or sell duplicates off. My house is only so big and my interests change. Buying a beach house three years ago gave me a whole new arena to collect for with a vintage beach vibe. Having that to collect for has been the best!

"My house is a reflection of my vintage love of collections, holiday and the quirky. I am also a fan of holiday decorating. I like things in multiples. My love of holidays has evolved into my business Magpie Ethel, for which I craft items to celebrate each occasion. Each item I make has a vintage component to it—hence the need to keep hunting. It is a vicious cycle!"

HONOURING THE PAST

I like that I can have items that make my house and me unique. It is a memory and often one of a kind. I really enjoy the stories behind each item. When I am at a flea market or estate sale and I hear the story behind something I will often spend time writing it down and tucking it in with the item. It is my way to honour the past.

Erv's
50¢
75¢
35¢
KEEP THIS COUPON

MANNING BOWMAN
SUNSHINE JANE
PEANUT
BUTTER

JUNE

"I hunt down and hoard supplies, as everything I make has a vintage component to it. What makes my art memorable is that component. I can take the smallest doodad and give it new life. I really enjoy that immensely—recycling something that otherwise would be tossed or not enjoyed."

@magpieethel

CHOICE of STAND
CHOICE of STAND
CHOICE of STAND
CHOICE of STAND
CHOICE of STAND
Glov-Ett
SHOES FOR ACTIVE FEET

ENTREPRENEUR

Junk Bonanza

At home with the flea market entrepreneur

KI NASSAUER

"I'm drawn to a vintage-inspired life because designing and decorating with vintage gives you an opportunity to create your own style. Every vintage piece has a history and I enjoy adding to the story!"

As the original "junk lady," Ki Nassauer has been dubbed the "Martha Stewart of vintage" and "America's most famous junker" in extensive media coverage. She has crafted a career from junk since 1999, scouring flea markets, salvage yards and streetside piles of cast-offs for materials to create tastefully inventive furniture and decorative accessories. Her creativity has earned her nearly 215,000 followers on Facebook.

Ki was one of the first to realize the potential revenue in converting junk into cool stuff. After her "test" garage sale grossed $11,000, she founded JunkMarket, monthly sales that have morphed into Junk Bonanza, three-day shopping extravaganzas twice yearly in Minneapolis. Each Bonanza showcases wares from hand-picked dealers nationwide who deliver best-of shopping experiences for lovers of antiques, vintage, architectural salvage, and one-of-a-kind and artisan-repurposed treasures. The three-day events also include special appearances, workshops and giveaways.

One of Ki's hallmarks is her joy of connecting those who comprise her deep national network of vintage dealers, artisans and junk aficionados. She is able to realize this in her role as editor-in-chief for *Flea Market Style* magazine. *Flea Market Style* chronicles the beauty and utility of the vintage-inspired life with six issues per year, available on newsstands.

The co-author of *Decorating JunkMarket Style* and *Junk Beautiful, Room by Room Makeovers*, Ki also produced a regular column in *Country Home* magazine and has made hundreds of public appearances nationwide. Before shifting to a career in junk, she owned and operated successful clothing stores, and freelanced in product design for several national retailers.

Ki has savoured every step along the hike to the top of the junk pile and she preaches the gospel of junk through consulting, public appearances, interviews and magazine signings. She is happily committed to ensuring that repurposing remains sustainable, functional—and always fun! ✻

VINTAGE LIFE

"Vintage living is my hobby, profession and business! Whether it's my morning flowered vintage juice glass, a project I'm working on for *Flea Market Style* magazine or cooking on my O'Keefe & Merritt range, I'm constantly reminded why I love vintage!"

MODERN CONVENIENCE

Modern technology has helped to make vintage more accessible. Being able to shop for vintage online and gather inspiration from Instagram has been a welcome addition from when I started in the vintage business. Modern technology also makes it easier to collaborate with other creatives and artists in the vintage industry.

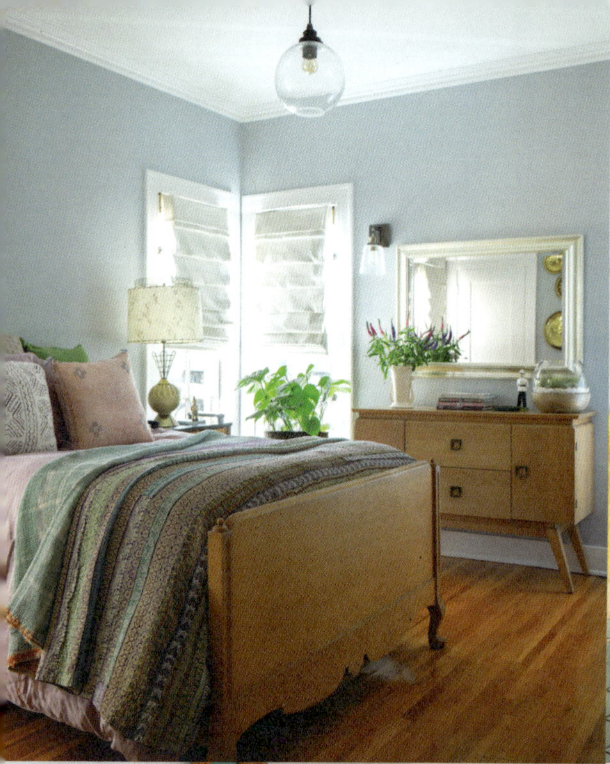
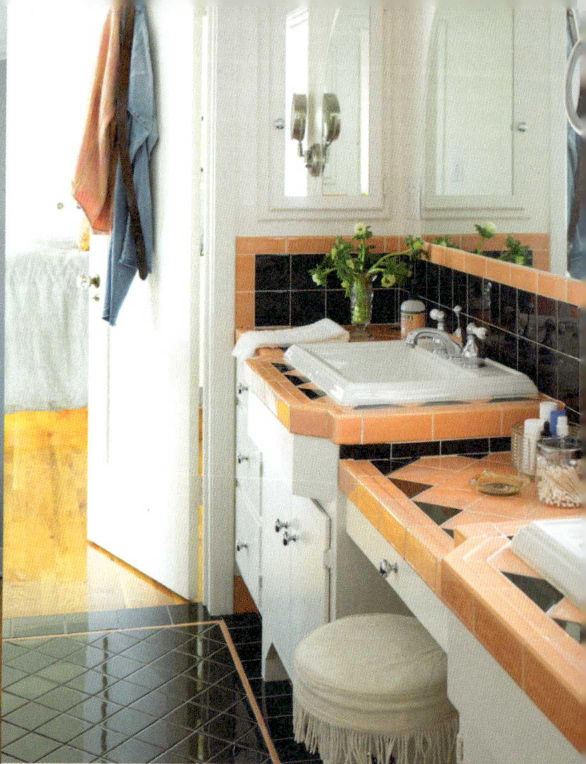
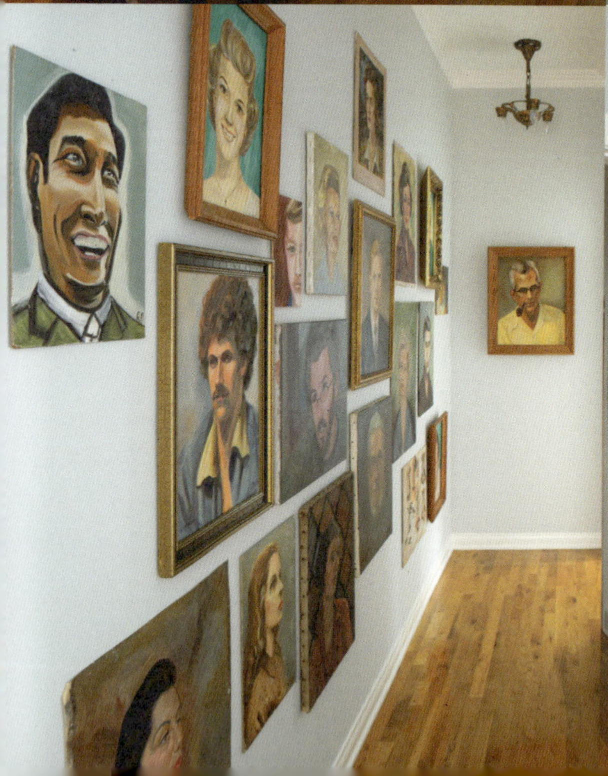
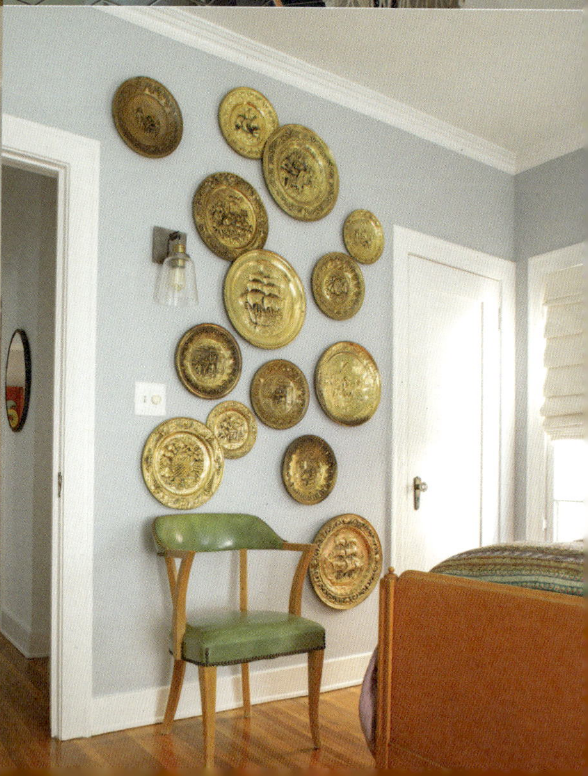

"My eight-foot marlin is my most prized vintage possession! It travelled from Minnesota to California and hangs proudly in my living room. Finding this marlin was like finding the holy grail to me! Next up on my list to bring home is a coin-operated Sandy horse for my grandkids to ride!"

"I have a passion for quirky, off-the-beaten-path, colourful vintage items that make you smile. Some of my favourites include pieces from carnivals and the circus—particularly game wheels! My vintage style at home might not be for everyone, but it sure gives visitors something to talk about!"

JUNK BONANZA

"'Flea market' is an enduring aesthetic because it's never boring! There will always be the thrill of the hunt for one-of-a-kind items that fill your home with character. It's an aesthetic where anything goes, which allows everyone to create their own personal style."

104 VINTAGE LIFE

kinassauerstyle.com
@kinassauerstyle

WASHINGTON
Evergreen State
ARKANSAS
RHODE ISLAND
VERMONT
PAINTED DESERT Ariz.
MEXICO
LONG HORN
TEXAS
MASSACHUSETTS
OREGON
The Sunset State
OKLAHOMA
STATE FLOWER
MISTLETOE
MISSISSIPPI
Navajo Trail
TENNESSEE
INDIANA
YUMA
ARIZONA
MONTANA
UTAH
JACKSON HOLE
AERIAL TRAM-WAY
GRAND TETONS
WYOMING
Zion National Park
NEBRASKA
IDAHO
NEW MEXICO
LUCKY ME! I VISITED
Carlsbad Caverns
NEW MEXICO
NEW HAMPSHIRE
Old Man of the Mountain
ILLINOIS
CONNECTICUT
IOWA
WYOMING
First National Bank
YORK FLORAL CO.
SPECIALTY SERVICE CO.
RENT YOUR TOWELS AND LINEN
Realtors WEDGWOOD Insurance
BECK HALE & BECKNER
Merry Christmas
and a Happy New Year
WICHITA FALLS, TEXAS
BOOTHE'S SWEET SHOP
Hoosier Pride
Money When You Need It
PARSLEY FLAKES
CRESCENT
MACE
CRESCENT PURE SPICES
TWO OUNCES
SPRINX
MARJORAM
LEMON PEEL
KINGS CANYON NATL PARK
GRANTS PASS, ORE.
CHICAGO ILL.
SAN ANTONIO
STONY CREEK VILLAGE
SEQUOIA NAT'L FOREST
AIR FORCE ACADEMY
IDAHO
PETRIFIED FOREST
ARIZONA
SHASTA DAM
HOUSTON
COLORED PENCILS
LEAD PENCILS
DIXON ANADEL
COLOR PENCILS
VENUS UNIQUE
Thin Lead
COLORED PENCILS
Blaisdell
NICK

COLLECTOR

Squirrel Vintage Shop

Buying and selling with an eye for design

RUTH ROSENFIELD

"I've become part of the creative, funky, passionate group of buyers and sellers, most of whom started as collectors like me."

Ruth Rosenfield started shopping at Pasadena-area flea markets when she was still in high school. "We had a couple of really good ones," she recalls. "I went every weekend and got hooked. This is where I really started to appreciate and collect vintage. There was so much visual eye candy and inspiration in vintage items, and it helped me develop my taste level being exposed to so many examples of good design."

She attended art college and moved to New York City to work in advertising. "I kept going to pretty much any flea market I could find, mostly the great 47th Street flea. I wasn't making enough money as a junior art director to buy much, but I just loved the experience of looking. I was also fascinated by the people who sell and buy at flea markets and the whole vintage culture. It's a decidedly creative environment."

In the past 30 years, Ruth has worked as an art director and creative director in three cities and at seven advertising agencies—all the while continuing to collect vintage. Now that she is settled in Mill

Valley, California, buying and selling is a hobby. "I've found that the process of finding great vintage items, researching their history, and photographing and selling them fills my creative tank and I carry that juju into my day job."

Ruth acknowledges that her profession has informed her passion for vintage. "When your job depends on coming up with creative, unique and visual ideas on a deadline, you do everything you can to fill yourself with inspiration. You read every magazine and book you can, watch movies and TV shows of all kinds, expose yourself to art, culture and ideas wherever and whenever you can. Immersing myself in the wide world of vintage, in person and now online, has helped fill me with ideas that I have used throughout my career. And now it has helped me create a side business of buying and selling vintage, and connected me with so many interesting people and places. All these experiences have just added to my creative arsenal." ✺

ECO-CONSCIOUS LIVING

Another aspect of the vintage business that really resonates with me is that we're saving so many items from the landfill. I am very eco-conscious, and to me this idea of reusing something old (and better looking) is the epitome of green living. I see myself as doing a form of recycling: not only passing on great looking, functional, unique items, but by buying and selling vintage I'm doing our planet a big ol' favour.

SQUIRREL VINTAGE SHOP

PRIZED POSSESSION

My most prized is something that came to me as part of my family history and I didn't even know it existed. It's a 1930s multi-drawer oak countertop display cabinet made by the Weber Lifelike Fly Company, from Stevens Point, Wisconsin, to sell fishing flies, the kind that would be on the counter at a general store. The story goes that my great uncle was a travelling candy salesman, based in New York. (He would often send us boxes of samples!) He brought this cabinet home from a trip to the Midwest and it lived in his basement holding bits and bobs of hardware until he passed away. It went to my uncle and then to my cousin, Susan. She was out visiting us from the east coast and observed all the vintage goings-on in my house and said, "I have something in my basement for you." And voila! This box arrived and it was love at first sight. I couldn't believe something so beautiful could be from my own family. And it's an advertising piece on top of everything else. It's something I would have *killed* to find at an estate sale. It sits in a very prominent place in our house and it's currently holding my vintage typewriter ribbon tin collection.

110 VINTAGE LIFE

GREAT DESIGN

My vintage passion is anything that features great design, fantastic typography or bold colour. Even better if it contains all three. While I admire people who can limit themselves to a neutral palette, that's not me. I pick things for their graphic qualities, not really for their value. I will usually bypass something that I know will fetch a big profit, if I wouldn't personally want to own it. My taste is definitely a bit funky. You can often find me in the garage or outbuilding at an estate sale, digging for something really old, cool and hidden. I love to find things that have been repurposed and are useful. And, of course, I'm especially drawn to items that are forms of advertising for places and products. That can be something as simple as a vintage coffee can or a great old hand-painted sign. Those are the things that really connect with me.

111

Superior Quality
WASP
521
PAINT RIT!
THRIFTY
GUARANTEED
100% STYRENE
TB-1420
ROYAL

"I love to scour estate sales near and far, and the discovery of finding the most unusual and fantastic items."

ART DIRECTION

In my world, art directing and vintage collecting are completely interconnected. I began taking photographs after every estate sale or flea market to make a visual record and reminder of what I bought where (I loathe a spreadsheet). And being an art director, I had to make the photographs look good. I discovered the art of the flat lay and realized it was just like an advertising layout. I love making flat lays of items of a similar kind, but also find it a fascinating challenge to use items from just one estate sale. I see it as an homage to the people whose house I was in and the interesting lives they've led. I started posting these photos on Instagram, getting followers and great feedback. I've found that what I started choosing to buy at estate sales and fleas became informed by my idea of how I'm going photograph them. Sometimes, I find myself formulating what the photo is going to look like even as I'm in the frenzy of a sale. Often I'll be attracted to an item, or reject it, based on how I can art direct it either in my booth at a flea market, or on Instagram. Using my art direction skills has really helped bolster my vintage brand. I've even started selling prints of my flat lay photos.

SQUIRREL VINTAGE SHOP

"I'm drawn to the unique typography, graphics and illustration of lard tins, an everyday pantry staple. Lard was produced regionally, so I love to search for and collect tins from all parts of the country. I mostly find them being reused in garages and workshops filled with nails or other useful parts. I appreciate that these simple objects lived a second life. They went from the kitchen to the workbench, my two favourite rooms to search at any estate sale!"

@ruthsrosenfield

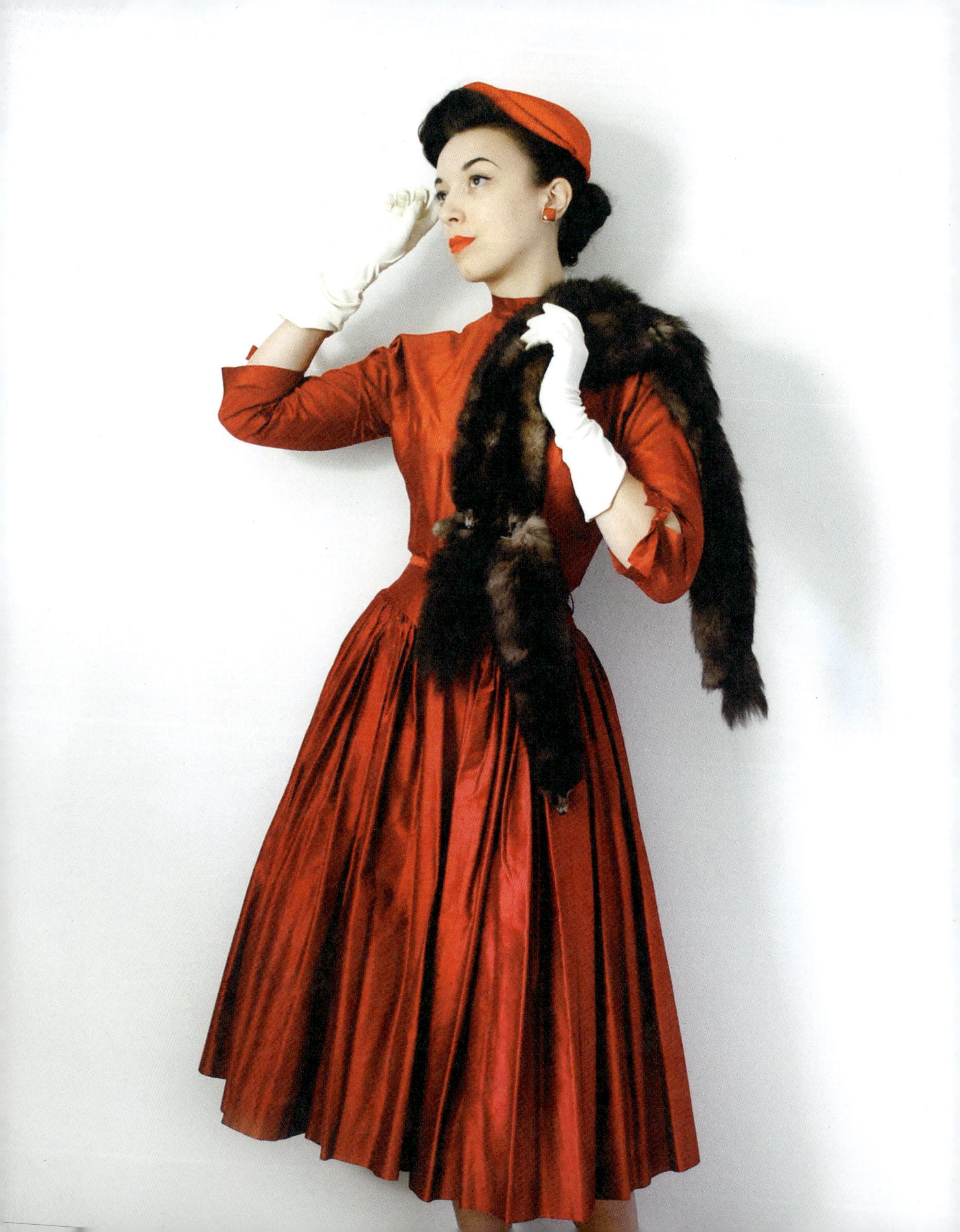

FASHION

Vintage Rose Girl

An artist, musician and historian, Eliza wears vintage with style and substance

ELIZA SCHNEIDER-GREEN

"Because I wear my vintage clothing regularly, I associate each dress or suit with specific events or moments in my life. The love I have for each garment is tied to my memories of where they were worn."

Eliza Schneider-Green is an artist, photographer, writer, singer-songwriter and student of art history and museum studies in Tallahassee, Florida. "I am constantly surrounded by the sounds and styles of the past," she says. "I've always felt that there's this cohesiveness within my life, with vintage acting as the thread that runs through my education, my hobbies, my interests and my passions. At this point, I'm not sure which one inspires the other more. They are inseparable."

"When I'm studying the major art movements of the 20th century, I can't help but also think of what was happening in the world of fashion, since art and fashion are constantly influencing one another. When I'm playing with my band and singing jazz and blues from the 1920s and '30s, I'm imagining the world in which these songs were sung for the first time. When it comes to styling for my photography projects, I'm always choosing vintage garments and hairstyles over modern ones, as I'm at my most creative when I'm surrounded by the things that I love."

In her early days of collecting vintage, Eliza says she "gobbled up all the fluffy prom dresses and beaded ball gowns I could find that were within my teenager budget." But around 2014, she began collecting 1940s and '50s suits and day dresses to build up a daily wardrobe that fit her lifestyle. "I've always been fascinated by the wartime fashions of the late 1930s and early 1940s, as well as by the influence of Christian Dior's New Look on postwar style. And hats play a large role in these revolutionary years of style, as they were used to accentuate the drama of an outfit, or to add a touch of glamour to an otherwise ordinary suit."

VINTAGE ROSE GIRL 119

"To me, a vintage-inspired life is simply living with a deep appreciation for the styles, technologies and events of the past."

"The architectural elements of a good hat are hard to ignore—especially the gravity-defying tilt hats from the late 1930s and the make-do-and-mend styles that emerged out of the mid-1940s as a result of rationing. Hats are wearable works of art—three-dimensional sculptures that make an outfit complete. In my years of collecting and wearing vintage, I've never felt completely dressed until I have on a hat, and beyond the style and drama and practical reasons for wearing them, they act as conversation starters. A suit is just a suit until you add a pop of colour or dash of a veil, and then, all of a sudden, that suit is transformed into something complete, with the hat acting like the exclamation point on the end of the sentence."✤

LIVING HISTORY

Vintage is the antithesis to fast fashion and the disposable fads that come and go with the seasons. While style evolution is nothing new, the magic of a well-tailored suit or simple black dress can be found across most decades in the 20th century—the overall style from the 1930s to the 1960s might be different, but the idea is the same.

There's a joy and attention to detail in vintage clothing that cannot be matched by most modern styles. The texture of cold rayon, whimsy of 1940s novelty-print dresses and innovation of post-WWII designs are intertwined with both the personal stories and the national histories that we've grown up with.

Vintage clothing acts as living history, something that can be touched and worn and studied, alongside the narratives from textbooks and historical documentaries, and the stories from our parents and grandparents. Just like when visiting an ancient Roman temple, or seeing a beloved painting in person for the first time, I have a visceral reaction to holding a vintage dress in my hand, knowing that it's a vessel for the memories of all the women who have come before me. What has it seen? How many weddings, funerals, first dates, life-altering days and ordinary days has this dress been worn for?

Each piece is a visual anthology of someone's life. And each time I wear it, I'm adding to the collective memory. I'm adding my own experiences and emotions and giving life to something that has outlived the women who first loved it. And that, to me, is nothing short of magic.

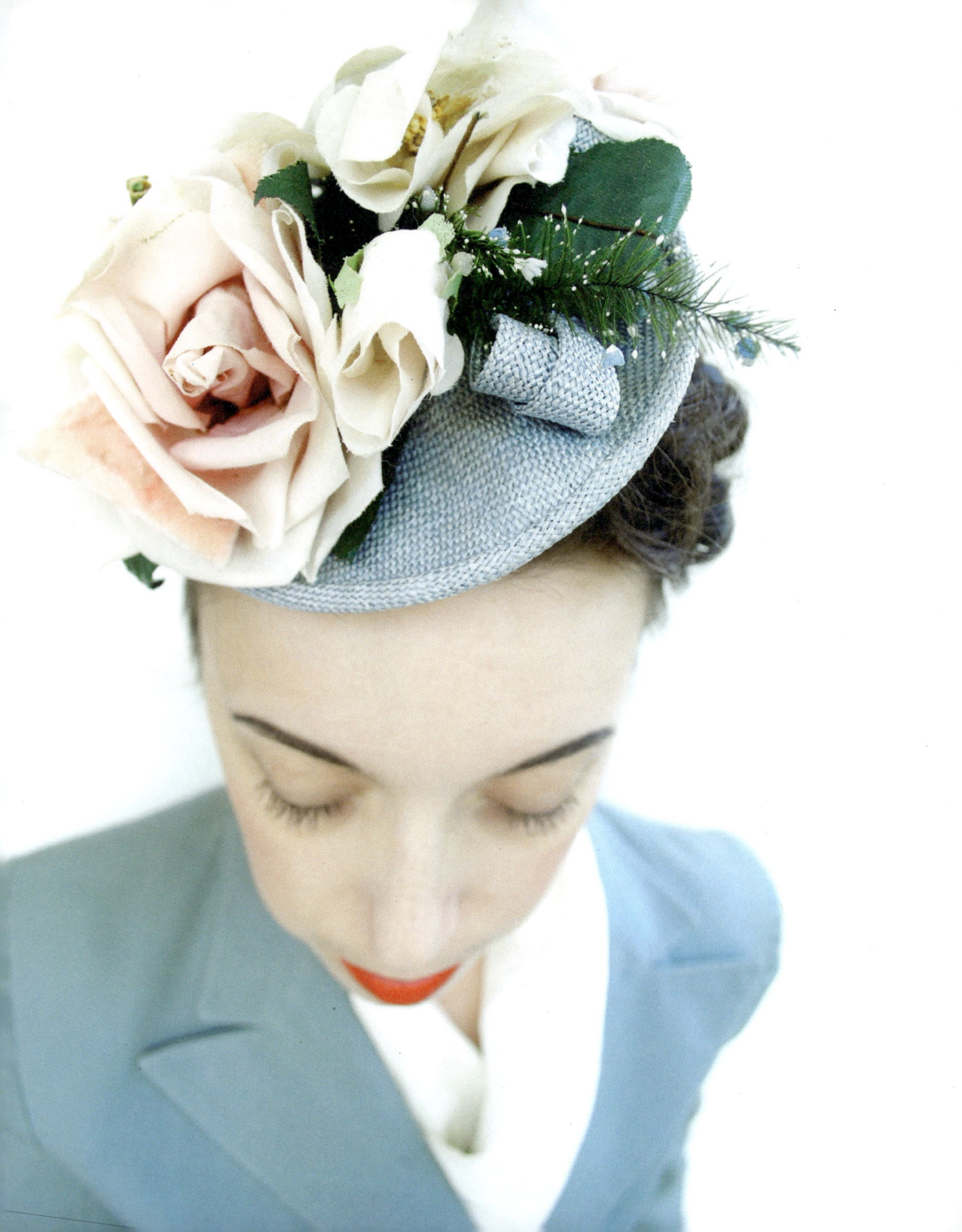

BEYOND AESTHETICS

I can't count the number of times I've had a deep conversation with a complete stranger that began with "I just have to ask where you got that dress…" or "my mother had a hat just like that when I was a child…" Bonding with someone in such an intimate way simply because of the clothing I wear isn't something I take for granted. But beyond these conversations, I find it ironic that the way that I connect to so many of my friends, purchase my clothing and deepen my knowledge of the past, exists in such a modern capacity. And this combination of the old and the new is what I find so fascinating about the vintage community.

My appreciation for modernity is intimately linked with my knowledge of the past, and the most memorable conversations I've had are not about past styles, but about the differences between our lives today and the lives of our mothers and grandmothers. We live in a time that is, by many accounts, more open-minded and welcoming to previously frowned-upon viewpoints and ways of life. However, the harshest realities of humanity haven't magically disappeared just because we possess tools that previous generations didn't have. I believe that the first step in reconciling your love of vintage must be recognizing your privilege to live in the time that we live in, while also being aware that we aren't living in a magic bubble where the racism, sexism and close-mindedness of the past has ceased to exist. And this is where the opportunity to educate lies. You should not be apathetic to the hard-to-swallow events and mindsets of the past if you are going to appreciate the aesthetics—and in only viewing it aesthetically, you miss an opportunity to start conversations.

ONE HUNDRED HATS

I began the One Hundred Hats project in the summer of 2015 after purchasing my fiftieth hat. The project was my way of cataloguing and documenting the 50 that I owned, while looking ahead to the 50 that I would eventually add to my collection. The first photos were taken on my iPhone—I sat on my front steps and propped up a white backdrop behind me and took the photos selfie-style. When I posted them on my Instagram, there was an overwhelming amount of interest from my followers and encouragement for me to continue, which took me by surprise! I started getting private messages from followers on nearly a daily basis, sharing their own collections and stories about hats they owned. Since beginning the project, I've had people send me hats from their own collection for the project— and I don't take that for granted!

Nowadays I have around 83 hats total (I've lost count!), and use a Nikon D3000 on a tripod and two spot lamps, and take roughly 200 photos for each hat. But I still shoot each photo in my carport, propped up against a white background. I don't believe that you need fancy equipment or a professional studio to create art. You just need to be creative in how you use what you have, and be patient with the process. Every photo that I take has minimal editing—I don't believe in altering my photographs beyond recognition. If there's a hair blowing in front of my face, it stays. If there's a mosquito on my cheek (a common occurrence in Florida), it stays! If there's cat fur on my collar, it stays! I prefer realism in my photographs, rather than polished perfection.

When I first began the hat project, my hair and makeup were far more modern than they are now. I have a background in ballet and theatre, so I've always had a knack for doing my own hair and makeup, but I've had no formal training. Most of what I've learned about vintage hairstyling and makeup is through experimentation and studying first-hand sources—magazine ads, photographs and historic videos on YouTube. So now I have my go-to 1920s, '30s, '40s, '50s and '60s makeup and hairstyles, and I've gotten it down to an exact science!

When I decide to shoot a particular hat, the first thing I do is have a look through my closet and choose an outfit. I always stay loyal to the decade—if I'm shooting a hat from the early 1940s, I'll wear an outfit that is from the early 1940s, with the appropriate hair and makeup, and undergarments. I believe in historical accuracy above all else with my photographs. There's an emotional reaction I have to an outfit that is historically accurate. Something just clicks, and I feel a complete understanding for the era, when each element—the hat, the hair style, the outfit, the undergarments, down to the lipstick shade and eyebrow shape—is working together. At that point, taking the photo is just documenting the cohesiveness.

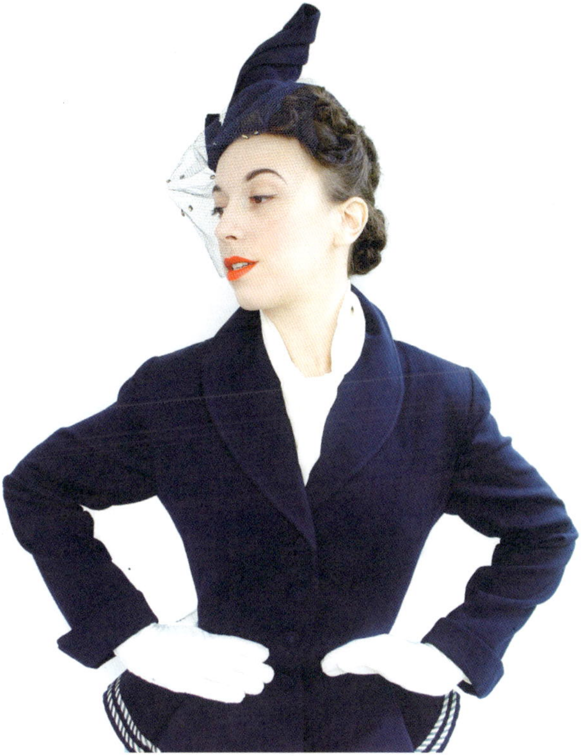

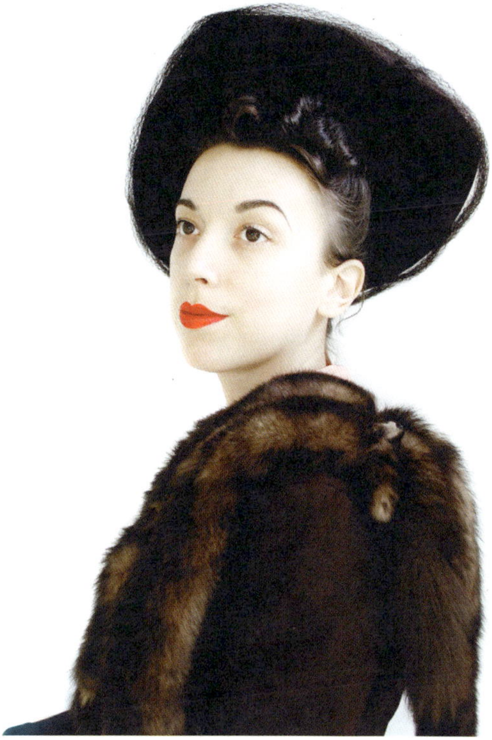

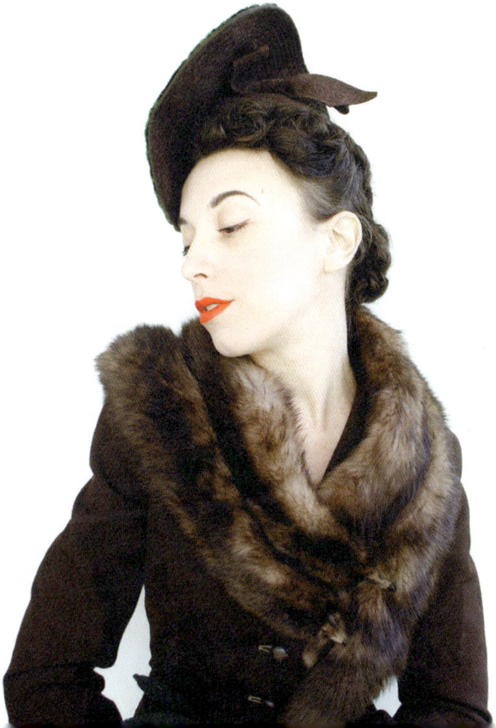

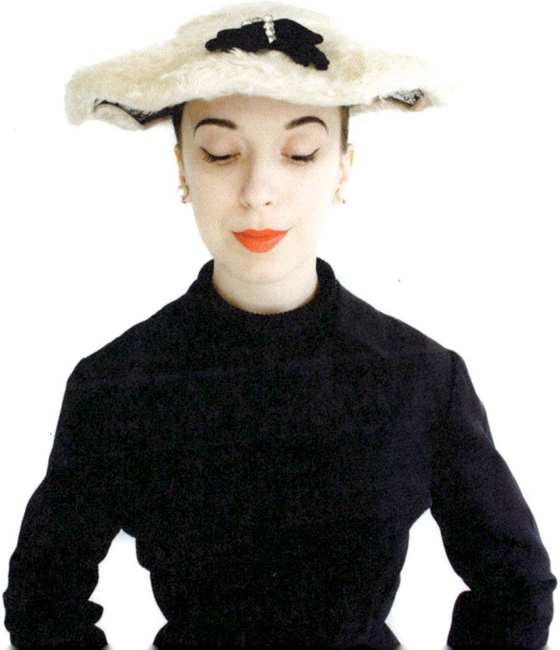

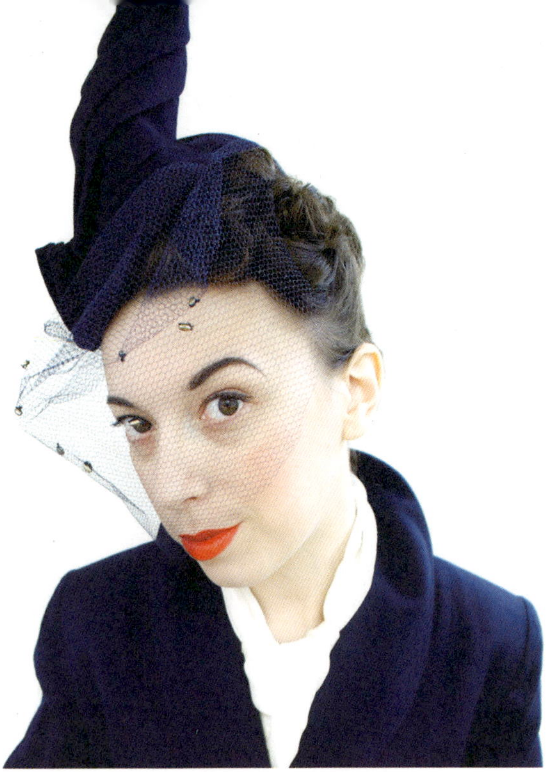

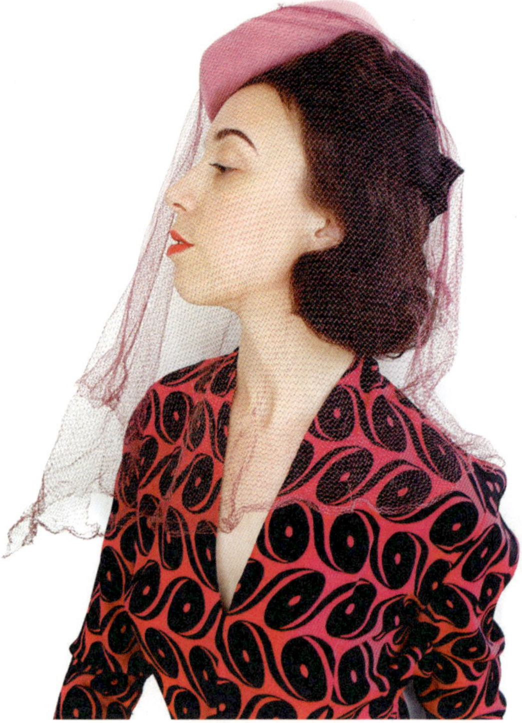

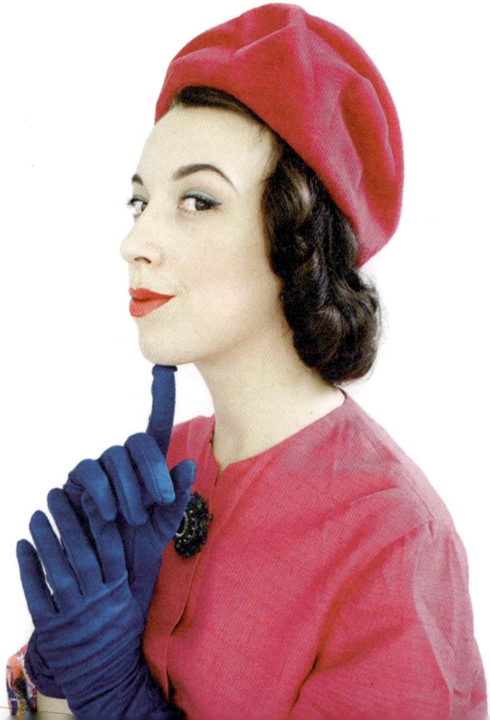

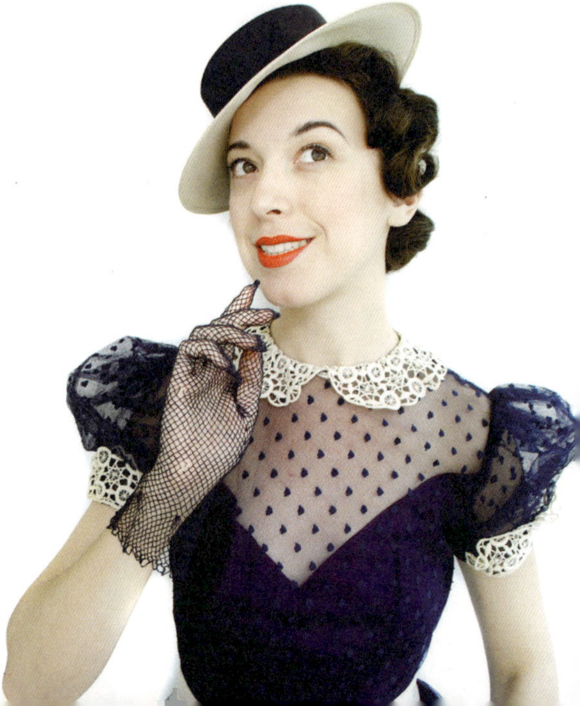

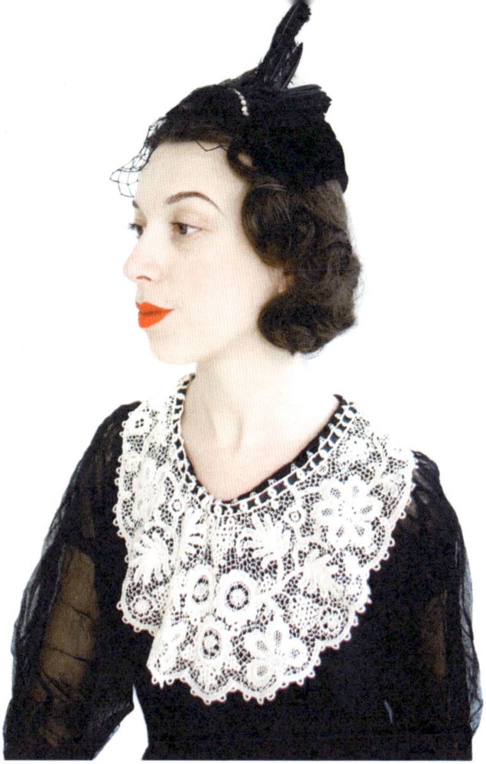
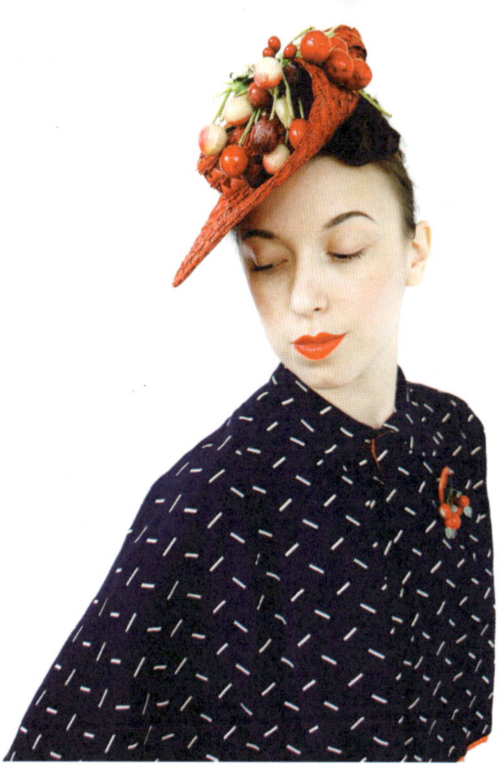
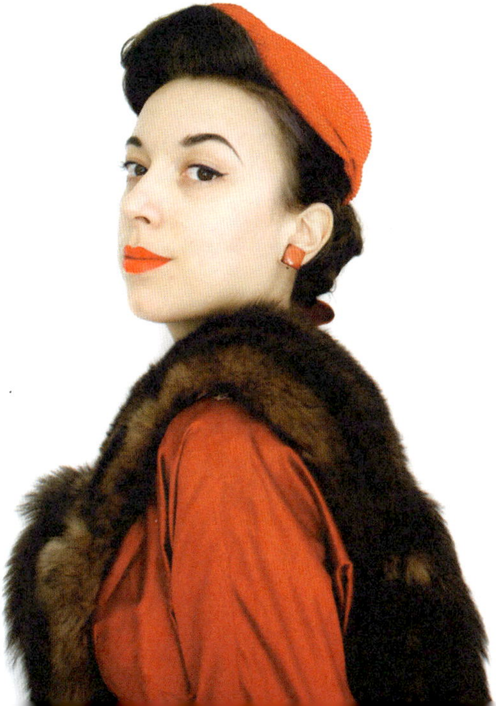
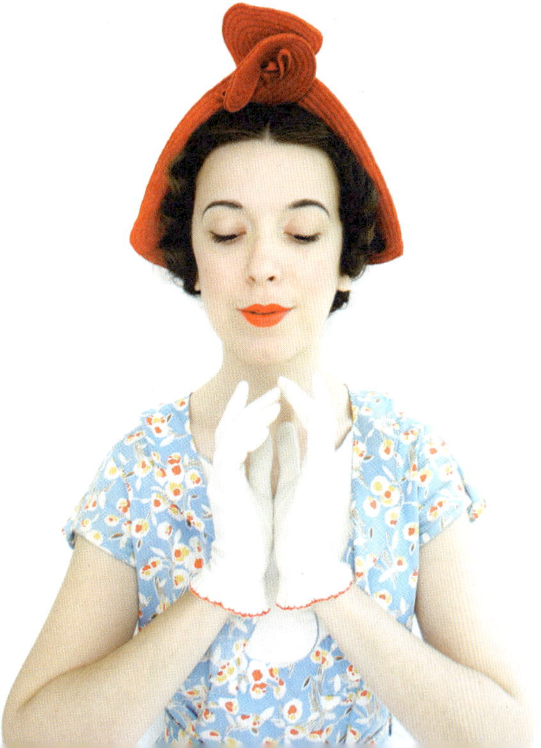

"There's a certain feeling I get when I listen to old music, and it's the same feeling I get when I wear a dress from the 1930s or hold a book from the 1860s. It goes beyond nostalgia—something like a homesickness for a time that I have never lived through (not in this life, at least), and it permeates every part of me. I have a background in ballet and musical theater, and grew up with my grandfather's collection of jazz records and my mom's collection of Rolling Stones, Beatles and Carole King, so music has always been a deep part of my life. I was in a folk band for several years and quickly came to love Americana and country music from the first half of the 20th century. But my love for music and love for vintage feel most intertwined when I sing jazz and blues from the 1920s and '30s. I step into a different realm when I sing those songs. As a songwriter, I'm heavily influenced by southern gothic literature and the music I grew up listening to. Patsy Cline, Dolly Parton (who my guitar is lovingly named after), Kay Starr, Billie Holiday, Lee Morse, Django Reinhardt, George Gershwin and many others were the soundtrack to my childhood and are now the soundtrack to my adulthood. When I'm singing a song written in 1931, wearing a vintage dress and sharing my love of music with people who appreciate it, I feel that my life is in perfect harmony."

vintagerosegirl.wordpress.com
@vintagerosegirl

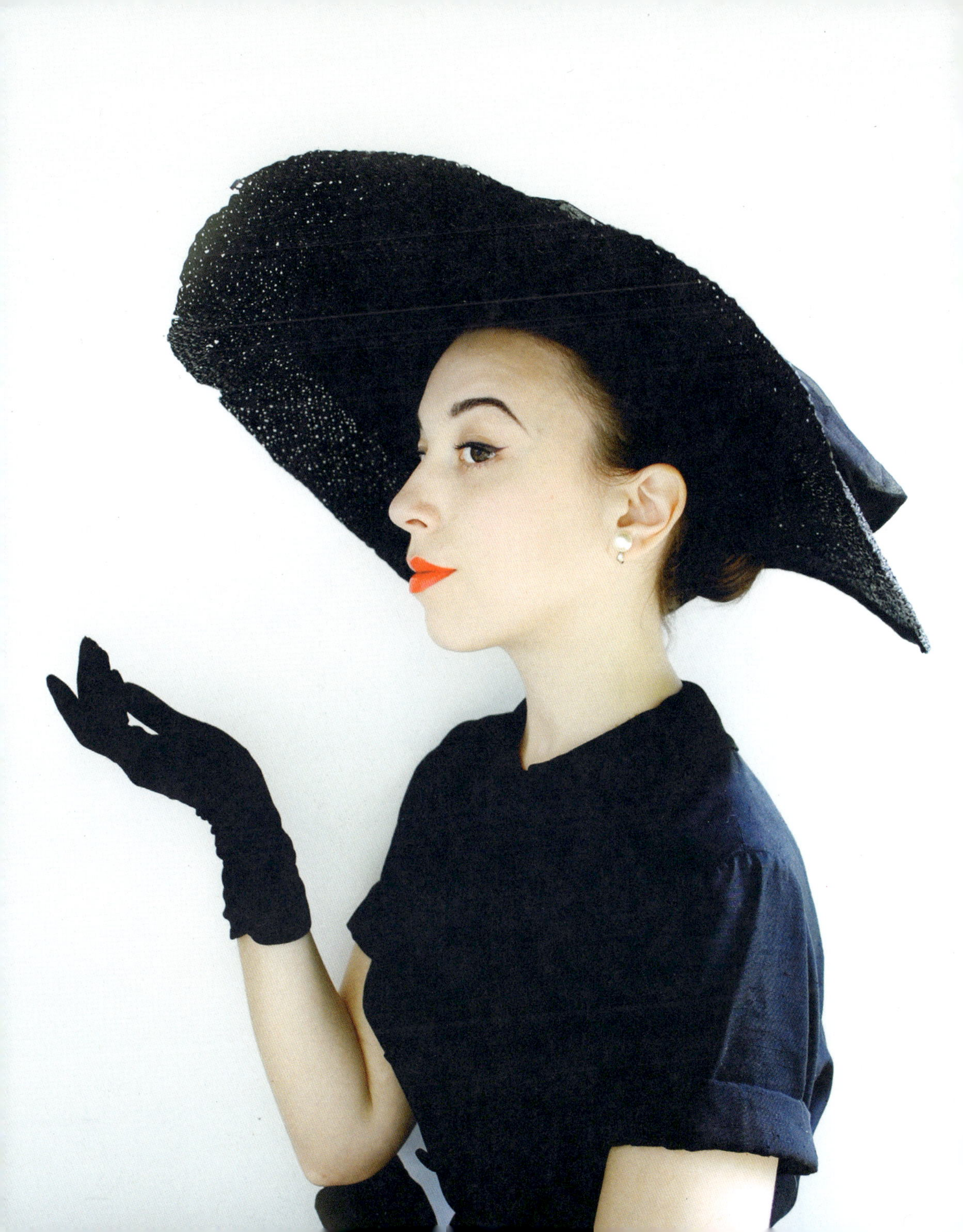

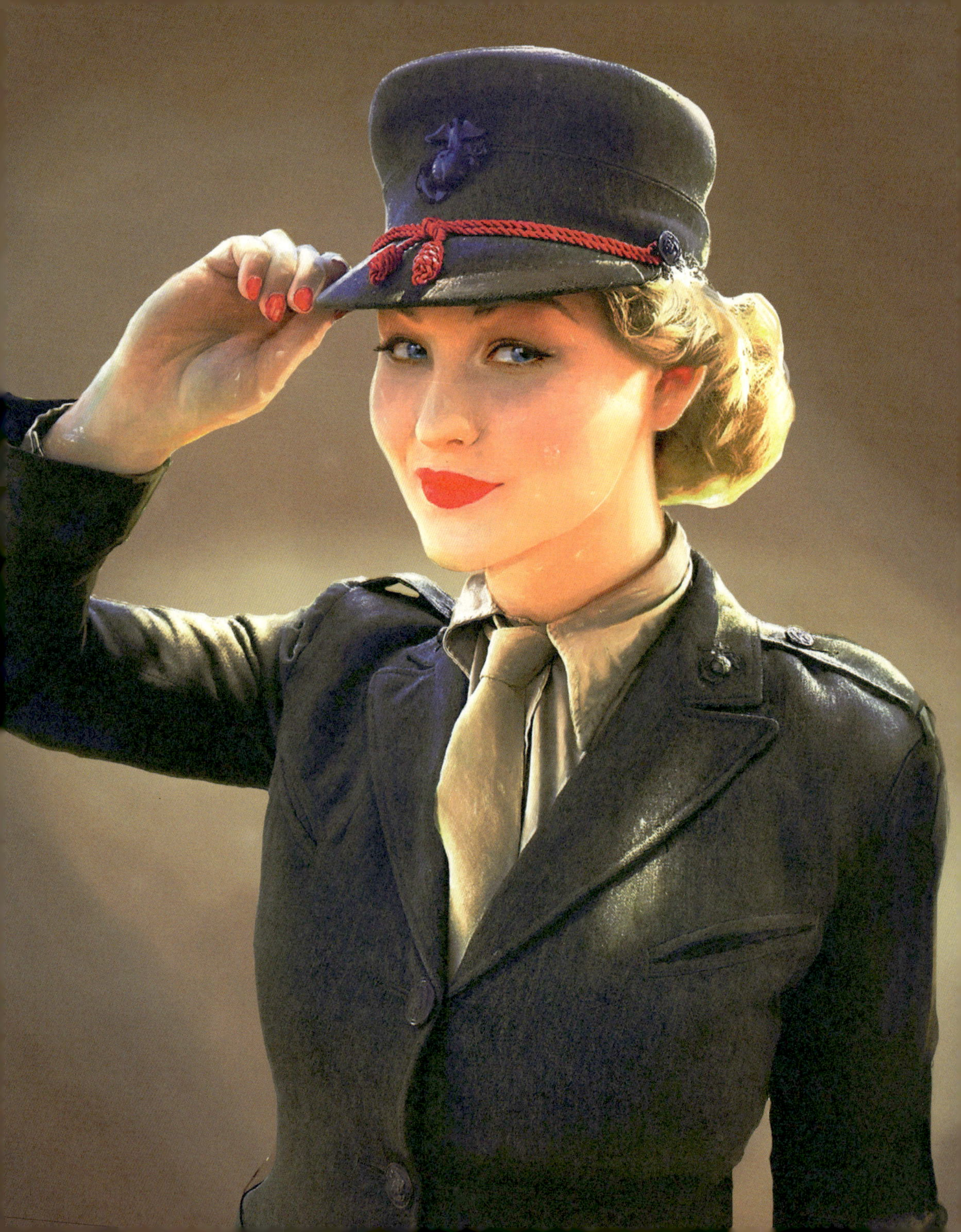

COSMETICS

Bésame Cosmetics

Vintage-style makeup for today's woman

GABRIELA HERNANDEZ

Gabriela Hernandez emigrated from Argentina to the United States in her early teens, but a memory of her grandmother's beauty routine in Buenos Aires informs the ethos of her cosmetic company to this day. "I would literally sit in awe," describes Gabriela, remembering how she watched her grandmother apply makeup. "She was so meticulous with every line, every soft stroke of the brush, powder lightly flitting through the air, her perfume lingering as she floated through the door. She taught me that makeup should be an experience, not a chore. I went on to grow in my appreciation and admiration for the simplicity of old Hollywood glamour, the softness of classic beauty."

A background in graphic design and photography coupled with a large collection of antique beauty products and packaging inspired Gabriela to found Bésame in 2004. "I wanted to make a product that really captured the essence of what was beautiful in the antiques I had from my grandmother's collection, but also was usable for women today."

It took a couple of years of experimentation and development to produce her first small lipstick. "At first I only intended to do this as a side project, since I already had a graphic design studio to take up most of my time. This is something I did because I loved it, so I took my off-time and worked on developing the look of Bésame, from the product to the colours, to the packaging and message of the brand."

Bésame literally recreates colours of the past; Gabriela identifies trends of the past and sources colours from old makeup to be as authentic as possible. "I wanted to look at the past because I thought that they had really valuable insight into how products were made and how little it took to make a woman feel beautiful. I wanted to go back to that simplicity, and that's why it was important to make the products look like they belonged in the period and give women the fantasy of actually being there."

"Designing our products is really one of the joys of having Bésame, since I am a designer and photographer; it's really the side of the business that I enjoy the most. I like making the products, designing the cases and the graphics in the boxes—putting these things together is like bringing out things from the past and giving it to people today. It's a fantasy really, but it's very convincing when it's done well, and it does make a difference in making women really feel beautiful when they apply the products as well as when they wear them. Searching for beautiful vintage makeup and adding it to my collection is my passion, since they provide the inspiration for all of our products."

"Fifteen years later, I can still remember what it was like to watch my grandmother. Every day is a reminder of her and of the women everywhere who we encourage and empower to feel like their most authentic and beautiful selves—inside and out." ❋

"I think my most prized is the first vintage lipstick I purchased, which is the one that inspired the shape of our lipstick that we still use today. It was also the first colour we produced, Bésame Red, when we started the company in 2004."

ERAS OF BEAUTY AND GLAMOUR

I am partial to the 1930s as my favourite looks to recreate. I just love the fashion of that period. It was before WWII, so fashion was still very important, even though people did not have a lot of money after the Great Depression. The people with money definitely wanted to show it off, so fashion was really at a high-point in terms of design and materials. Makeup manufacturing was really getting into its own at that time with the creation of the Pan-Cake Make-Up and wearable looks that people could put on as a daily-use product.

At Bésame we stick to periods from the 1920s to about the 1950s. We have some colours that were in use in the 1960s but that's where we stop as far as our products and our shades. The colours from these early years are really very versatile and can be used for a lot of different vintage and modern looks, since they remain classic after all these years. We make the colours and products that looked great on many women in the past, and they still do today. The care in the manufacturing and design of products in the past is what appeals to me the most, and what inspires me to create modern counterparts to these beautiful items.

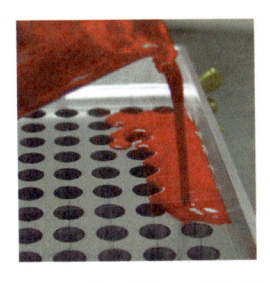

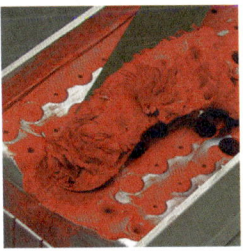

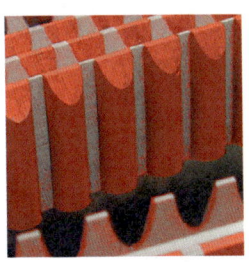

VINTAGE LOOK

Vintage makeup is really more simple than most people think. If you look at the cosmetic bag, let's say of a woman in the 1930s, you would only find four to five items inside at the most. The majority of women probably had three items in their bag, consisting of lipstick, rouge and a powder compact. Cake mascara, a pencil for brows and an eye shadow that would match the outfit she was wearing completed the look. The vintage look is really more about grooming then it is about makeup, so if you want to do looks from the past, concentrate on your hairstyle, your eyebrows and your overall grooming. Paying attention to these details will really get you closer to the vintage look. It wasn't really all about the makeup but everything around it that mattered.

BÉSAME COSMETICS   135

PERFECTLY PACKAGED

I still design everything that we do. A lot of my time is spent on product development, formula and packaging. I spend a lot of my time on that side of the business because all the pieces have to be designed. It takes us a while to design because a lot of time we move pieces to fit within a collection. There isn't anything that exists and looks the way that it needs to look, so a lot of the things are made for us from scratch. It makes our product look definitely more unique than other products. But it's a lot of fun, because we get to play with moulding things and making pretty boxes and pretty appliqués. These days with 3D printing and moulding techniques that exist we can just do all kinds of really wild things. It's kind of endless what we can do, which sometimes makes it harder, because there's just so many choices. But we're still focused on the product, what would make sense, and what would people want. I always go with, "Would I want this? Would I buy this?" If I would buy it, then other people might as well. If I don't like it, I definitely don't make it, that's for sure. (excerpted from an interview on HelloGiggles.com)

besamecosmetics.com
@besamecosmetics

137

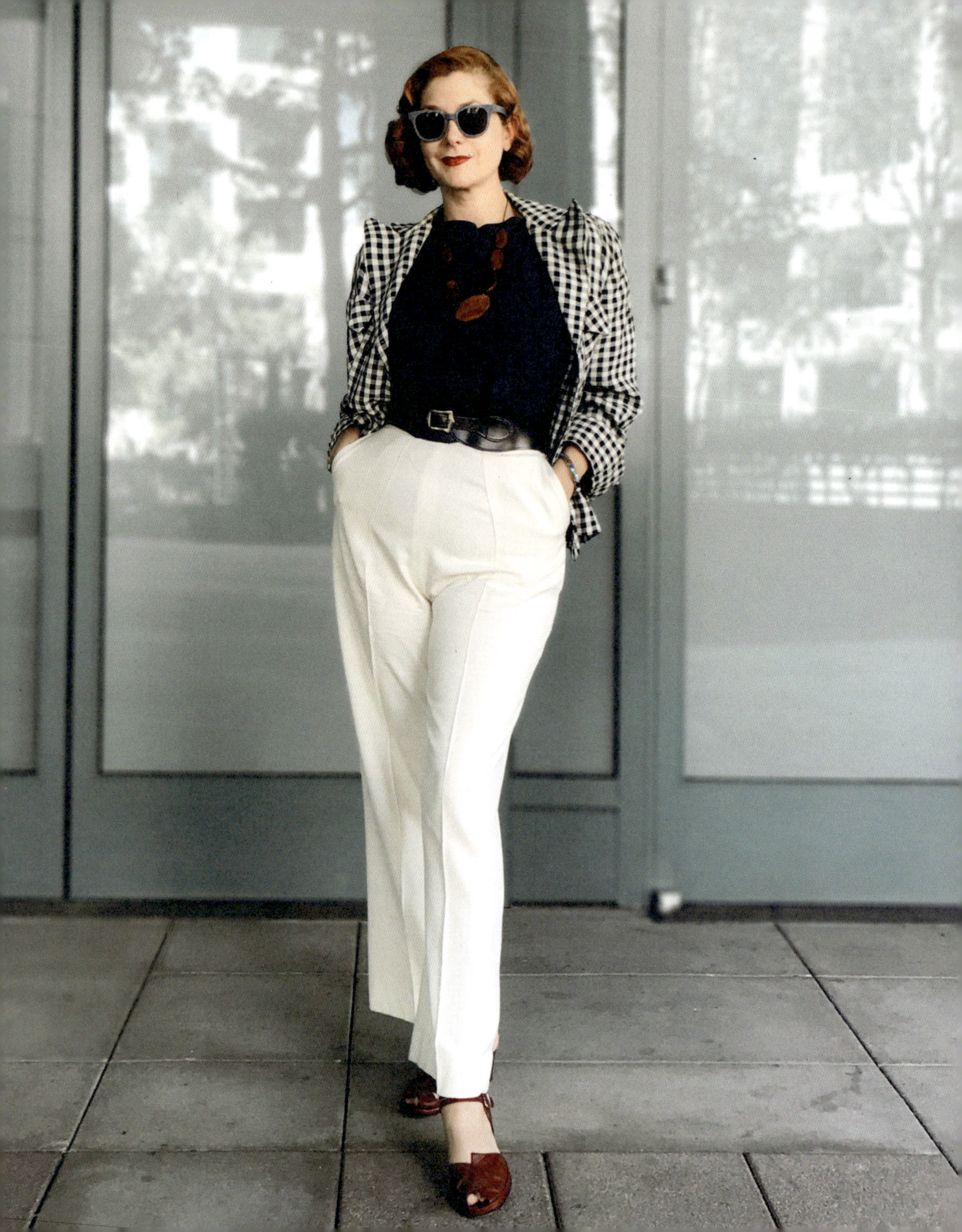

PERSONAL STYLE

No Accounting for Taste

A vintage wardrobe for everyday living

JESSICA PARKER

"Wearing vintage every day feels like taking a stand against the labour practices and environmental damage created by the modern fashion industry. It feels like making a small, everyday choice that not only helps me develop my own style, but is in line with my values as well."

Jessica Parker is an art director living in Los Angeles, California. "I've always loved old things," she says. "Old art, architecture, furniture, housewares, books… I love old things in part because they have a story that isn't readily apparent, a story that is only partially written." About a decade ago, Jessica's love of old things eventually lead her to explore style: "I went from a scarf or dress here and there to an everyday all-out-vintage wardrobe."

Jessica's experience with contemporary mass-market clothing had been unsatisfying. "I remember one day in particular, trying on a pencil skirt in a large chain fashion store. The skirt fit me in the hips, but was far too large in the waist. The salesman suggested I could always get it tailored, but I thought, why? Why would I spend money to alter something that wasn't exactly right that was made in a way I couldn't support with a level of quality I wasn't confident in, only to have the colour feel dated in two years? At that point, I realized I would rather wear clothes that already fit my proportions and were made in a manner and with materials difficult to match today, even if they felt dated. Even better, let them feel so dated that they're never in nor out of fashion, but they're my style."

"I discovered in vintage clothes a vast resource that allowed me not only to indulge my love of old things on a daily basis but also to develop a personal style that I was able to document through Instagram. Uncovering the stories behind what I wear has led me to find a whole community of like-minded vintage wearers who were also curious about who made their clothes, 70-some years ago."

Intrigued by the history of vintage fashion labels and designers, Jessica documents her research online on her blog, No Accounting For Taste. "I started digging into the history of vintage fashion labels and designers around 2012 as online research tools became more robust. Through newspaper and magazine archives, city directories, trade publications and census records, I began to piece together the stories behind my wardrobe, posting the original advertising or editorial content for my outfits where possible. I love learning about the people behind the clothing I wear, particularly in an era where fast fashion has become the norm." ❖

TRUE & FUTURE VINTAGE

Researching the people and stories behind the clothes I wear is important to me because it deepens my appreciation for them. Knowing how something came into being and who came up with the ideas to make it happen means that every time I pick it up to put it on in the morning I have someone to thank, someone to honour. And by telling these stories, I hope to inspire in others the same curiosity and gratitude that I feel. I hope that people who enjoy reading these stories will be more conscious about where everything in their lives comes from, not just their clothing. So now, even though I'm starting to wear more modern clothing as I get older, I'm far more conscious of where it comes from than I was before I started wearing vintage. Today, if I buy modern, it comes from independent women designers, produced locally and ethically, and it feels a little like living a story that someone will uncover 70 years from now.

RECONCILING THE PAST

It can be difficult. Much of the editorial and advertising content I'm interested in is from the 1940s or very early 1950s, and this is not a time in American history of which I'm particularly proud as it concerns marginalized groups. People looking into the vintage community often conflate our dressing vintage with a desire to return to a pre-civil rights America, but that's not what we want (anyway, it's not what I want). I think what we appreciate is a lost craft. Local design and manufacturing, high-quality textiles and thoughtful construction—these garments have lasted 60-plus years and rarely need more than the occasional reweave or reinforced seam. In them, we see the possibilities of human ingenuity and resourcefulness, of a pride in craftsmanship that is extremely rare in the modern world.

"I try to keep my day job separate from my vintage interests, despite the fact that I wear vintage to work every day. People I work with are sometimes surprised when they discover my Instagram, and people who follow me are sometimes surprised to learn I have a regular, non-vintage-related job. I haven't yet figured out how to make a career out of research, so piecing together these stories has become a time-consuming but addictive hobby."

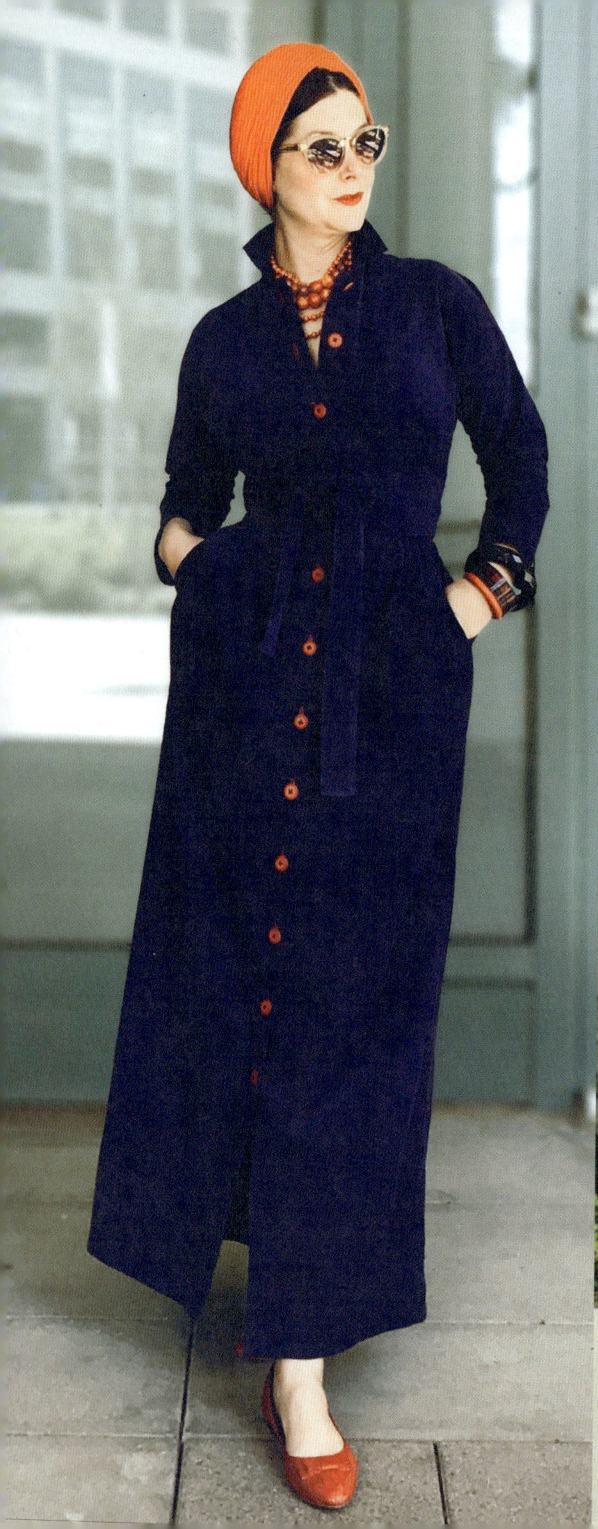

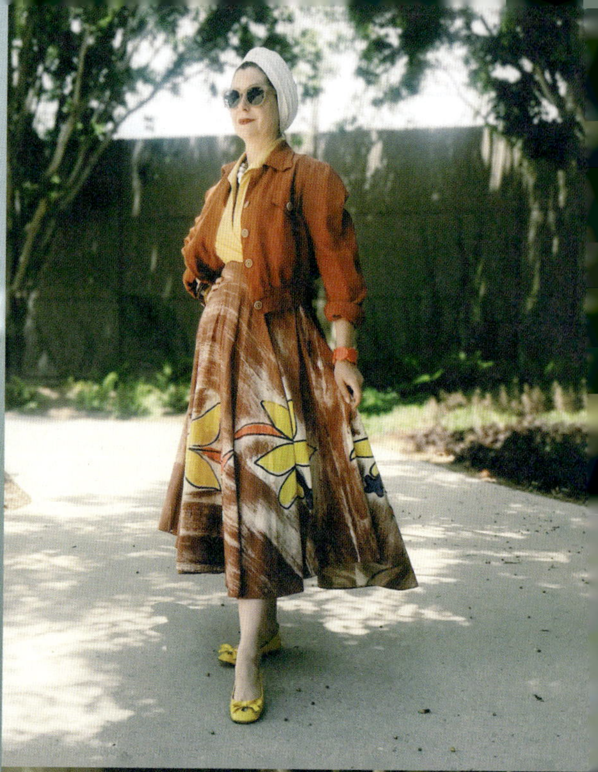

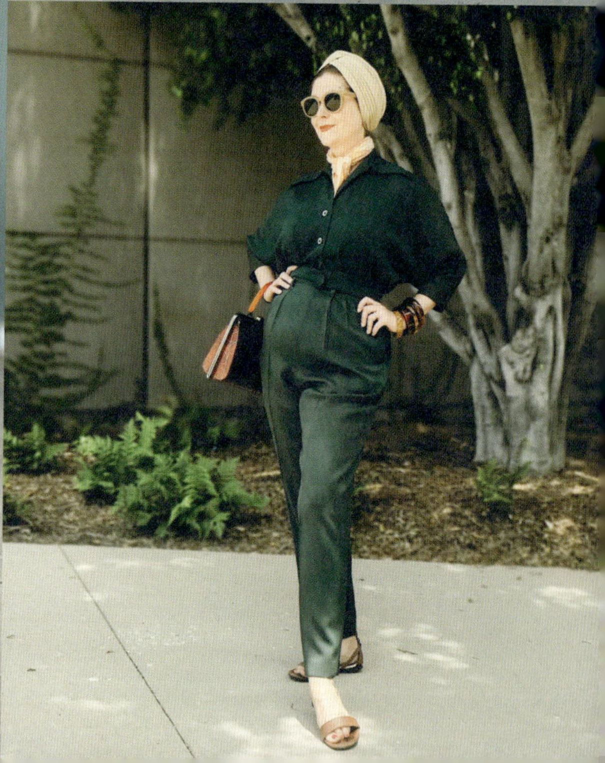

noaccountingfortaste.com
@noaccountingfortaste

Patti Blau

ILLUSTRATION

Patti Blau

An artistic flair
for the past

PATTI BLAU

Based in Miami, a locale she describes as a "sustainable version of living on vacation," illustrator and designer Patti Blau's colourful imagery does seem to emerge from a place of relaxed joy, tinged with nostalgia. "As an artist, my artwork has always been about memory," she explains. "I use objects as visual reminders to take the viewer back in time. I especially love vintage objects that represent childhood, such as vintage school graphics, toys, globes, puzzles, paper dolls and things that remind me of my own childhood."

Patti grew up in suburban New York. "My family also spent time upstate in the country. It was there that I discovered the many antique shops and wonderful old barns full of industrial pieces and old farm furniture. It was our weekend ritual to go out exploring, and that was what really started my vintage life." She went on to study art and painting at Parsons School of Design in New York and Paris. "I loved living abroad and studying different languages and cultures. Those experiences had a big influence on me and I still love to travel and explore new places."

She lived in the Big Apple for a time, working as a prop stylist and costume designer in the film industry. "For my work, I was always looking for objects and pieces, some to use for production, and others for artistic inspiration." She continued to paint and, after moving to Miami, started a stationery company, writeables.com, that drew upon her personal collection of vintage greeting cards. "Back then, prior to everyone having a computer and cell phone, the challenge of finding the graphics and recreating them was a special one, and the company was very successful."

Her art and illustration is inspired by her love of vintage objects and fashion. She is intrigued by what we surround ourselves with and why we surround ourselves with it; these personal choices are a recurring theme in her artwork. "I love interior design and am really amazed by the millions of combinations of objects and furniture we create, no two exactly alike. I love fashion design, and the combinations of clothing we select and how we wear them. I am really interested in the spaces we occupy and the objects we place around us, both for utility and for decoration." ❊

"Although I adore many, probably my favourite vintage period is mid-century. I consider mid-century design to be the iconic definition of an object. When I think of objects for a design, I don't think so much about what the newest version of that object may be—in my mind, I'll first always go to a vintage icon. Many modern conveniences just do not have the line, shape and style of mid-century design. There is something classic about it that makes it always in style. Since it is iconic, it's timeless and mixes easily with contemporary design."

"When I watch old films, I always find myself admiring Art Deco interiors. The scale and beauty of that time period no longer exists—people seemed to have much more space around them and filled that space with oversized, generous objects and furniture that really added beauty and elegance to the interior. Sweeping staircases and vases full of flowers, sleepwear with feathers and men with top hats; it really was an era of opulence. I enjoy reliving that era through film and art, and it is really an inspiration for me."

HI-TECH MAGIC

In terms of style, I like to mix vintage with modern. As an illustrator, I like to create vintage-style imagery on a hi-tech digital screen. I really appreciate the magic of the digital world, and the millions of things you can do with the computer in design. Often my work is about creating digital content directly for digital media, so it works perfectly, and the design programs offer so many options in terms of styles that it cuts the work time in half, and that doubles the creativity. It's really amazing that the same colours are always available, and the brushes have so many choices. I am constantly discovering new resources online for learning the craft, and I really appreciate all that modern technology has to offer.

"My artwork is often about categorizing objects. Whether I create an environment or a room to place them in, or just make a list of them, I am usually talking about objects and their relationships to us, or to each other."

150   VINTAGE LIFE

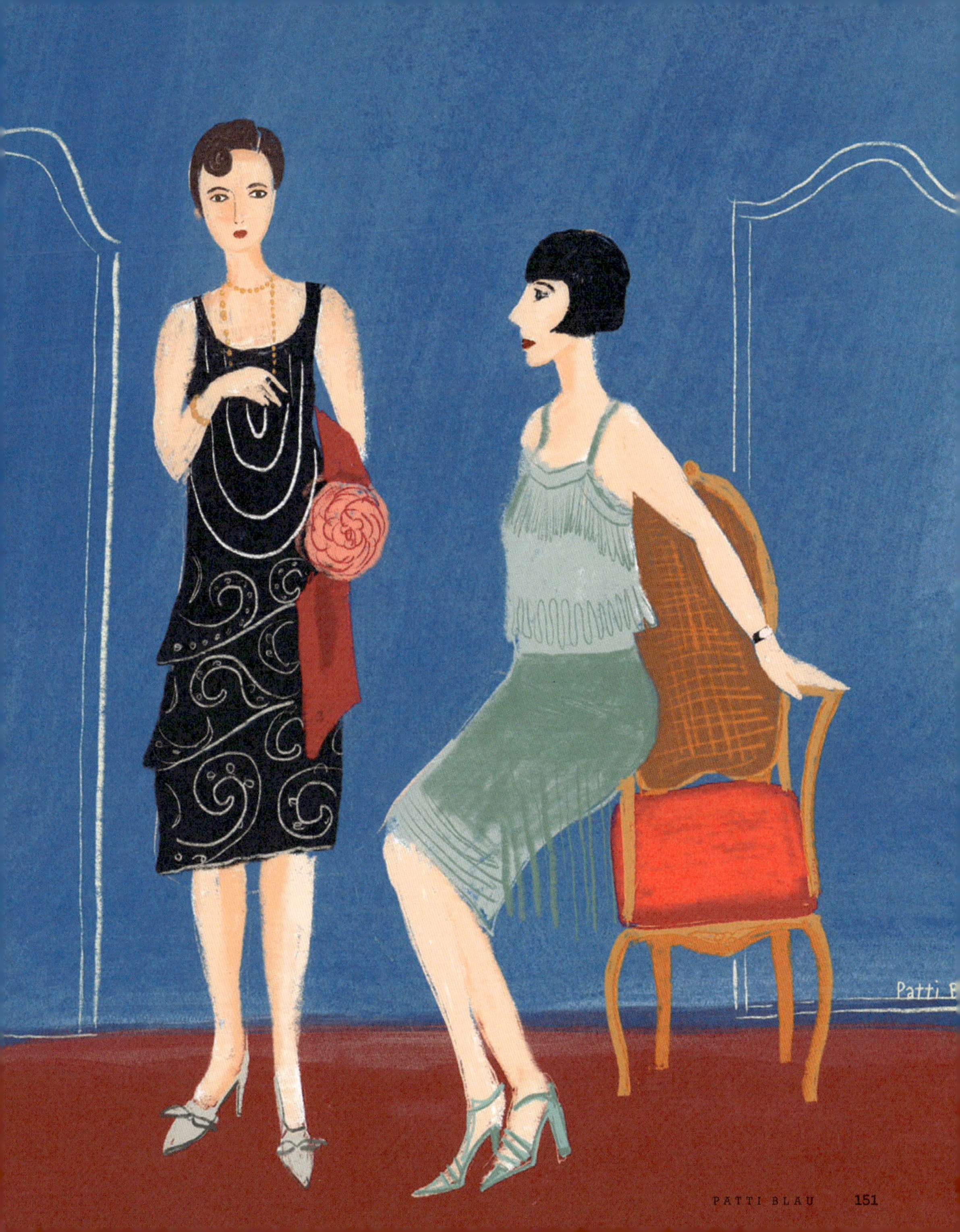
Patti B

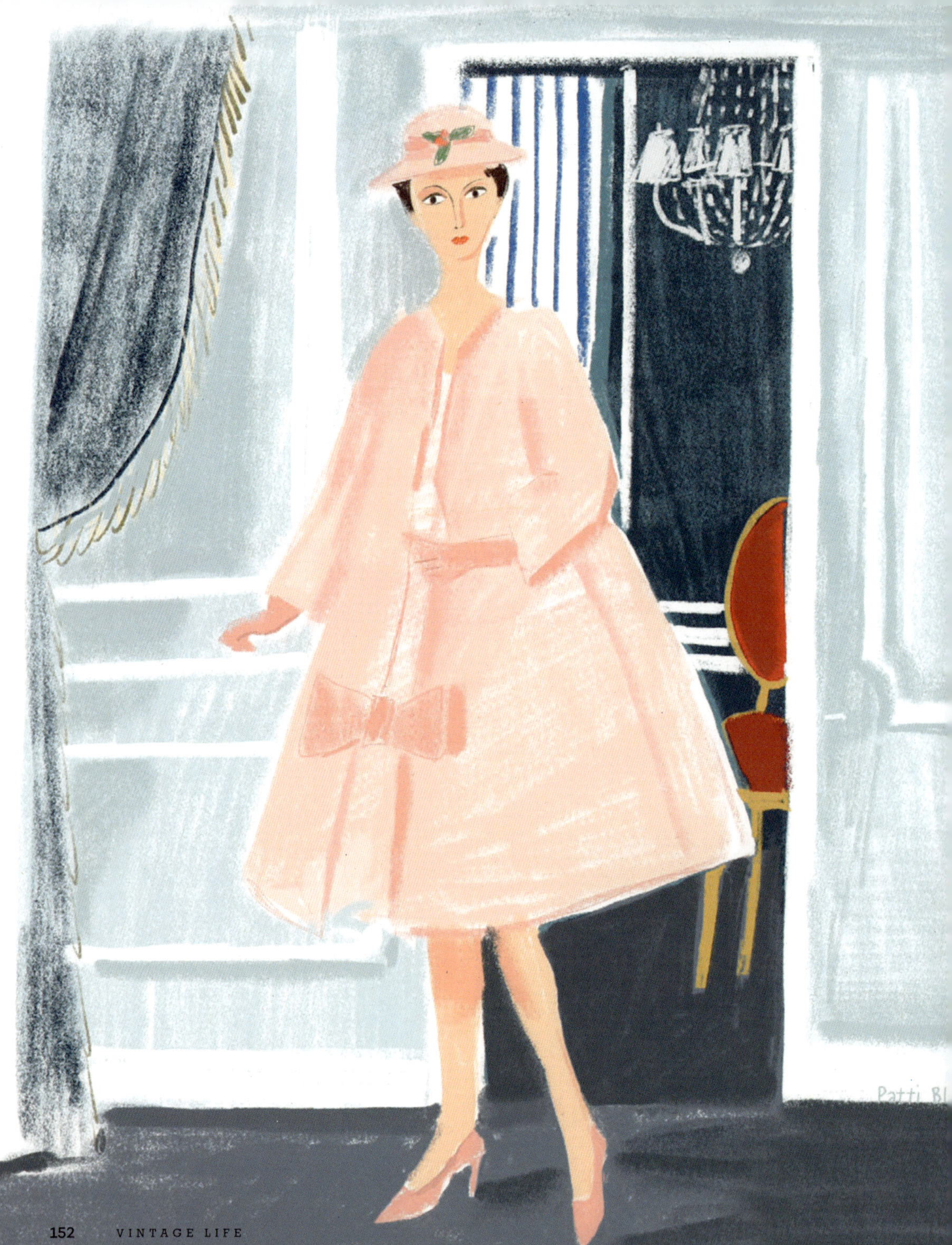
Patti Bl

"I love fashion design, and the combinations of clothing we select and how we wear them."

PATTI BLAU   153

HOME STYLE

My home is an eclectic mix of the things that inspire me. My studio is full of books for reference mixed in with vintage objects that are either for sale on my Etsy shop (vintagebeach-kids) and temporarily visiting, and those that have a permanent place. Every object I own or sell has a history, and I select them for either their design or graphics, so everything I find has a value to me.

I have small vignettes around the house to display some of my collection. I rarely change anything, so I am not a person who, for example, makes holiday displays—once it's there, it stays. These are my personal objects, things I enjoy seeing daily. They include a selection of things I love. I mix all of that with a sort of island farmhouse feel. I have old painted wooden farm cabinets and tables, and my rooms are painted in earth tones. In with this mix is also all of our modern conveniences. My home seems like one big art studio, and although the artwork on the walls changes often, the vintage feel is always there.

pattiblau.com
@pattiblau

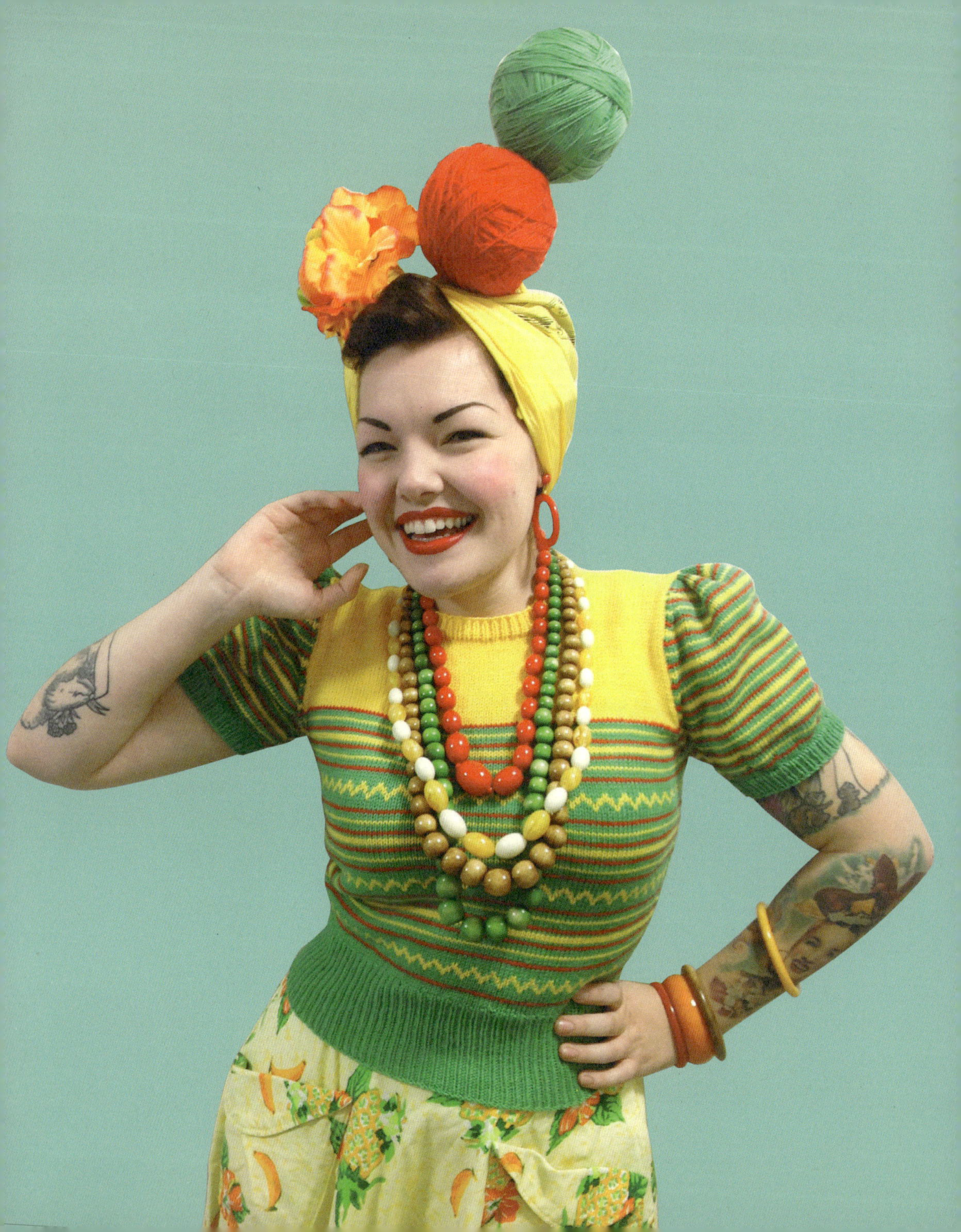

VINTAGE KNITS

Sydney Crabaugh

Fun, fashion and self-expression through knitting

"Oftentimes, I can situate myself in a vintage bubble that the modern world cannot interfere with. I easily forget that I stick out in a crowd of grumpy New Yorkers on the subway, and wonder why people stare at my garishly colourful outfits."

"Apart from clothing, my passion for vintage has been diverted to a keen study of early film. I have known that cinema studies was my career path since I was 20 years old and saw *Sunrise* (1927) for the first time, and have since gone on to receive my master's degree in film history from NYU. I tend to focus on 1920s to 1950s Hollywood film and Weimar-era German film. I strive to be a film archivist, rescuing old, forgotten reels and bringing them back to life."

Sydney Crabaugh's vintage passions fall in two very compatible categories: clothing and film. "Clothing has always been the most tangible way for me to connect to an era, as I can buy a dress or a hat and imagine the woman who wore it when it was made. Any vintage piece I own with a known history holds a particular fondness in my heart." When Sydney can't find a desired garment in her size, she makes it. "Luckily my adoration for film and knitting pair together quite well, as I am usually working on my latest vintage piece while screening an old film!"

"I have never been drawn to 'modern' life. Throughout the years I have shied away from the mainstream, never finding excitement in liking the same things that most people like. I teetered around different phases in middle school and high school, but everything changed when I saw the film *Gentleman Prefer Blondes* (1953). The colours, the outfits, the way that Jane Russell talked and the way that Marilyn Monroe moved... it all clicked for me. I remember looking at the fashion and hairstyles thinking, that's what I want to look like."

Shortly after, she picked out a special dress at a local vintage store. "My grandmother cut my hair and taught me how to set my curls. I remember the exciting, fitful sleep in my sponge rollers and the big reveal the following morning. I remember putting on stockings and having trouble zipping up the delicate metal zipper of my dress. And most importantly, I remember applying bright red lipstick to wear outside of the house for the first time. The comfort I felt when I stood back and regarded myself in the mirror is one

"Nearly all the comments I receive are positive, but the occasional stare of confusion and disapproval makes me giggle. I'm content to live in the vintage realm I've created for myself, regardless of how others perceive me!"

that I haven't looked back from. I knew my identity had found a home."

"I felt a sigh of relief from my soul," she describes of this transition to wearing vintage in 2008. "I knew that the silky rayons and fuzzy wools from bygone eras better reflected how I wanted to present myself to the world. Since then, I have found every possible way to connect with earlier decades, particularly the 1940s and 1950s. Having always been a creative type, vintage knitting became my primary outlet for incorporating vintage styles and colours into my wardrobe."

She knits almost exclusively from vintage patterns. "It is an absolute delight to take a pattern from the eras I love and recreate it with my own hands. To think that a knitter from 1943 has made the same sweater that I just finished... what a dreamy thought!" On Instagram and through classes and retreats, Sydney shares her passion with others. "I also hope to write my own vintage-inspired patterns in the coming years!"

"As far as technology goes, I don't think I would be where I am today if it wasn't for the wonderful vintage and knitting communities I have found through Instagram. Social media can be toxic and mind-numbing at times, but I have an endless supply of gratitude for the friends it has brought me. Through Instagram, I have connected with countless others who also lead vintage lives, developing sincere friendships and bonds with many of them. I now have an entire online community of people who understand this integral part of me and feel so lucky to have found them." ❖

PERFECT PLAID

One of the most exciting moments, since I've been collecting vintage pieces, was when I found my 1950s Pendleton suit. The Pendleton 49er, a type of plaid jacket that was created for women in 1949, is my most collected vintage item. Over the past few years, I have become obsessed with collecting all of these incredible jackets in the myriad of colour combinations. A few years ago, I stumbled upon a 1950s women's Pendleton pants suit that was exactly my size. It is so rare to find an intact two- or three-piece Pendleton suit from this era, not to mention with trousers!

KNITTING COMMUNITY

This April I hosted my first Vintage Knitting Retreat! A group of us trekked to upstate New York to stay in an 1860s farmhouse and knit by the fireside for a long weekend. During the retreat, I taught courses on knitting vintage garments, how to decode old patterns and how to perfectly fit a vintage garment for different body types. We also took a trip to a local farm to meet the new lambs, and had evening theme nights! It was such a treat to be able to share my knowledge of vintage knitting with other enthusiasts and to help others make a successful garment.

The community of vintage knitters is small but mighty and is growing by the minute. I get so excited when other vintage knitters pop up on Instagram and Ravelry, and see how they are interpreting vintage patterns I have yet to see knit up by contemporary hands. Our little niche group keeps growing, and I cannot wait to welcome the newcomers into this magical world!

```
"I have been lucky to have
only worked in yarn shops for
the last eight years, which makes
it quite easy to dress in vintage
both on and off the clock. Being
surrounded by fibres, colours
and other creators on a regular
basis has only fed my inspiration
for my own knitting projects. I
feel so grateful to work in a field
where I not only feel comfortable
to be who I am, but also get to
speak to others about my passion
for knitting, vintage knitting
and yarn."
```

SYDNEY CRABAUGH

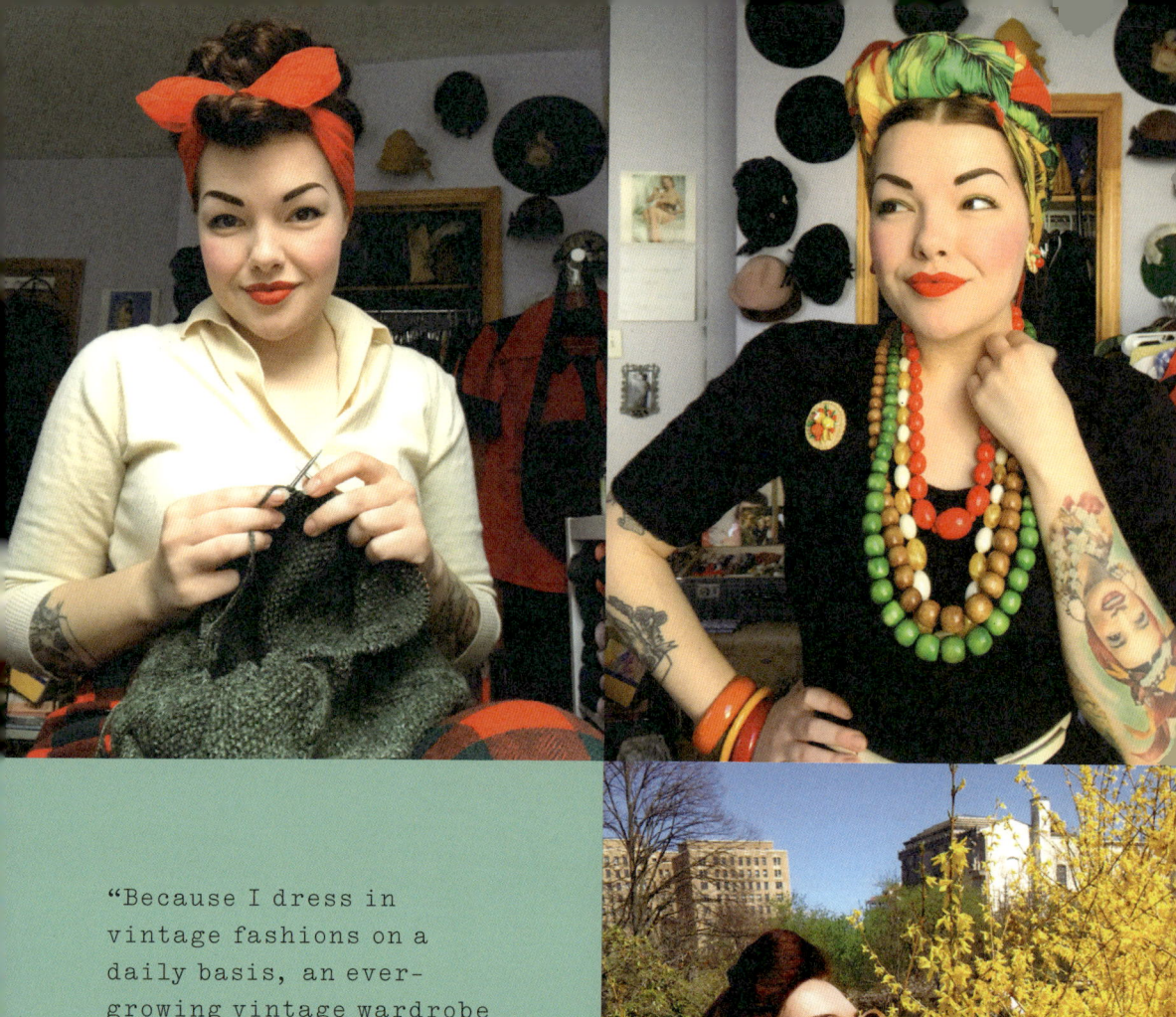

"Because I dress in vintage fashions on a daily basis, an ever-growing vintage wardrobe is critical. I love the thrill of entering a thrift or antique store, not knowing what sorts of treasures are there to uncover."

@squidneyknits

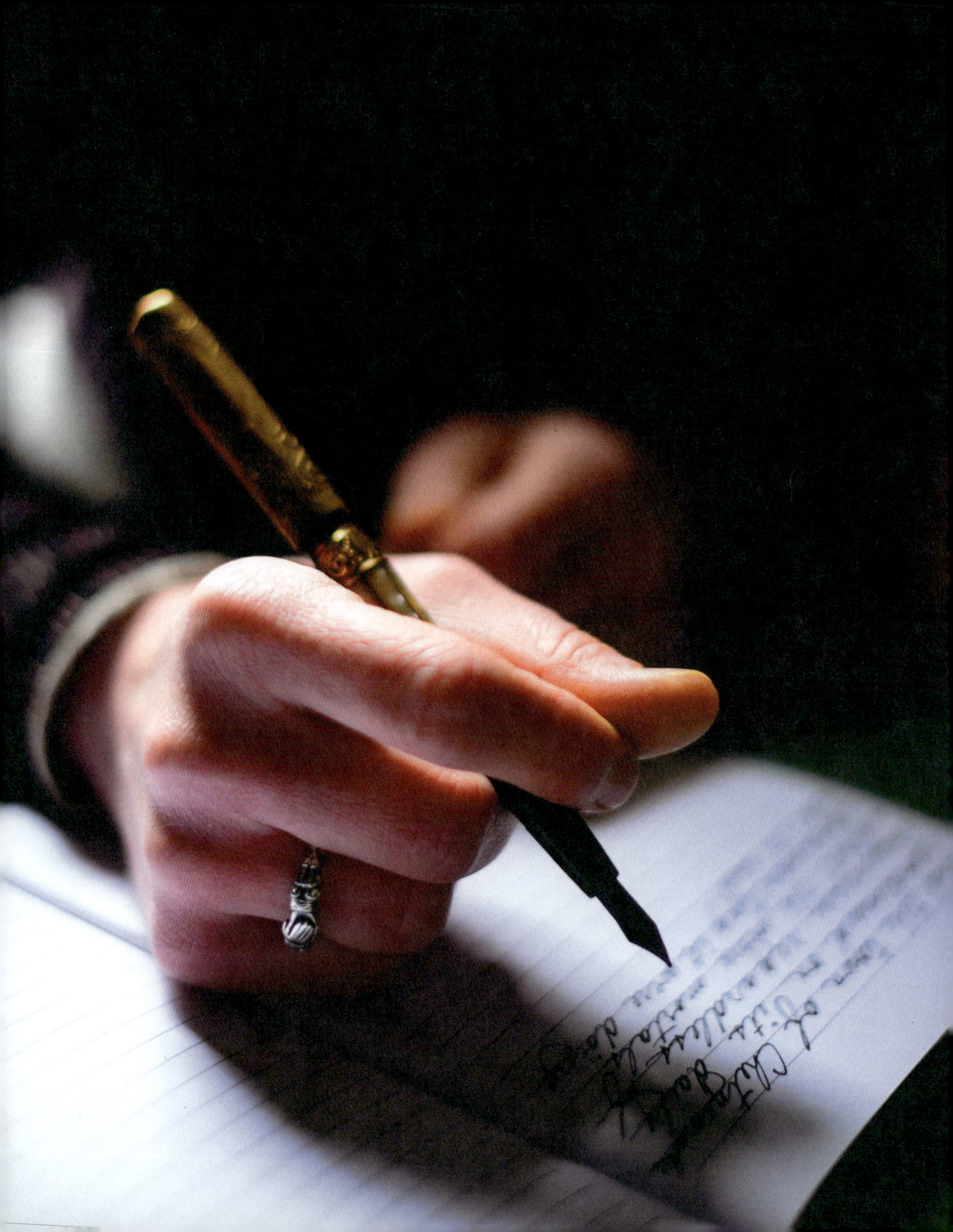

IMMERSED IN HISTORY

This Victorian Life

A married couple committed to living an old-fashioned life

SARAH *and* GABRIEL CHRISMAN

"Bicycles have been my favourite way to engage with the world from early childhood. Bicycles encourage mobility and exploration, and also give the rider true freedom— at our own speed, under our own power."

– Gabriel Chrisman

Though many of the folks profiled in this book are engaged in a vintage life, none are as thoroughly immersed in the past than Sarah and Gabriel Chrisman. The couple live, as much as possible, in the late 19th century. "When I was a little girl," explains Sarah, "I had two big dreams: to live in the Victorian era and to be a writer. My husband Gabriel, who shares my passion for history, grew up in a family who considered first-hand experiences to be the best form of education. When I told him about my dream of travelling back in time, his response was, 'Why not?'"

In Port Townsend, Washington, the Chrismans live in a house originally built in 1888 to 1889. As you can imagine, a house of that age had seen many generations and renovations. "Our house was a bare shell when we moved in, and over the years we've been working to return it to its original Victorian splendour," Sarah says. "The Victorians felt that the home is the foundation of all good things, that the concepts of home and love are inseparable. The house itself, and the objects within it, are all celebrations of the love within these walls. It is a private, sacred space, and a sanctuary from the outer world."

"Over the years, we've replaced increasingly more everyday items in our life with their Victorian equivalents. The light that I write by, and by which Gabriel reads to me on quiet evenings, is provided by antique oil lamps. The only electric lights in our home—used when company visits—have hand-blown glass bulbs that are copies of the earliest light bulb patents. We cook on a wood-burning stove using recipes from antique cookbooks, and many of these recipes work their way into my books. An antique icebox keeps our food fresh, and I empty the meltwater from its drip tray every evening."

Faithful to the attire of the era, Sarah wears a corset 24 hours a day. She has written a book, *Victorian Secrets: What a Corset Taught Me about the Past, the Present, and Myself*, that explores how this undergarment transformed her body and perceptions. "The clothes we wear every day are all copies of antique

THIS VICTORIAN LIFE 167

"In the 19th century, there was a philosophy that we should have nothing in our homes that we do not know to be useful or feel to be beautiful—preferably both. Our surroundings have a subtle yet unavoidable influence on us, the way that water shapes stone, and we, therefore, have an obligation to ourselves to make sure that those surroundings forward goals to which we truly aspire." — Sarah A. Chrisman

19th-century garments," Sarah says; "in some cases, we own the originals, while other clothes are modelled after antique photographs or fashion plates in our collection. Every little detail in our lives is as deeply historical as we can make it, from the antique ewer and basin I use to wash every morning when I greet the day, to the 19th-century eyeglasses that are the last thing Gabriel takes off at night before we go to sleep."

The details of their daily lives are shared in Sarah's other nonfiction tome, *This Victorian Life: Modern Adventures in Nineteenth-Century Culture, Cooking, Fashion, and Technology*. Sarah also writes an ongoing series of historical fiction and Victorian Cycling Club romances entitled Tales of Chetzemoka: "Interacting with all these little everyday details of history on a constant basis gives me a wonderful framework of knowledge on which to base my stories." In addition to Sarah's writing, the couple offers historical consultations, speaking engagements and research assistance.

Gabriel studied computer science in college in the 1990s but found that technology was ultimately alienating, so he countered his studies with history. "I have always been fascinated by technology, and especially by our relationship with technology," he says. "I have explored this complicated interface in many ways over the years—through bicycles, computers, late 19th-century technology, libraries and archives." He switched course: "I entered the information school for a master's degree in library science, creating my own emphasis for archival studies. My studies and interests drew me towards a more comprehensive lifestyle, in which my principles, skills and goals all came together as an integrated whole."

168   VINTAGE LIFE

Sarah's academic background is in cultural studies. "If I had to distill my entire university education into a few sentences, I would say that it's one thing to study a culture in a classroom, and quite another to visit another country and live amongst its people," she says. "While we can't travel to the past in the same way we travel to different lands, we can still learn a great deal about the past by experiencing its details firsthand."

When asked how they reconcile their love of vintage with the modern world, Sarah responds: "The word 'reconcile' implies a need to restore amity between two antagonistic forces, but the past is not the enemy of the present. There's no contradiction in living in a way that helps us understand where the world came from in order to understand what it is now, and where it's going in the future." ❊

"A great deal of the technology that has become ubiquitous in the modern world can be traced back to inventions and concepts from the late 19th century. Studying the complex dilemmas these technologies brought into the world with them helps us understand problems still faced by people today.

Innovations in travel like the locomotive, the steamship and the bicycle led to increasingly diverse societies, as transport became easier for people and goods. It also led to greater social mobility: as working-class people bettered themselves, they moved from positions in one subculture of society to another.

There are a lot of parallels between the late 19th century and life today. This makes it a fascinating time to study—and to write about! I love using my books to point out all the things the past had in common with the present, and to share the wealth of information that it holds for all of us."

"My favourite room within our house is my writing den, where I spend most of my time each day. It holds as many bookshelves as we can fit inside it, filled with antique volumes for research for my stories. My desk is an heirloom from Gabriel's grandmother, and I bought my mother-of-pearl fountain pen with part of the advance from my first book. Next to my desk is a basket full of notebooks, each one dedicated to a book in the series I'm writing. Whenever I come across a good quote or interesting piece of information that I think I can work into a story, I'll jot it down in the notebook I'm saving for that story. Then when I write each book, I use the dedicated notebook for that particular story, and my notes are all conveniently where I can find them."

INSIDE STORIES

The most reliable accounts of any scene come from eyewitnesses, and the very best come from actual participants. An author who reports what others have done is merely an observer, but since I have an inside view of the action I can invite readers into the true hearts of my characters. The stories in my historical fiction series are a complex weaving of personal experiences and research in antique primary sources. To write them I put together passages from my own private diary, historical diaries written in the 19th century, and antique books and magazines. All the characters in my series take their inspiration from antique photographs in our private archive, and they've each taken on their own personalities as the series has progressed. They're all good friends to me now.

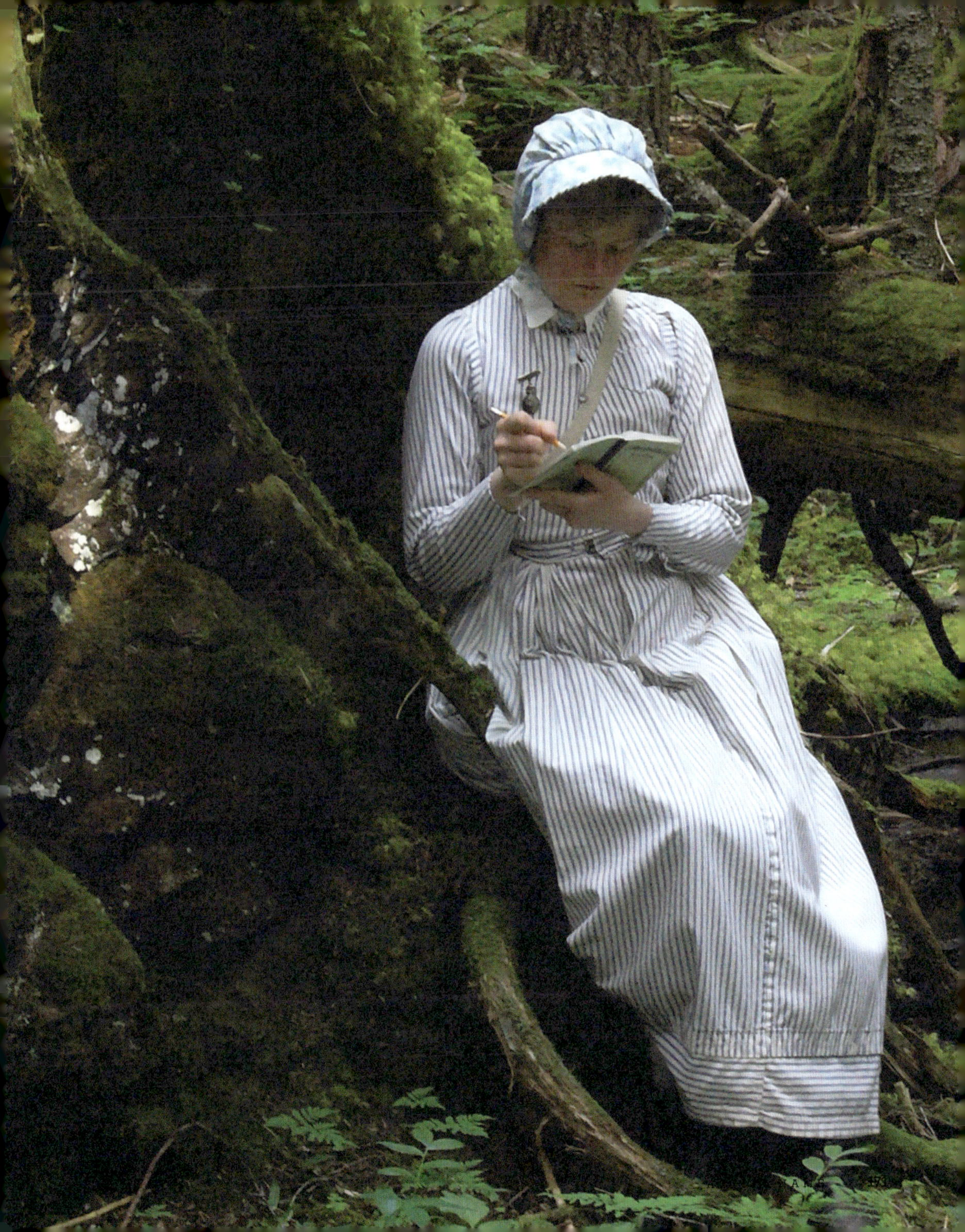

TALES OF CHETZEMOKA

My Tales of Chetzemoka series follows the adventures of a group of friends in the 1880s and '90s. Each book focuses on different individuals within their community, so readers get to see society from a lot of diverse perspectives. The challenges faced by a young widow running a dress shop are substantially different from those confronted by a bookish sea captain's daughter, a trained nurse or an investigative reporter, but in the course of the series, we get to see the viewpoints of all of these.

Chetzemoka is based on Port Townsend. (Port Townsend was named after a British aristocrat with whom an early explorer was trying to curry favour; I took the liberty of renaming the town after the leader of the local Clallam tribe who allied his people with the pioneer settlers.) The landmarks in the stories are real buildings and places that are still here; I'll often take my notebook out to the location where a scene takes place and write it there so that I can record all the details. Researching the town has involved everything from long hours spent in the county archive reading old business ledgers and newspaper clippings to hunts through local antique stores to find schoolbooks used by children here in the 19th century.

Each of my characters has their own private history, and learning all the details of these is one of my favourite parts of writing. The antique books that Gabriel and I collect are crucial primary sources. To write Nurse McCoy, for example, I read 19th-century medical texts, articles written by trained nurses in the 19th century and writings on invalid cookery from cookbooks of the time. To get her distinctive voice just right, I read humorous novels and satires from the period. As I read I take notes, and the character gradually emerges with her own strong and opinionated personality.

At the end of each of my novels are appendixes, everything from 19th-century recipes for the foods mentioned in the story to lists of further readings about the topics discussed in the book. It's always my hope that my stories will inspire readers to pursue their own interests in history and engage more deeply with a time that has so much to teach us all. Happy reading!

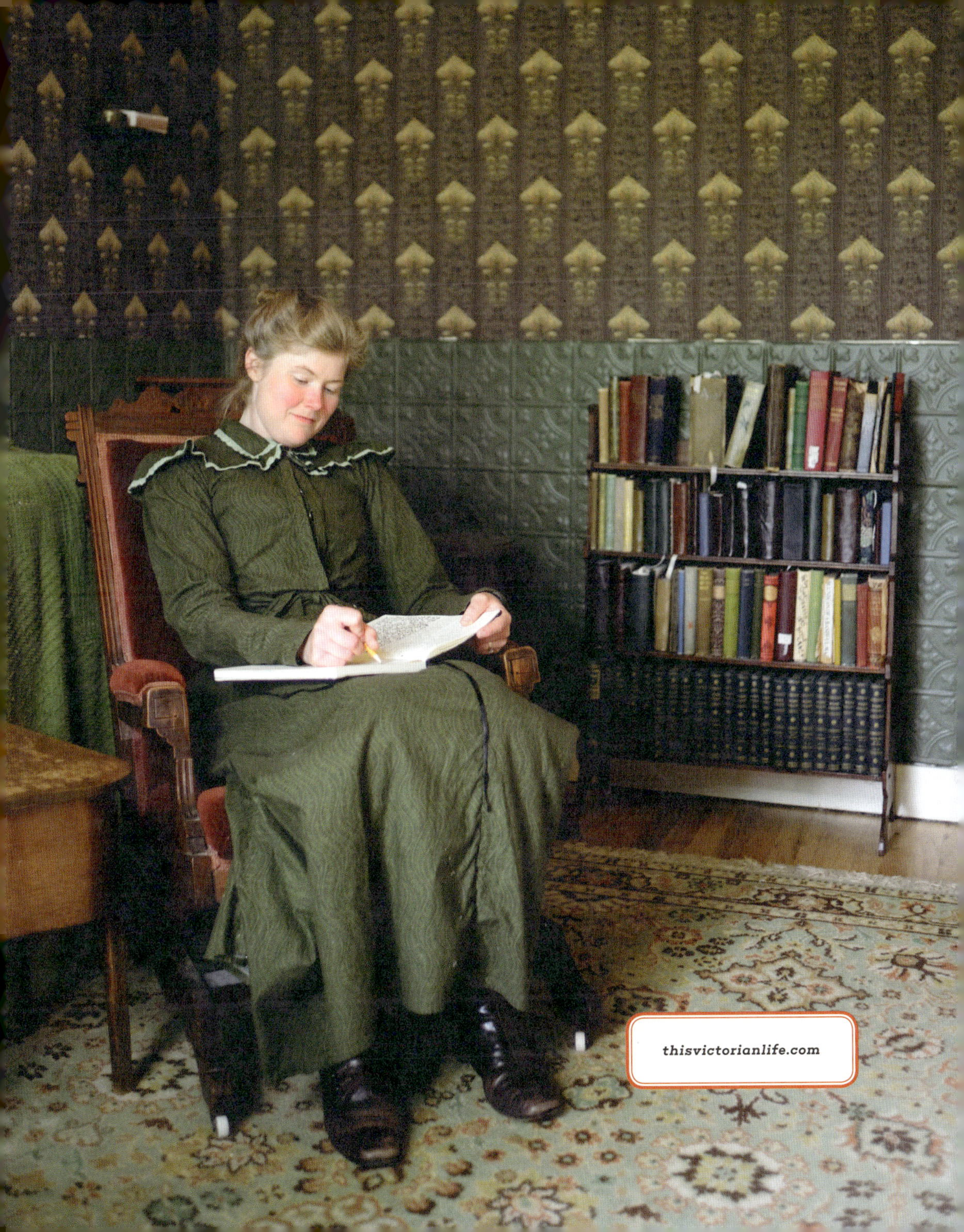
thisvictorianlife.com

DENOYER GEPPERT SERIES
DENOYER-GEPPERT SERIES
J. L. RANTA
VANCOUVER
B. C.

RETAIL

Stepback

Nostalgia for sale

ROBIN MUXLOW *and* CHRIS SWITZER

Robin Muxlow and Chris Switzer opened their retail store, Stepback, in February 2005. The couple had always talked about having a shop, but a casual stroll in their Vancouver neighbourhood of Kitsilano one day led to the discovery of a suitable space. "So we took the plunge and rented the space." A musician, Chris had been touring the world with various bands and singers, but he knew he was going to have some downtime. Robin, a graduate of the University of British Columbia with a master's in architecture, was looking for a challenge. "We had been avid vintage shoppers for years, both growing up with parents who collected antiques, and thought having our own small business with two young children at the time was a good way to keep Chris close to home."

The shop has grown—and their family has, too, with a third child. Stepback has moved a few times since those early days, but the things they love about the past haven't changed: "The quality of items from the past, the craftsmanship," says Robin. "Things were generally built to last or be repaired or mended if they broke. It's more sustainable. You hear people say, 'They don't make them like they used to.' This isn't necessarily true. There are a lot of well-made, quality products out there; they are just more costly. Everyday consumer items used to all be made to last, but that's not the case now."

"Chris and I both love vintage books. I collect school readers and school-related paraphernalia: charts, maps, flashcards. Other collections include trophies, hand-tinted black-and-white landscape photographs, 1930s to '40s rayguns... the list goes on!"

When it comes to shopping for Stepback, they know what their customers like. "It's seamless, we only source, sell or pick things for the shop that we love ourselves." After a particularly good haul of picking for the shop, they'll post sidewalk stacks of vintage suitcases, crates, typewriters and chairs to Instagram, getting their customers buzzing for the next new old thing to make it into the shop. ✣

"We get to reduce, reuse and repurpose almost everything we use in our lives or sell at the shop—old idea but timeless and timely!"

STEPBACK 177

QUINTESSENTIALLY CANADIAN VINTAGE

There are obvious things like snowshoes or bearskin rugs, but things like ceramics from Medicine Hat, Alberta, in particular, seem to always come up. From Medalta crocks to colourful Hycroft and Medicine Hat potteries dishware, they seem to always resonate with collectors.

"We bought a 1924 one-room schoolhouse in the Shuswap to convert into a retreat and to house our collections."

GRAY BEVERAGE
GRAY BEVERAGE
GRAY BEVERAGE
GRAY BEVERAGE
Peek Frean

FIRST AID CABINET

Life
POP SHOP
ZINFANDEL
OAKLEY
OAKLEY CALIFORNIA
PEPSI-COLA
NAPHTHA

GRAY BEVERAGE

stepback.ca
@stepback_ca

Tools of the Engraving trade

PRINTING

Artistry Engraving

Operating a
third-generation
print shop in
Chicago

PHILIP GATTUSO

"Within the world of ink on paper and design, interests change like the wind, but people generally have a deeply rooted respect for traditional design when it comes to engraving. We see typography, colours, paperweight and finishing techniques changing throughout the years but the overall layout stays the same. Recently, it seems quite a few people are taking a step back, thinking about what stationery was and how they can adapt modern design within that platform."

A third-generation printer, Philip Gattuso works at his family-owned and operated print shop, Artistry Engraving and Embossing, in Chicago, Illinois. "My maternal grandparents, Thomas and Dorothy Johnsen, founded the company in 1955 after working at Marshall Field's in the engraving department," Philip says. "My dad began working at the shop full time in 1983 and my mom started in 1988. Upon graduating from the Milwaukee Institute of Art and Design in 2014, my wife, Holli, and I started our full-time positions."

Engraved stationery was once the standard on most fine corporate correspondence, giving it a distinct, slightly raised surface. "Engraving is the act of scratching, scraping or cutting into a surface," Philip explains. "With the use of a graver, one can cut figures or letterforms into metals, stones or other hard substrates. The end result can then be inked and pressed into a sheet of paper using intense pressure, creating an image with a unique look and feel that no other printing process can replicate!"

"What was once over 100 engraving shops in Chicago has dwindled to less than 100 engraving shops in the world," remarks Philip. "As a family, we continuously push to keep the engraved stationery trade alive and well, but things have been difficult and we've been forced to employ different printing processes within the last 15 years. It's by no means a bad thing to have letterpress, foil stamping, offset and digital printing capabilities in-house, we just took great pride in exclusively offering engraving and it was a hard reality to realize it simply wasn't possible any longer."

"I can't wait to see what the future holds for the engraving industry. Things are changing very quickly, and as shops continue to go out of business, something needs to happen. Something needs to change. All I know for certain is that I will continue to engrave stationery until I am physically or mentally unable to." ✽

Wishing you a Merry Christmas
and a Happy New Year

OLD TECH

I would have to say the vintage possessions I prize the most would be our fleet of C. R. Carver die stamping presses from 1919. They went out of business in the 1930s, so these presses definitely aren't being produced anymore and most of them have long since been destroyed. Parts are hard to come by but we've been very lucky having acquired four of these presses at various times throughout the last few years. They are a very important part of our business and my life, and without them I wouldn't be able to produce half of the work I do.

PRESERVING A PASSION

My biggest draw to vintage objects and technology is simply preservation. Cotton-content onion skin paper isn't being produced anymore, half-inch hand-engraved steel dies are a thing of the past and most engraving shops recycle them, and the engraving industry is currently floundering around the world. My main goal is to educate and carry the engraved stationery industry into the future.

The process of engraving has so many limitations that it's very difficult to produce something that's never been done before. This aspect of the process, in my opinion, causes people to get bored with engraving a lot easier because they don't have the artistic freedom they would with other print processes. On the positive side, this forces us to try new things and, since we no longer need to hand engrave our plates, we are able to use programs like Illustrator to create more precise and in-depth work.

```
"I mainly run a C. R.
Carver die stamping press
that was created in 1919,
and if it were up to me,
it's the only press I'd
ever run again. Besides
running a vintage press
I also collect vintage
blank paper, letterheads,
stationery and half-inch
hand-engraved steel dies."
```

"My life and my profession are one and the same. Most of my vintage collections can also be used around the print shop as examples, display and inspiration; helping us to fine-tune our craft so it continues reflecting the past yet pushes into the future. I use old letterheads to remind me of what is possible, old steel dies to remind me of how hard I must continue to work, and old machinery to make things that bring joy to others."

artistryink.com
@artistryengraving

PLEASE SUPPORT YOUR LOCAL STATIONERY ENGRAVER

AS A PRINTER I DEAL WITH THE RELATIONSHIP INK HAS WITH PAPER. EVERY RELATIONSHIP IS DIFFERENT; TYPE OF PAPER, PRINT PROCESS, DESIGN, HUMIDITY, INK OPACITY, ETC. ENGRAVING, ALSO KNOWN AS DIE STAMPING, IS MY PRINTING PROCESS OF CHOICE. A PROCESS ONCE RESERVED FOR THE WEALTHY HAS PROVEN ITSELF TO BE FAR MORE VERSATILE THAN PREVIOUSLY THOUGHT. IT IS A KIN TO LETTERPRESS IN THE FACT THAT THEY ARE TRUE OPPOSITES IN JUST ABOUT EVERY SCENE OF THE WORD. ARTISTICALLY, I TREASURE THE LINE THAT SEPARATES THESE TWO PRINTING PROCESSES BUT WHERE ONE HAS FLOURISHED THE OTHER IS FIGHTING FOR SURVIVAL. THIS ONGOING PRINT SERIES IS ABOUT THE TOOLS OF THE LATTER; THE TOOLS OF THE ENGRAVING* TRADE.

FOLLOWING IS A LIST OF PRESS PARTS THAT I INTERACT WITH EVERY TIME I SET UP AND RUN A JOB ON A 4.5" X 9" CARVER DIE STAMPING PRESS.

PART No.	DESCRIPTION OF PART
069	BED CONNECTION LOCKING PIN
076.5	DIE CHUCK WRENCH PIN
0123	SLIDE CONNECTION LOCKING PIN SPRING
0124	SLIDE CONNECTION HOLD UP SPRING
0154	DIE CHUCK WRENCH
0180	WIPING PAD REWIND FRICTION DISC STUD
0189	DISTRIBUTOR ROLL ADJUSTMENT SWIVEL STUD
0190	DISTRIBUTOR ROLL ADJUSTMENT SCREW
0192	DISTRIBUTOR ROLL ADJUSTMENT SWIVEL COLLAR
0213	DISTRIBUTOR ROLL SHAFT
0277	SHIFTER LEVER FRONT
0342	SHIFT LEVER BACK
0500	DIE CHUCK SCREW FOR NO. 734
0501	DIE CHUCK SCREW FOR NO. 919
0520	UPPER TOGGLE PIN (NEW STYLE)
0521	LOWER TOGGLE PIN (NEW STYLE)
0522	TOGGLE ROLLER PIN (NEW STYLE)
0591	COUNTER BLOCK PLATE 4.5" X 9"
D1208	THUMB SCREW FOR FOUNTAIN BRACKET CAP
01237	TOGGLE ADJUSTING PINION
01259	REWINDER SHAFT
01262	REWINDER TUBE
01612	FOUNTAIN ROLL SHAFT (LARGE ROLL LARGE FOUNTAIN)
01613	FOUNTAIN ROLL SHAFT (SMALL ROLL LARGE FOUNTAIN)
01614	INK FOUNTAIN PAN (LARGE FOUNTAIN)
252	WIPING PAD ADJUSTMENT WORM GEAR
254	WIPING PAD ADJUSTMENT HAND WHEEL
409	WIPING PAPER CORES
457	PLUNGER
472	SLIDE HOOK CONNECTOR
481	HAND WHEEL
824	WIPING PAD CONE
1126	COUNTER BLOCK 4.5" X 9"
1453	TRIPLE CAM CLAMPING SCREW WRENCH
1458	TOGGLE ADJUSTMENT RING
1481	DIE CHUCK SHOES (BACK RIGHT, FRONT LEFT)
1482	DIE CHUCK SHOES (FRONT RIGHT, BACK LEFT)
1556	TOGGLE ADJUSTMENT BLOCK (COMPLETE)
1563	TOGGLE PIN BUSHING (CENTER)
1564	TOGGLE PIN BUSHING (BOTTOM)
1565	TOGGLE PIN BUSHING (TOP)
1566	TOGGLE (LOWER)
1567	TOGGLE (UPPER)
1587	COLLAPSIBLE REWIND TUBE END RIGHT HAND
1599	COLLAPSIBLE REWIND TUBE END LEFT HAND
1776	REWIND HAND WHEEL
1823	WIPING PAPER FEED ADJUSTMENT ARM (OLD STYLE)
2095	LARGE ROLL FOR LARGE FOUNTAIN
2096	SMALL ROLL FOR LARGE FOUNTAIN
2098	FOUNTAIN DRIVE GEAR 7/8" HOLE (FOR LARGE ROLL)
	HOW DESIGN LIVE 2017

THIS IS A CARVER DIE STAMPING PRESS USED IN THE PRINTING OF ENGRAVED COPPER & STEEL PLATES. MANUFACTURED BY THE C. R. CARVER COMPANY, OF PHILADELPHIA, PA., IT WAS FIRST PERFECTED IN 1892 AND ADVANCED UPON UNTIL AROUND 1931 WHEN THE PLANT WAS SOLD AT AUCTION.

THE CARVER PRESS USED TO CREATE THIS PRINT WAS MANUFACTURED AROUND 1919 AND CONTAINS A PRESS NUMBER OF 1239. IT IS THE NEWEST CARVER ARTISTRY POSSESSES.

Engraving is embossing with ink

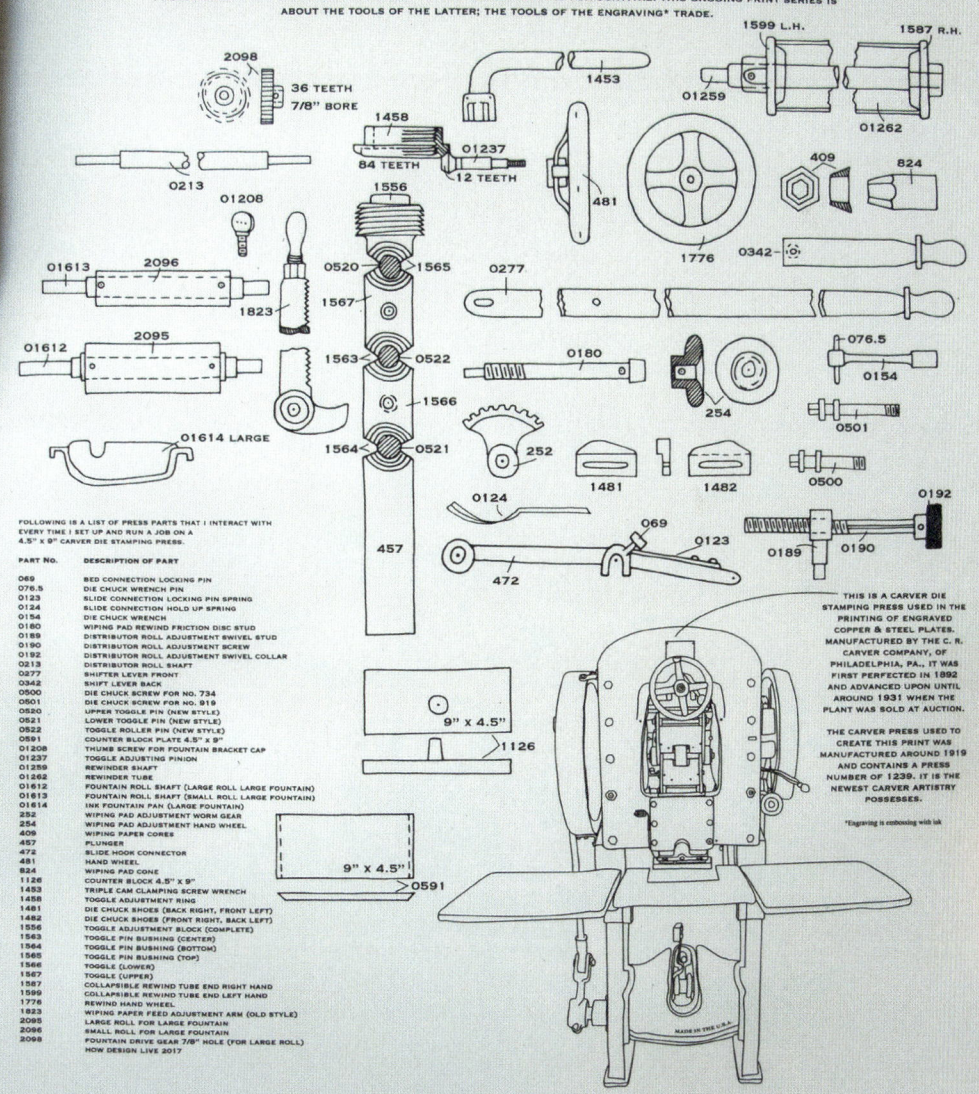

357/650

Tools of the Engraving* trade №2

Paper: Neenah Paper - CLASSIC CREST® Double Thick Cover BARE WHITE 130DTC (352 g/m2) 16pt Eggshell · **Engraving & Illustration:** Philip Gattuso at Artistry Engraving & Embossing Company, Inc. · Chicago, Illinois · www.artistryink.com

ARTISTRY ENGRAVING 189

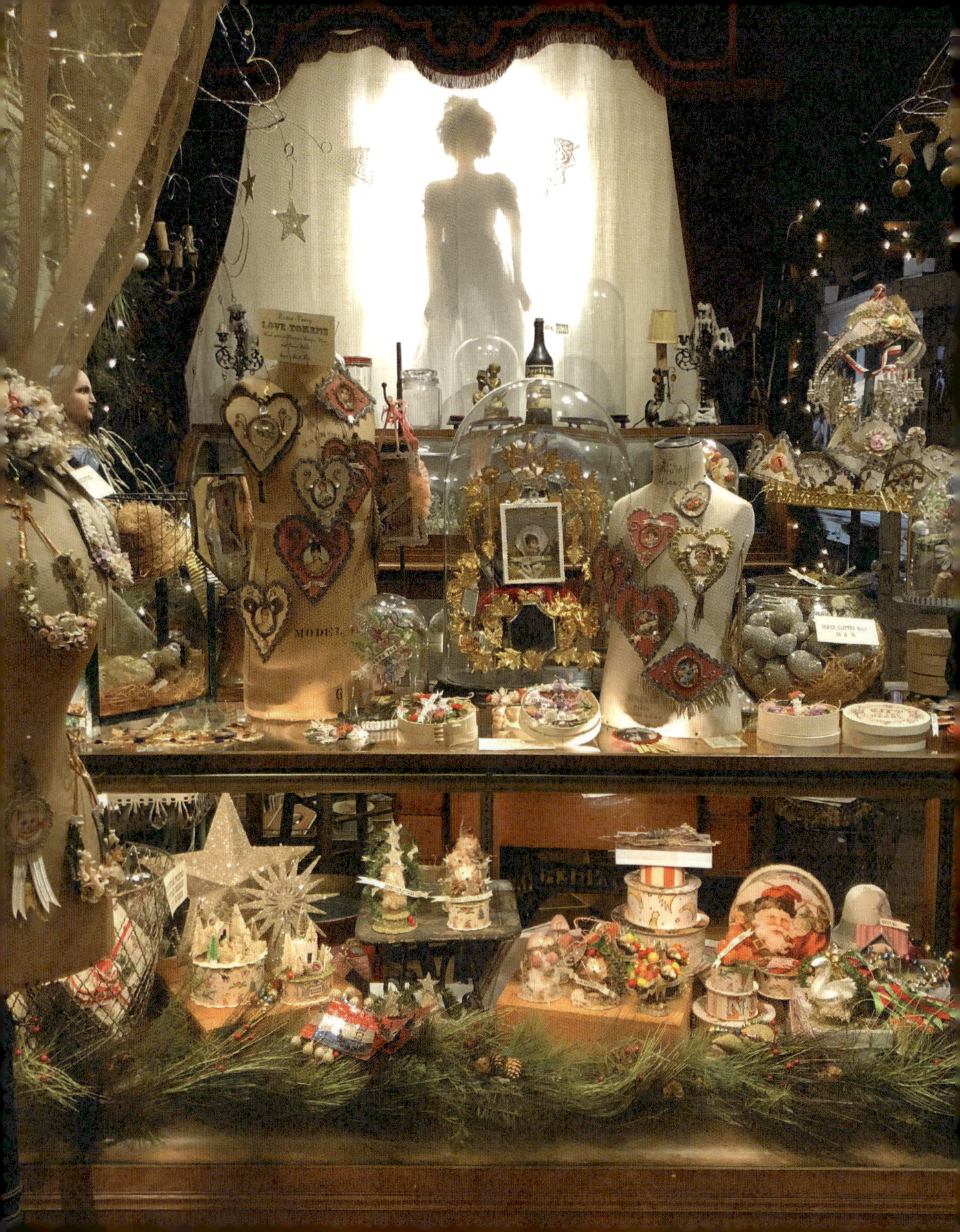
LOVE TOKENS
MODEL

RETAIL EXPERIENCE

Theatre of Dreams

Setting the stage for fantasy and delight

WENDY ADDISON

"Everywhere you look in my little kingdom, you will see antique collections that inspire me."

Wendy Addison's unique world is one of vintage Victoriana fantasy that is sprinkled with glass glitter and messaged with the gothic wood-type–inspired font Ironwood. This is the Theatre of Dreams, a business that she started in the 1990s. "It was a way to put forth my imaginary vision using techniques and materials from the past," she says. "I combined my fine art training and my love of antiques to construct whimsical paper gift items, optical toys, fantastical wire work, shadow puppets, paper theatres, letterpress goods, illustrated books and fine art drawings."

"I started out as a fine artist when I was very young, and along the way became proficient at paper marbling, bookbinding, box making and letterpress printing." She describes Theatre of Dreams as a "stage" allowing her to give vision to her imaginary life, which exists in her home and studio. "In the last 22 years, I have lived and worked in a magical little town (Port Costa) on the banks of the north San Francisco Bay. My retail store and home are in an 1880s storefront and my studio is in an old grain warehouse."

"I have been collecting antique paper and ephemera for 40 years and have an amazing collection of graphics. I adore antique mechanical tools, and my home and shop are full of antique gas lights, hand-run Victorian-era tools, such as a treadle sewing machine, hand-driven letterpress, wind-up puppet shows and hand-cranked laundry wringers, which I use for mounting paper. I also collect and use antique linens, clothing and cookware!"

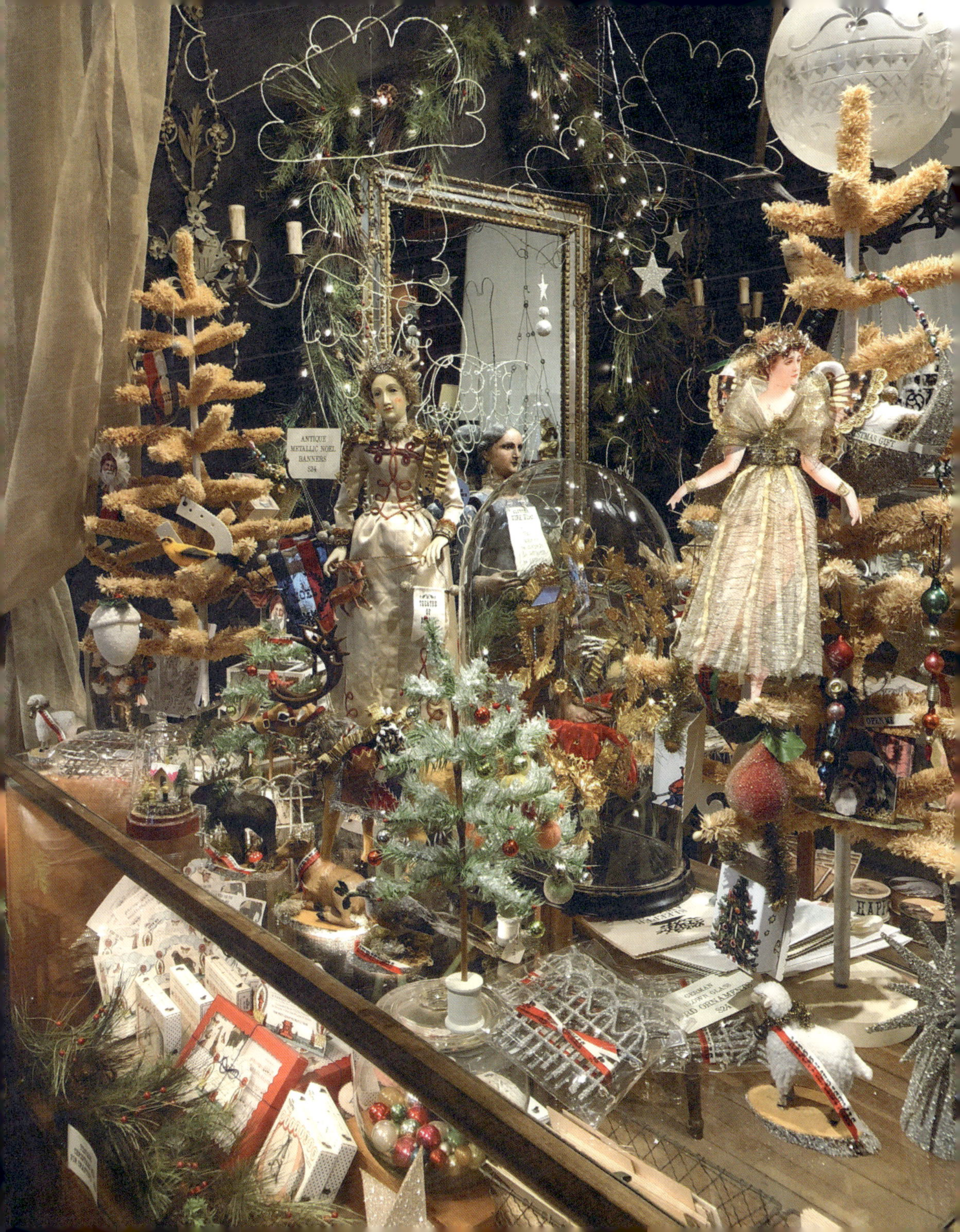
ANTIQUE
METALLIC NOEL
BANNERS
$24

Basing her giftware designs on antique materials, Wendy often uses antique die cuts from the 1870s as well as old newspapers, sheet music and vintage crêpe paper. "I also use antique tinsel and glass beads at Christmas time."

Her shop is full of unique and intriguing delights of fantasy. A few times a year, she also hosts vintage sales of her own treasures and ephemera. A recent sale was declared an event of "the weird & the wonderful, the practical & the fantastical, the usable & the inexcusable!" She packed up her regular shop goods and restocked the tables and shelves to the rafters with antiques. "I have curated this sale especially for artists, designers and craftspeople," she says. Guests are invited to dig through piles of antique textiles, beads, buttons, trims, millinery flowers and ribbons, books, prints, paper ephemera, objects from French flea markets, old Dennison stationery goods and crêpe paper, sewing stuff, wallpaper, and inspiring and "indescribable oddities." ❈

HOLD TO LITES ASTRONOMICAL

INTERIORS

POST CARDS TRADE CARDS

ANATOMICAL HALLOWEEN CHRISTMAS

CIRCUS BALLET COSTUME

"I find that antique objects speak to me. Things that have been held, and used, and loved and cared for—for decades—seem to carry with them the spirit of human-ness that is warm and comforting."

CIRCUS
IS COMING!
DE LA MANO
THE CHAMPION
THE CHAMPION
PRESTIDIGITATEUR
AMBIDEXTROUS COMEDIAN,
ARCH ILLUSIONIST AND HUMORIST
A NIGHT OF MYSTERY!
TWO HOURS OF FUN.
PROF. DE LA MANO
"MENE, TEKEL, UPHARSIN"
THE ENCHANTED CROSS
AH SIN'S LAUNDRY
THE SECOND SIGHT MYSTERY!
PYRAMIDS OF EGYPT.
THOSE SINGULAR CARDS
THAT BEWITCHING MONEY
GOOD MUSIC IN ATTENDANCE
FOR PARTICULARS SEE SMALL BILLS.
ADMISSION, 25 CENTS.
WHAT
GHOSTLY
MUSE
SPEAKS!
BY WHAT
MACHINERY
OF
DREAMS
DOES
SHE
DANCE
?
ON WHAT
SHADOWY
STAGE?
PORT COSTA
TOWN WIDE
YARD SALE!
PRINT SIDE
GOES DOWN

"As we live in a progressively more cold and electronic world, the more people are drawn to my shop and the evocative environment I have created. Things that are antique or vintage and also handmade have a warmth and humanity that is more and more attractive to people—they need an antidote to the impersonal modern world we live in."

wendyaddisonstudio.com
@thewendyaddison

TINSEL TRADING
EST 1933 NYC

We present a treasure trove of antique & vintage materials for the creative soul. Please take a moment to touch the texture & enjoy the visual of this moment in history.

TINSEL THREAD SPOOLS
This thread was made in France almost 100 years ago and is the base material for all things TINSEL. These threads are for hand work only.

FULL SPOOLS PRICED AS MARKED

CORDONETTE 3 PLY $24 HANK

PASSEMENTERIE

Tinsel Trading

Continuing a family business of selling antique trims and finery

MARCIA CEPPOS

"Three generations of trim collectors obsessed with buying up old stock has resulted in one of the largest collections of antique trim in the world."

Tinsel Trading is a third generation passementerie store founded in 1933 in Manhattan's garment district. Passementerie refers to French decorative trimmings such as tassels, braid, fringes and ribbons.

Marcia Ceppos started going to her grandfather's shop when she was just eight years old. Her grandfather's interest in this particular industry began after World War I as an employee of the French Tinsel Company. "The main product was metal threads in an array of styles, colours and sizes also known as 'tinsel,' and made in France," describes Maria. "It's not surprising that he gravitated towards threads; after all, his father was a tailor. Metal thread, however, was an unusual choice for an ambitious young man to start his career with. Years passed and Arch J. Bergoffen, my grandfather, purchased the company in 1933, changed the name, and thus began Tinsel Trading Company."

The colours, glitter and textures appealed across the generations. At age 11, she began actively assisting in the store. "I would travel with my older brother from Queens to Manhattan, by subway, on Saturdays to help out," says Maria. "Throughout high school and college, I worked every opportunity I could, learning as much as possible about the business. By the time I was 18 years old, I was hooked. I knew that I wanted to make my life at Tinsel Trading, surrounded by the glistening beauty of antique trim."

Her grandfather diversified Tinsel Trading's offerings by acquiring anything decorative and old. "He bought ribbons, buttons, tassels, fringes, raffia ornaments and anything else that attracted him—even

Brazilian beetles from the 1930s—in all colours and fibres. If it remotely fit into his idea of a creative decorative item, he wanted it." Hundreds of boxes would arrive at the store. "Several pieces of each item would be put on a shelf to sell, but the rest went into the basement, one box piled on top of another, blocking aisles and passageways, and mostly sitting unopened and unmarked for years and years. My grandfather was a pack rat and thank goodness he was."

"When my grandfather died in 1989, it became my job to make sense of thousands and thousands of items and organize it all. I wanted to introduce to the world the wonders and magic of an amazing collection of vintage that spanned over 70 years and the introduction of contemporary goods in the same genre."

With attention from Martha Stewart's television show in its heyday and then the advent of shopping via the Internet, Tinsel Trading has successfully navigated through the decades. "As a businesswoman, I have to use modern-day tools, computers, cell phones, etc. I use them to spread the word mostly through Instagram and my website."

In 2009, Tinsel Trading welcomed designer Wendy Addison (also featured in this book) as creative director. "Her imagination has brought a panoply of rich new possibilities to the world of Tinsel," says Marcia, "and her visual sense has revitalized our retail store." Due to ever-increasing rents and a desire for change, Marcia moved Tinsel Trading to Berkeley, California, in 2017. "We got lucky and found a beautiful storefront with big display windows and shade trees along the sidewalk." And there's lots of parking—"a big plus after 84 years in New York!" ❋

METAL TRIM

Metal trim made in France, Germany and Belgium before World War I is our specialty. These materials were made during the golden age of handwork and were destined for opera and ballet costumes, lavish evening gowns by couture houses, as well as military dress uniforms. I also have a passion for antique ribbon work, beaded flowers and antique buttons. I am a self-confessed hoarder of these items!

"Since my work and my home are all about Tinsel, I am surrounded by it everywhere I live and work! I spend my 'off' days hunting and gathering in flea markets for more antique trim."

tinseltrading.com
@tinseltrading

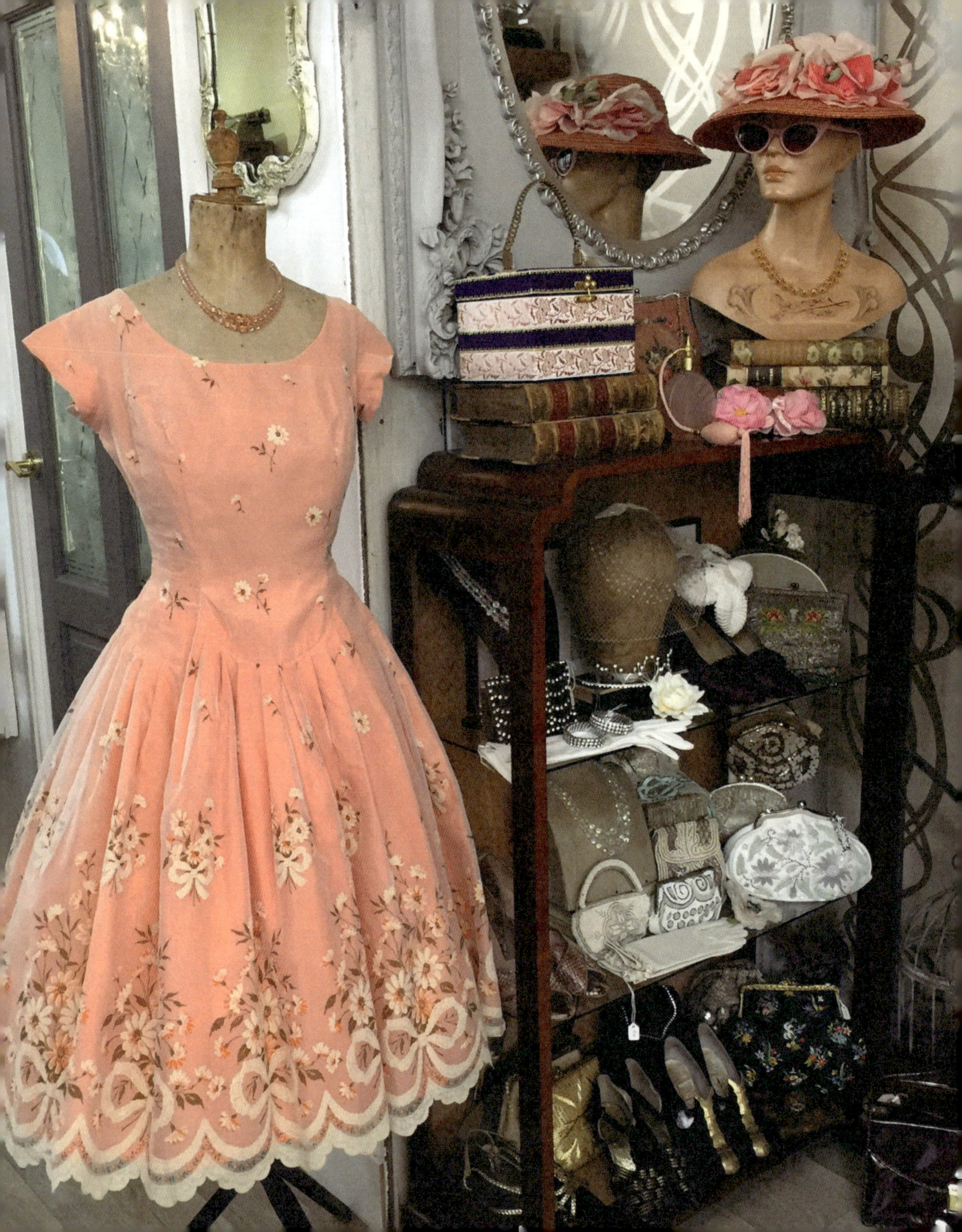

CLOTHING & HABERDASHERY

Donna Flower Vintage

"Having a shop is so wonderful. Creating an emporium of vintage loveliness has been a dream come true and when I hear customers gasp and say 'Wow' as they walk through the door I feel like my job is done."

—Donna Flower

PORTRAIT BY STEVE NUTH

DONNA FLOWER and **JASMINE BENNETT**

Donna Flower Vintage

"There is an excitement when I find vintage furniture, homewares, old fabrics or clothing; I just don't get that same buzz from walking into a store and buying something new. It's wonderful to have an item of clothing or something made from vintage fabrics that makes your outfit unique, a one-off, especially if it was handmade."

Since leaving her childhood in the English Somerset countryside and heading for Los Angeles and then back to London, Donna Flower (and yes, that's her true given name) has longed to return to the countryside.

"I moved to Devon from London when pregnant with my second child (19 years ago). It was my dream to move back to the countryside, where I grew up. I was at home with a new baby, in the middle of the countryside, with my friends still in London. With more time on my hands, I turned to sewing and started making things with my vintage fabric finds. Patchwork and quilting became a big love of mine at this time. I only wanted to make quilts from vintage fabrics and started buying feed sacks on eBay, which was in its infancy at the time, from the USA. I was fascinated with the history of feed sacks during the depression years. These were not part of our cultural history in the UK, and so I thought that there would be a similar interest overseas in typically British fabrics such as Sanderson, Liberty, Laura Ashley, William Morris, etc. I started selling my excess fabric on eBay and it was a huge success."

The demand led to the development of her own website. "I now supply designers; costume makers for film, TV and theatre; museums; gallery owners; and hobbyists. My website was run alongside textile and vintage fairs, and twice a year I would host an open house where I would transform my house into a vintage emporium, with people travelling far and wide to visit."

"I am a single mother of three children, aged 14, 19 and 29, with the youngest two still at home with me. Five years ago I opened my first brick-and-mortar shop with my daughter, Jasmine Bennett, in my home town of Barnstaple. Donna Flower Vintage now sells vintage fabric, textiles, haberdashery and vintage clothing." ✽

DONNA FLOWER VINTAGE

PASSION FOR TEXTILES

My first love and complete passion is vintage fabrics and textiles. I cannot get enough of them. The very thought of them makes me excited. The prints can tell you a lot about what was going on in the world at the time they were produced and are a good record of social history. I have been collecting fabrics for over 20 years now. I have vintage haberdashery cabinets that house most of my collection, along with a stock room that is bursting with fabrics on shelves from floor to ceiling. I have 19th-century fabrics to 1980s fabrics in my current stock but have to say my favourite era is the fabrics of the 1950s. The 1950s prints show that the world was looking forward, after the Second World War when restrictions were lifted. Technological advances meant that fabrics could be mechanically screen printed. Colours were brighter and more vibrant. The designs include atomic patterns, space travel, science, rock and roll, and the growing teen culture. Fabric designs and fashions were exciting, fun and kitsch.

VINTAGE FABRIC

PRIZED POSSESSION

There have been many, many heart-stopping, excited, inner-squealing moments, but I have to say I was so delighted to have found my vintage haberdashery cabinets. I used to have a photo torn out of the *Sunday Times* magazine of a vintage haberdashery shop and dreamt for years of having something like it. I found an advert in a local paper, some 15 years ago, of a shop that was closing down. They had been an old wool shop and key cutting service and the owners were retiring. They had an old shop counter and glass-fronted cabinets for sale. I drove for two hours to the venue to view these items, bought them for a very small price and had them collected and delivered to me the next day. They have been in my home and now in my shop and are very much admired.

DONNA FLOWER VINTAGE

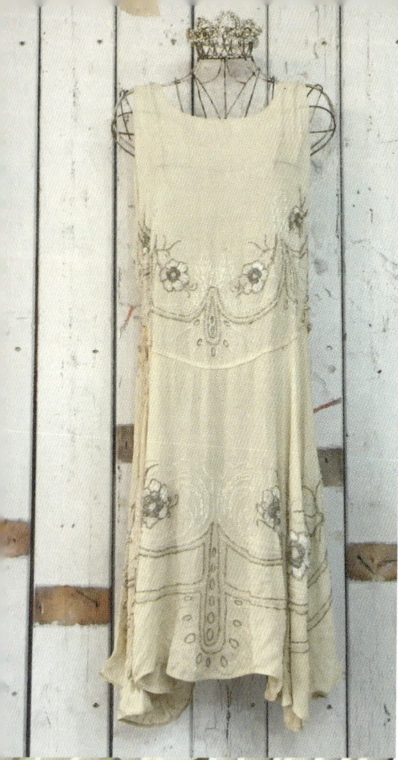
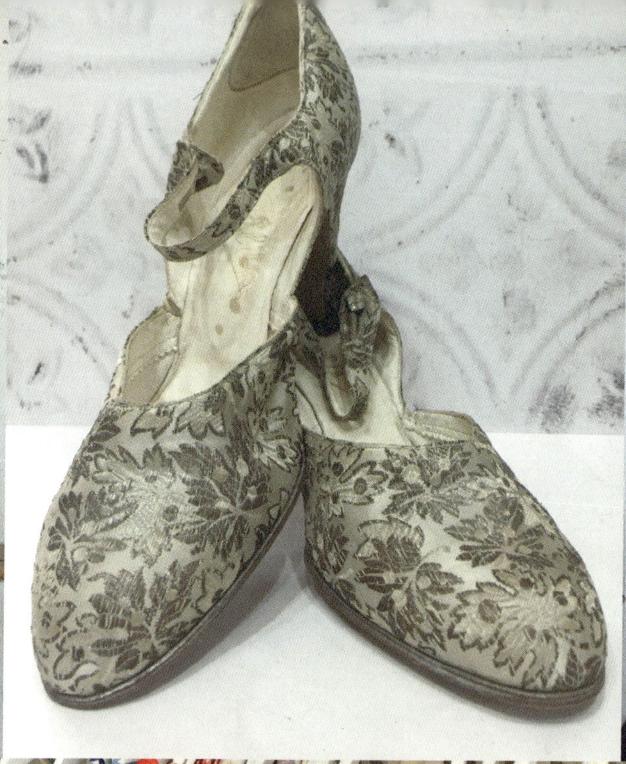
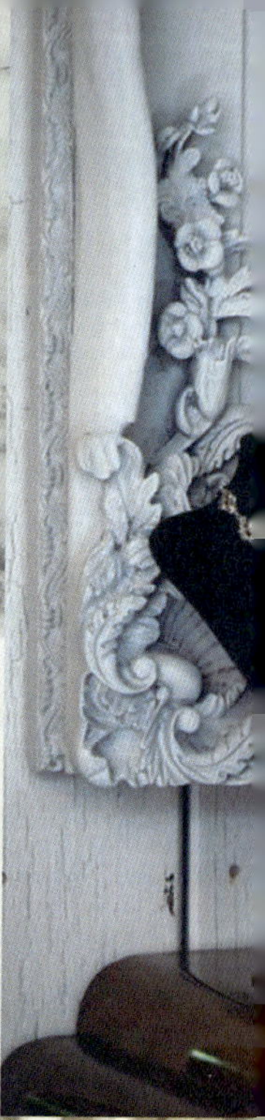
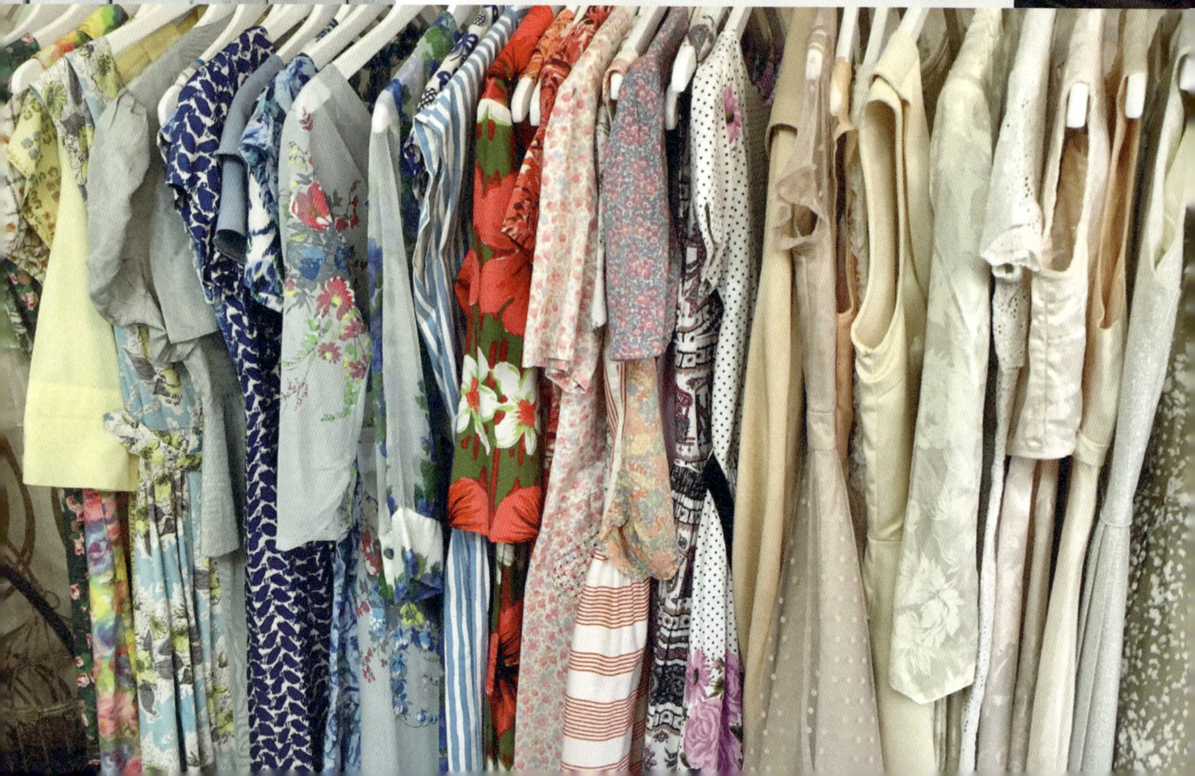

"I adore anything old. I am drawn to the history of what they have meant to others, where they have been, what they may have seen."

donnaflowervintage.com
@donnaflowervintage

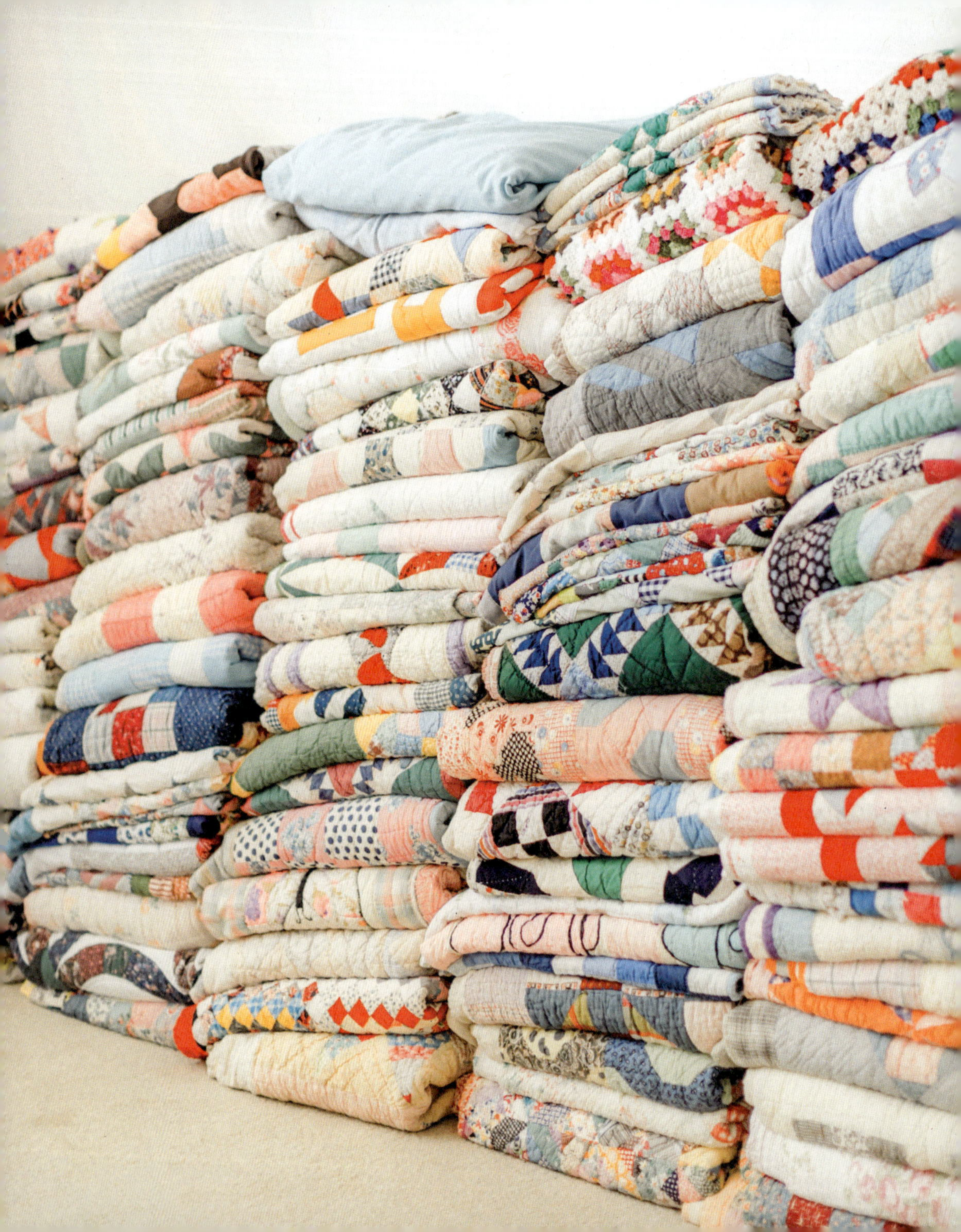

QUILTS

Stitched and Found

A photographer
(and new mom)
selling old quilts

HANNAH KELLY

"I am married to my high school sweetheart and we just welcomed our first child at the end of 2018. We live in Nashville, Tennessee, where I am a wedding photographer by day and a quilt hoarder by night. We spend our time downtown attending Predators games or at church with our dearest friends."

Having grown up in rural southern United States, quilts have been part of Hannah Kelly's everyday life. "I lived on a dairy farm, with my grandparents just a quick walk down the road," she recalls. "My grandparents made their own clothes, and quilts to keep warm. My grandmother made quilts until she was older and I grew up with family quilts displayed proudly on our walls. My mom tells me stories of sitting with her grandmother, stuffing cotton balls into the cherries on a cherry tree quilt they were making."

Hannah is a wedding photographer by day and a "quilt hoarder by night," she jokes. "I started several businesses while in middle and high school that helped me pay for college." In fact, she is an entrepreneur and has a busy business reselling vintage quilts. "Over the past three years, I have bought and sold over 5,000 vintage quilts. I have shipped quilts to all 50 states and over 10 other countries. I love that these lost treasures have been given a new life with these families all over the world."

Hannah says she has a deep appreciation for the anonymous makers who dedicated hours of their time and attention to these: "The products I sell are 95% vintage quilts. I wouldn't have the business I have without someone in the past spending the time to make each of these quilts."

The appeal of old quilts is in their history; even if their precise provenance and personal stories are lost, they are imbued with nostalgia and, one imagines, love. "A new quilt lacks the history and story of an old quilt. So many old quilts are made out of feed sacks, and this type of fabric just can't be replicated today. It takes years of love and wear for a quilt to have that 'feel' and a new quilt simply can't provide that (for now!)."

"So, so much history is wrapped up in quilts, their patterns and their purposes." ✣

"Every single quilt is a one-of-a-kind piece of artwork full of history. Each one is different, whether by the unique stitched, detailed pattern, or choice of fabric. I love snuggling up with an old quilt and thinking back on the other hands that held it and made it. Who was it made for? How long did it take?"

A KEEPER

My most prized possession is a quilt made by my grandmother. She gifted a quilt she made to each of her 10 grandchildren when they were married. The quilt I received is extra special because it was pieced by my great-grandmother and quilted by my grandmother. After my great-grandmother died (before I was born), my grandmother found these quilt pieces in her belongings and took them to make into a finished quilt.

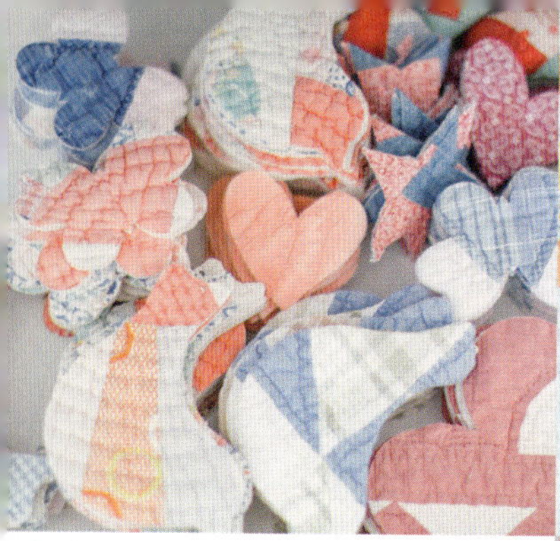
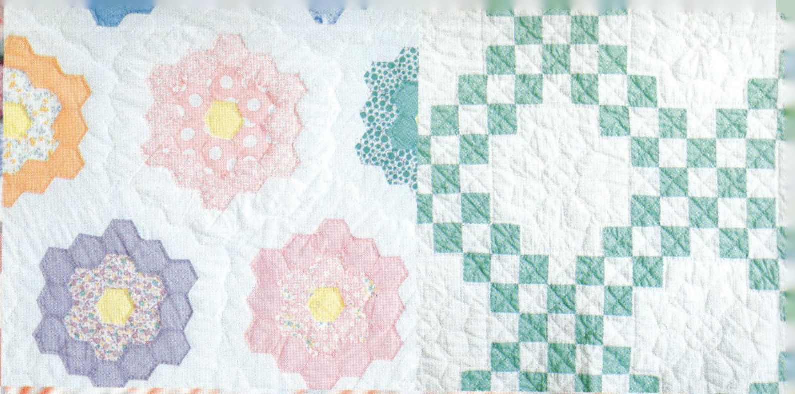
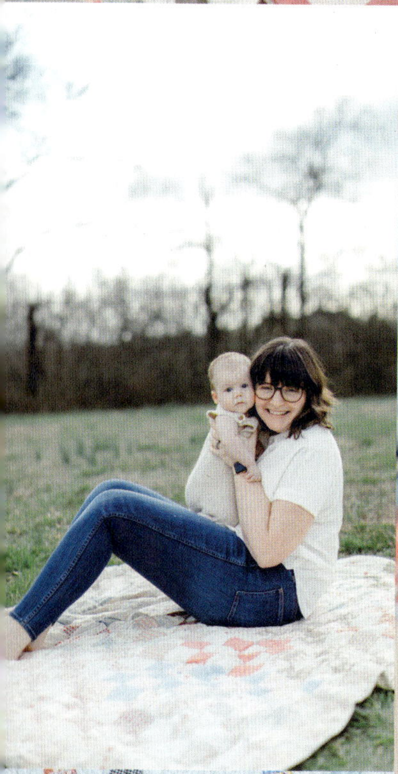
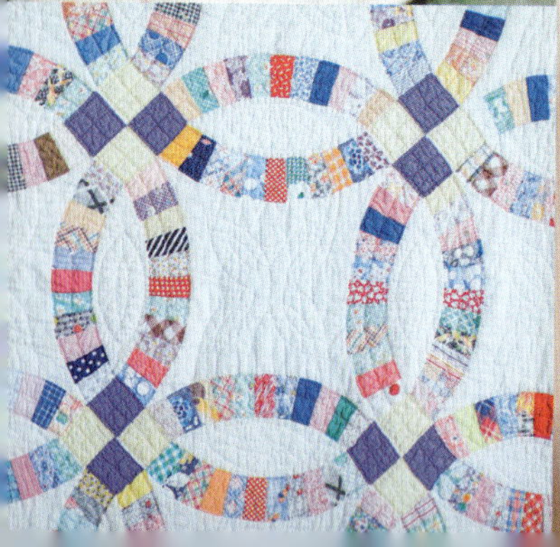
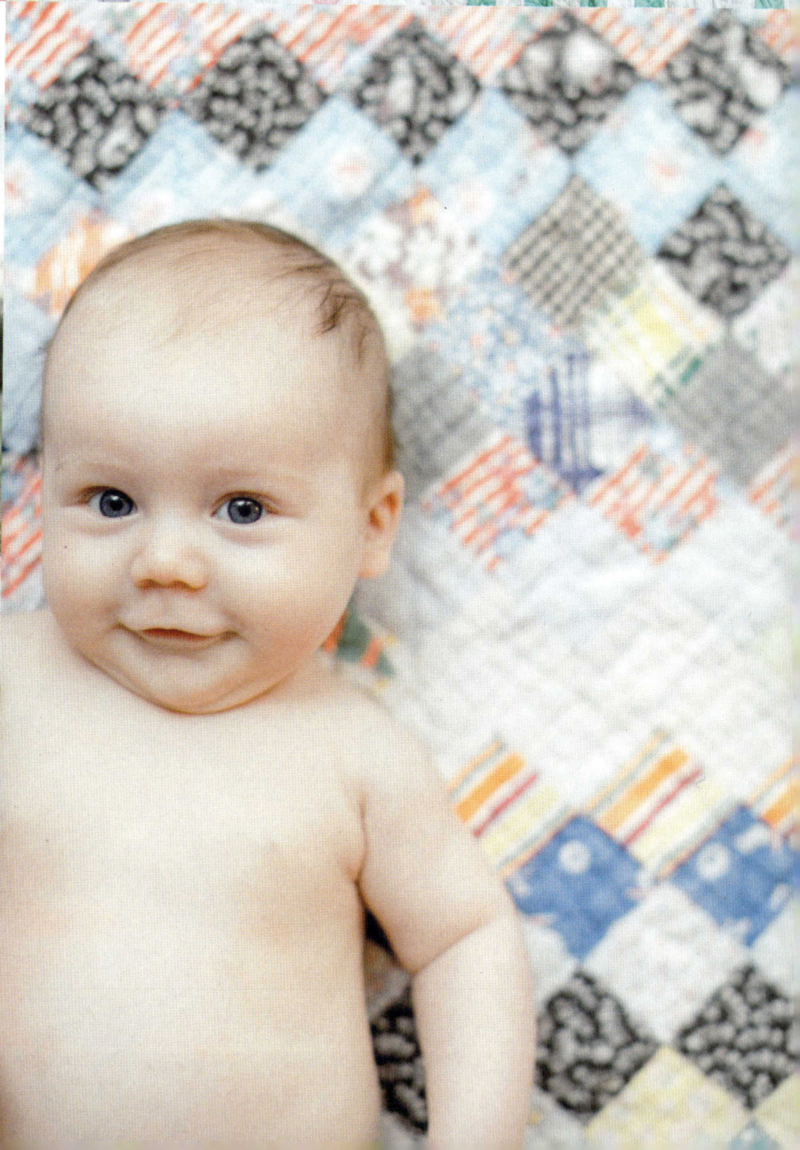

"I sell a large number of my quilts to other photographers. They use them in their photo sessions. So, these quilts are also going into homes that may not have 'loved' quilts but now they get to learn more about them and enjoy them too."

stitchedandfound.com
@stitchedandfound

THE FLOYD COUNTRY STORE
HOME OF THE FRIDAY NIGHT JAMBOREE
circa 1909
2055
OPEN

THE FLOYD COUNTRY STORE
Loitering allowed

MUSIC & COMMUNITY

The Floyd Country Store

Heritage and tradition in the Blue Ridge Mountains

DYLAN LOCKE and HEATHER KRANTZ

PHOTOS BY BRETT WINTER LEMON, GINA DILG AND J. PARKS

"When someone comes into the store for the first time, they are floored by how everyone seems to know each other. There are older folks who have been coming to the store for 30 years and who rarely ever miss a Friday night. We are inspired by the way we witness the culture passed down organically. We consider ourselves caretakers of these traditions, which bring meaning and great joy to life in Southwest Virginia."

L ocated on a plateau of the Blue Ridge Mountains in southwestern Virginia is the small town of Floyd—population of less than 500. The Floyd Country Store, owned by Dylan Locke and Heather Krantz, is and old-time destination with a lot on offer: a store, cafe and music venue dedicated to the traditional music and dance of the Appalachian region. "Our building was originally Farmer's Supply and opened in 1910, and operated mostly as a general store through the 1900s. In the late '70s, a tradition of musical friends getting together around a potbelly stove at the Feed and Seed next door formed what became known as the Friday Night Jamboree," explains Gina Dilg, the store's marketing and project coordinator (she and her husband Jason are also regular performers at the venue).

"Three string bands play on the stage every Friday night for a room full of dancers and onlookers in the store itself, and the street fills with groups of old-time, bluegrass and folk musicians." The Floyd Country Store is not only a hub for the community, but a destination for tourists to experience a "place out of time." The Floyd Radio Show broadcasts the charming sounds of Floyd over the Internet and as a podcast. "Our old-timey variety show is reminiscent of Prairie Home Companion. The show began in 2011, and takes place every month from September through May. We invite three musical acts (usually old-time, bluegrass or folk) for a Saturday night show full of music, stories, comedy skits and wacky sound effects. The show is performed both for a live audience and for listeners around the world."

"There is a lot in the traditional music, dance, storytelling and ways of life that connect people on a much deeper level than we are used to in our modern era. Technology goes over the top with how much information we are able to access, or how many people we can be in contact with while still remaining completely isolated."

Across the street is County Sales, a record store that boasts one of the largest selections of old time and bluegrass recordings. "The dedication to the music and to those who love it is the reason that Dylan Locke revived County Sales, the record store that ran for 50 years, primarily through mail orders and phone calls. Even in our modern era, many of the folks who got their music through County Sales never did buy computers, but still want to purchase music and learn about new releases and reissues of classic recordings. Even though digital music is now the most prevalent, these albums don't come with the liner notes that tell the story."

While music might feed the soul, visitors to the Floyd Country Store Cafe won't leave hungry; they can enjoy southern favourites like Brunswick stew, collard greens and skillet cornbread, made from scratch. "In the summertime, the benches in front of the store fill with kids eating ice cream cones, and in the winter months folks pick up their homemade pies and sides for holiday get-togethers. The Floyd Country Store is a community gathering place centred around good food, local artisans, mountain music and dancing."

"Both the owners, Heather and Dylan, and many of the staff at Floyd Country Store and County Sales are old-time and bluegrass musicians, and can be found playing on the stage or in the street on warm nights. Some of us get done with work duties only to stick around because friends show up with instruments," says Gina. "We carry the musical and dance traditions on at the store, not because they bring in tourists, but because we love the music and the connectedness that comes with it." ✤

TEACHING MUSICAL TRADITIONS

Although old-fashioned country stores are abundant in our part of the world, our passion is driven by the musical traditions that bring folks together from all walks of life. In the early 1900s, families homesteaded here on what is called the Blue Ridge Plateau, scraping a living from farming and forestry. These families were so tightly linked to their neighbours and music was a huge part of existence. Fiddles and banjos were played for regular social dances and work parties, church services, weddings and funerals.

Our musical heritage puts our town on the map, and many people come down the Crooked Road (Virginia's heritage music trail) looking to experience music and dance in our small town of Floyd. Of course, it is one thing to present this music at a dance every week, and another to make sure that it is handed down and appreciated by generations to come. Many of the older generation of mountain musicians have passed on, and folks don't learn the music in the same way that they did when the music was in its heyday.

The regional sound of the way people play fiddle music in Floyd and neighbouring counties is still heard on our stage, passed down through the generations and still being taught to young students through our education program, the Handmade Music School. Two local musicians and historians, Mac Traynham and Andy Buckman, have mastered very specific regional styles of playing and teach workshops, lead jams, give historical presentations and mentor students, keeping the tradition alive in the most dynamic and real way.

floydcountrystore.com
@thefloydcountrystore

COUNTY SALES
RECORD STORE
NEW & VINTAGE
MUSIC BOOKS
DVD VINTAGE CD
VINYL

CIRCUS
TRADITIONAL
SIGNWRITING & LINING
FAIRGROUND ART & DESIGN

SIGNPAINTING

A. Goodwin Signwriting

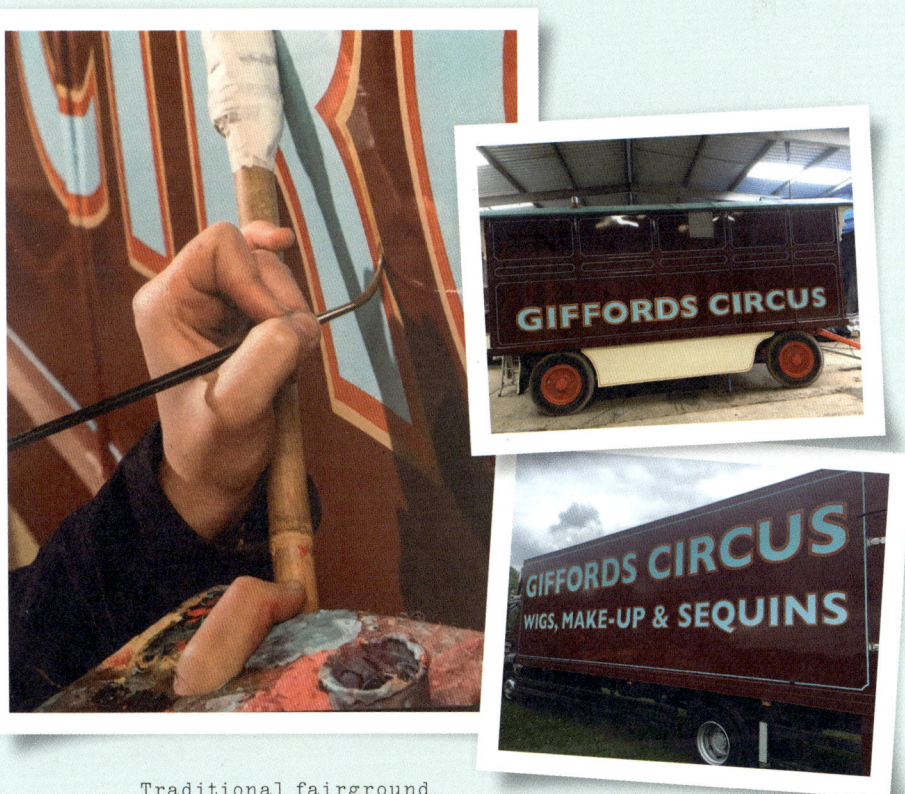

Traditional fairground graphics and vintage restorations

AMY GOODWIN

PORTRAIT BY JULIAN CALDER, ADDITIONAL PORTRAITS BY MARK LORD

"I'm drawn to signwriting not only due to being surrounded by it throughout my upbringing, but because of its methodical application: how a sign is built up through stages, how it evolves within its application and how, then, I've potentially added another layer or story to a history."

Amy Goodwin's passion for the past began in the British steam fairground industry: "The art and the traditions; the way of life, the stories that are passed down over generations and the sense of community; the rides and the steam engines—and this is embedded in the approach to all of the work I undertake."

It's an interest that is very personal: Amy spent the summers of her youth travelling with a steam fairground. The experience, she says, "has heavily influenced my practice as a traditional signwriter and fairground artist, thus the traditions and heritage of the fairground industry—the elaborate and visual typography, flamboyant colours and meticulous lines—is now reflected in both commissions and my own practice," she explains. Amy was first taught signwriting by showman Joby Carter of Carters Steam Fair, a family-run travelling fair reknowned for its

"Word of mouth is the strongest form of communication in this industry, thus this was the most powerful tool when beginning my career as a signwriter—and still is!"

beautifully restored and decorated rides from the late 1890s through the 1960s. "All my signwriting work is undertaken using traditional methods—by hand, using no tape, nor digital assistance."

Drawn to this community, Amy desires to do her part in keeping this unique industry alive. "The way of life is simpler, full of vibrancy and communication, of transience, and yet of hard work and physical graft," describes Amy. "I believe this is what has instilled my work ethic in me. Furthermore, the fragments of fairground art, which you might find in antique shops, appeal to me: I collect them and then extensively research their history, to find out which fairground they originated on, who painted them, etc."

"My completed projects include extensive restoration and paintwork commissions across the heritage, fairground and circus industries, including steam engines, living wagons and fairground rides, alongside the design and production of one-off bespoke signs, in collaboration with individuals and businesses."

"My practice-led PhD is looking to re-establish the identities of fairground women, by constructing an archive as illustrated space, holding traditional signs and works on paper, which tells stories of the women's lives. This study is informed by both my fairground upbringing and experience of working as a female signwriter in the industry." An integral part of this research is gathering the oral histories of women from the 20th century: "stories that have been passed down through generations and could have been lost. Part of the PhD is concerned with archiving these stories so they become a part of fairground history, creating identities for the women." ✻

"I feel there has been a resurgence of traditional signwriting and subsequently an admiration and respect for the craft. I feel my approach of undertaking all of the stages traditionally is acknowledged and appraised. This is particularly true when viewers realize it is all undertaken by hand, with no tape—that is always quite a satisfying reveal."

FAIRGROUND FRAGMENTS

I'm not only concerned with practicing the craft in this traditional way but am passionate about collecting old fragments of fairground art. This is expanded by my extensive work in the preservation industry, particularly on steam engines. Within this discipline, my passion is working to old photographs of the steam engine in question, recreating the original paintwork, effectively remaining true to both the application of the craft and the visual finish.

ITS **HANCOCKS**

WINKLEIGH **BOUGHTONS** AMERSHAM **ENGINEERS** DARTMOUTH

a-goodwin.com
@a__goodwin

Using vintage
element, motifs
and materials in
creative projects

Maker

PHOTO BY GINA JOHNSON

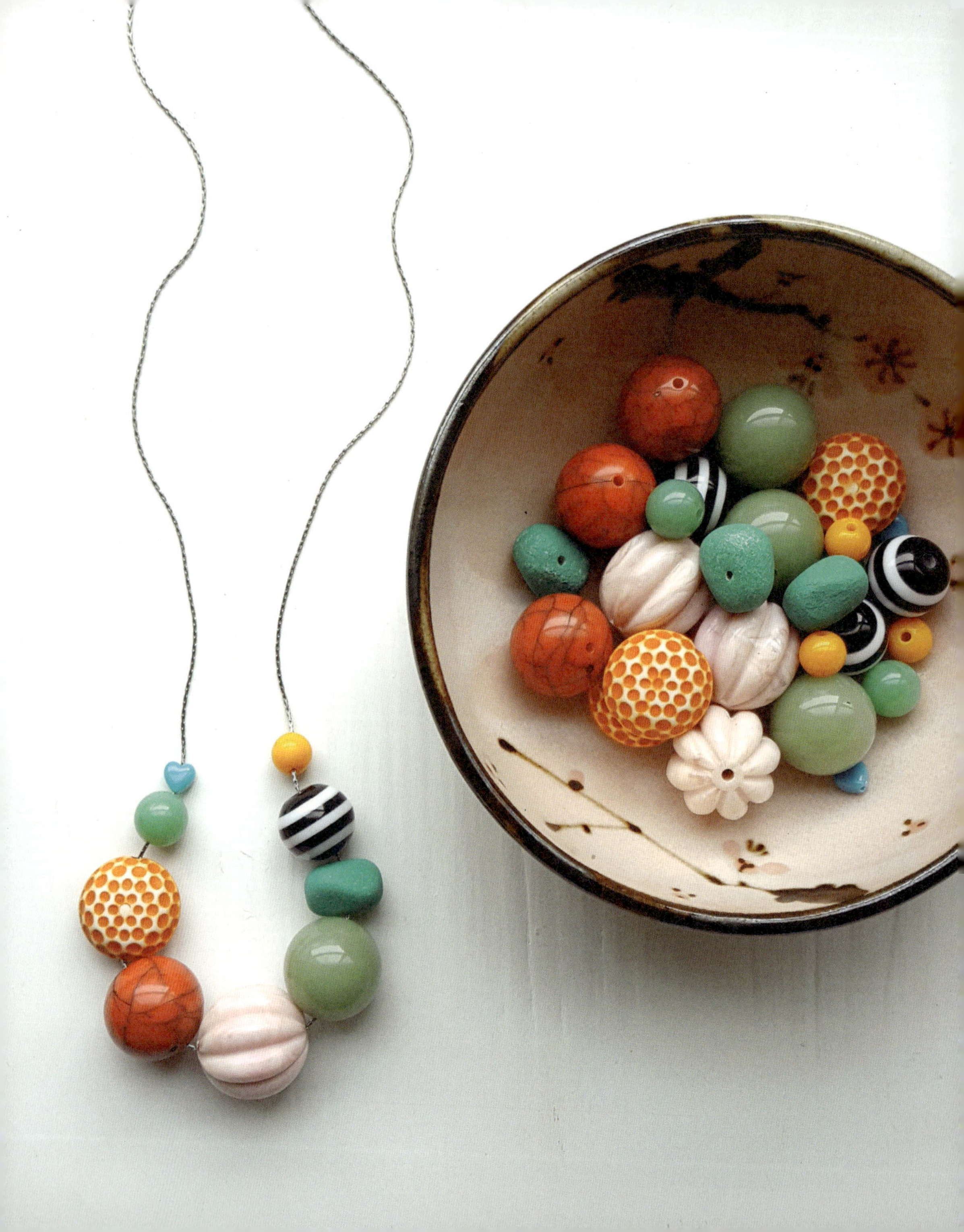

ARTIST · MAKER · CREATOR

Vintage Bead Jewellery

by

KATERI MORTON

"Jewellery is a form of narrative. The pieces we respond to and choose to wear are part of our story of self. In using vintage materials, I feel linked to the stories of both wearers and designers of jewellery who came before me. Whether I'm using a three-strand purple costume necklace from a friend's great-aunt, or a stash of never-used deadstock beads from a factory closeout, I get to work in a river of story and colour and help to keep it flowing. Over the years, my favourite projects have been custom requests from clients who have a treasured piece of family jewellery that they'd like recreated into something contemporary."

Kateri Morton makes brightly coloured jewellery using vintage beads. "Nearly all the beads I use are Lucite or plastic, either from deconstructed costume jewellery or unused deadstock that I purchase from collectors and dealers. From my very first purchase of vintage costume jewellery, I've been beguiled by the colours, details and craftsmanship of my materials. Vintage Lucite is a high-quality product, and it's easy for me to get lost in the tiny world of a single marbled round bead. Because they're plastic, these small works of art have a very long life ahead of them in the world. I curate them into settings where they are celebrated and create joy. I have a definite love affair with my collection of beads. I hope I'm only the middle part of their story, and that after they're done being my jewellery they'll have another life as something else." ✳

"I use a number of vintage items in my photo styling. Imperfect things have my heart, and I love to use dented, chippy, tarnished or verdigris objects as foils for my bright, glossy finished pieces of jewellery. They provide good visual contrast and a sort of anchor to the starting point of my work: the continued life of vintage things."

urbanlegendjewelry.com
@katerimorton

No. 3030 Quarter Size Case

KATERI MORTON 241

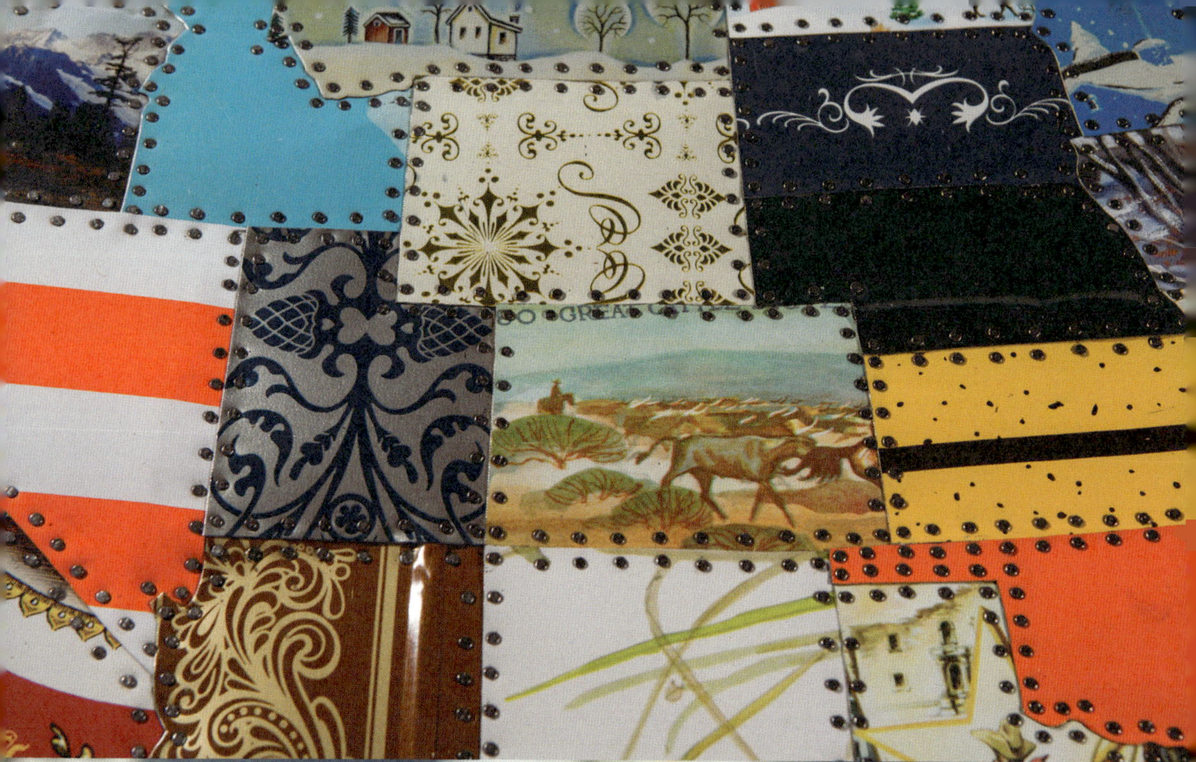

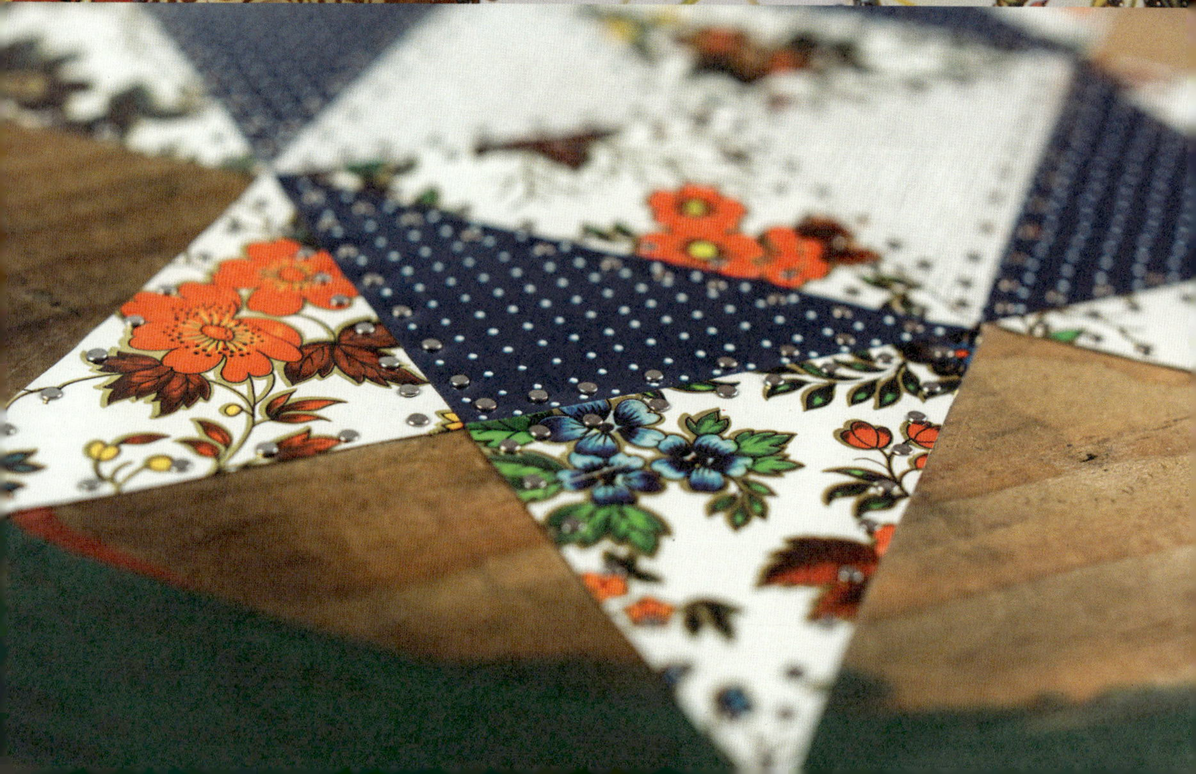

ARTIST · MAKER · CREATOR

Tin Patchwork

by

KIM FOX

Kim Fox's creative materials are typically old and discarded. This might not seem like the start of something great, but for Kim, they're markers of beauty. "I love the patina of age," she says. Kim makes "quilts"—patchworked constructions out of vintage decorative tin canisters. "They would have held cookies, tobacco, soap or other items." Snipped tin pieces are nailed onto salvaged wood substrates from a variety of sources. "My favourite salvage guy I know has found me terrific things like an antique glass-cutting table from an old hardware store or moulds from the now-defunct Jeannette Glass factory here in Western Pennsylvania. I also gladly search dumpsters and estate sales for interesting pieces to work on. My great love is taking things that no one wants anymore and giving them new life in my art." ✻

"I am as drawn to the laborious aspect of creativity as I am to its unpredictable outcomes. I gain almost as much from the process of cutting apart tins and sourcing the wood as I do from the assemblage of the art itself."

"I maintain as many of the old markings, production codes, measurements, etc., on the salvaged wood as possible because of what they add to the aesthetic. Old tins are also so much more interesting than contemporary packaging because the art was the focus, whereas modern packaging has to include so much information, like ingredients, warnings, instructions, etc."

VINTAGE LIFE

workerbird.com
@workerbird

The
ReBOOKery
House Beautiful
GREAT PARTY GIVING
HANDYMAN'S
BOOK
Little Lu
HELLO
ROCK
Summer

1 2 3
JUGGLE
WITH
ME!
A COUNTING BOOK
Prayers
FOR CHILDREN
A LITTLE GOLDEN BOOK

Bunny
Button

TheReBOOKery
The
ReBOOKery

ARTIST·MAKER·CREATOR

New Old Books

by

GINA JOHNSON

From her home in Peculiar—a western Missouri town with a population of less than 5,000 where the slogan is "Where the 'odds' are with you"—Gina Johnson turns her collection of vintage books and textiles into one-of-a-kind scrapbooks. "When my children were young, I began collecting Little Golden Books to read with them." The collection grew—not only for the benefit of reading to her children, but because they reconnected Gina to her own childhood. The children grew out of the books, but Gina's appreciation did not waver. "My first 'rebooked' journal was a mini scrapbook I made about my boys and their summer shenanigans." Using a worn book to build upon, the end result was more fulfilling that she could have imagined. "That journal led me to discover how to link my love of everything old with my inherent need to create." ❈

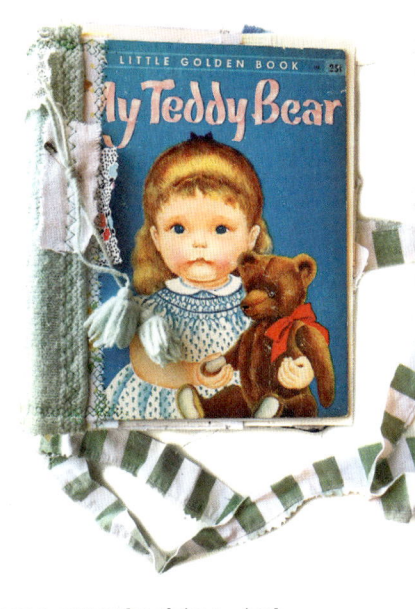

"I began scrapbooking. And while I loved the hobby, I felt that it was too sterile. I wanted to figure out a way to marry both the physical aspect of memory keeping (photos, memorabilia, stories) with the more abstract part—feelings and emotions."

"Growing up, I spent a lot of time with my grandparents. My 'country' grandparents were frugal and resourceful farm folk who had a passion for going to sales and collecting antiques. Their house was like a quirky museum full of some of the most unique treasures I'd ever seen. From a very young age I practiced their principles by saving, collecting and cherishing many treasures. My 'city' grandparents were makers. They made donuts and pizzas, clothing and quilts, furniture and rocking horses. Their creativity and ingenuity was embedded deep within my soul and it wasn't until I started creating journals that I was able to release this magical energy. Every time I create a journal, I truly believe my grandparents are with me—looking over my shoulder, gently nudging me to carry on with the priceless lessons they taught me. Each one of my creations is a collaboration of love between me and my childhood memories. I love combining old with new. When I use thrifted materials in my creations, I feel I'm adding yet another layer to the story I'm about to tell."

248 VINTAGE LIFE

"The journals I make always include something from the past, whether it is my great-grandma's Dresden plate quilt blocks or my Grandma Neva's collected felt."

therebookery.etsy.com
@rebookery

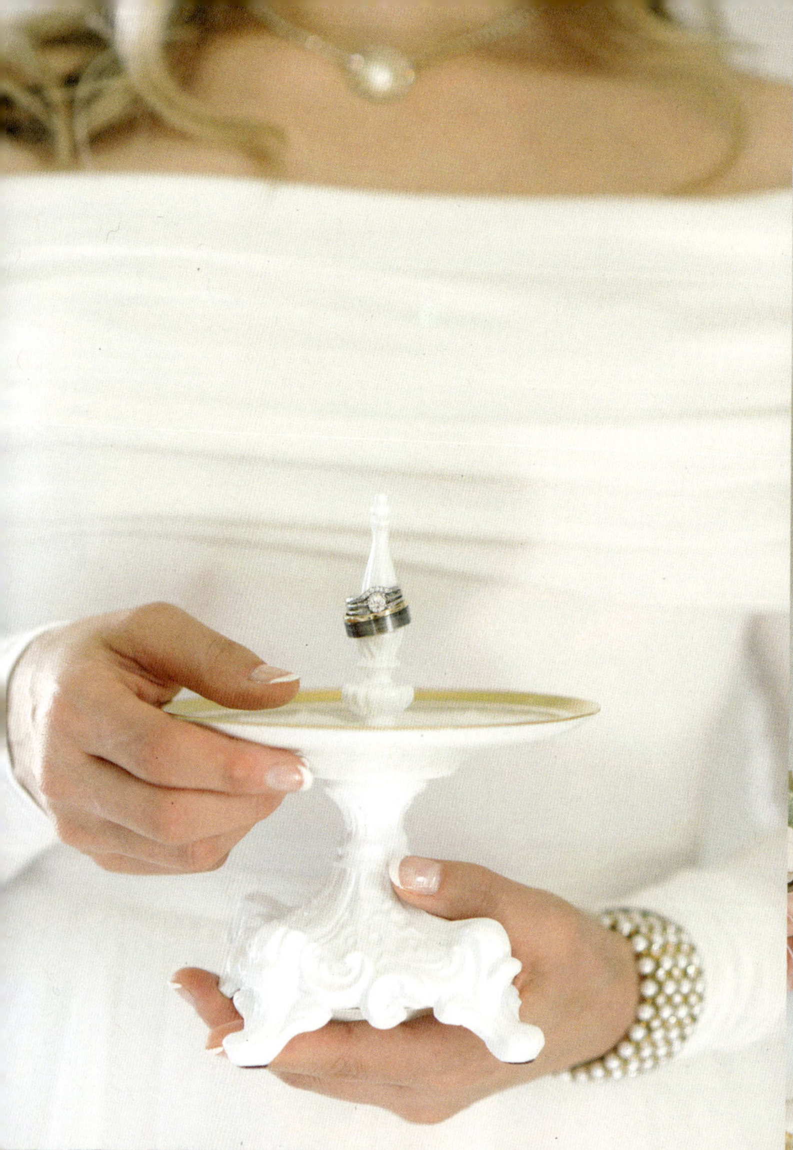
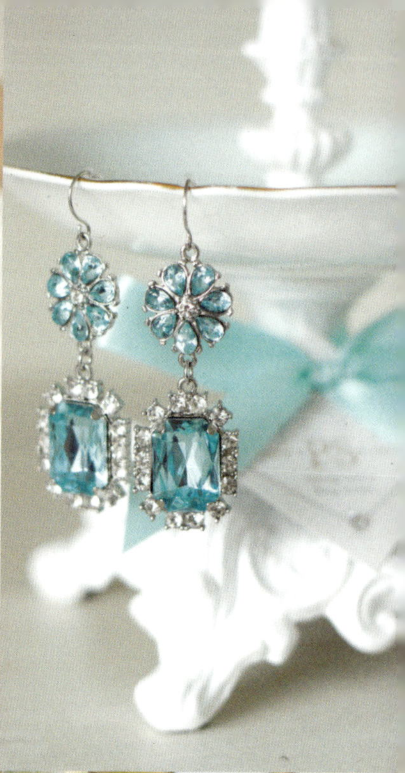
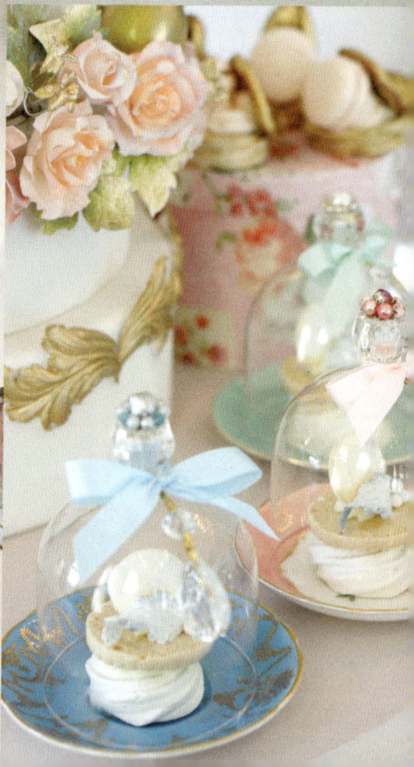
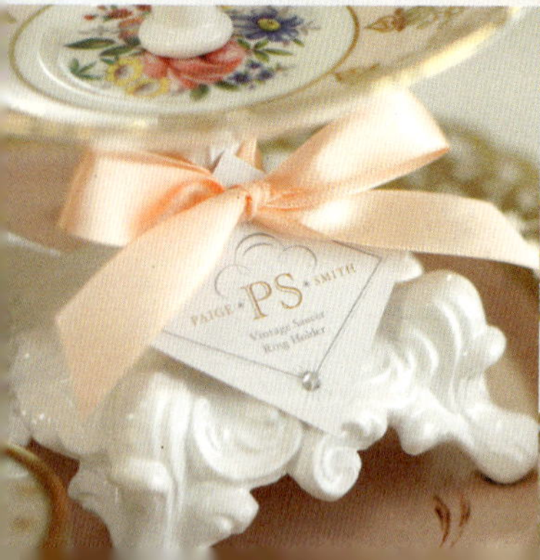
PAIGE
PS
SMITH
Vintage Saucer
Ring Holder
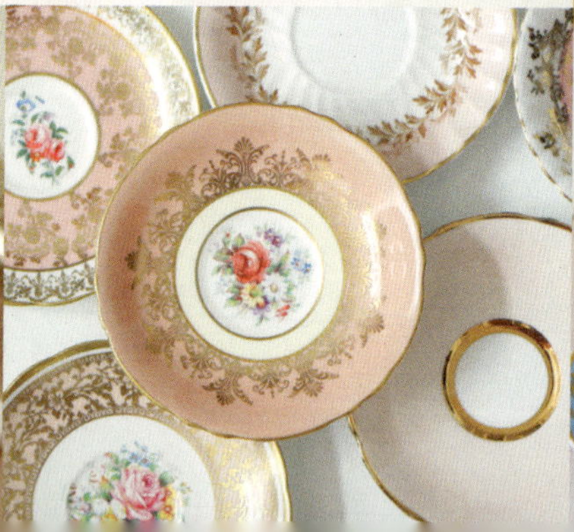

ARTIST · MAKER · CREATOR

Cherished China

by

PAIGE SMITH

"My personal mantra is to only ever repurpose single saucers that are missing their matching cup. I rescue them from flea markets and thrift stores—found close to home and abroad. Many stunning saucers have been 'inherited' from the estates of other life-long collectors."

While on a three-month sabbatical from her job as a web designer, Paige Smith wanted to get back to making things with her hands. "A collector at heart, one of my greatest loves is for beautiful vintage china saucers," she says. The idea of a ring holder made from vintage china began to take shape. "My initial prototypes were created using all things vintage: lamp bases, finials, chandelier teardrop crystals, old lady clip-on earrings and charms." She gives as second life to orphaned saucers by repurposing them into jewellery holders and mini dessert domes. "To streamline production, the saucers predominantly remain as the 'something vintage' in both products."

"It's a fulfilling endeavour to repurpose china saucers in a new way beyond their original purpose and need. For customers who have received china from a loved one, it's very special to create new pieces for them to pass on to the next generation." ✤

"In my home studio, nearly 700 saucers are stacked neatly in the drawers and shelves of my French cabinet. Dating back 50 years or more, the saucers come from well-known English manufacturers: Royal Albert, Aynsley and Paragon to name a few. I'm always in awe of the stunning beauty and seemingly endless array of colours and different designs of china patterns. Saucers in pastel colours and intricate gold patterns catch my eye and heart the most."

"I'm in my happy place when I am designing new work—matching colourful satin ribbon to the saucers and seeing the personality of each piece come to life."

PAIGE SMITH   253

"I've had to overcome some fear in regards to using large power tools. In making a ring holder, I use a tabletop drill press to create a small hole in the centre of the saucer. For most people, the idea of drilling through china is daunting and scary. But with patience and practice, I've learned that despite its dainty appearance, china is quite durable. After years of drilling holes through hundreds of saucers, I've also saved the little 'donut holes' of fine bone china. It is so interesting to capture just a few fragments of the manufacturers' markings on the back of the saucer."

heirloomkeepsakes.ca
@paigesmith_heirloomkeepsakes

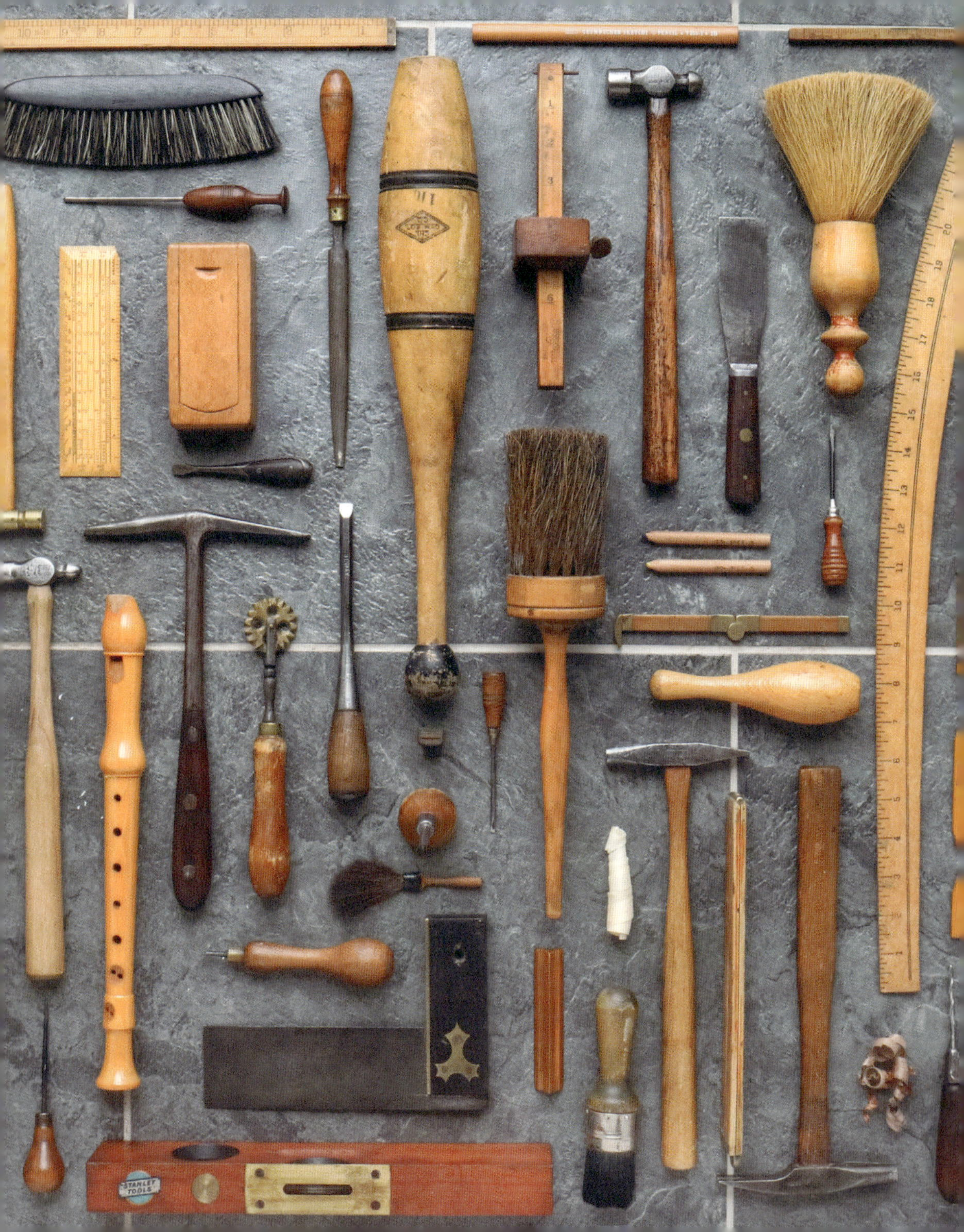
STANLEY TOOLS

ARTIST · MAKER · CREATOR

Curated Collections

by

DEBORAH HUMPHRIES

Artist, designer, collector and archivist Deborah Humphries combines her skills and interests by photographing carefully arranged compositions of objects. "Knolling is compelling, soothing, structured and interesting to our eyes and brains. It's easy to make sense of it at once, and then it engages us to discover each item individually and as a whole."

"Knolling" is, in fact, the term used to describe flat lay photography, in which items are arranged with a defined sense of order, originating from a janitor who worked for Frank Gehry (a Knoll furniture designer as well as famed architect). "As Andrew Kromelow cleaned the fabrication shop each night," explains Deborah, "he would gather the tools left out and set them all in a clear, flat space." He positioned each tool at 90 degrees to another, considering the space in which they existed. His coworker Tom Sachs coined the term in 1987 and wrote parameters for the technique, with the aesthetic reaching peak popularity and visibility today with the rise of Instagram.

"A complete story can be relayed by the image. The reason for the grouping does not need an explanation, although adding context exponentially increases the layers of meaning. The fine art of knolling satisfies all the elements of art expression: balance, proportion, emphasis, variety, movement, rhythm and harmony. And tools satisfy our primal need to create and work with our hands." Knolling tools is a nod to this particularly artistic and organized janitor. ✽

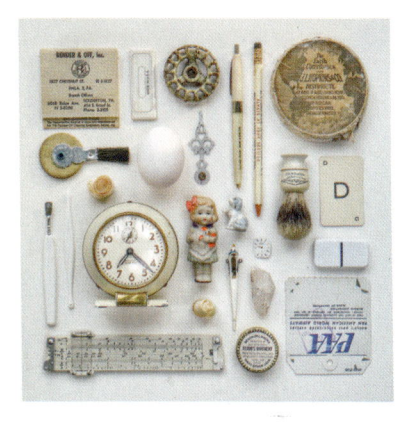

"The simplest tools carry their history and meaning with them. Well used and well loved. Grouping these together by type, brand, handle or material style not only retells the story but adds to it. All of this speaks to my heart and soul. The memories that many of these tools invoke, inspire me to share and continue collecting."

258 VINTAGE LIFE

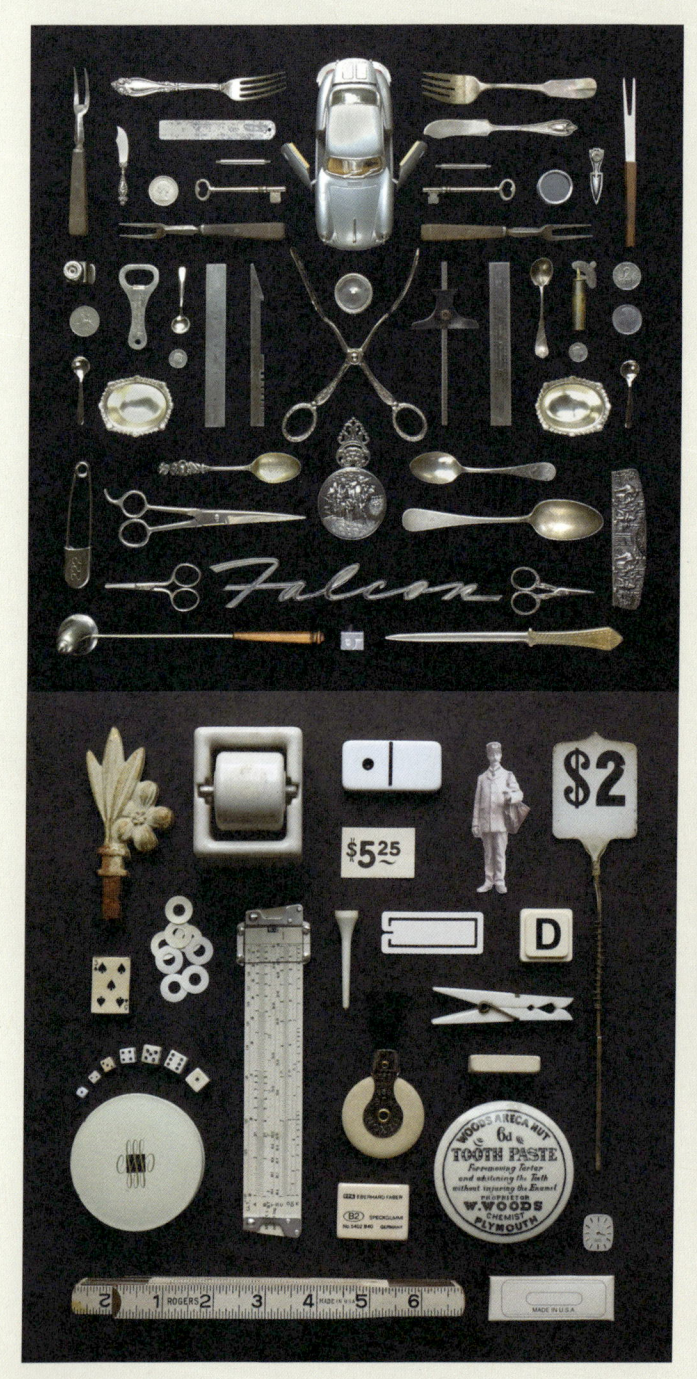

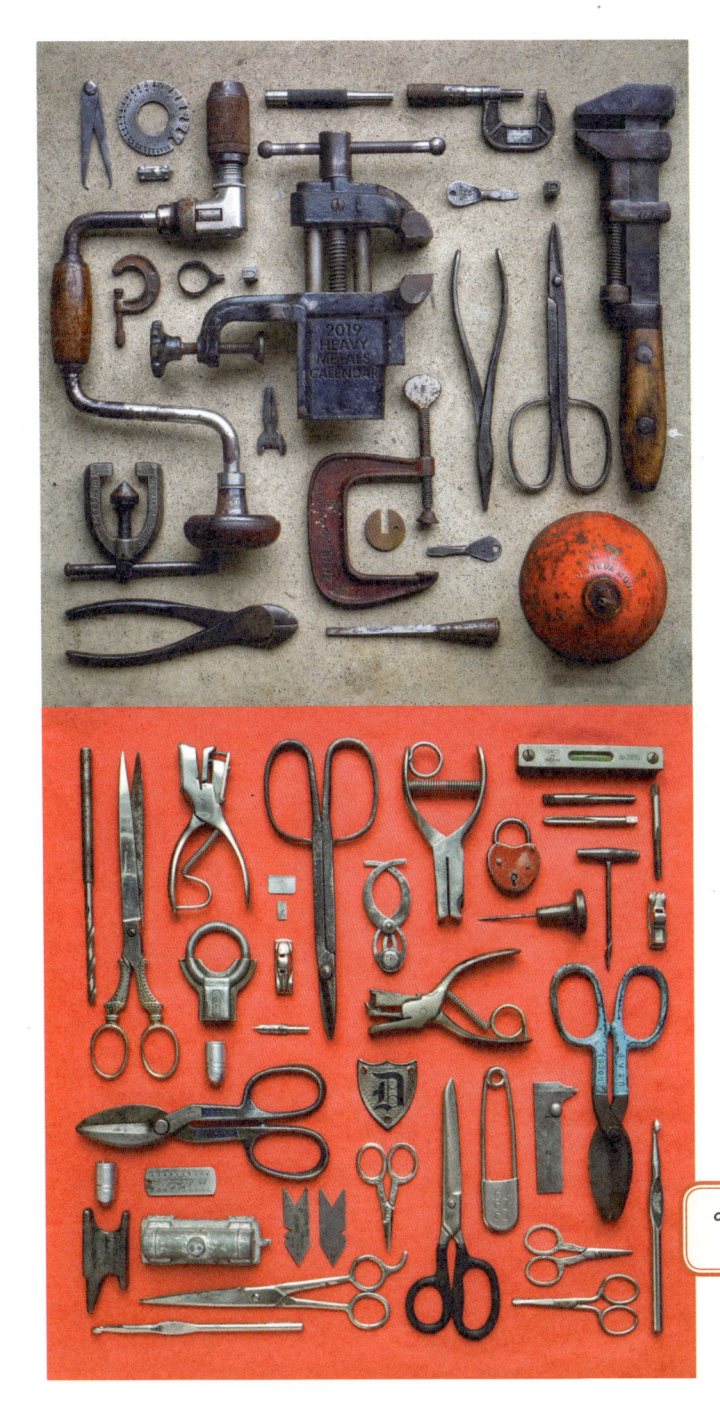

"Out of necessity, my parents shopped second-hand stores, so I've had vintage (old) items around me my entire life. I grew to love things that were already worn a bit or broken in. They seemed to be better quality than what we could buy new—and this is still the case today. Later, when I inherited an ancestral archive of family letters, photos, furnishings, clothing, art, music and instruments dating to the early 1800s, I was never concerned that the storage was a burden, yet I was unsure what I could do with the archive. Thankfully, I discovered Instagram and joined with collectors and keepers in sharing these treasures and others found."

deborahhumphries.com
@djhinva

DEBORAH HUMPHRIES 259

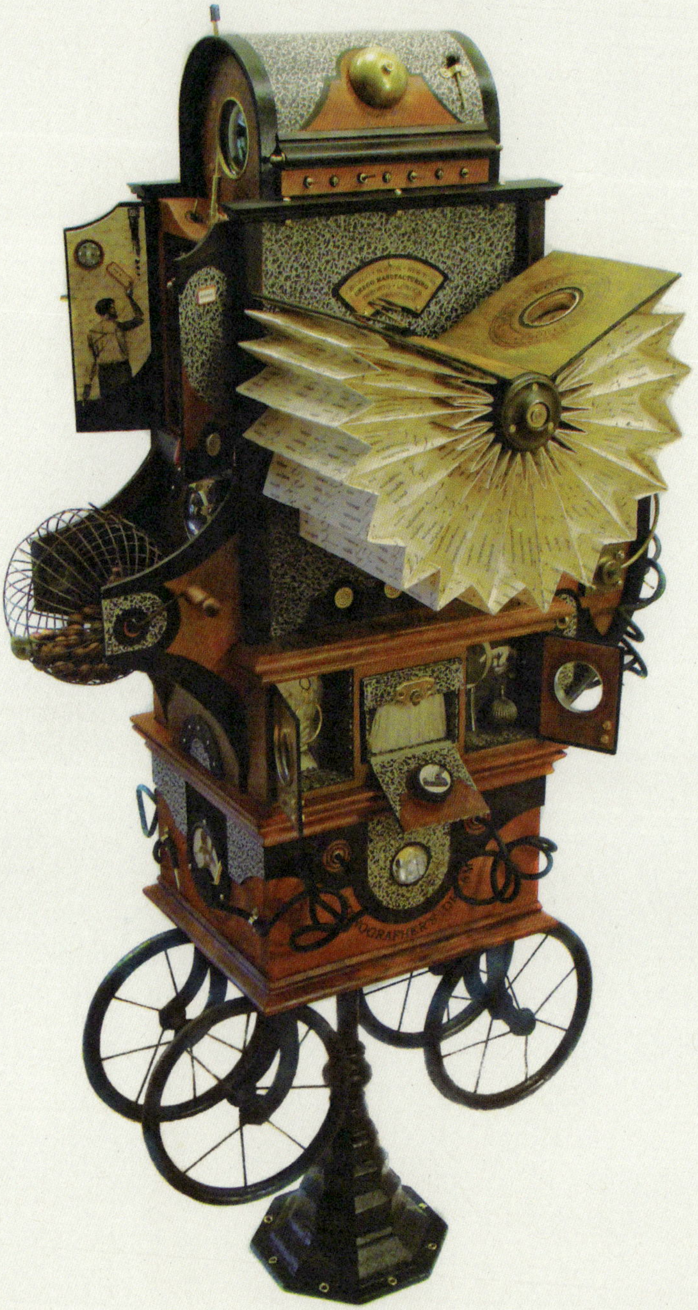

ARTIST · MAKER · CREATOR

Artistic Artifacts

by

NANCY CALLAHAN

"Some pieces rely on childhood memories of growing up in a family of seven children in rural America. These pieces rely heavily on collecting, enhancing and arranging vintage artifacts to evoke a particular time and storyline. These staged installations amplify both personal and universal memories."

She describes herself as an "artist who makes artifacts," but through her sculptural book objects and installations, Nancy Callahan is a storyteller who constructs pseudo-historical narratives. With the deed to her house dating back to 1830, Nancy could indeed to said to be living in the past, and it's a time period that informs her visual language. "If you were to visit you would find a curious mix of vintage furniture and odd bits and bobs I have pulled in from the past. Bones, beetles and bird nests rest under bell jars; wood spindles and newel posts lean in corners; discarded postal scales, typewriters and adding machines perch on shelves alongside pencil sharpeners, check-makers and magnetos. Stacks of old dictionaries, atlases, antiquated textbooks and classroom primers can be found tucked here and there. Dig deeper into the drawers of card catalogues, oak flat files and wood boxes of all sizes and you will find the treasured parts and pieces I have collected and use to make my work: glass test tubes and lenses, mechanical clock parts, rusty springs, pulleys and casters, discarded wood handles, spools, finials, gears and gauges. Then there is the ephemera: Victorian die-cuts, faded tags and torn labels, flash cards soiled from use and outdated topographical maps—all these items quietly wait their turn." ✽

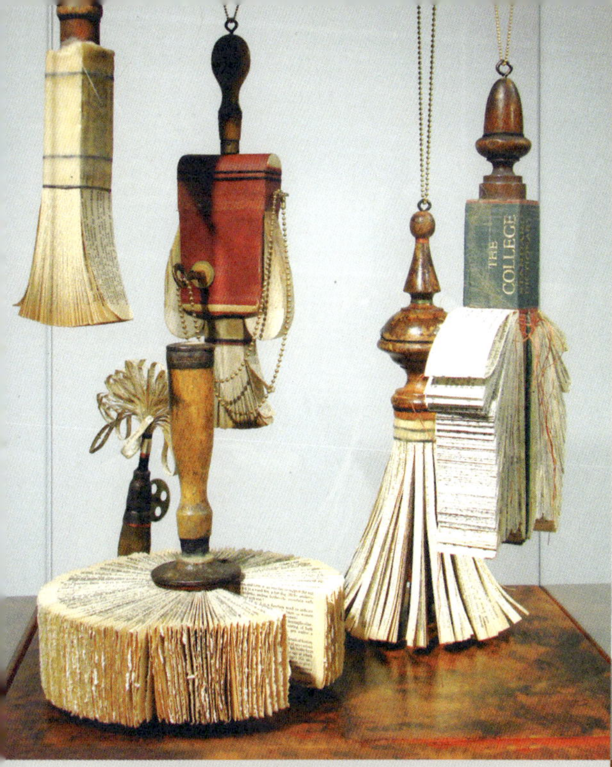
THE
COLLEGE

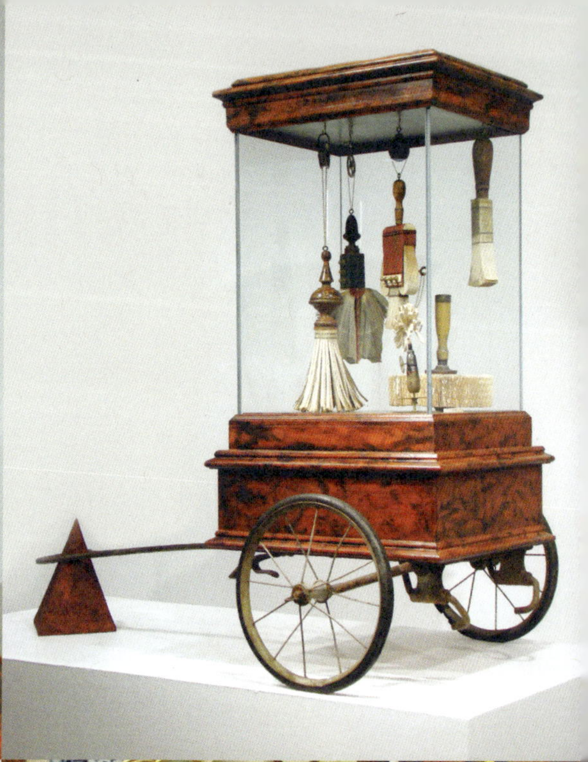

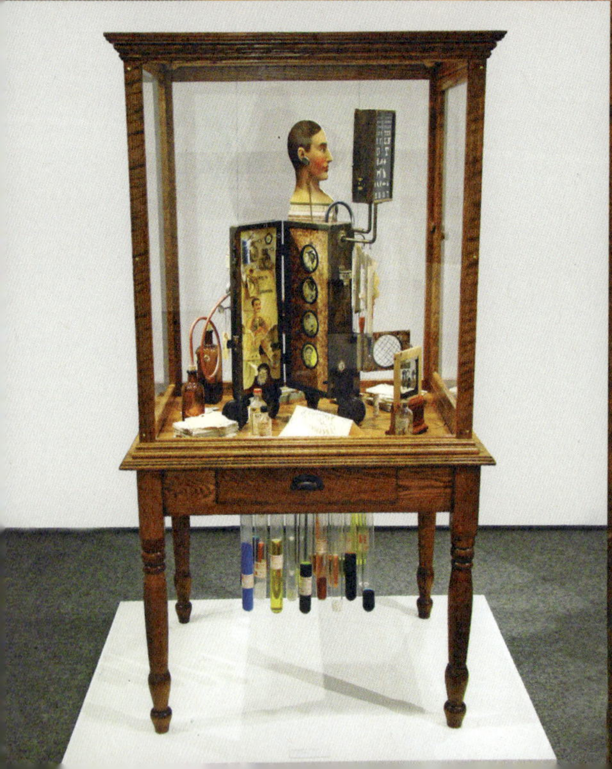

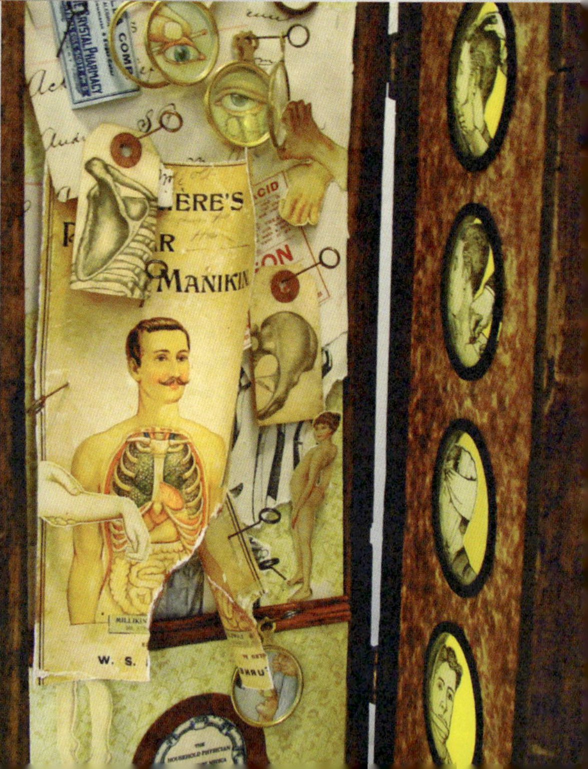
CRYSTAL PHARMACY
ERE'S
MANIKIN
ACID
W. S.

"Recent work is inspired by early architecture, inventions, board games and, most importantly, the people connected to them. I call this series The Traveling Museum of Curious Matters. Imagine, if you will, a museum that exists in the future where the curator has the uncanny ability to travel back to the late 1800s or early 1900s and pluck artifacts from the dreams of unsuspecting dreamers. Once procured, these unique objects are pulled through a time portal to the present. After viewing, these relics will be returned to the minds of their dreamers. These items often seem curiously familiar, but you, the viewer, cannot quite imagine what they are, where they came from or how they work. In these pieces, I create my own artifacts by combining vintage parts and pieces along with hand-built components."

NancyCallahan.net

I know, I know, I should have kept a journal.

ARTIST · MAKER · CREATOR

Collages of the Past

by

AMY DUNCAN

Amy Duncan is a mixed-media collage artist. "I'm inspired by remnants of the past, blending vintage odds and ends with simple graphic images to produce original compositions. With my work weaving together the elements of time and history, with colour, texture, pattern and tone, it's not uncommon to find used envelopes, scraps of receipts and letters, leftover wallpaper, forgotten photographs, old book pages or snippets of torn maps as components in it."

Within old, rusted, dilapidated and forgotten objects, Amy finds stories that she "teases" out through collages. "I sense there is something more than their mere physical presence and it is this essence that I desire to capture. A rusted key, a broken clock, a torn ticket stub, a chipped teacup... items are often tossed aside with the idea that they are no longer useful. But below the surface, there's a story: the rusted key opens a treasured lockbox, the clock once chimed in a childhood home, the ticket stub was a wonderful vacation trip, and the chipped teacup was grandmother's favourite. The most ordinary of objects can tell a story; you just have to listen." ❊

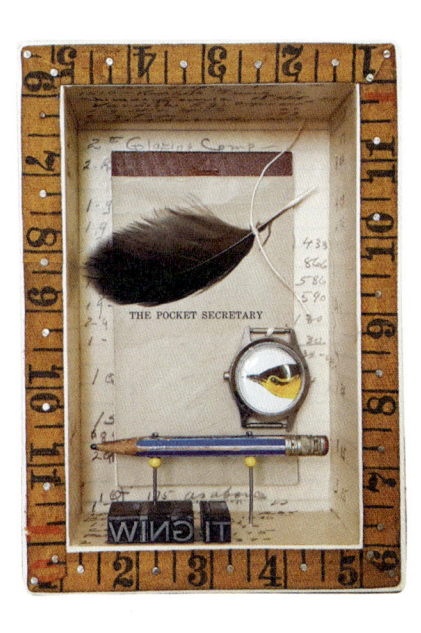

"When things are new and shiny, they may be useful but they are lacking soul—no story, no history, no connectedness. By focusing on well-loved ordinary objects—scrutinizing their surface, examining the details, evoking a memory—I'm able to tell a story that gives new life to remnants of the past."

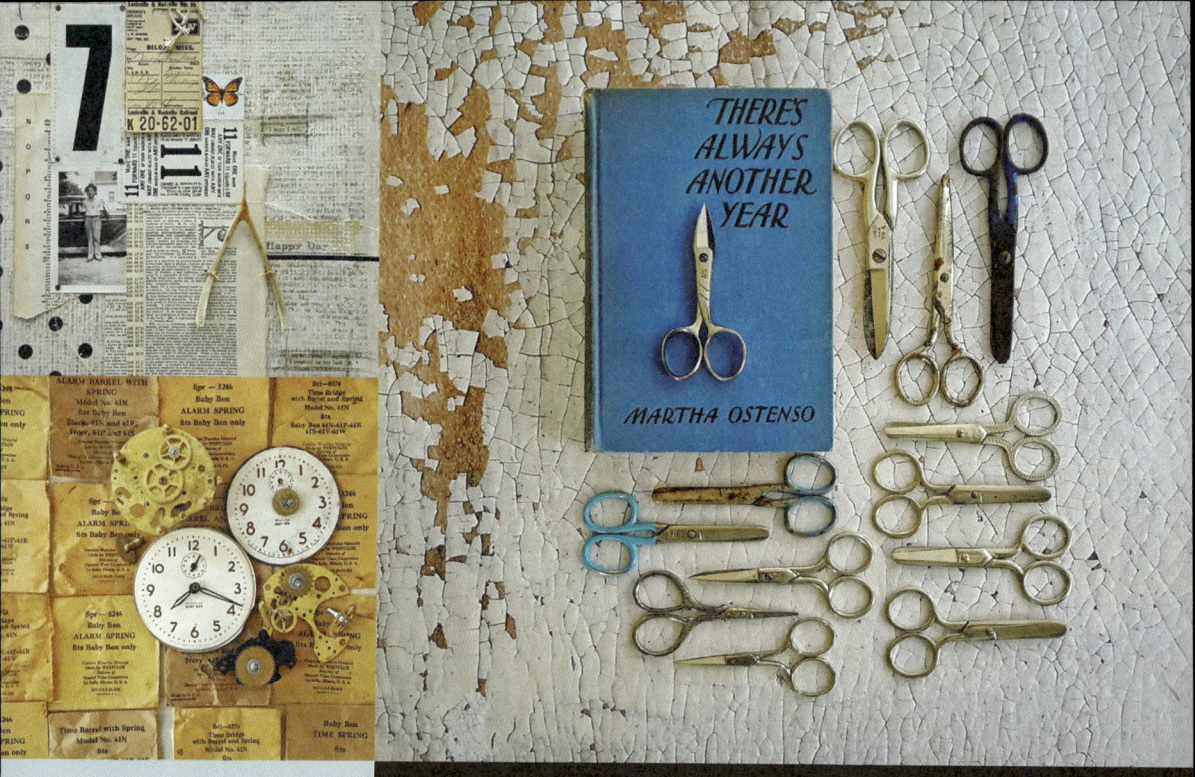

"I have quite a
collection of
materials that
are constants
in my work and
represented
often in my
compositions—
old clocks
and all their
parts, sewing
paraphernalia,
anything used
for measurement,
locks and keys of
all shapes and
sizes, eyeglasses
and encyclopedias,
dice and dominos,
buttons and
bobbins, stencils
and silverware."

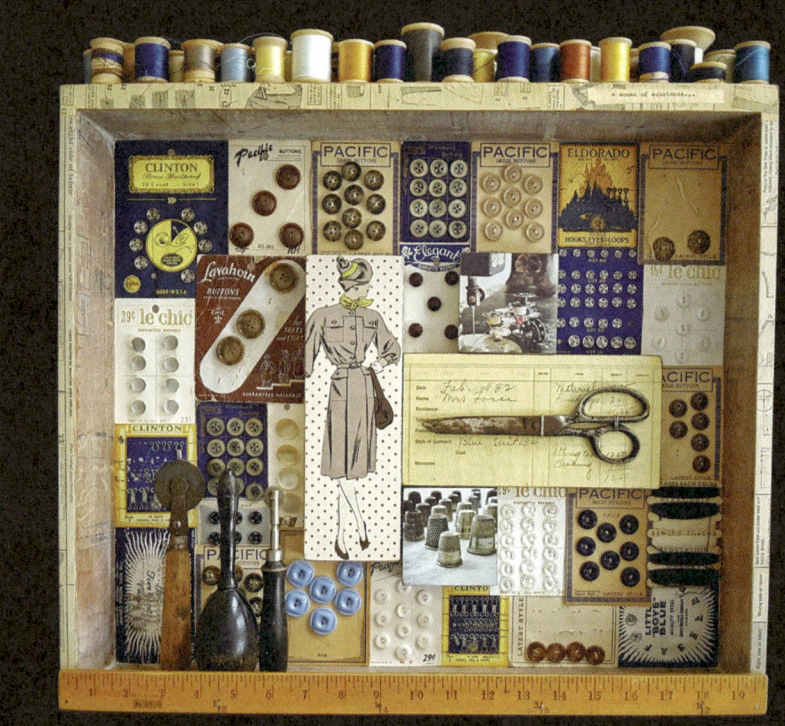

266

CUISINE ARTISTIQUE
ÉTUDES DE L'ÉCOLE MODERNE
URBAIN-DUBOIS
OUVRAGE EN DEUX
PARIS
HOTEL DU PALAIS D'ORSAY
9 QUAI ANATOLE-FRANCE
PARIS 7e
SUR LES RIVES DE LA SEINE
FACE AU JARDIN DES TUILERIES
ON THE BANKS OF RIVER SEINE
FACING THE TUILERIES GARDENS
XO
61

EAGLE SKY BLUE 740½
VILMORIN-ANDRIEUX & Cie
PRODUCTEURS
DE GRAINES DE SEMENCE SÉLECTIONNÉES
4 QUAI DE LA MÉGISSERIE 4
PARIS 1er
is, for you
happy with me.
ADMIT ONE
ADMIT ONE
Young, Edward, 1683-1765
Night-thoughts
Butterworth, A.M. William Blake,
mystic. 1911.
edition...pub. by Edwards, New Bond
Street, London, in...1797."
44 Points to Ponder
look
find
PUBLIC HIGH SCHOOLS
Seattle, Washington
QUARTERLY REPORT
OF GRADES
LIST OF WORDS FOR SPELLING CONTEST
11
E
F P
T O Z
L P E D
E D F C Z P
D E F P O T E C
1
2
3
4
5
6

studiofourcorners.com
@studiofourcorners

"In a world full of stuff, we owe it to ourselves and to the world around us to reinvent and redistribute things that have become obsolete."

ARTIST · MAKER · CREATOR

Upcycled Accessories

by

CHRISSY SMITH

"I think it's important in this day and age to reuse as much as we can. We overproduce with devastating effect. We need to value what is already here and use our creativity to enrich our environment."

Using found and upcycled fabrics and artifacts, Chrissy Smith makes bags, clothes and homewares to sell in her vintage stall in a local antique market in the English coastal town of Seaford. "Reusing and remaking is my absolute mantra," she says. "To repurpose things is ethically sound. It enables creativity in its purest form, doesn't waste the world's resources and produces unique pieces of work and art." Chrissy uses leather, mid-century fabrics and tapestries to create one-off bags. "I upcycle soft furnishings, lamps and small pieces of furniture, giving them a modern twist with chalk paints and vintage fabric upholstery. I make lampshades from 1950s fabrics. Old cashmere jumpers become hats, cowls and hand warmers." Even old powder compacts from the 1950s have been repurposed to hold handmade lip balm. "If I see potential in something I will pursue the idea. To have the freedom to do that and pass it on to someone else is, to me, my finest achievement." ✼

"If you are interested in anything vintage you need to be a forager: you have to enjoy the process of gathering pieces from a wide variety of sources. Flea markets, junk shops, charity shops and even the municipal dump! The thrill of the chase, the bargain, the potential you see in something that—to others—is just garbage."

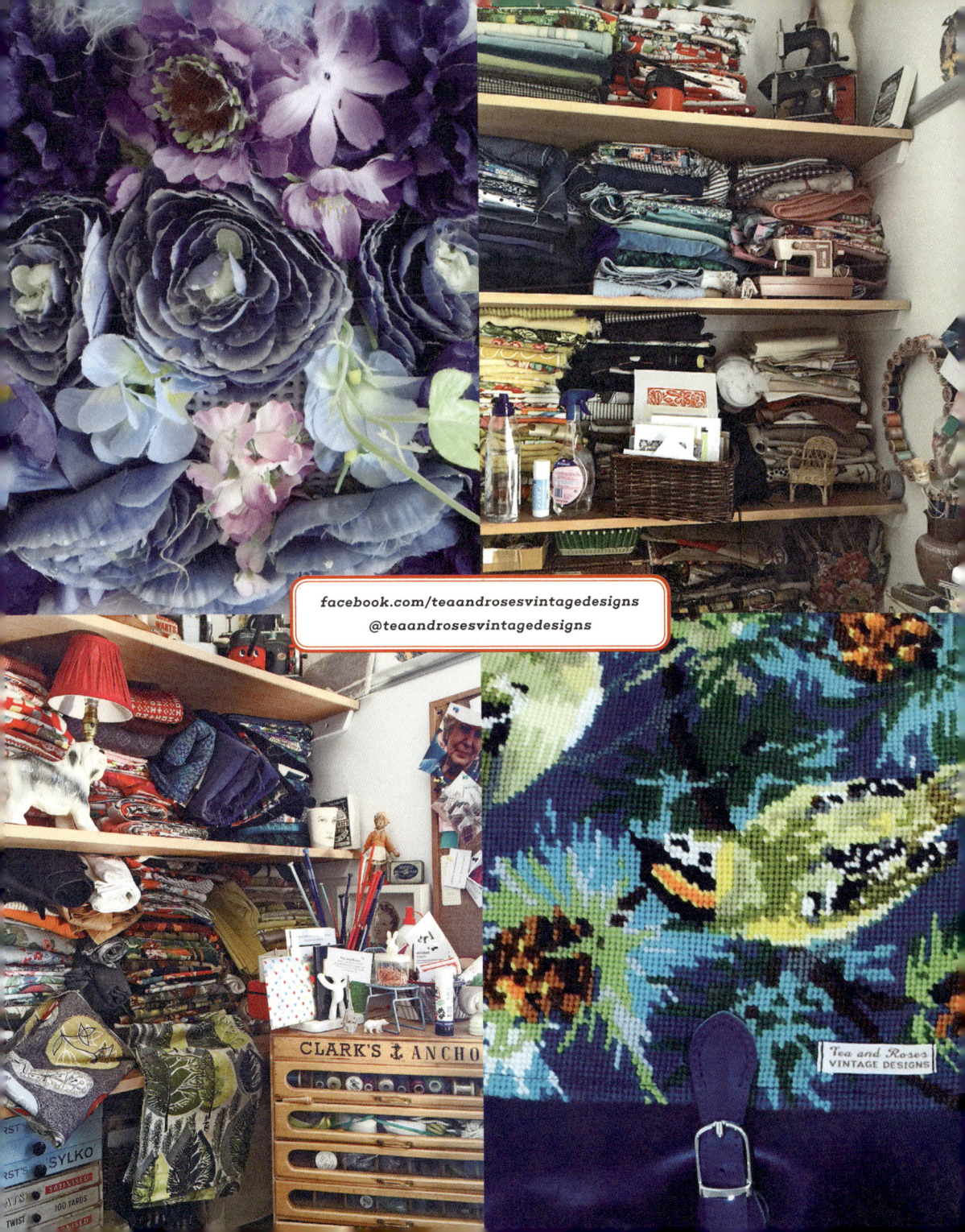

facebook.com/teaandrosesvintagedesigns
@teaandrosesvintagedesigns

Tea and Roses
VINTAGE DESIGNS

118

ARTIST · MAKER · CREATOR

Analogue Photography

by

COLLEEN RAUSCHER

In today's age of instantaneous everything, to use film cameras makes a statement about slowing down and being more mindful when taking pictures. "Returning to documenting the world with film is a bit like opening a time capsule," says Colleen Rauscher, for whom analogue processes allow her to experience the anticipation and patience required in film photography.

"I take, develop and print analogue photos of primarily historical architecture, architectural details and urban landscapes with 'vintage' film cameras. I'm fascinated with historical architecture and materials, and have a profound respect for the technique and craftsmanship that people used to use in their work. My photographs are a way to preserve, highlight and experience these structures and spaces within cities as fragments of memories: elaborate, incomplete, fleeting."

Colleen experiments with different cameras and film sizes. "I'm currently collecting vintage cameras to further experiment with, to see what results I can achieve. So far I have a Rolleiflex from the 1960s, a Brownie Starflash, a Corina 2 from the former Czechoslovakia and an Olympus Pen half-frame from Japan. I have been experimenting with taking double exposures on a Holga camera, and occasionally incorporate these images into a mixed-media/photo transfer collage with found vintage objects or materials." ✣

"I feel that utilizing processes without all the new technology lends more authenticity to my work, inviting the element of chance and the unknown to contribute to a piece that is unique."

"The Holga is an inexpensive plastic toy camera, made in Hong Kong in the 1980s for working-class families to take everyday pictures. This low-tech, medium-format camera uses 120 mm film, which produces a square image, rather than the rectangular format of regular 35 mm film. It is valued for its low-fidelity 'authentic' effects, such as vignetting, blurs, light leaks and distortions in the final picture, which is difficult to achieve in the digital photography world. Other examples of low-tech cameras include the Diana, Polaroid and pinhole cameras."

colleenrauscher.com
@colleen_rauscher_art

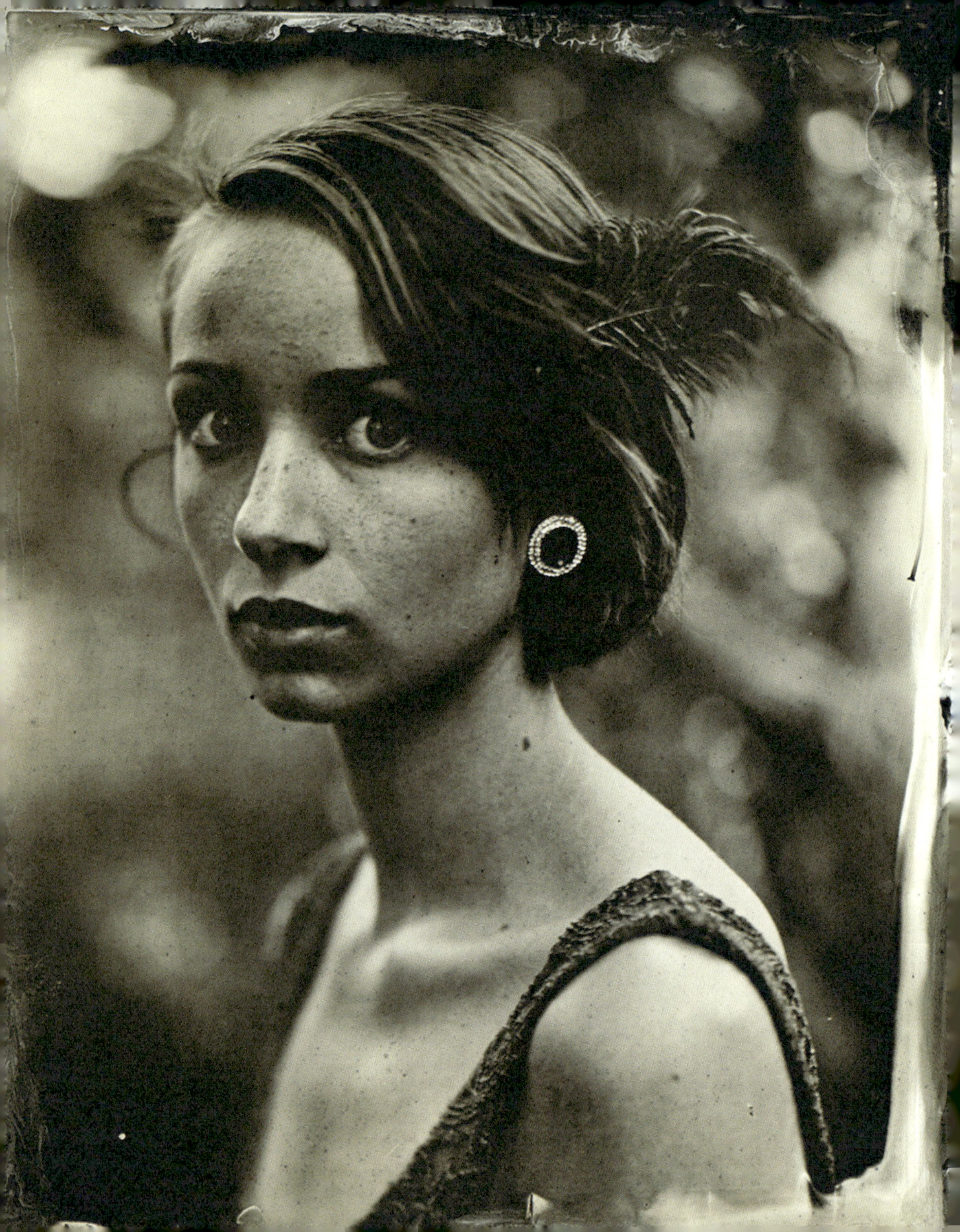

Wet Plate Photography

by

TEKOA PREDIKA & MICHELLE RAINEY
RAINIKA PHOTOGRAPHIK

Tekoa Predika and Michelle Rainey love old cameras and the stories of the past that they hold. "As we started to collect a few vintage cameras we were inspired to learn how to use them and to delve into the history of photography. All vintage cameras and the lenses are unique, and they have their own personality when it comes to creating a photograph."

Using processes of analogue photography from the Victorian era, the couple makes wet plate collodion tintypes on metal plates. "Wet plate collodion photography has a distinctly unique look all of its own," says Michelle. They also create ambrotypes on glass plates (using vintage medium- and large-format cameras) and cyanotypes on paper, textiles and glass. "Cyanotypes, another early process that dates back to 1843, are often known and loved for their deep, intense Prussian blue hues. We make cyanotype photograms, directly printing plants and flowers and other collected or found objects, as well as cyanotype prints using photographic images from glass plates or film."

Building on the tradition of travelling tintype photographers from the 1850s, they have fashioned a travelling darkroom out of a 1970s Triple E Surf Side trailer so that they can creative tintype portraits at events, festivals and artisan markets. In an ongoing project, Tekoa is documenting modern-day homesteaders in the Kootenay region of Canada's British Columbia. ✻

"The way the plates are made by pouring a handcrafted film directly on the plate minutes before sensitizing it in silver and exposing it to light gives the images a painterly quality. Often there can be evidence of the hand of the maker, drips, scratches, even fingerprints. The film speed is very slow so exposures are long and there is no grain, so images have a real softness to them. The plates are quite silvery, as they are sensitized in a bath of silver nitrate. The collodion 'sees' the UV light spectrum in a way that results in a haunting, timeless quality to the images."

280 VINTAGE LIFE

RAINIKA PHOTOGRAPHIK 281

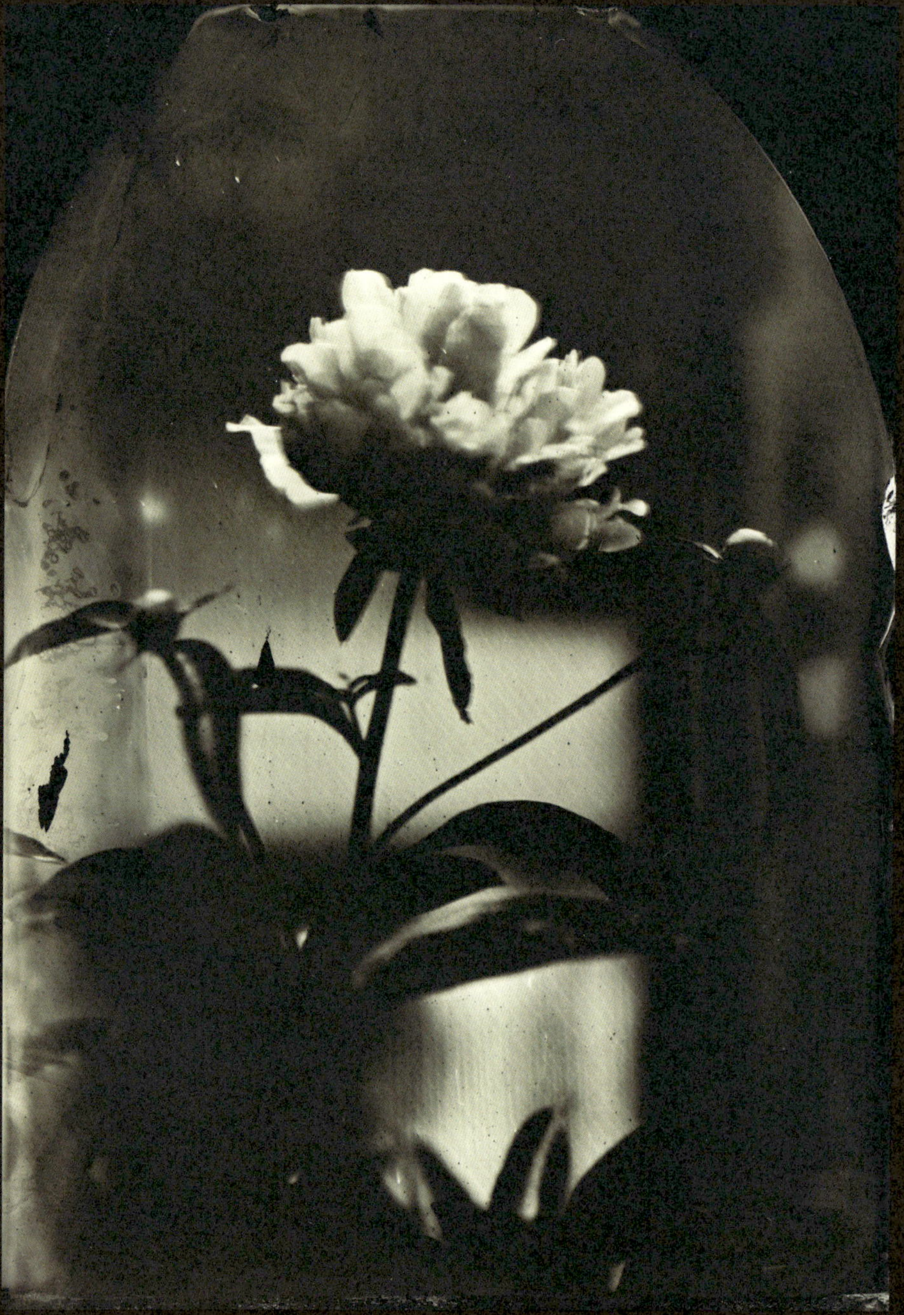

rainika.com
@rainika_photographik

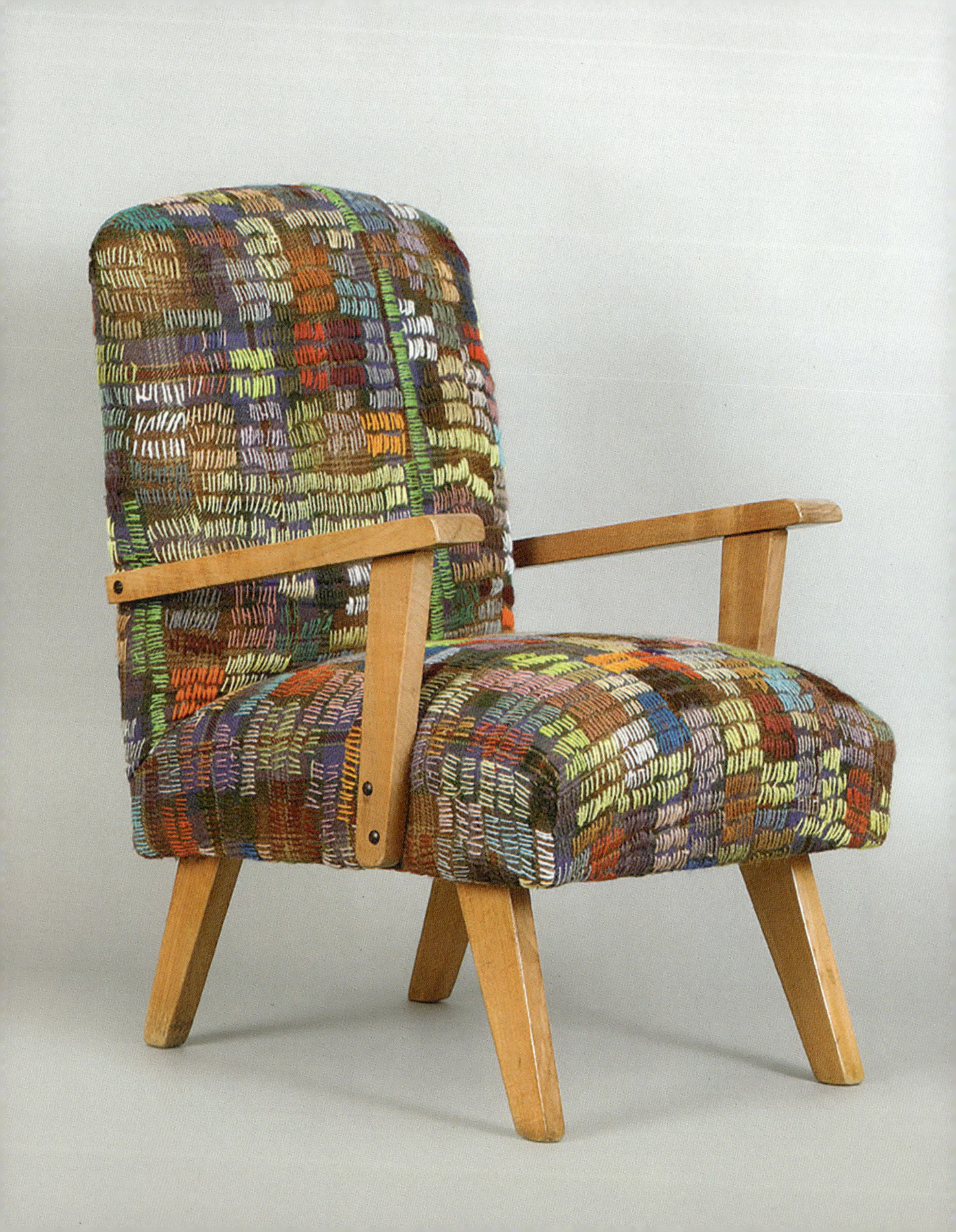

ARTIST · MAKER · CREATOR

Textile Allsorts

by

MELANIE HILL

When it comes to candy, allsorts are a sweet and eclectic mix of colourful licorice confectionery. Melanie Hill's Textiles Allsorts is also a treat: a gorgeous mishmash of beautiful vintage textiles, all mixed up and stitched together. "I only use recycled and reclaimed fabric," she says. "I like the old worn quality of them, the faded colours and patterns, plus the quality is far superior to current products." She makes stools with cushions of repurposed vintage quilts and fabric yo-yos (also known as Suffolk puffs), and recovers furniture. "I like to make practical items to decorate the home such as lampshades, cushions, footstools and bedheads, whatever I can cover to cheer my home and other peoples'." She also creates soft sculpture animals from patchworked pieces. "I feel the vintage elements bring a point of difference and uniqueness to my work." ❊

"The hunt for the vintage and unusual products is part of the fun. Sometimes I have to think outside the box for a way of including vintage pieces in my work."

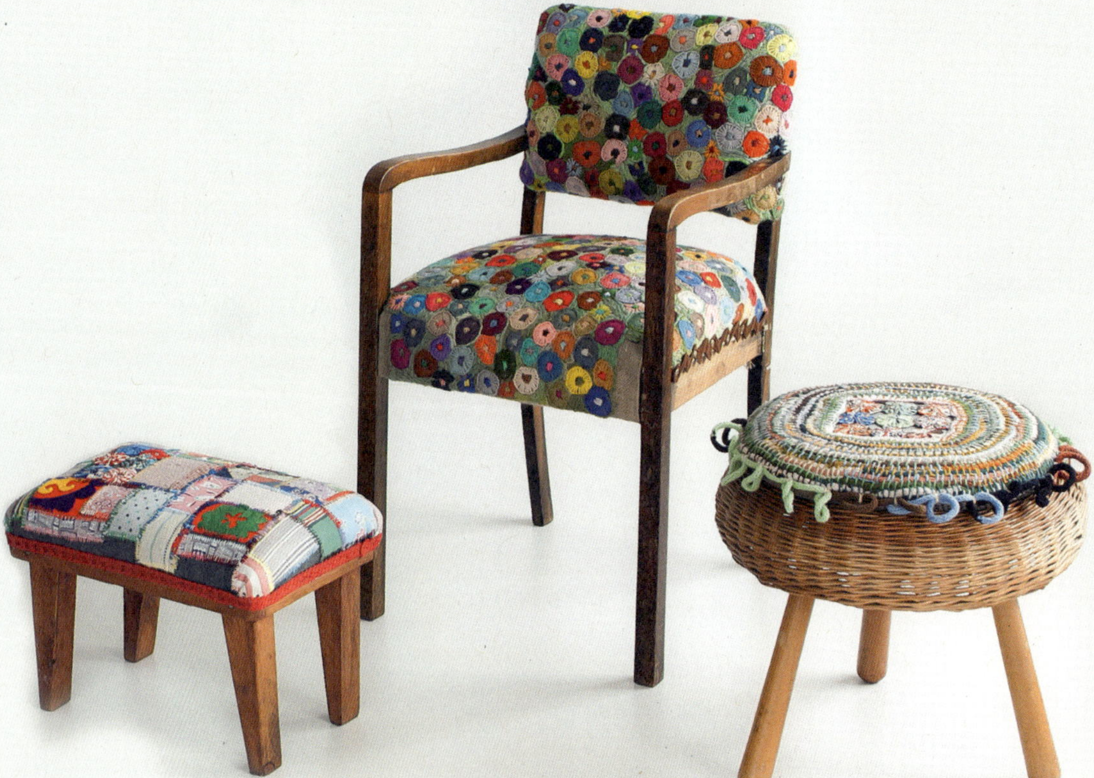

MELANIE HILL 287

The RYLMA Mending
COTTON MENDING
COATS CHAIN
FILOSHEEN
CHADWICK'S
WOOL and NYLON
For Reinforcing and Mending
COATS
SPUN NYLON
FOR HOSIERY MENDING
Y389
NO DARN
EIGHT
EXCLUSIVELY DYED TO MATCH & MEND ALL HOSIERY
Della Darn
WOOL
Fast Colours for
Darning and Embroidery
50 YARDS
4 STRAND MENDING
455
"EMANESS"
Eagley
COLOUR 428
STITCH IN TIME
HOSIERY MENDING
DARNEEZI
PERI-LUSTA
DARNING THREAD
SPECIALLY PREPARED FOR FINE SILK HOSE
Matchall
HOSE MENDING
BARBOUR'S
WAX THREADS

textileallsorts.com.au
@textileallsorts

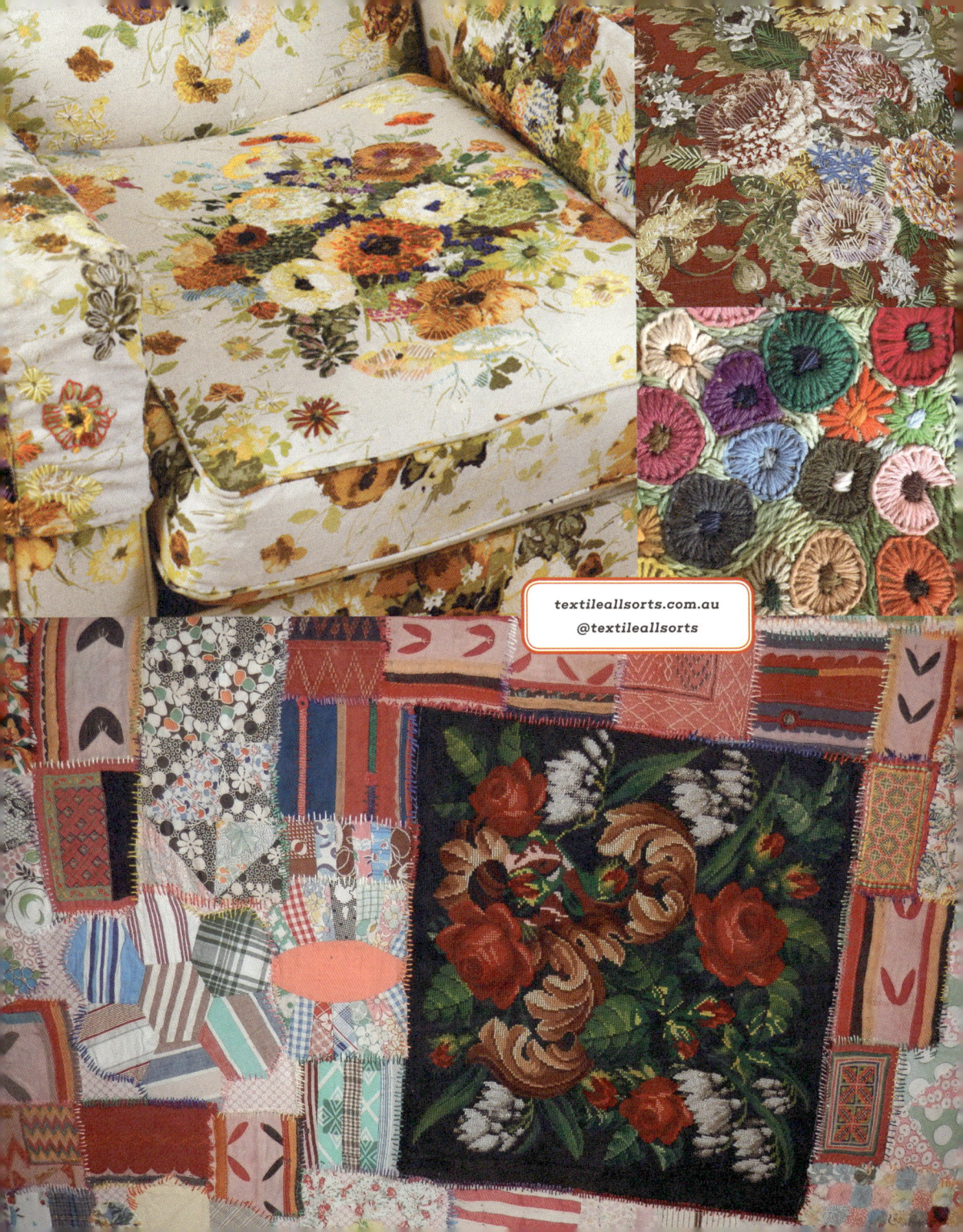

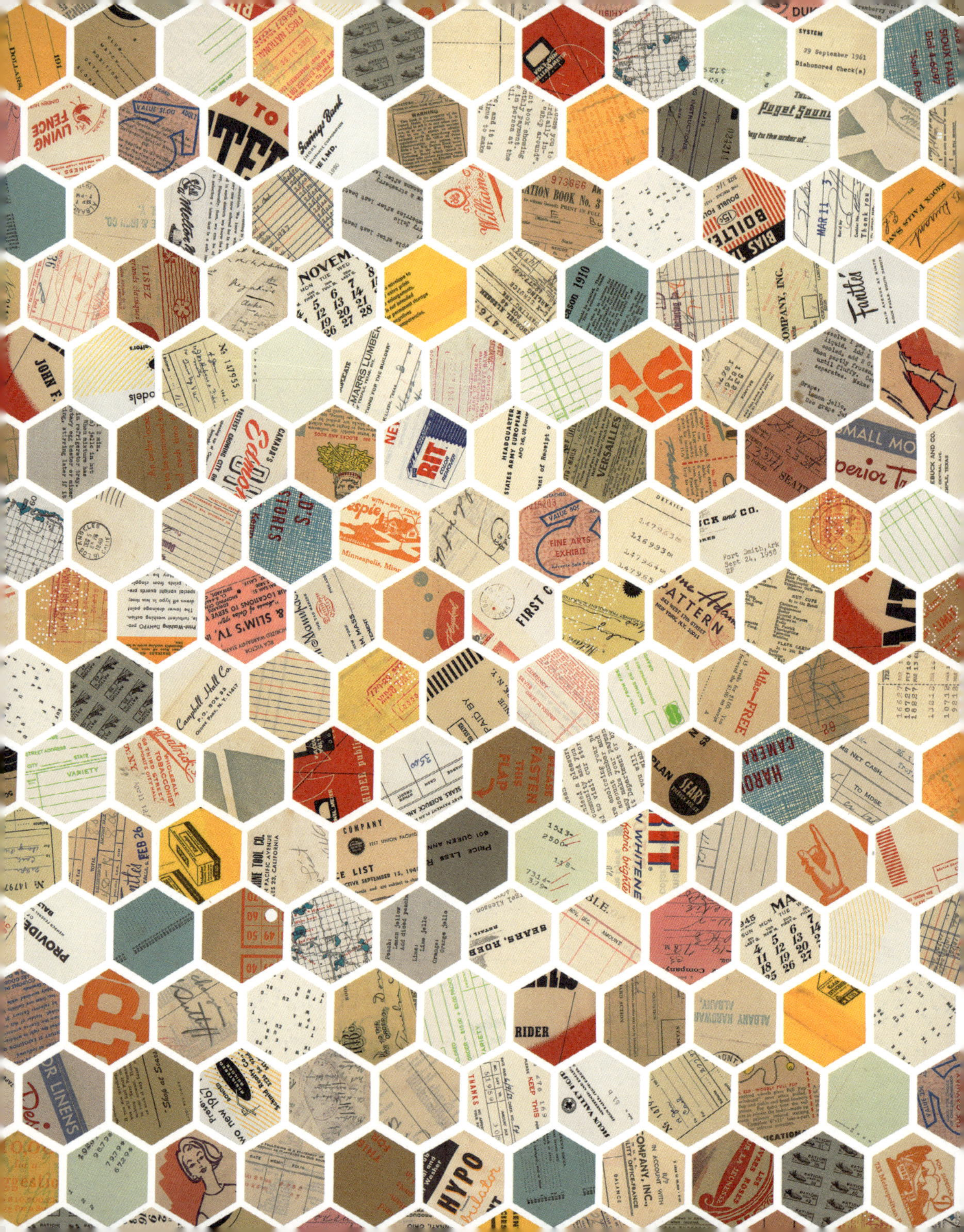

ARTIST · MAKER · CREATOR

Ephemeral Artwork

by

NELL NORDLIE

Paper ephemera is one of the most accessible vintage items one can collect, particularly if you're interested in mundane everyday papers. A large portion of Seattle-based collage artist Nell Nordlie's stash is comprised of remnants from her grandparents' lives. "Cancelled personal checks, bank statements, utility bills, instruction manuals for tools, department store receipts are plentiful evidence of both tedium and adventure," she says. "I make flat and sculptural collages using vintage photographs, books, ephemera and packaging. While I mix some new materials into my work, I'm most excited to incorporate the collections that I've amassed; sorting through piles at antique stores and flea markets is a fun part of the process, as is rediscovering little bits of paper in boxes and drawers at home."

"I appreciate the history and expressive visual texture of found materials. The pre-existing marks and imagery lend humanity to work that could otherwise feel too hard-edged or simple. When choosing materials, I search for humour, beautiful negative space, typography, well-composed images of banal reality, quirky outfits, machine-made perforations, misspellings, bold graphics, personality, delicate surfaces that have accrued character over time, lines, dots and dashes."

Sometimes the precision of her craft belies the handmade process. Her collages are cut by hand and meticulously adhered with glue, thread or tape. "While it can be difficult to cut up irreplaceable items, I constantly remind myself that experimentation and play always lead to valuable outcomes." ❋

"My process is often tedious, as I hand-cut all of my collage pieces, but using paper that is already rich in colour and pattern is a kind of efficiency that I embrace."

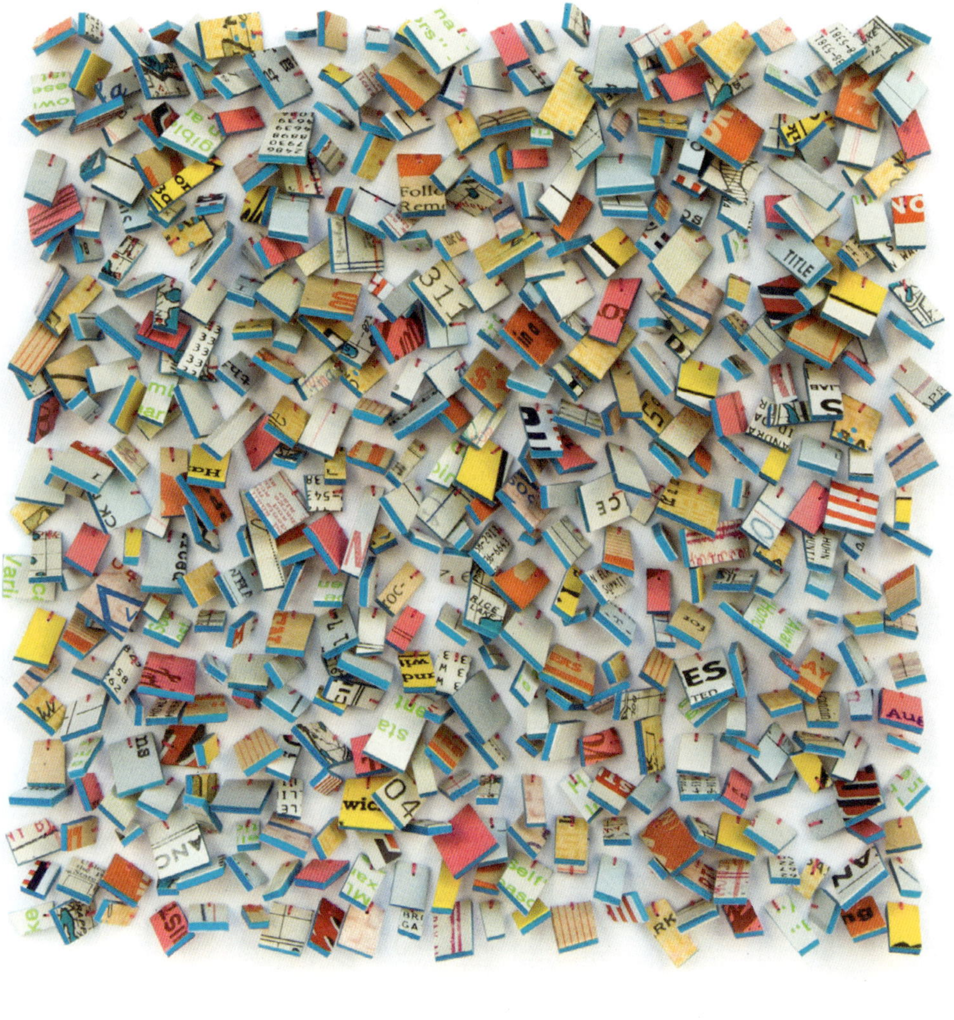

NELL NORDLIE

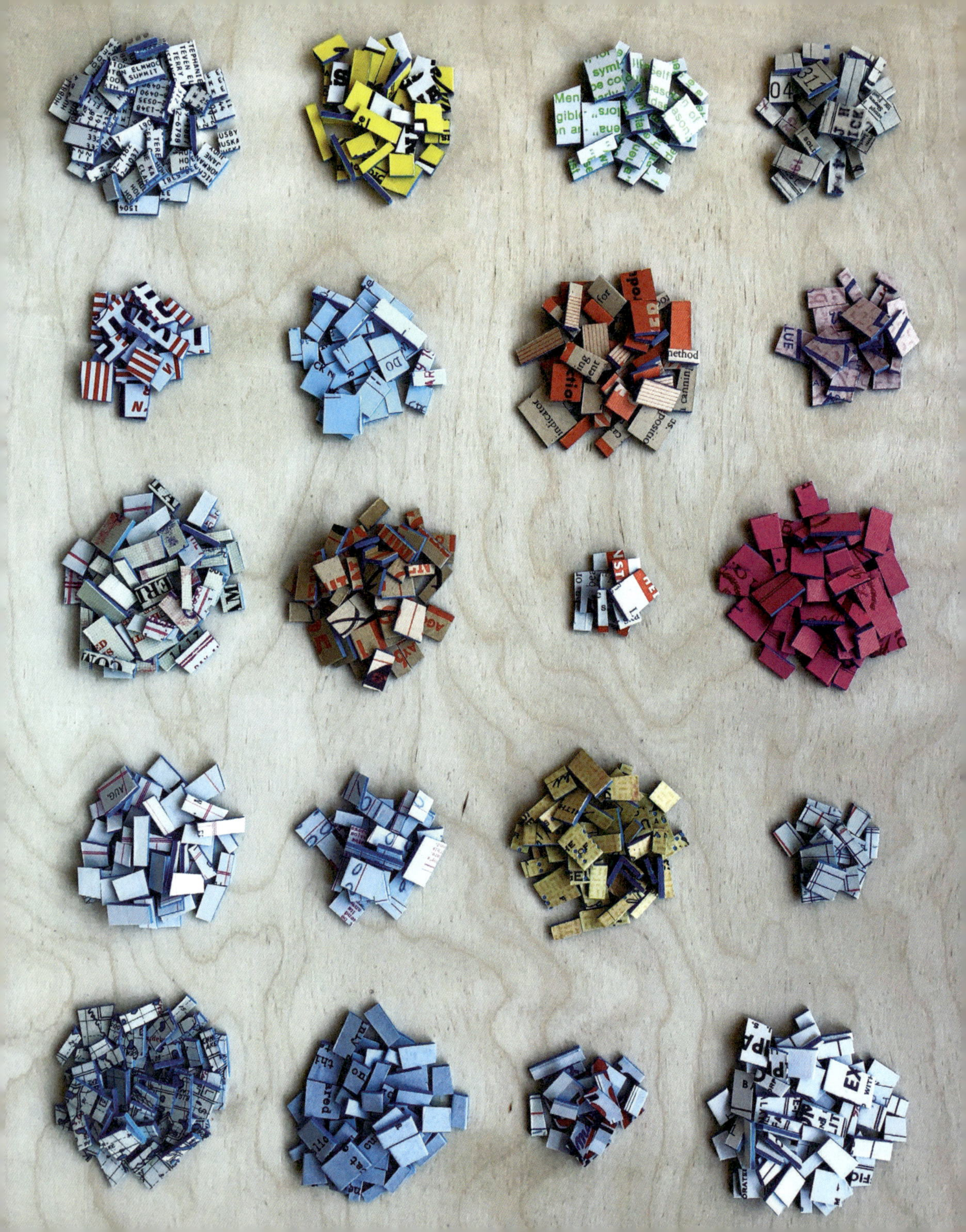

nellnordlie.com
@nellnordlie

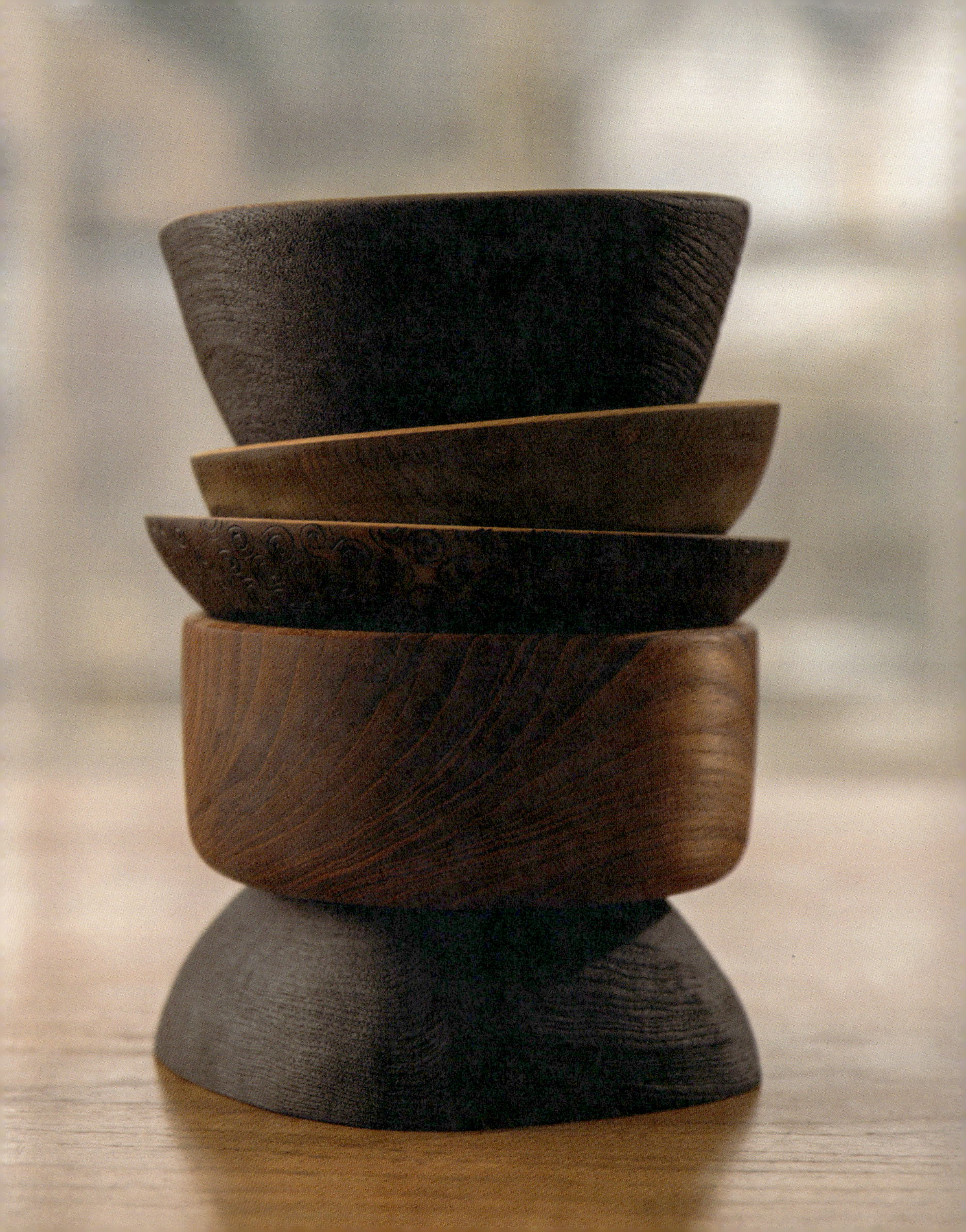

ARTIST · MAKER · CREATOR

Renewed Bowls

by
JULIE WONS

Calgary-based graphic designer Julie Wons is on a quest: "To rescue and renew vintage wooden bowls." Think old salad bowls, hewn and turned. "The mid-century modern era was a heyday for wooden bowls, and a steady supply can still be sourced today. The wood species range from teak bowls designed in Denmark and made in Thailand to maple bowls from Canada and Japan. The bowls in my collection are around 70 years old. Some show their age with lifelong cracks exposed during removal or with new cracks that erupt during the process of charring."

Julie finds their timeless shapes, utility and range of wood species all appealing qualities. Each bowl gets a full makeover; decades of finish and wear is scraped off and each bowl is sanded down to bare wood, revealing waves of grain, texture and colour. "Then the fun stage of renewal begins," says Julie. "The bowl interiors are left natural and a brand new surface treatment is applied to the exterior. The exterior treatments are inspired by a neutral palette and based on traditional processes—either branded, charred, ebonized, pickled or natural. To complete the makeover, the bowls are finished with a mixture of mineral oil and beeswax, protecting the wood but remaining tactile." ❊

"The actual work of removal and renewal is very rewarding—from sanded to ebonized to finished—but the idea of reviving these vintage bowls so they can perform a function in daily life for decades to come is pure magic."

VINTAGE LIFE

@wonswork

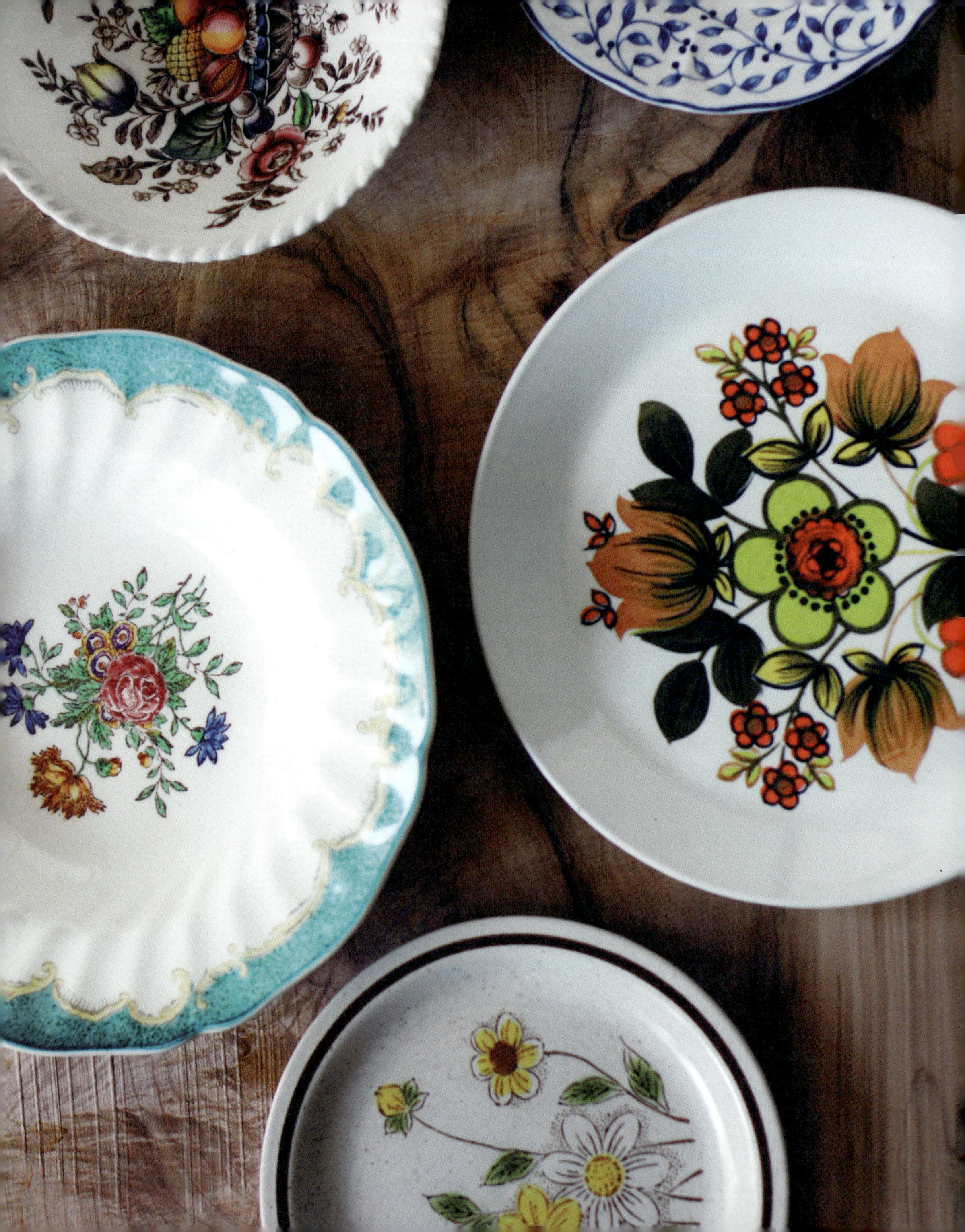

ARTIST · MAKER · CREATOR

Dish Watching

by
CHANEL MARTINEAU

"There is an element of mystery to vintage items and their colours. They tell a story of a moment in the past, and that really fills me with wonder."

As a young kid, Chanel Martineau was mesmerized by the items that graced her family's little cottage in the woods. "From the drapery to the dishes, every piece dated from the 1970s or before, each unique in colour and shape. It's clear to me that this is where it all began, my love for vintage items, especially dishware! All the good memories I had of this little place were the reason for that impact, just the sum of a lot of love, family and some funky colours!"

Inspired by these dishes, Chanel incorporates their colour palettes and motifs, such as a retro owl, into her surface pattern designs. "I incorporate a vintage feel in my work by using muted hues, I think it creates a retro vibe. Through my work, my goal is to translate that mesmerizing feeling over to others." ✤

chanelmartineau.com
@mrsmixedmedia

CHANEL MARTINEAU   301

99
94
93
ALMONDS
23
A
Dick Naylor
HIPP
92
THE BOTTLE
98

3

30
Coca-Cola

13
20
18

ARTIST · MAKER · CREATOR

Shadow Boxes

by

JESSICA JEWETT

The object is king, declares Jessica Jewett, an artist in Bath, United Kingdom, who makes three-dimensional shadow boxes. "It sows the seed, inspires the story or theme, and the scene gets built up around it," she says.

"I have always collected interesting and beautiful things. However as the things accumulate on the mantelpiece, they have to fight for attention from the clutter of the everyday and end up getting lost and overwhelmed by the jumble of brighter and shinier things of modern life. I found that I could give them space by giving them a box of their own, in sympathetic surroundings that let their voice be heard."

A box constructs a space around an object or grouping: "A frame to keep the hurly-burly out, keeping the moment undiluted or unintimidated by the loud and brash," describes Jessica. "My first love has always been making boxes. Call them assemblages or shadow boxes or 3D collage; I just called them boxes. I come from a family of artists, but went to study medicine, and later qualified as a psychologist. However, the drive to make and worship the beautiful has grown stronger over the years and has finally won out. And now I focus on making and putting my collecting habits to good use." ❋

"An old atlas with colourful cross-sections cutting through the earth, or a battered dinky toy truck, an evocative lead oak tree or a handful of old radio valves, now obsolete. All have had past lives and I like to create a new space for them and a new chapter to their story."

"The vintage things that I collect most avidly are old toys, die-cast lead figures, board games, cigarette cards, matchbox labels, old tinplate windup toys, dinky toy cars, decorative playing cards, play figures, maps, stamps and even old tools. These vintage finds seem to carry so much depth to their story. They were made with care, with an eye to detail and design, and have survived several lifetimes of play, use or even neglect. They are not objects of any great value, but to me they are things of great beauty and with a little space and a helping hand, maybe others can see this too."

skylarkprints.com
@sky_lark_prints

"I scale my pieces and my surface designs to invite the viewer to take a step closer to see and feel the thoughtful details."

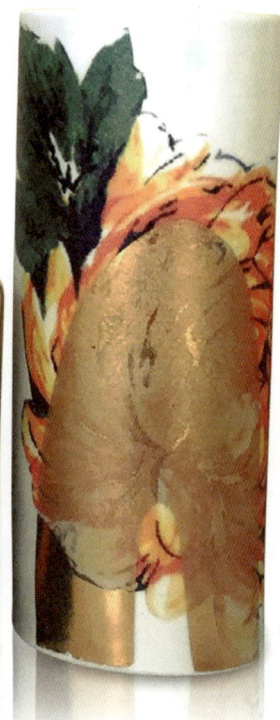

ARTIST · MAKER · CREATOR

Handkerchief Vases

by

ANDREA CHRISTIE

"It is my intent to create ceramic works of art that tie a sense of time and memories to the physical nature of the hand and earth. By using slip cast and hand-built functional objects, I am able to explore the conversation between form and surface."

Through her ceramics, Andrea Christie explores symbolic images and patterns that relate to the domestic, the familiar and the incidental. "Most recently I have made a body of work that was inspired by my mother's collection of about 200 vintage ladies handkerchiefs," says Andrea. These porcelain vases are decorated with custom-printed floral decals designed with motifs from these vintage fabrics and enhanced with gold lustre overlays. "I intend to honour the textile designers and illustrators of the past by scanning in a beautiful detail from a vintage handkerchief." She manipulates and enhances the motif in Photoshop and makes the decals. "I want to bring a piece of these lovely and intimate pieces of history out of the dresser drawer and put them into the hands and homes of new owners."

"The ceramics inks that create the details fire to a subtle texture, which influences the gold overlay, and recalls the texture of the fabric in the original textile. My work is intended to nestle into domestic spaces and evoke a celebration of the material, the trace of the artists' hands and the timeless beauty of functional porcelain objects. These vases are a labour of love and are produced in small batches of around 10 to 20 in a run." ✤

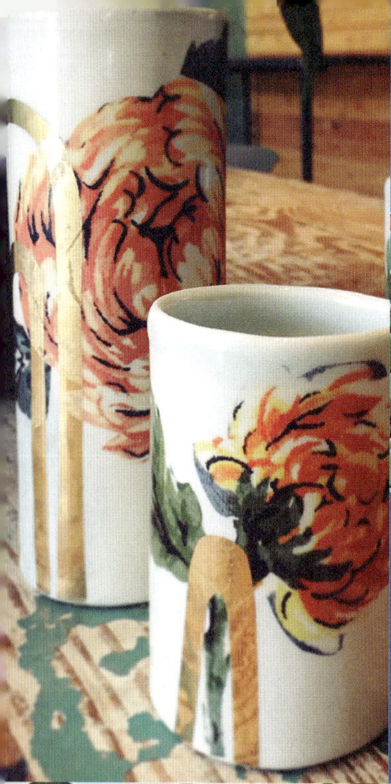
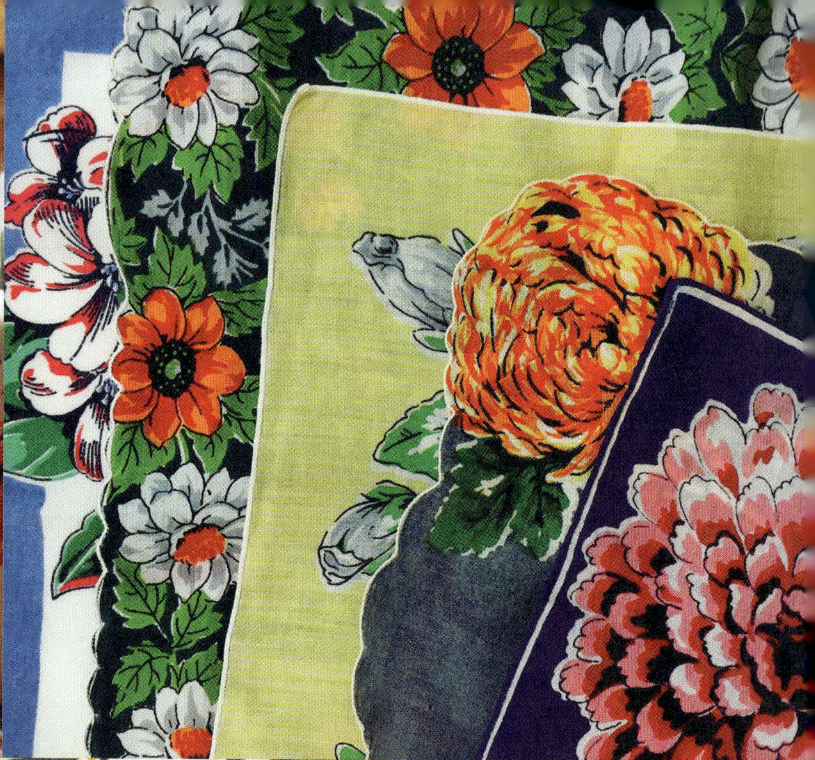
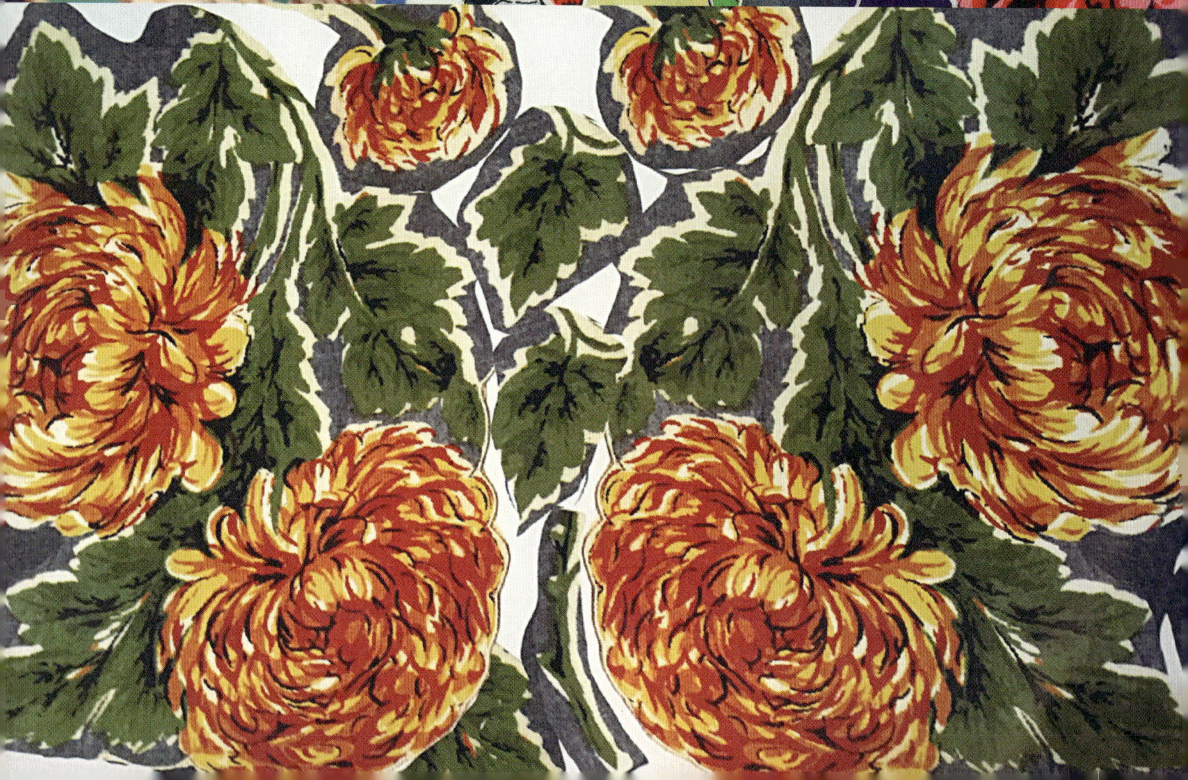

christieceramics.com
@andreachristieceramics

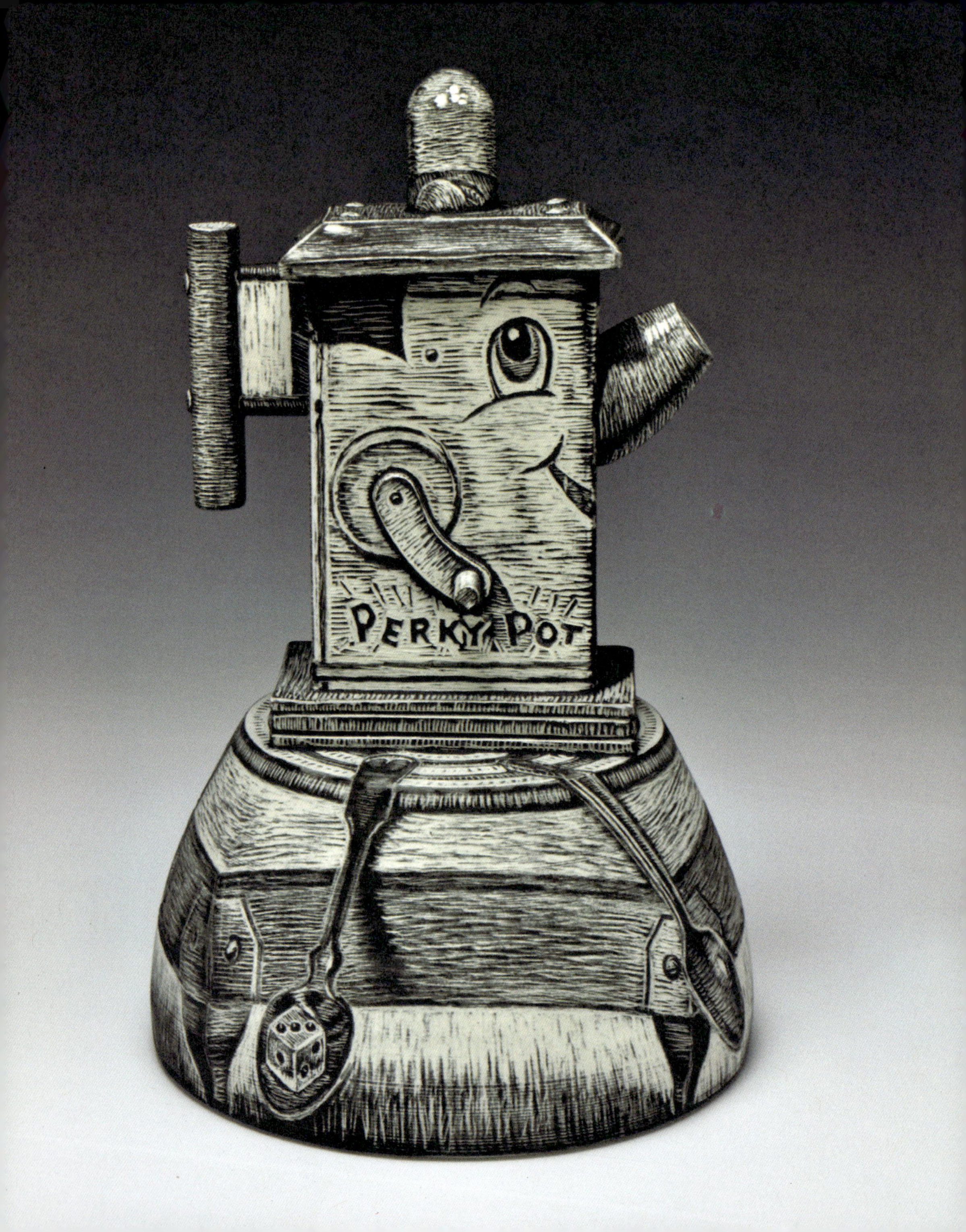
PERKY POT

ARTIST · MAKER · CREATOR

Toys as Sculpture

by

CHRIS THEISS

Chris Theiss makes narrative ceramic sculptures that combine his love of drawing with three-dimensional form. "I liken it to having my cake and being able to eat it, too," says Chris of the combination of expressions. "Toys are my absolute favourite objects to incorporate into my sculptures," he says. "I'm particularly attracted to the Fisher-Price line of pull toys from the 1950s and 1960s. They are just so visually fun! I also feel that toys add the idea of play to my work, which is something that I've always admired with artists and designers such as Alexander Calder, and Charles and Ray Eames. When I sculpt or draw old or vintage toys within my sculptures, they become characters that help drive the narrative. A shelf in my studio is jam-packed with these inspiration objects, waiting to be the focus or perhaps have a supporting role in my next ceramic story. Who will it be?" ❉

"Vintage objects have been an essential part of my work for as long as I've been dealing with my immediate surroundings and personal space, and using it as my subject matter."

CHRIS THEISS 311

"Both the hand-building process of slab construction and the surface technique of sgraffito are very old indeed. Sgraffito, meaning 'to scratch,' is essentially the process of scratching or carving through an applied surface layer of contrasting material into a base material such as wood, plaster or clay. It can be traced back to ancient Islam. It found its way to southern Europe during the Italian Renaissance, migrated to northern Europe and eventually found its way to the American colonies by way of German potters."

mrsgraffito.blogspot.com

Is Konijn te klein?
Claudia Verhelst
Erik van Os en Elle van Lieshout Ik weet een mop!
maan roos vis AVI M3 naar zee! Lieneke Dijkzeul
Ik rijm, rijm, rijm
Dirk Nielandt Heksenclub
Lijkt zij op mij? Bas Rompa
kan mijn jas in de was? Bas Rompa
Spin en Spook
Erik van Os en Elle van Lieshout wat een mop!
Zon op mijn neus
Chris Winsemius Hier waak ik!
Kriepie
Reine De Pelsmaeker - Claudia Verhelst beer bros vindt een bal
Kriepie
Kriepie

COCO POPS

ARTIST · MAKER · CREATOR

Imagination at Play

by

CLAUDIA VERHELST

"I use these vintage toys for colour inspiration for my illustrations. Not only for the colours, but also for the shape, the story behind it."

An illustrator in Kruibeke, Belgium, Claudia Verhelst specializes in picture books and books for first readers. Inspired by vintage toys, she surrounds herself with their happy colour, with collections displayed throughout her studio. "I collect vintage toys because they make me smile—they are poetic, beautiful and have great colours," she says. "It's working in an environment full of colour and happiness that gives me energy and inspiration."

The toys not only inspire colour palettes, but provide company for the imagination, too, as Claudia guesses at the histories of the objects (and of their previous owners). "I have a very large collection, including squeaky toys, rubber toys, tin toys, tin boxes, plastic toys, old Fisher-Price toys, Educalux toys…" And the list goes on. "We look for them in thrift stores, flea markets… Even my children and husband join in the search. I attach great importance to the environment, buying fewer new things, less polluting, and reusing old vintage things is one of the things that contribute to that." ✣

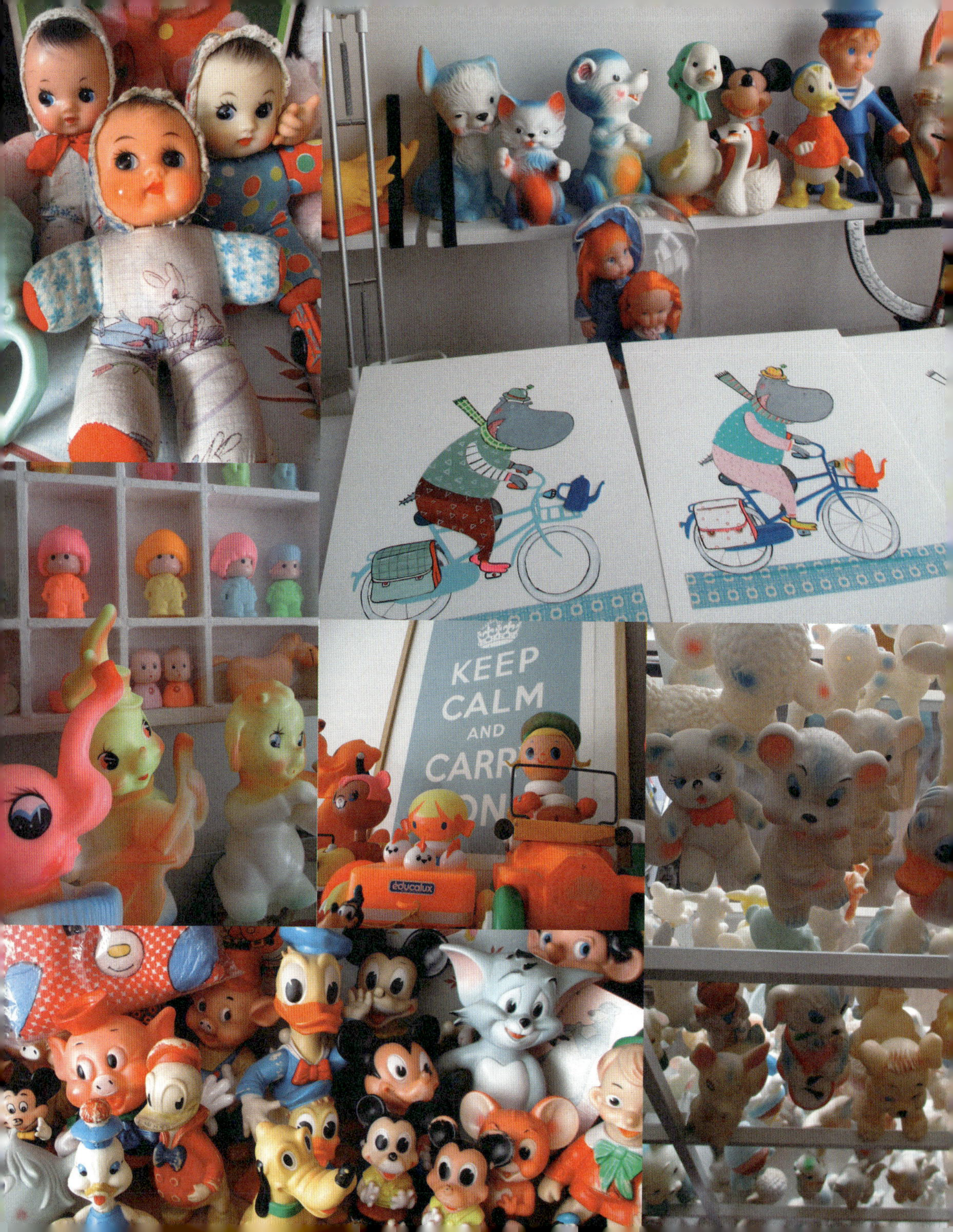
KEEP
CALM
AND
educalux

claudiaverhelst.blogspot.com
@claudia.verhelst

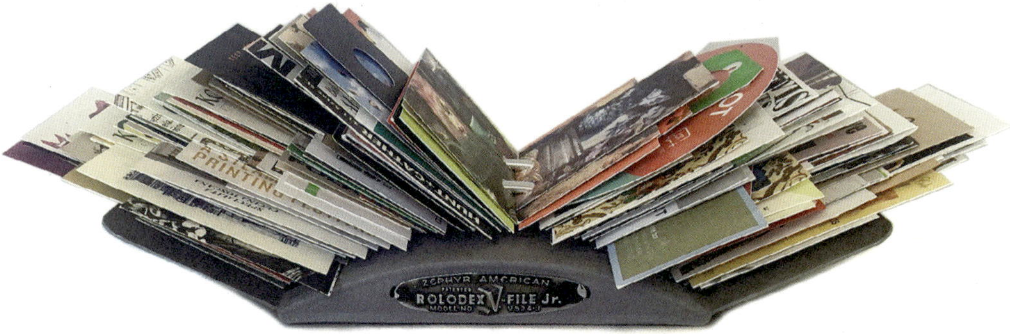
ZEPHYR AMERICAN
ROLODEX
FILE Jr.

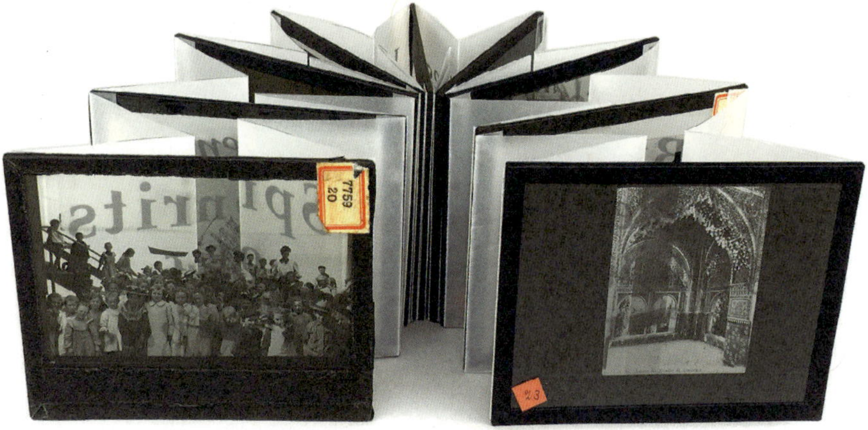
7759
20

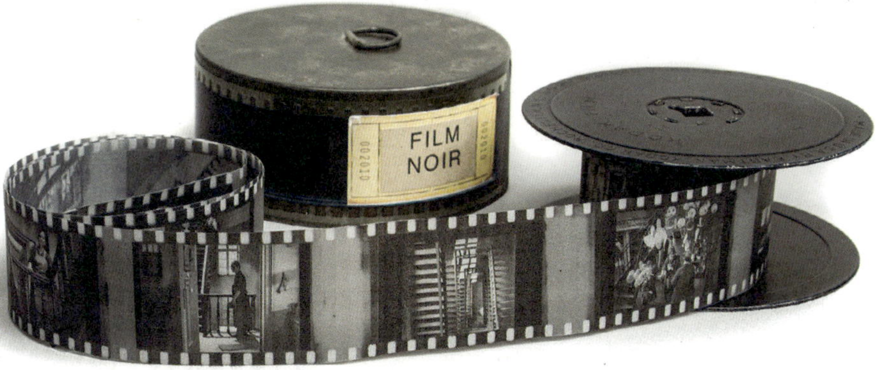
FILM
NOIR

ARTIST · MAKER · CREATOR

Non-Traditional Books

by

MARGARET SUCHLAND

Margaret Suchland is a collector of found objects and artifacts; items that she uses in making her non-traditional books. "I search for ephemera and vintage objects that appeal to me and that I find inspiring to work with or that spark an idea. A metamorphosis sometimes occurs when I come upon a vintage item and I can instantly see the object's potential for a new life." Sometimes, inspiration does not come immediately and the object remains in the care of her collection for years before just the right application presents itself. "In my work, I am interested in the passage of time and what remains. I explore the effects of time on memory and identity. My work reflects my interest in ephemera and vintage objects because of the effects of time evident on them; the worn edges, random marks and muted colours. These are all subtle evidence of the human presence and passage of time. They portray a 'presence of an absence.'" ❊

"I enjoy the randomness and unexpected results found when joining unrelated materials. I receive great joy in giving new life to vintage objects that otherwise would be discarded."

320 VINTAGE LIFE

IMAGINATIVE
ADAPTABLE
GRACEFUL
COLORFUL
RESOURCEFUL
SENSUAL
DEFENSIVE
ENDANGERED
TENACIOUS
SELF-RELIANT
SPIRITUAL
DISTINCTIVE
JOYFUL
MAGICAL
NATURE SERIES

margaretsuchland.com
@margaretsuchland

KEEP THIS COUPON

KIJK-
MUSEUM
1183
20

Automaticket
ADULT | ADULT
81524
81524

ARTIST · MAKER · CREATOR

Nostalgic Knits

by

ANTONIA SULLIVAN

Antonia Sullivan creates charming, high-quality, 100% pure lambswool knitwear. "Under my label Sprig Knitwear, I design and create all my knitted garments from my home studio," she says. "There are varied stages in constructing the garments, including using vintage machine knitting tools such as transfer tools, weights and a card-punching machine, and my pre-loved linker."

The knitted patterns that adorn Sprig hats, scarves and wrist warmers are at once timeless and nostalgic. "My current collection is a range of knitted accessories embellished in Fair Isle patterns. These patterns focus on images of nostalgia, from Stick-of-Rock (a mint-flavoured confectionery) to vintage matchboxes, to hoop and stick games." One source of Antonia's inspiration comes from photos of her mother growing up in mid-century Britain. "These photos are mostly in black-and-white, yet are filled with delightful patterns and personality. My knitwear brings these qualities to life with vivid colours and playful decorations. This initial inspiration created the foundation of my practice and my knitwear label, which explores nostalgia and childhood memories."

"Every aspect of my knitwear resonates with a foundation of vintage influence and production. From the simplest stitch to the completed garment, my aim is to recreate the love and warmth that these nostalgic photographs produced." With attention to process, detail and quality, Antonia knits heirloom pieces that she hopes will be passed down for generations. ✤

"I first came across these photos of my mum with my grandma. Her husband (my grandad) had just passed away. She came around my house with bags full of photographs, and she went through each photo telling me and my family the story behind each picture and object—I was moved in a way I had never felt before. These photographs and stories captured, for me, what was truly important to us as a family and I had to respond to this in some way, eventually; knitting was the ideal discipline for this."

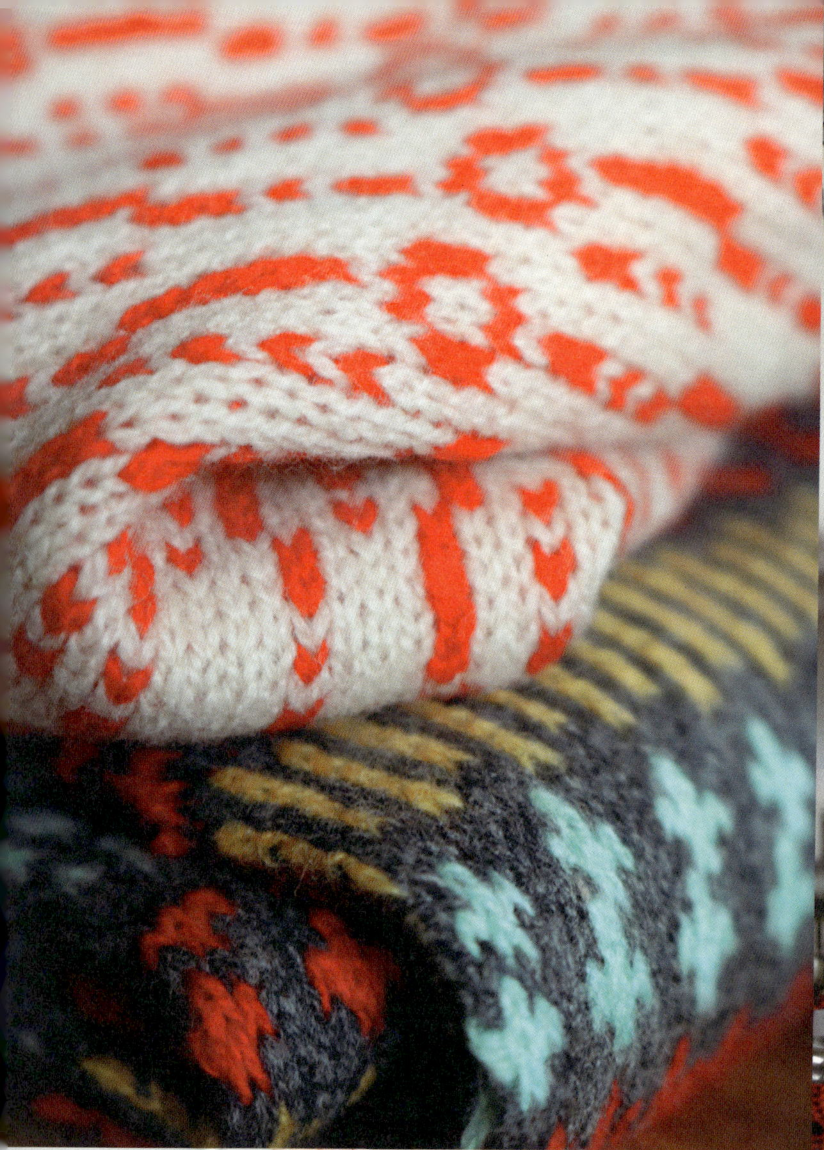

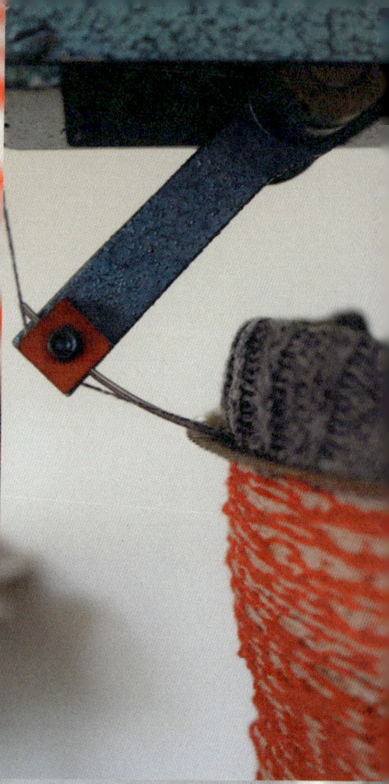

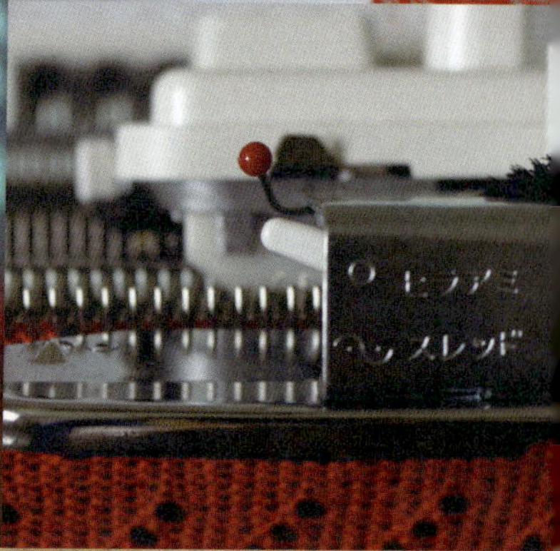
セラアミ
スレッド

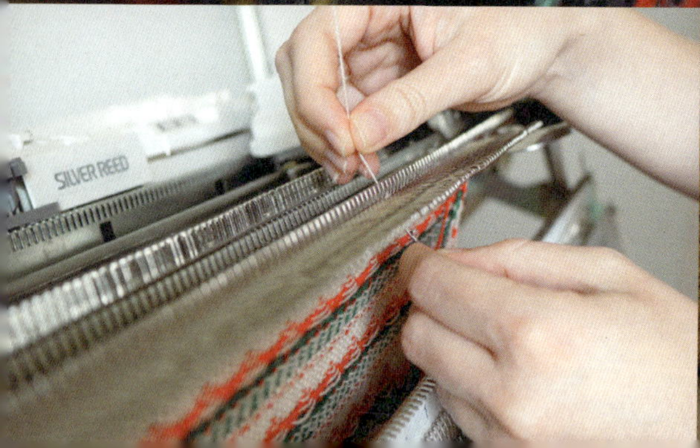
SILVER REED

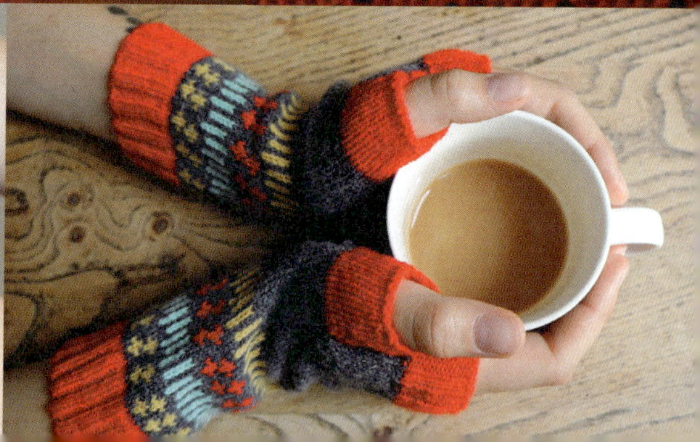

"My ethos focuses on wrapping my customers in love and bringing brightness on those bleak winter days with colour, softness and warmth—as though being hugged by those cherished memories."

sprigknitwear.co.uk
@sprigknitwear

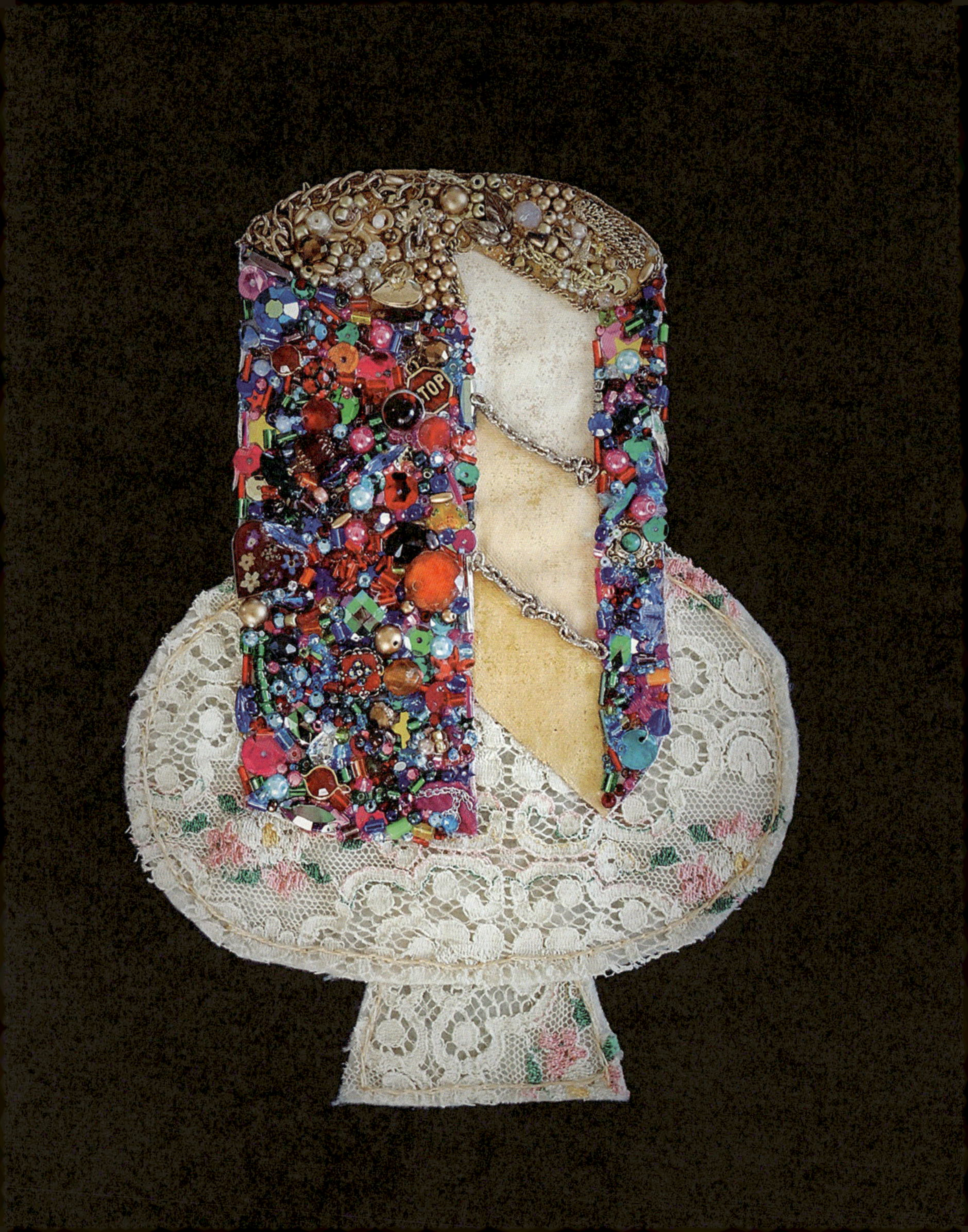

ARTIST · MAKER · CREATOR

Layers of Memory

by

SARA SANDLER

"I enjoy taking something old and 'unusable,' and turning it into something beautiful again, and breathing new life into something once forgotten."

Sara Sandler's exuberantly bejewelled cakes are joyful creations, and yet they emerged from a time of sadness. "Creating these cakes has been a long but incredible life-changing journey for me," Sara explains. "After the passing of my mother, I truly felt lost. Sitting with all of her fabrics and beads and jewels she had collected over the years truly inspired me to create again in an entirely new way. It not only keeps her memory alive, but just to be able to sit in my studio every day and create art with her things is just so special. I feel very lucky to have the connection to her on a daily basis in a creative way."

"I love the history and memories behind each scrap and antique bead I use in my cake constructions. I also disassemble vintage and antique jewellery to create 'sprinkles' and decoration on the cakes." With a nod to painter Wayne Thiebaud's cakes, Sara brings her background in collage and mixed-media into these textile creations. Using remnants, mostly from her late mother's stash of fabrics from the 1970s, she blends nostalgia with pop art. ✻

sarasandler.com
@sara.sandler.art

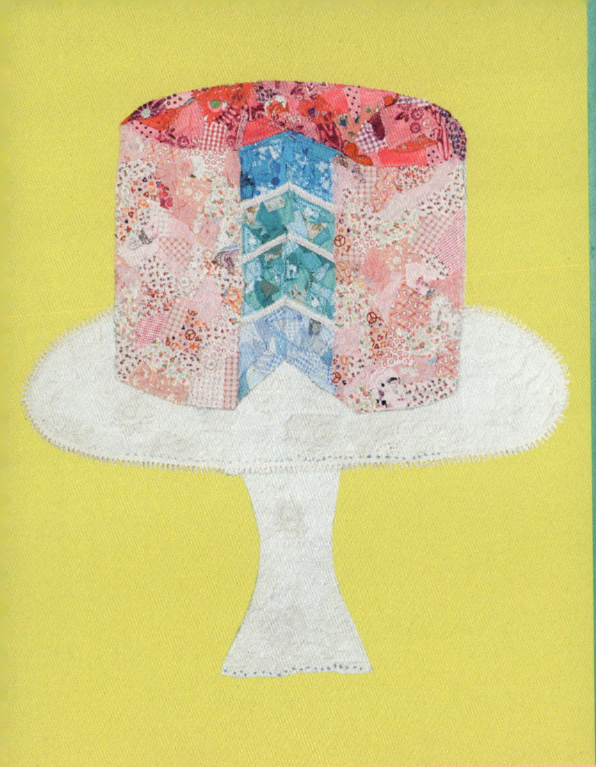

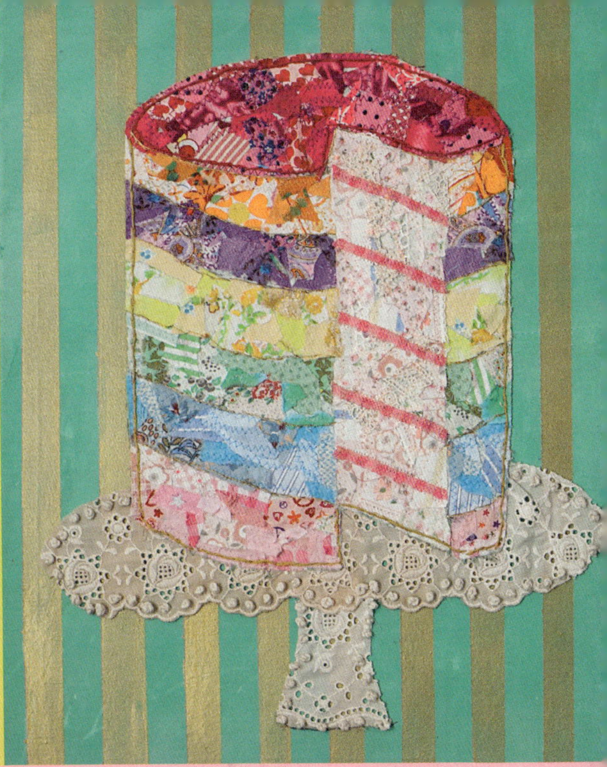

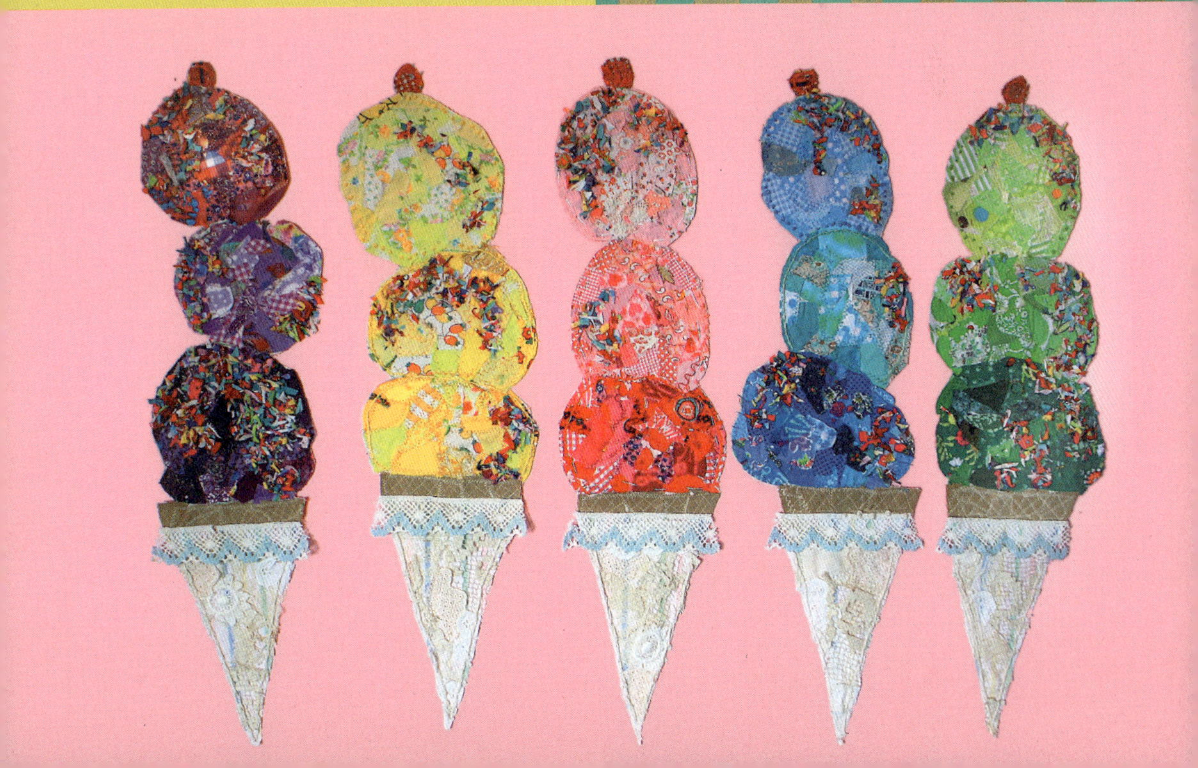

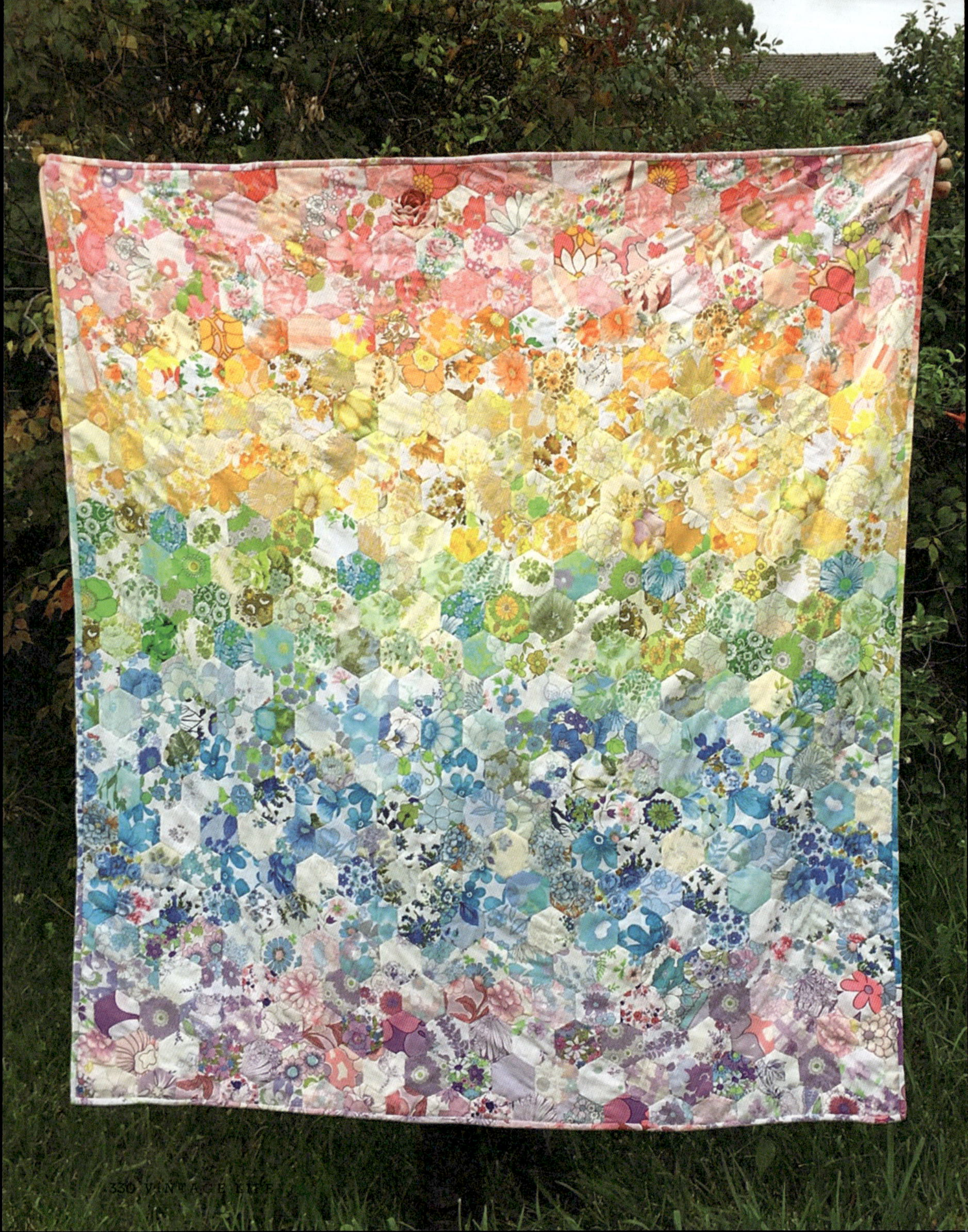

ARTIST · MAKER · CREATOR

Sheets of Style

by

THOURAYA BATTYE

"The bold patterns and colour of vintage sheets inspires every aspect of Amelie and Atticus' collection. From rainbow quilts to bright floral dresses, all pieces are designed to showcase the beauty of vintage."

Thouraya Battye's fascination with vintage sheets began over a decade ago. "My collection began in 2008 with my own sheet from my childhood, which I cut and began sewing bloomers from." She fell in love with their bright, beautiful patterns and began to look for them in thrift stores as a less expensive and sustainable choice of fabric. Under the company name Amelie and Atticus, Thouraya makes vibrant and unique quilts and clothing from vintage sheets and blankets. "With bold use of colour and pattern, these designs offer a taste of nostalgia in a unique and sustainable creation."

"I am drawn to rainbows, and in my practice, I find myself sewing rainbow quilts or quilts of a solid colour to showcase the stunning prints. I love finding new and unused vintage sheets in packets and am amazed that they are still out there. These are my favourite finds, along with the same print in a range of colourways, which worked together makes for a stunning quilt. My range includes vintage-inspired children's clothes, quilts and picnic blankets, all created from my collection of sheets and blankets. I love creating pieces full of nostalgia and they often find themselves in the hands of customers who grew up surrounded by these prints, which have left their mark in memories they can now hold."

Rosealee
sheets
Decorative Sheets
Rosealee
quality sheets
ALL COTTON
Sheridan
Decorative Sheets

amelieandatticus.blogspot.com
@amelieandatticus

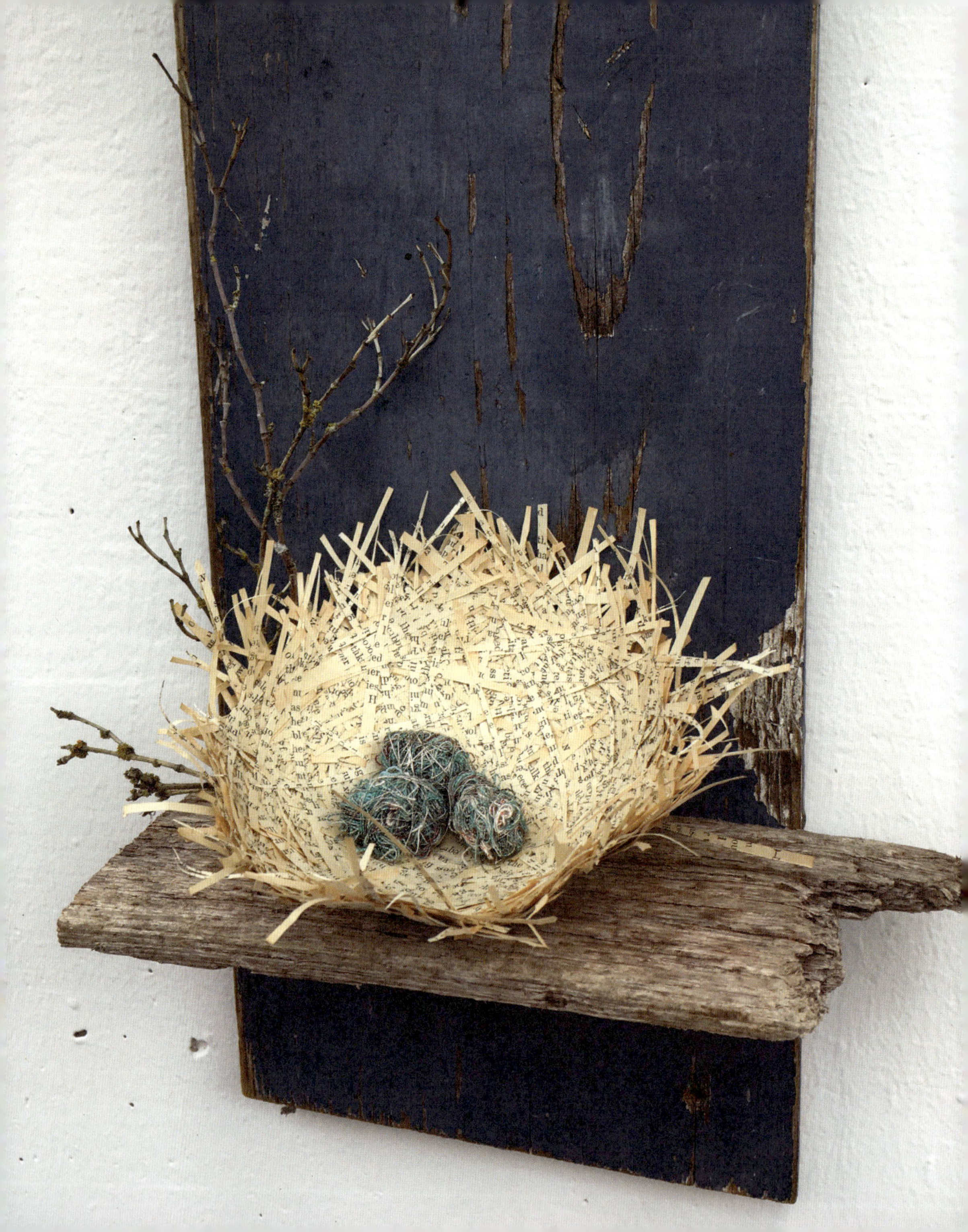

ARTIST · MAKER · CREATOR

Threads of Ideas

by

CAMILLE ESPOSITO

"The graphics on the spools inspire my work, as well as the wood forms. I have used the spools as part of a three-dimensional collage or shadow boxes."

Camille Esposito loves vintage spools of thread. "The wood, the graphics that are stamped on the ends in various colours, sometimes the spools are even a colour! And the thread, oh the thread!" she exclaims. "Such a diverse and inspiring palette of colours. Some seem part of the past; some seem very contemporary even though they are over 50 years old." If there's such a thing as painting with thread, then that's how Camille would describe her use of this creative supply. She also harvests pages from old books ("I feel less guilty when they are already loose and destined for the recycling bin."). The pages become elements of collage. "I use book pages for collage and to build nests. I'm not sure when I first felt inspired to build a nest out of book scraps but something about it, the words, the comfort that comes from books, is perfectly symbolized by a nest. I often fill the nests with eggs that I have made from thread. I am like a magpie, collecting bits and bobs, and making them new again." ❊

BELDING CORTICELLI
275 YDS
BEL-WAXED
MERCERIZED
BEL-WAXED MERCERIZED COTTON
FAST TO BOILING
25¢
BERKSHIRE & BECKET SILK CO'S
BUTTON & CARPET
FAST TO BOILING
SIZE 50 19¢
SHADE 1658
PURE SILK THREAD
ADAMS
50 YDS
COLOR 152
A
MERCERIZED COTTON
FAST TO BOILING
BEL-WAXED
15¢
J.&P. COATS
BOILFAST
BUTTON HOLE TWIST

camillesposito.com
@camillespositoart

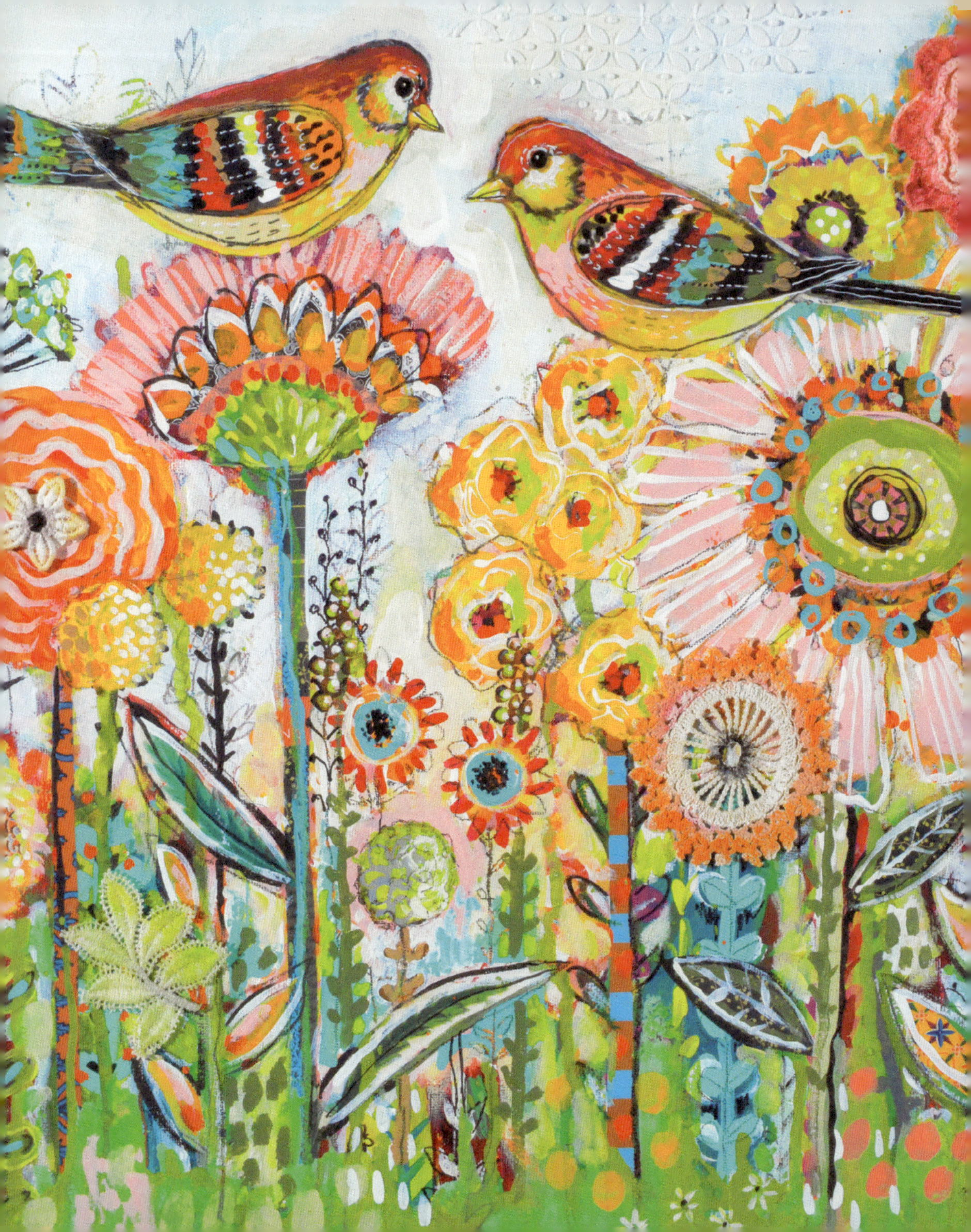

ARTIST · MAKER · CREATOR

Floral Doilies

by

LORI SIEBERT

In her mixed-media paintings, Cincinnati-based artist Lori Siebert focusses on florals and the beauty of nature. "Vintage elements are also often found in my work because of my love of texture and dimensionality versus a flat surface," she says. Lori collects a variety of vintage needle arts such as crewel work, crochet, embroidery and quilts. "When I made the connection that many of these beautifully stitched doilies and tablecloths are very flower-like in shape, the idea for a new series of images was born. I went on a mad collecting craze at several antique malls and flea markets to build my collection."

"When I work on these paintings, I go back and forth between painting the flowers and laying in the vintage pieces. I sometimes use the full doily and sometimes cut apart a tablecloth and use the floral pieces. I like to imagine the love, care and hours that someone put into these heirlooms."

Lori discovered an old book with instruction on how to make crochet flowers and she plans on learning this craft herself. "I am so excited about this direction in my work that I plan to take it even further. I have plans to create large canvases that incorporate even more of these vintage fibre arts. This concept combines all of my loves: vintage needle arts, fashion, fabric, texture and florals. It all started with the pretty doilies." ✽

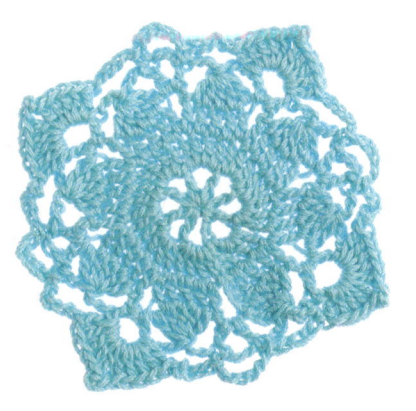

"I have been gathering all kinds of crocheted and embroidered doilies because they are very flower like. I am currently working on a series in which I am incorporating these beautiful handmade pieces from the past into my floral paintings. I am loving the mix of old and new."

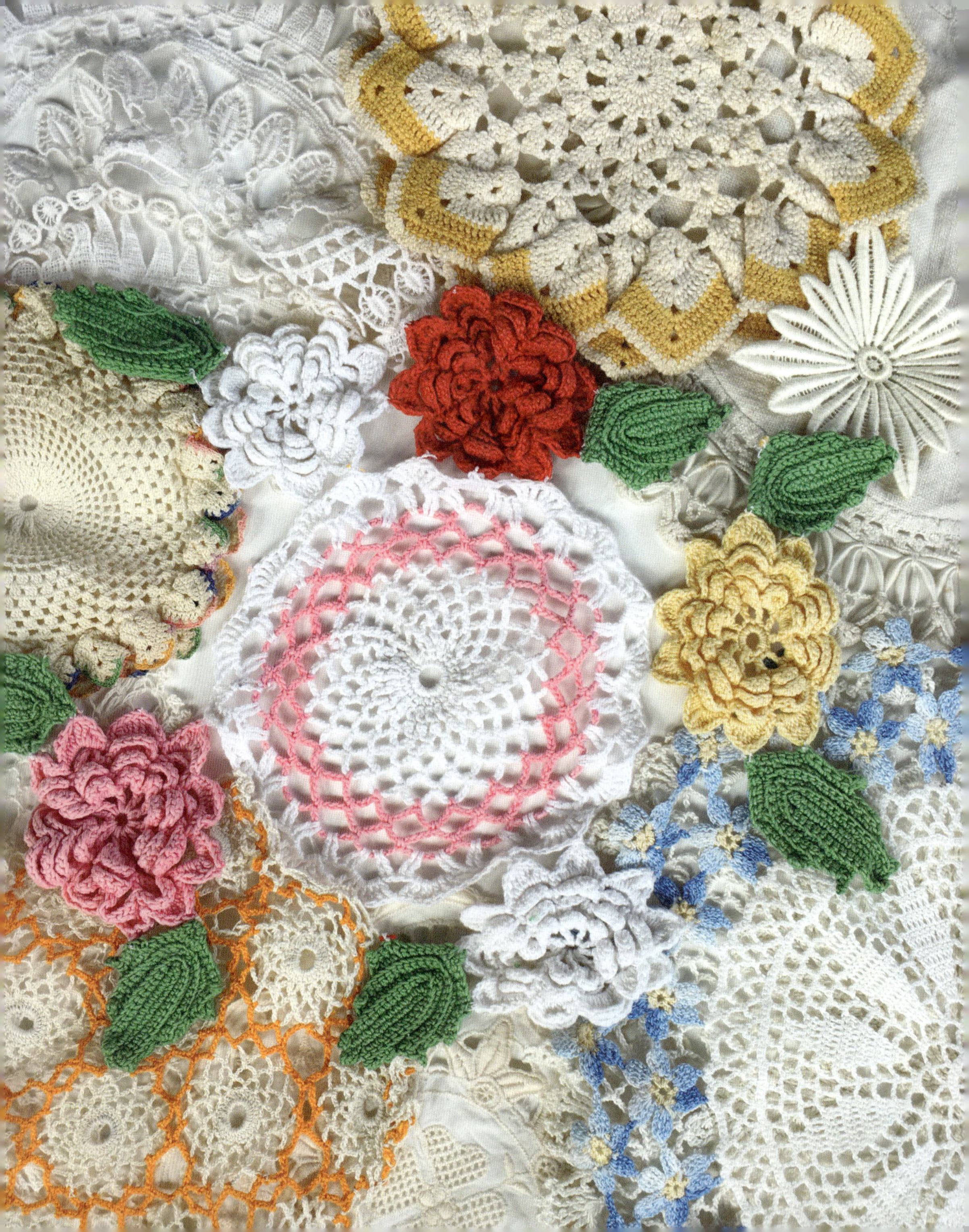

@lorisiebertstudio

Photographs

ARTIST · MAKER · CREATOR

Found Photos

by
CLARE ETHERIDGE

"Having a person, people or even a scene captured from years gone by to use as part of my art is an honour and a joy. The photos add an original and almost a storytelling element that I could not get as effectively anywhere else."

When creating art journal pages, Clare Etheridge loves to include old photographs. "The colour and quality of the photos is an inspiration in itself," she says, "especially when you consider that people at the beginning of the 20th century didn't take photos just for the sake of it—cameras and processing was an expensive hobby—so it was always a carefully considered photograph. Of course, not all of the photographs turned out exactly as intended and I think these are some of the most interesting—the everyday caught in black and white or sepia and still here to look at all these years later."

She will often start with the photo as the visual anchor to her page composition, drawing inspiration from its image and personality. "If there is any writing on it (front or back) that is always an idea starter. It is such a treasure to find descriptions, names and dates on the photographs. Images of 'well to do' ladies and gentlemen along with their pets or cars just beg me to either sketch from them or draw on them. I usually work with original photos in the belief that I am not disrespecting the photo or the subject, rather, giving it a new lease of life." ✽

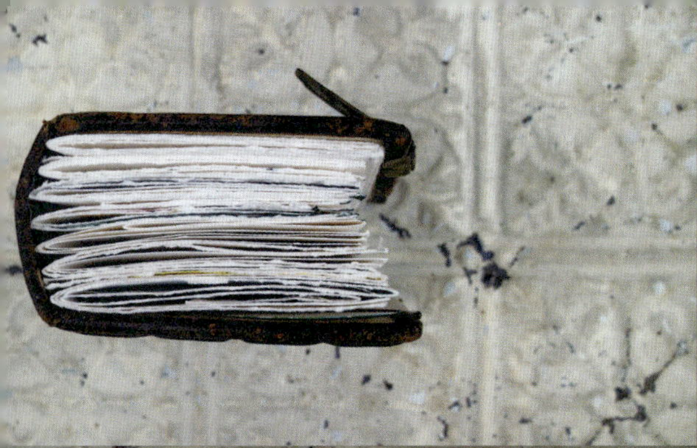
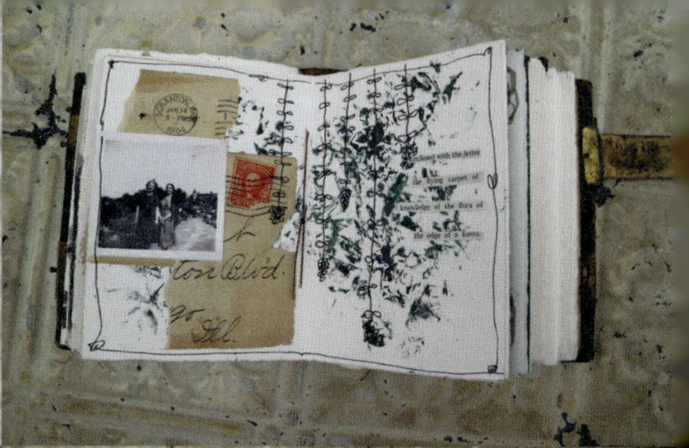
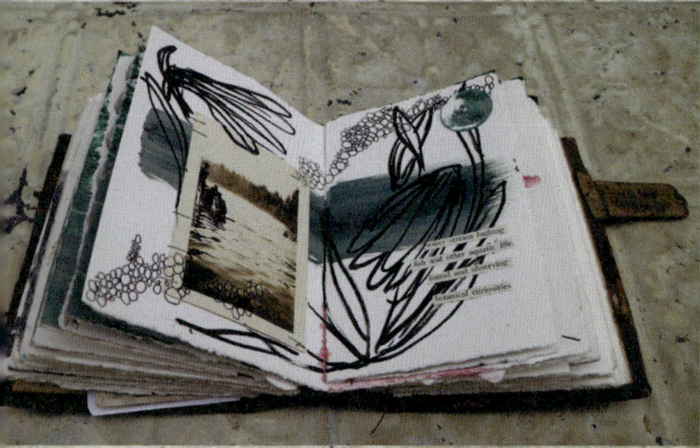
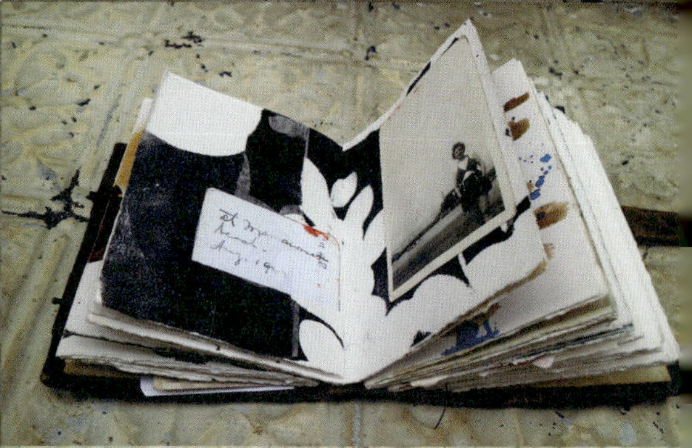
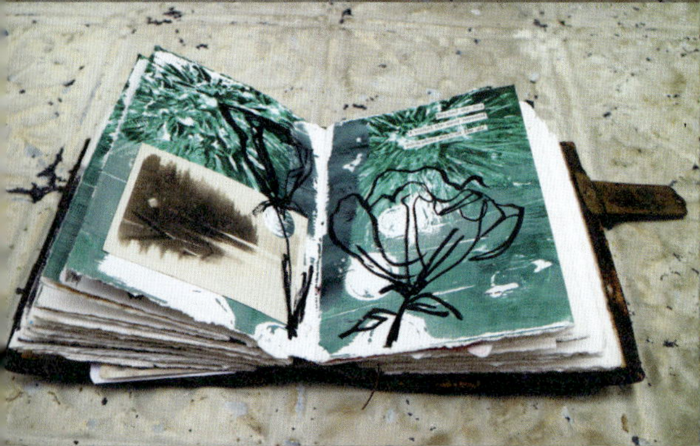
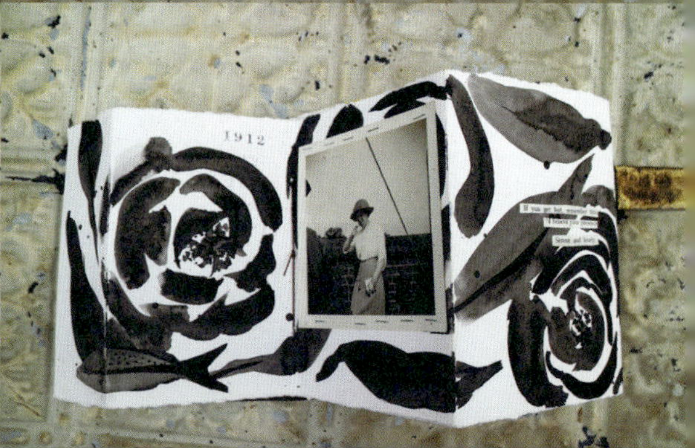
1912
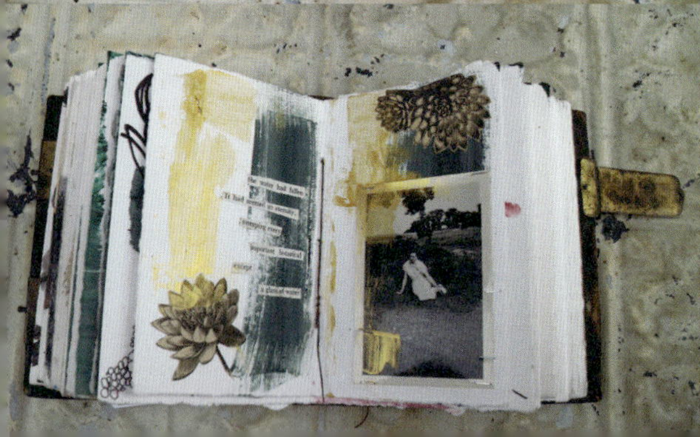
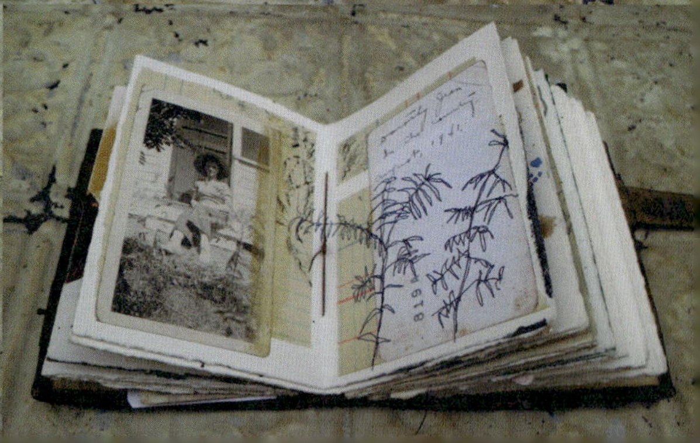

catseatdogs.com
@catseatdogsmakes

Decorating With Plants

TIME-LIFE
ENCYCLOPEDIA
OF GARDENING

ARTIST · MAKER · CREATOR

Paper Searches

by
SYDNEY ROSE

"I use scissors and glue to create playful, surreal compositions that combine and juxtapose images found in a variety of vintage magazines, reference books and storybooks."

Analogue is the past, but with more and more people tiring of our digital lives, it could offer a way towards the future. "I am an analogue collage artist," says Sydney Rose. "I choose to source most of my collage elements from vintage reference books and encyclopedias because there was once a point, not too long ago, when we relied on these books for unbiased, truthful answers about our world. It has been said that we are currently living in the age of information, with our technology allowing for instant access to answers for any question we may have. Search engine results present us with a mixture of truth and lies, which are often indistinguishable from one another and ever-changing. By isolating and combining these outdated images in new ways and with other materials, I am able to tell stories of human behaviour and habits, present observations of our knack for creation and destruction, and examine our ties to tradition and desire for endless progress. Through my collage work, I present to the viewer a new nostalgia—one that combines the fluid, haphazard nature of the Internet with images from a time when information felt more concrete." ❋

¼ INCH = 1 FOOT

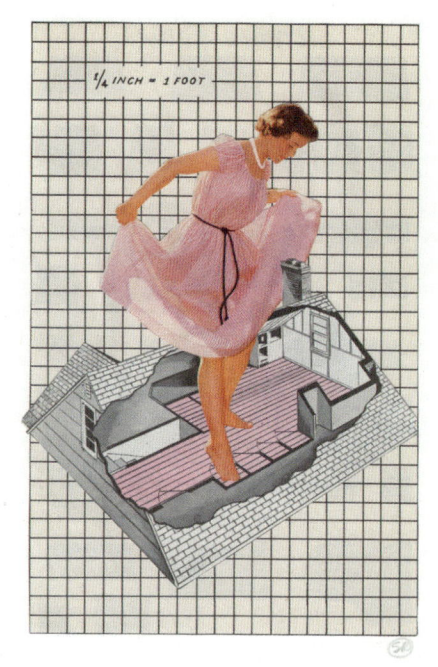

sydneyrose.ca
@sydneyroseart

and be ch
for years
WESTERN UNIC
A Western Union Telegraphic Gift Money Order makes a perfect . . . and most useful gift for a newly married couple.
ten their
rful day
cresc.
animando

ARTIST · MAKER · CREATOR

Collaged Quilts

by

SHARI SELTZER

"I procure paper quilt squares and elements at estate sales, thrift stores and the occasional dumpster dive."

Using the motif of a quilt, Shari Seltzer sews together imagery from vintage publications, advertising, maps, sheet music and dress patterns to explore gender roles and societal expectations. "I gather the images based on colour and thematic connections. I crop the images into squares that become the elements of the quilt. With those squares I compose a layout, testing different combos for visual balance and content. Once I'm satisfied with the composition, I tack down the images and hold them in place by using my sewing machine. I consistently create an edge with a blanket stitch, and I often use a zigzag stitch to connect all the interior squares. I select the colour thread that will complement the images."

Her preference is for imagery from the 1940s, 1950s and 1960s drawn from homemaking, cooking and women's interest magazines such as *Life* and *Better Homes and Gardens*. "In each quilt's theme, I often explore sewing, baking, homemaking and cooking, traditional female interests, but I also work with images from technical manuals and advertisements for men's products. As I 'quilt' I insert a narrative and play with how these everyday vintage images are viewed in a modern context." ✳

est features ever built into a refrigerator!
Niblets
FRESH CORN OFF THE COB
NEW

SHARI SELTZER 353

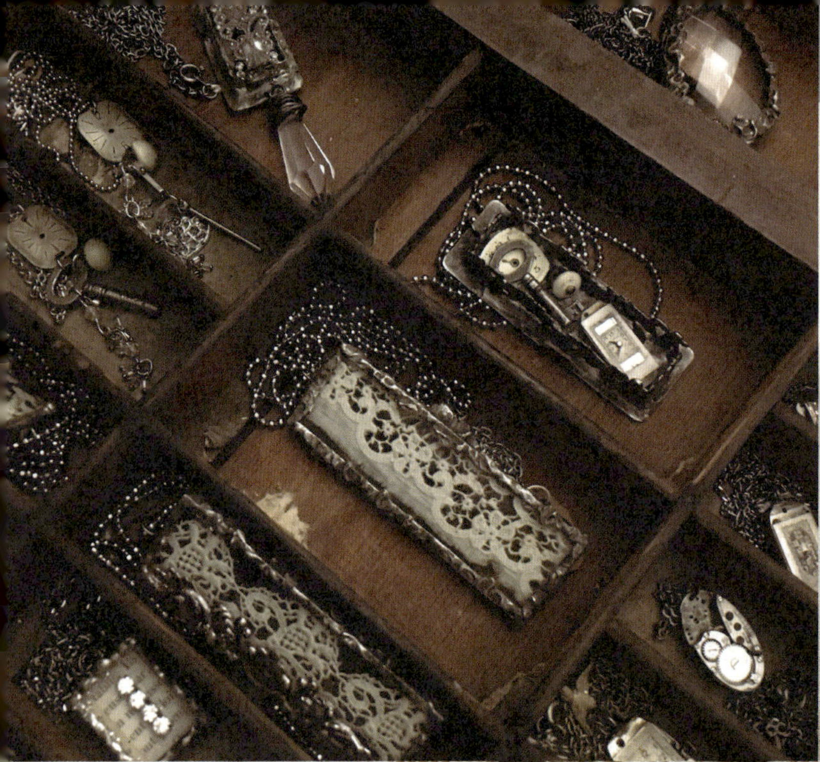

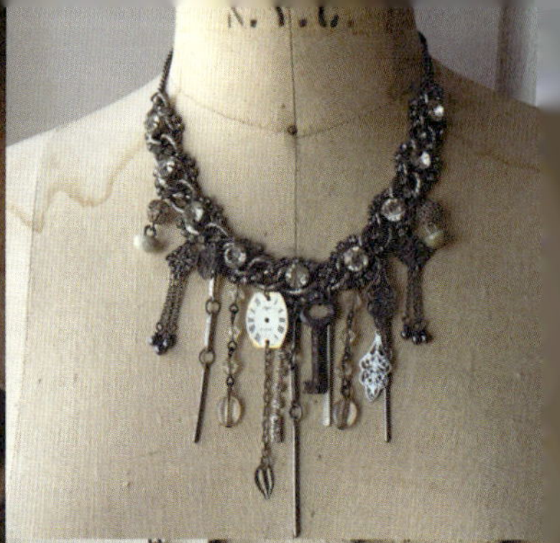

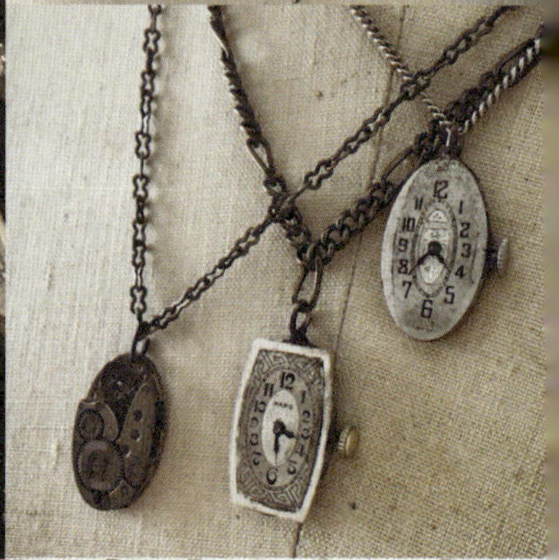

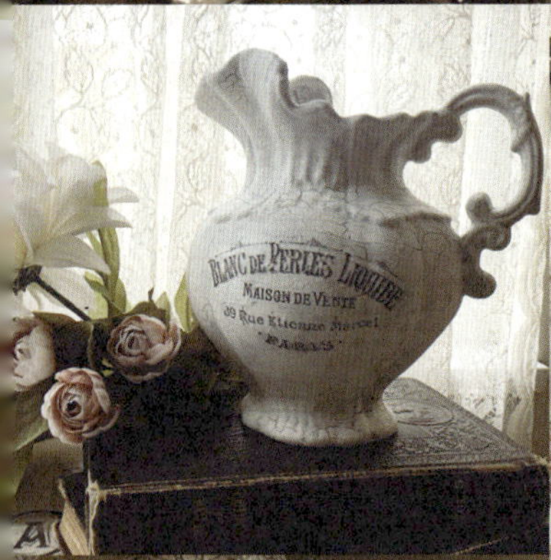
BLANC DE PERLES LIQUIDE
MAISON DE VENTE

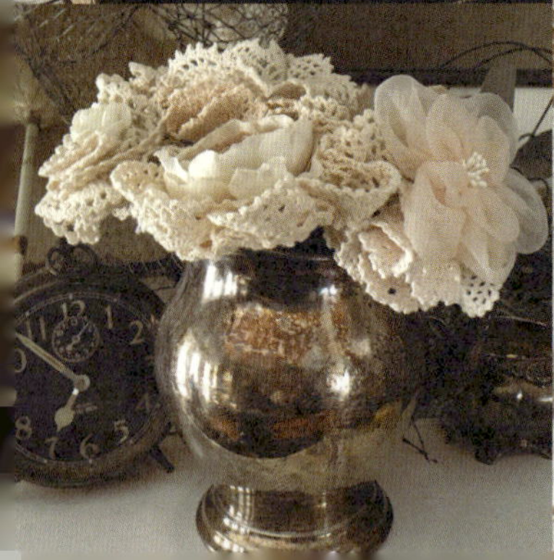

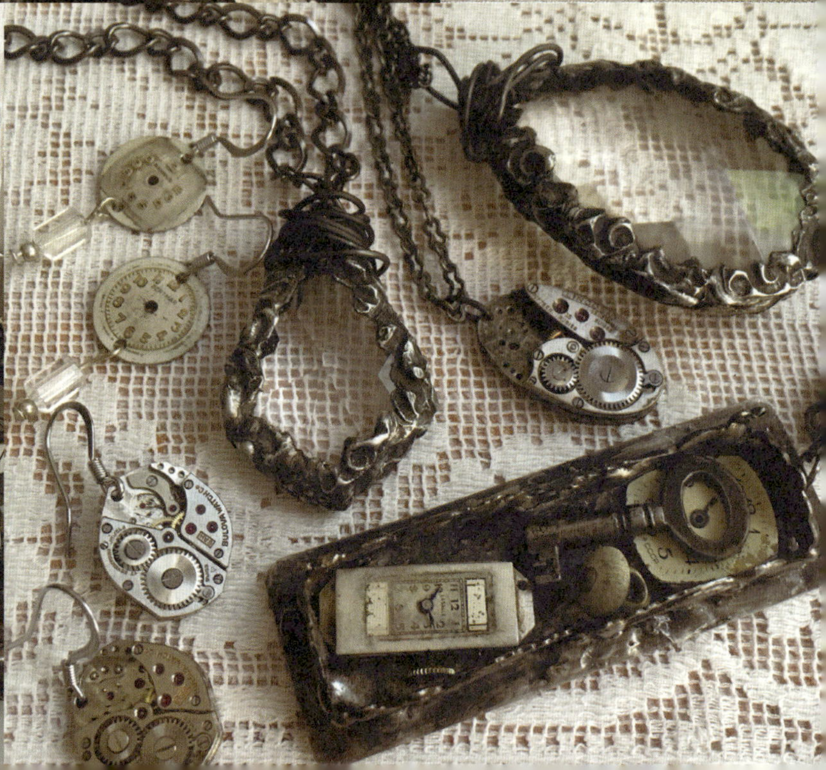

ARTIST · MAKER · CREATOR

Watchful Sources

by

LISA WINE

"The vintage elements I use enhance my products because they have unique details that spark conversation. When I first wore one of my leather cuffs made from an old leather belt people wondered what the silver badge on it was. This allowed me to go into a little history lesson explaining how chauffeur drivers in British Columbia used to have these badges attached to their hats for identification."

A vintage enthusiast who enjoys antique shopping and treasure hunting, Lisa Wine is always on the lookout for unique items to repurpose into home decor and jewellery. "When treasure hunting I am always on the lookout for small vintage items like watch faces, clock dials, skeleton keys, buttons and broaches to use for making necklaces or leather cuffs," she says.

A bit of shabby chic, a touch or crackle and an application of patina (real or faux) is part of the aesthetic. "Whether it's an old silver-plated teapot or ceramic pitcher I will crackle paint it and apply a decal to transform it into something more modern while maintaining a vintage look. My graphic artwork is sourced from many talented online graphic artists who sell their artwork to other creatives for use in their own projects."

She also makes statement necklaces embellished with charms and collected watch parts. "In all my work my effort is spent in updating an item yet maintaining a vintage look. There is something about a vintage item that always makes me wonder how it was made, how old it is and who owed it. There's history in a vintage item that can spark fond memories of the past." ❊

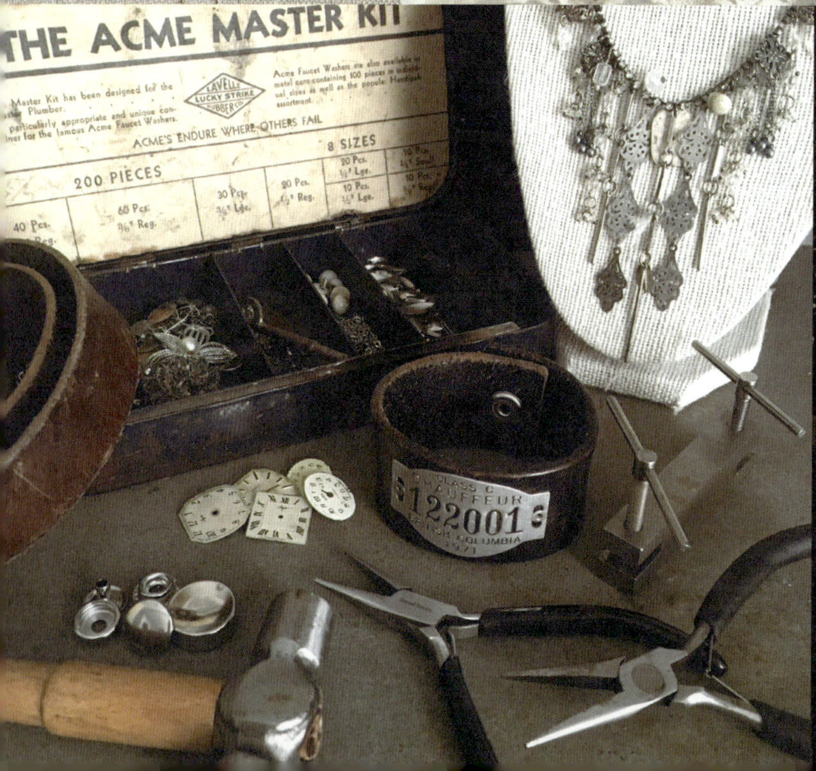
THE ACME MASTER KIT
ACME'S ENDURE WHERE OTHERS FAIL
8 SIZES
200 PIECES
122001

lisawinestudios.com
@lisawinestudios

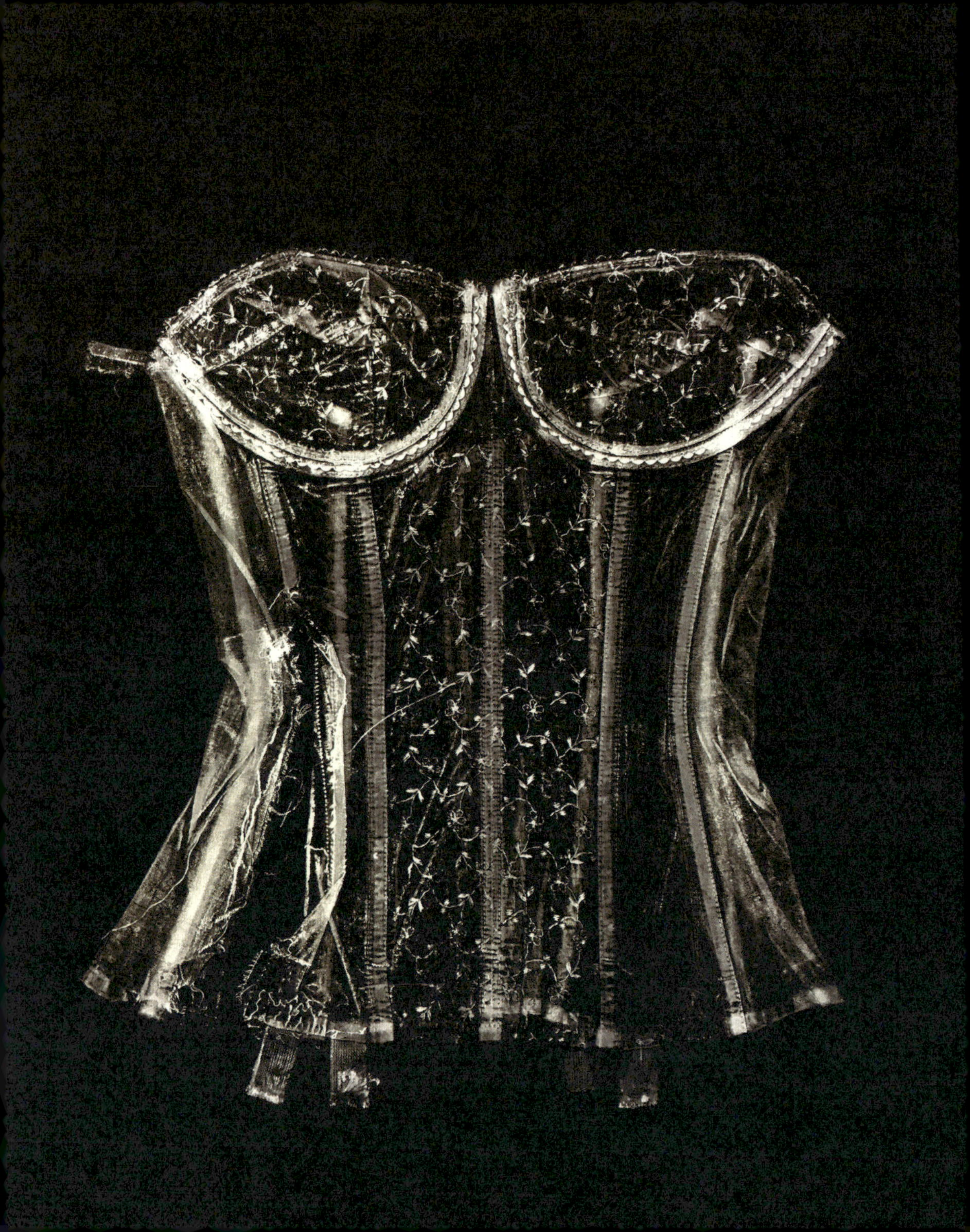

Monoprinted Undergarments

by

ROSE DELER

Rose Deler explores "the notions of female body image as shaped by evolving societal expectations." In her series of monoprints, entitled Pressure, she applies a thin layer of ink to vintage women's undergarments and accompaniments such as old girdles, corsets and gloves dating to the early 1960s and older. Placed ink-side down onto paper, it is fed through a rolling press causing a unique image of the garment to transfer.

"Throughout history, women have been judged by the shape of their figure. Consequently, a variety of contorting (and occasionally deforming) apparatuses were devised to physically mould and shape the female form to meet the ideal figure of the time—corsets and girdles to squeeze you in, hoops and bustles to push you out. As I come across these beautifully made undergarments, I try to imagine what the wearer might have been like. Was she a career woman, a homemaker? What was her day like, and how must it have felt when her binding undergarment would finally come off? As I roll these garments through the press, I am subversively pleased to be subjecting them to the pressure they had at one time subjected their wearers." ❇

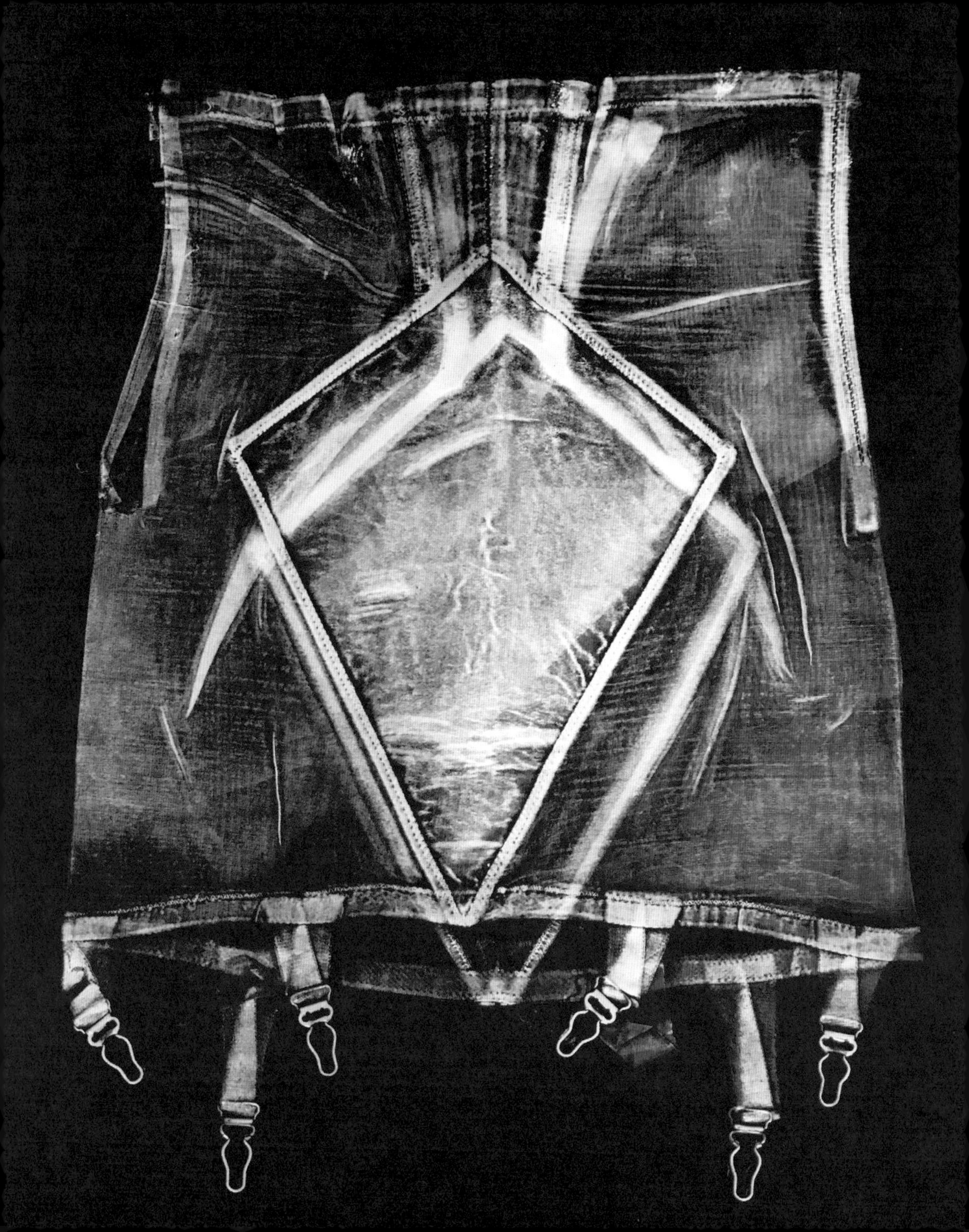

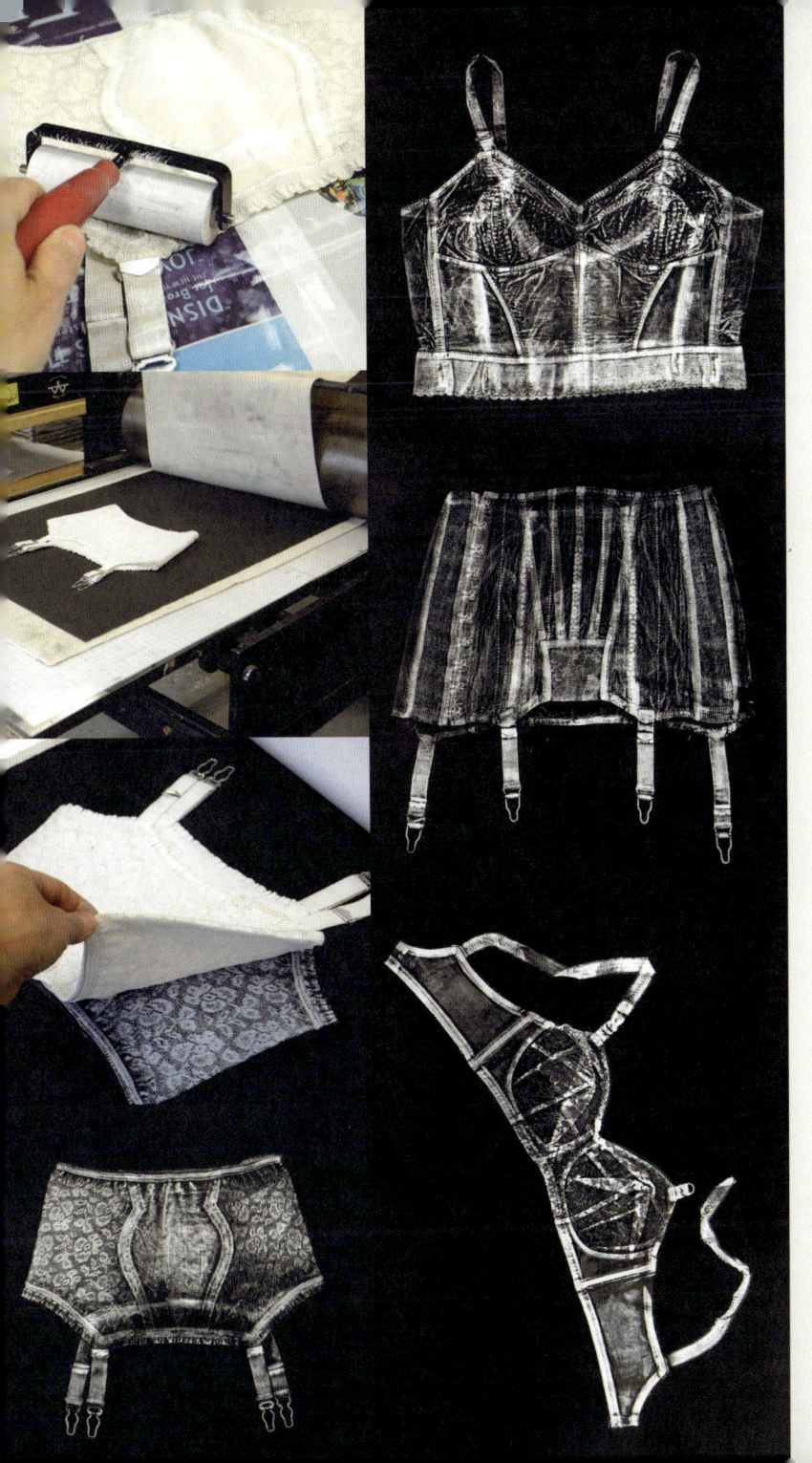

"Once the garment has been put through the process of printing, it is not long before it begins to come apart. The metal hooks bend flat, the metal garter clips cut through the elastic, and the fabric gets oversaturated with ink, losing its texture. At times I am amazed by the workmanship and beauty of these garments and reconsider whether or not to print them. I live with it for a while, hanging in my studio, appreciating this piece of herstory."

ROSE DELER

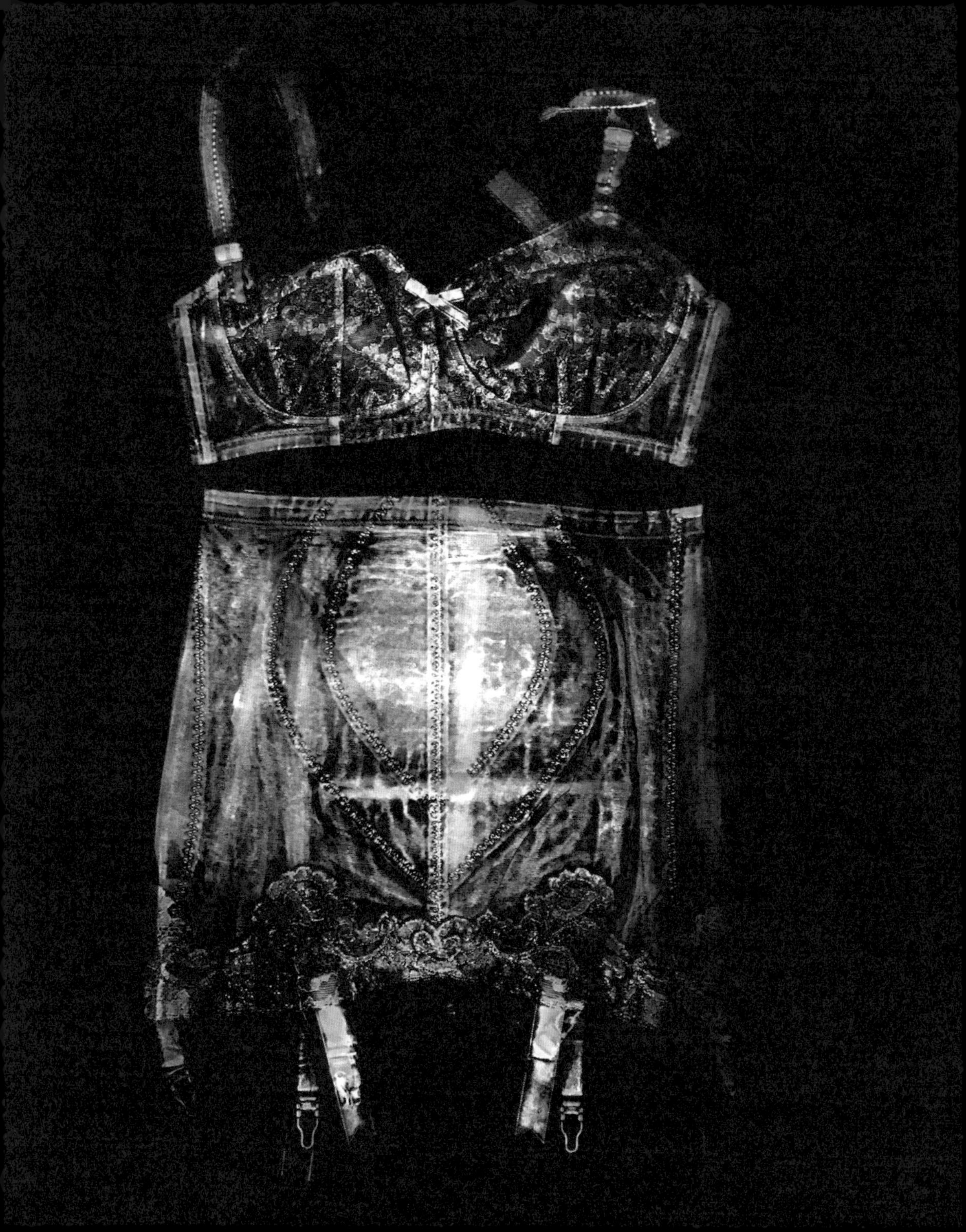

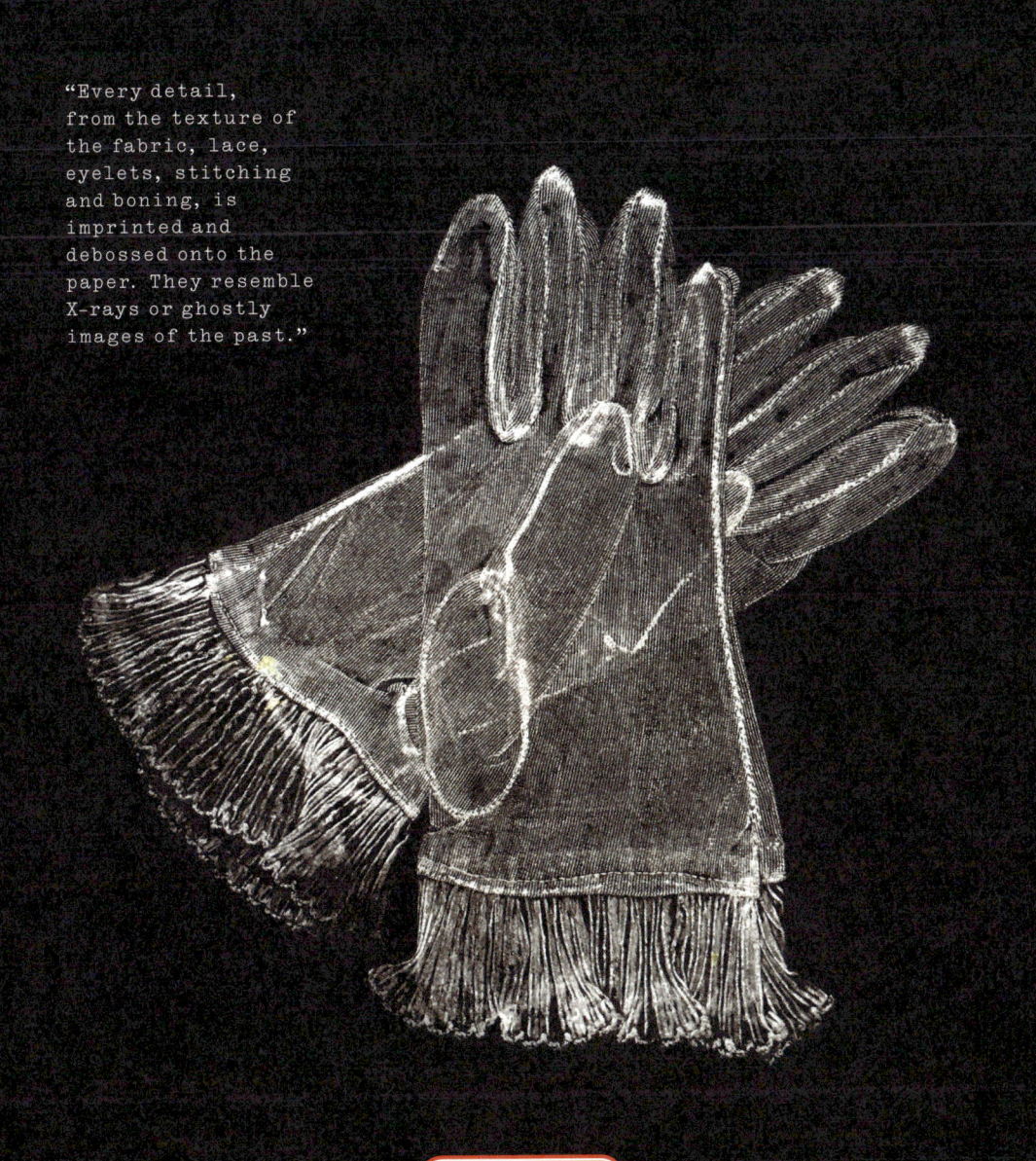

"Every detail, from the texture of the fabric, lace, eyelets, stitching and boning, is imprinted and debossed onto the paper. They resemble X-rays or ghostly images of the past."

rosedeler.com
@rosedeler

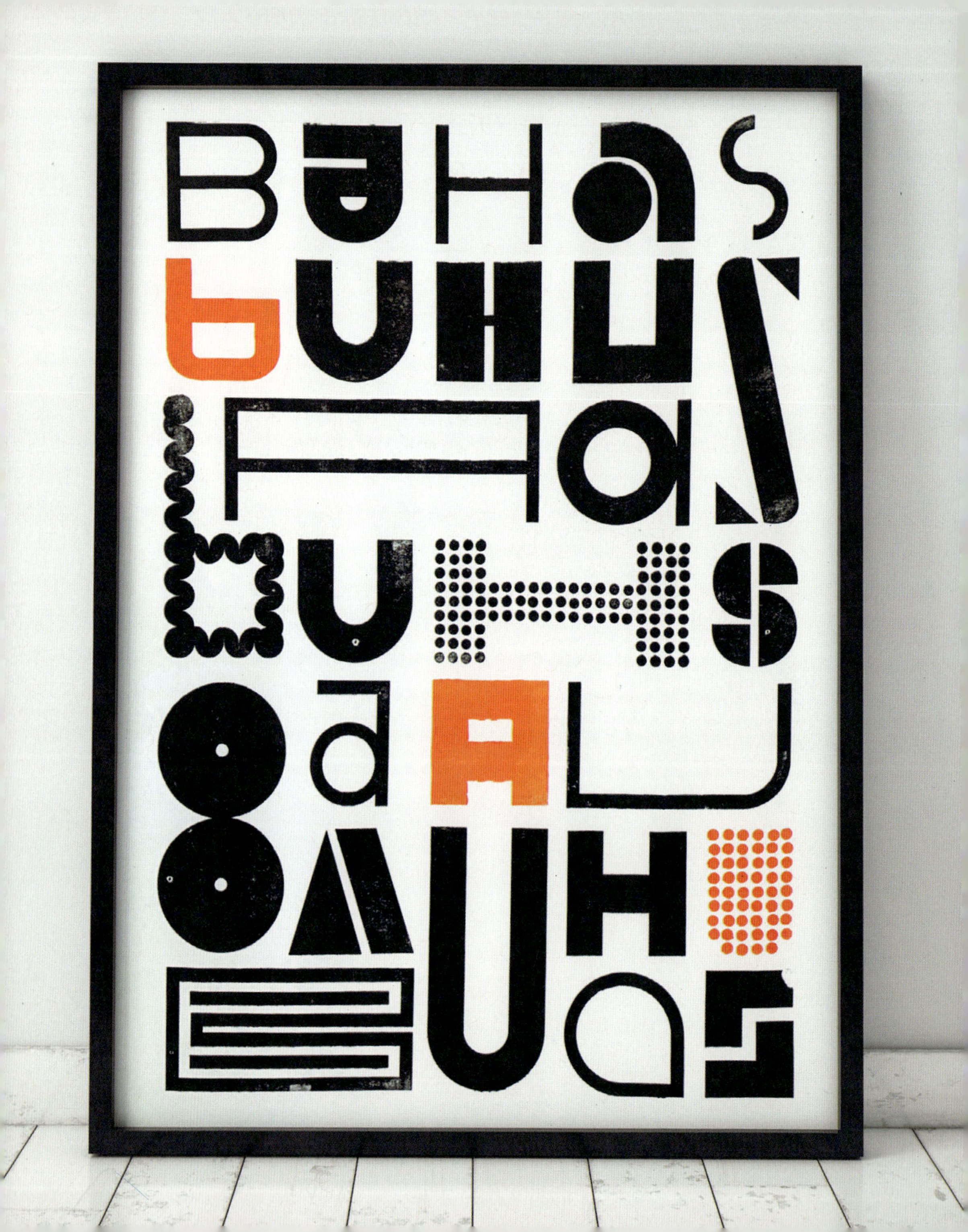

ARTIST · MAKER · CREATOR

New Art History

by

CABARET TYPOGRAPHIE

Cabaret Typographie is a letterpress workshop comprised of members Laura Dal Maso, Mauro De Toffol and Tommaso Pucci, and based in various Italian cities: Arezzo, Milano, Perugia and Venezia. The members share an experimental attitude and passion for typography and the history of art and design.

"We use vintage printing machines mixed with contemporary graphic design," says the trio. To achieve their large format posters, they may combine laser cut elements with traditional wood type. "Although the printing process is exactly the same as years ago, the combined results are very new."

A recent poster series is boldly typographic, playfully interpreting periods in artistic and designerly thought such as the Bauhaus and Fluxus movements.

The designers are careful to only do digitally what cannot be accomplished manually or traditionally. Vintage letterpress printing is interesting and challenging: "You know what you're putting on the machine—but not what the end result will be!" ❉

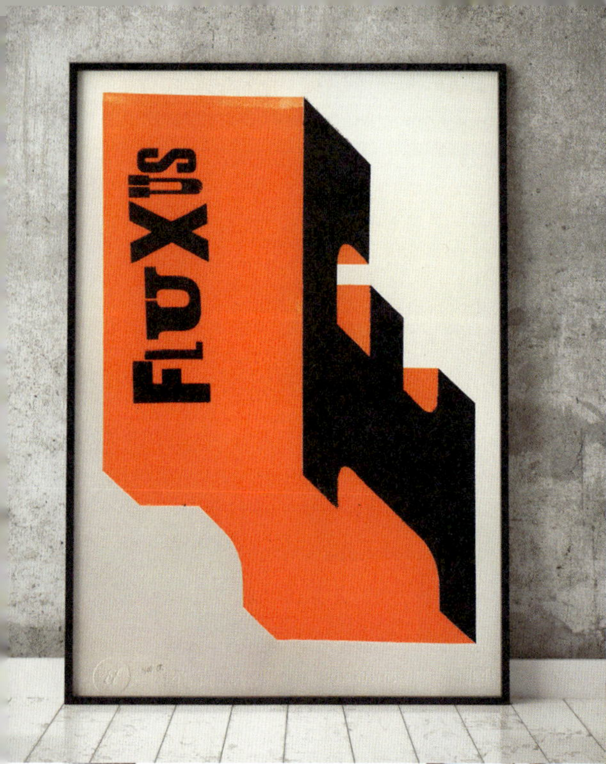
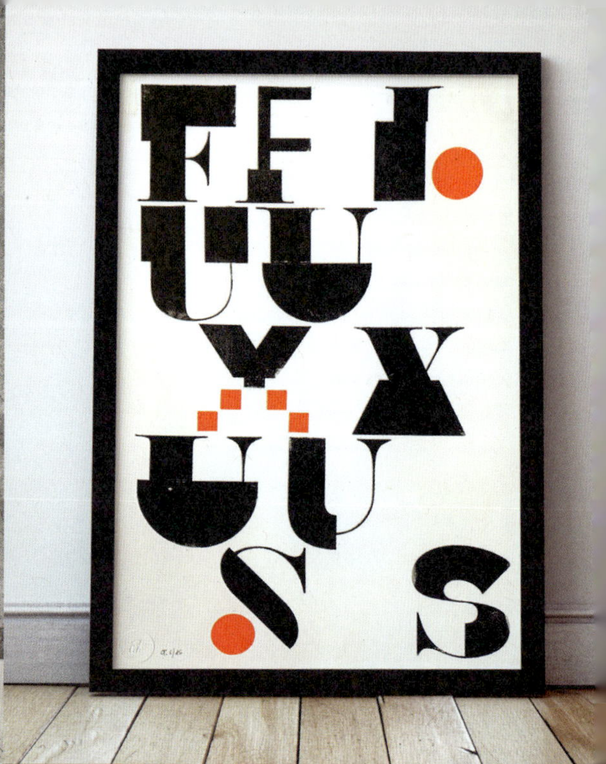
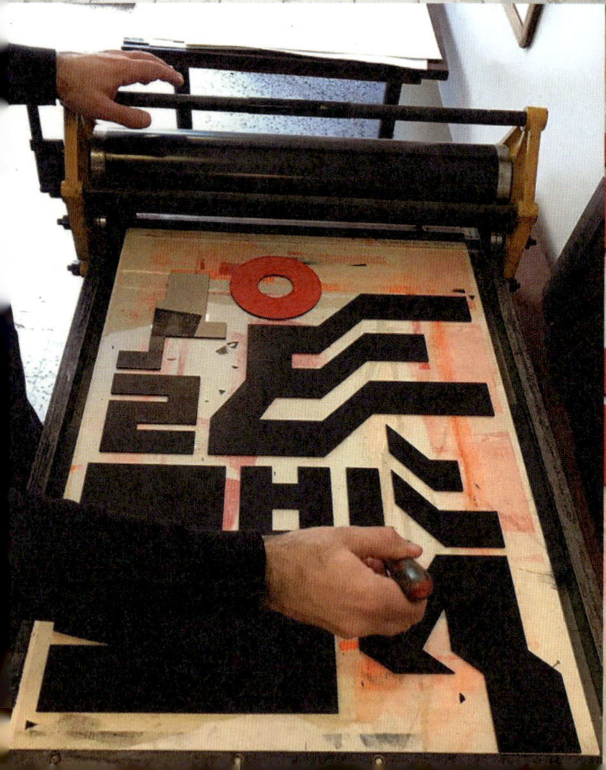
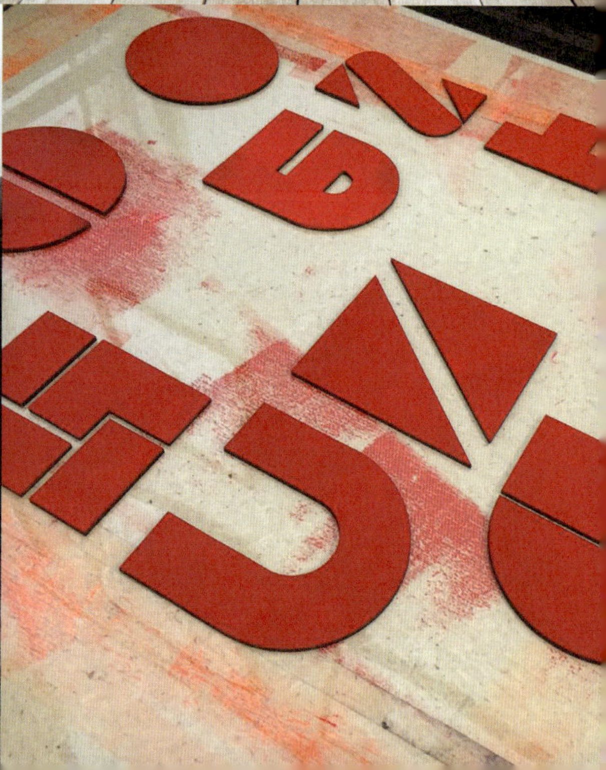

cabarettypographie.tumblr.com
@cabaret_typographie

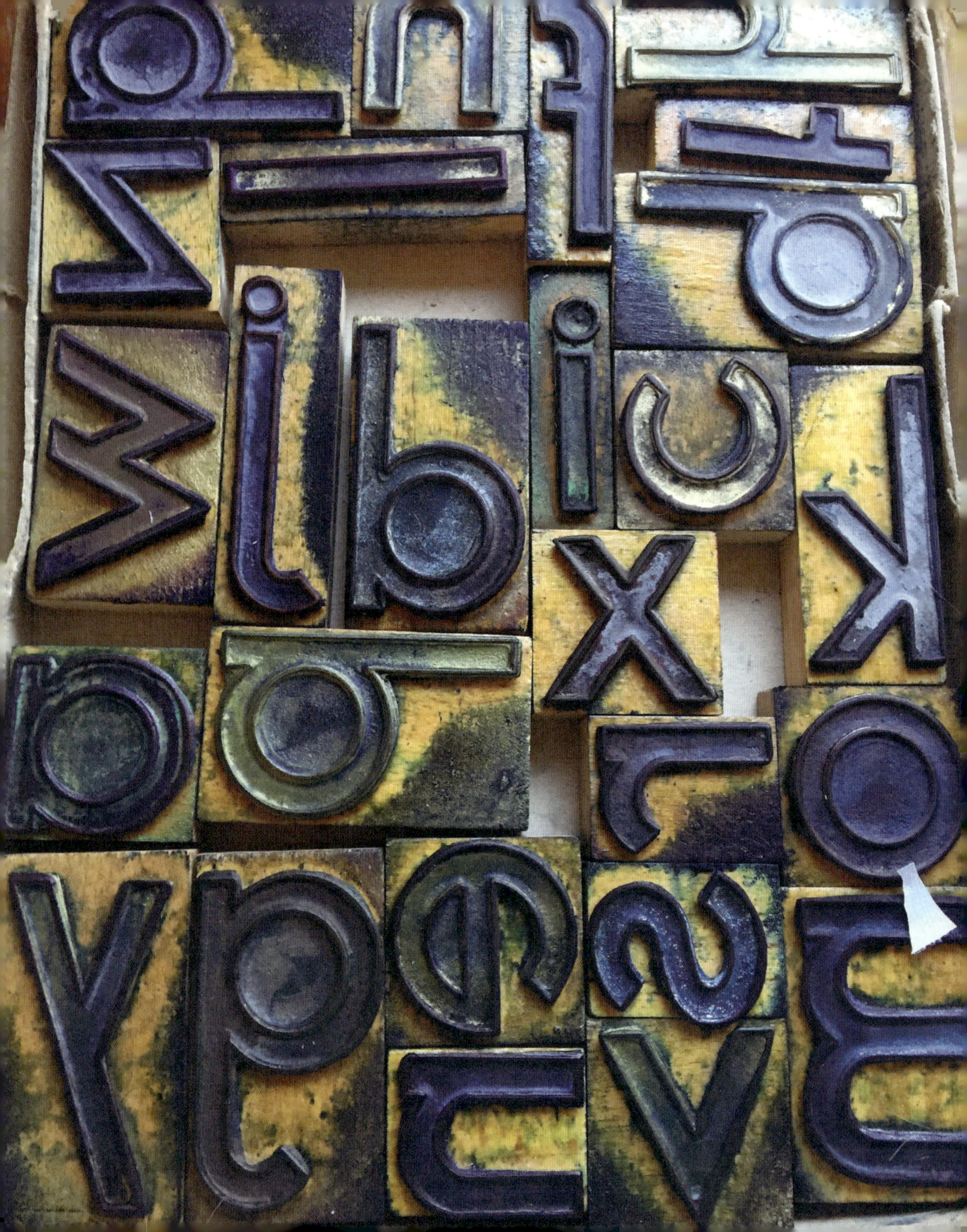

ARTIST · MAKER · CREATOR

Rubber Stamps

by

ILENE KALISH

"I do enjoy using modern stamps, but there is something about the vintage rubber stamp that can't be matched—sometimes it's the image itself that produces a great vintage feel or sometimes it's because the printing impression is much crisper on paper. They are also great for embossing. I enjoy collecting these sets, but even more, I love creating with them: cards, calendars, signage, banners and calendars are all produced regularly from my vintage stock."

Using vintage rubber stamps is a wonderful way to add some vintage flair to stationery projects. Ilene Kalish has just such a collection: "Most are from the United States and France, though I have stamps from around the world, including from the United Kingdom, Portugal, Spain, Australia and Canada. I have thousands of stamps—too many to count; and some are over 100 years old." Many originally came in sets, packaged for either teachers or shopkeepers, with full sets of uppercase and lowercase letters, plus numerals from zero through ten, and then dollar, pound and cent symbols. "I love the different fonts used and also all of the different 'dingbats' used to embellish the signs," she says. "The teacher sets really take you back in time—before the mimeograph or copy machine! My most prized set is called the Classroom Printer, made in Chicago in the 1930s. The set has over 300 stamps, the full alphabet and hundreds of words, and about 40 images—lots of farm animals and everyday objects. The set was designed for teachers to teach words and sentences to young students, and comes in its own special wooden case. Beyond that, I have many other sets: circus images, flowers, trees, transportation, sea creatures, hockey players, wild animals and shapes." ✤

MBRES ÉDUCATIFS
EAN-PIERRE
— PARIS —

ouse   nest

tor   tree

Ii Jj Kk Ll Mm

89 . + × − − $

@ilenekalish

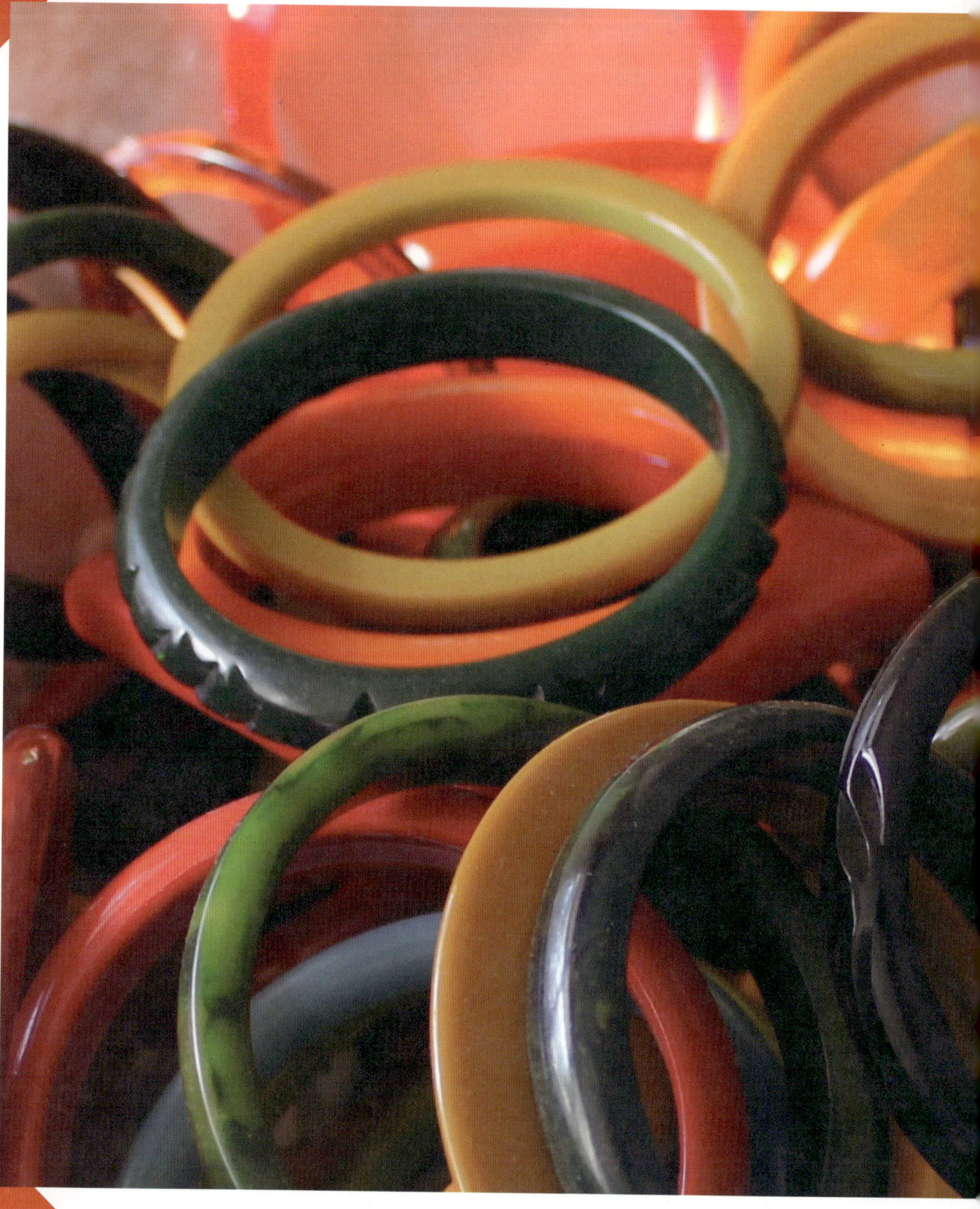

Object obsessions

"These colourful, clickety, bakelite bangles drive me crazy. An armful of them is an embarrassment of riches that I know is lost on most folks and I am probably relogated to the eccentric club. I love stacking interesting combinations of textures and colours for a special day out with friends or datenight. Whether it's the sound they make when they slide together or the tonal hues of another era, I am always looking for the next one at the right price to add to my collection."

— Nancy Gary Ward

artisticlicensefair.com

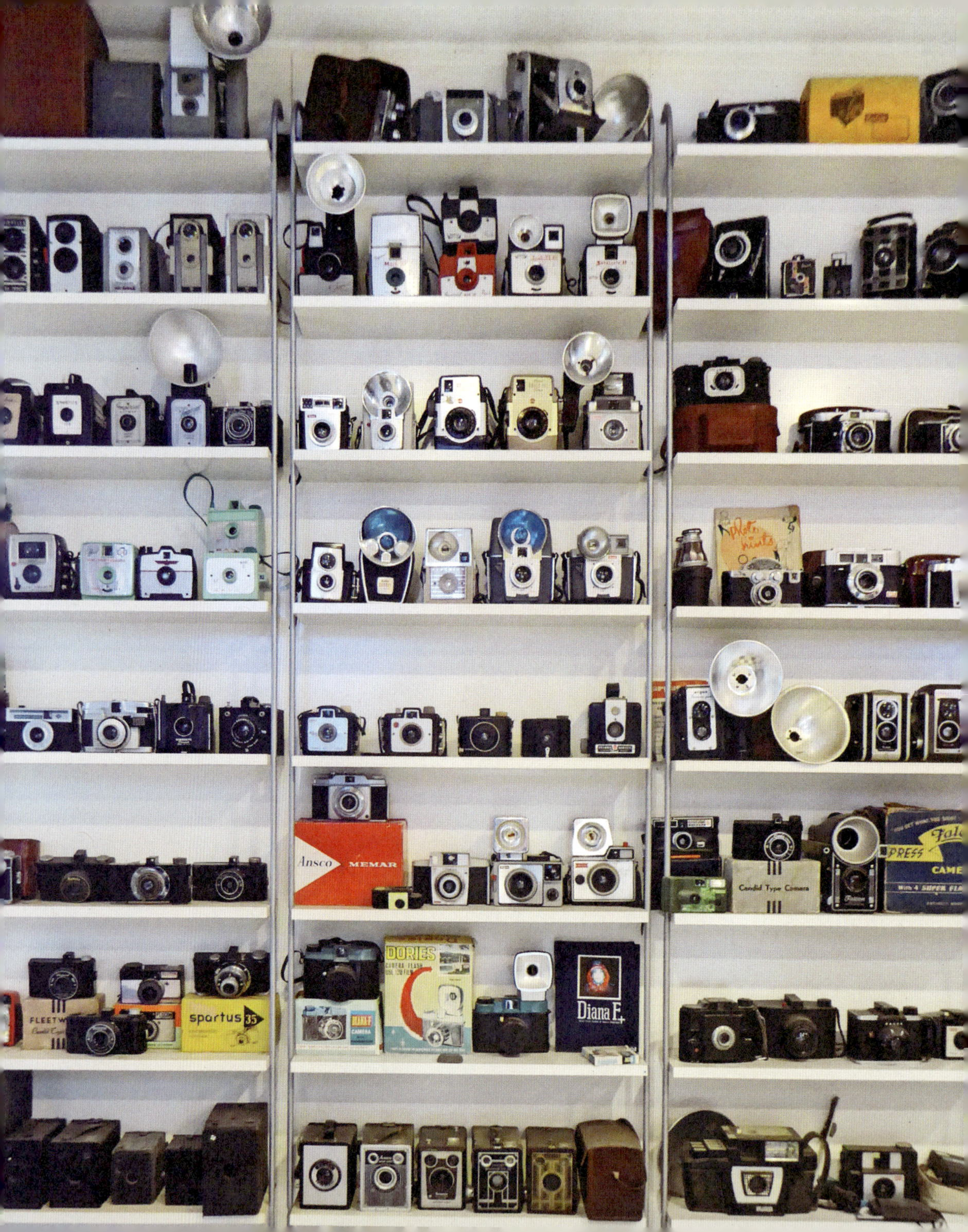
Ansco
MEMAR
DORIES
Diana F+
sportus 35
Candid Type Camera

OBJECT OBSESSION

Cameras

by

EILEEN SCHRAMM

In the late 1970s, while minoring in photography in college, Eileen Schramm began collecting old box and point-and-shoot cameras. "We had our own darkrooms and I could develop and print from all the odd sizes of film these cameras used," she says. "I would only buy ones that worked and were usable so I could experiment. Back then you could pick them up for less than a dollar." Film has disappeared from common use, and darkrooms have become rarer still. Even so, Eileen adds to the collection. "I still add the occasional one if the price is right. I have also received many as gifts, with comments like: This was my father's, I remember it from childhood and I didn't want to throw it away. Now they make me happy when I look at them from my desk or they elicit a gasp from someone seeing them for the first time." ❊

CAMERAS 375

DIE WOHNUN
ΕΛΛΗΝΙΚΗ
ΕΤ. ΕΝ. ΣΥΓΚΟΙΝΩΝΙΩΝ
Ich gratuliere.
EXPOSITION INTERNATIO
DE LA MUSIQU
GENEVE
A. WOLF
Frankfurt a/Main
Schweine-Metzgerei
Vilbelerstr. 18.
Telefon 2481.
AIR EXPRESS
RAILWAY EXPRE
AGENCY
KUNSTSCHAU WIEN 1908
NÄCHST SCHWARZENBERGPLATZ MAI BIS OK
PALAIS DU CINQUANTENAIRE
BRUXELLES
BAYERN
SIMPLICISSIMUS
CHRISTIAN THORSEN
BØRNEKONFEKTION
„PFEIL"
„Glühkörper
unerreicht in Haltbarkeit
und Leuchtkraft.
RE DE
ARIS
Ask
WESTERN

OBJECT OBSESSION

Poster Stamps

by

NIKO COURTELIS

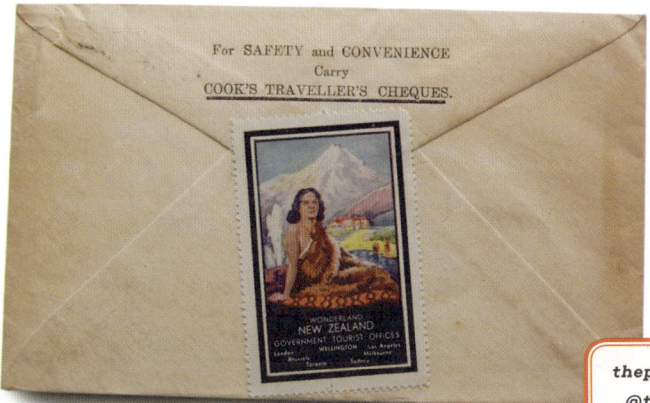

"These small, ephemeral items were often visually stunning examples of the popular art movements of the time. The iconic work of famed designers such as Lucien Bernhard and Alphonse Mucha can be found on poster stamps."

theportlandstampcompany.com
@theportlandstampcompany

Commemorative or promotional in nature, poster stamps are typically larger than average postage stamps but have no postal value. "They are relics, artifacts from another time," says collector Niko Courtelis, a partner at PLAZM design and a founder of PDXCC, the Portland Correspondence Co-op. "These miniature bits of analogue advertising were popular in Europe at the turn of the century. Their appeal, utility and popularity quickly grew, becoming ubiquitous in the United States in the 1920s."

"Not to be confused with postage stamps, poster stamps were used on letterhead and envelopes to promote brands and products, events and destinations," Niko explains. While some poster stamps were printed on low-quality paper, others were produced using sophisticated printing techniques, incorporating metallic inks, embossing and die cutting. The variety of techniques and graphic styles and typography is part of the collectible appeal.

"The subjects deemed important enough to appear on a poster stamp ranged from the sublime to the ridiculous. Some speak to the important innovations of their time: electric lightbulbs, pneumatic tires, air travel, fountain pens. Companies issued stamps as a series, meant to be collected as a set: animals, scenes of the world, folk costumes or ancient coins, for example."

Through another PLAZM venture, artists design and print their own custom pinhole-perforated poster stamps with the Portland Stamp Company. ✣

Heather

Chris DeVillier

Dené Oglesby

OBJECT OBSESSION

Postage Stamps

by

LAURA CAPP

"Vintage stamps are gorgeous miniature artworks, and when you have to select enough of them to equal 55 cents, you amass quite a gallery. Creating a harmonious colour palette that equals the current postage rate (and yet can still fit on a standard envelope) is a satisfying puzzle, and then when you pair such a pretty gallery of stamps with calligraphy it beats a No. 10 envelope with a bill inside every time."

@postscript.press
postscript.press

To receive a handwritten letter, addressed with a pretty stamp, is to receive a gift: the time and attention of the sender. "Handwritten letters are such an extraneous mode of communication these days," says Laura Capp of Postscript Press, a paper and lettering arts boutique located on the main street in Ashland, Nebraska.

"It feels like a luxury both to write and to receive them. So, when I've taken time to write—when I've sat down in concentrated thought and tried to hold complete sentences in my head, start to finish, without the convenience of the delete key and a cursor, it feels like the envelope should take a little extra time as well. Forget ballpoint pen and a standard Forever stamp. A handwritten letter deserves some extra pomp and fanfare, and what better way to put all those vintage stamps still in circulation to good use? What better way to celebrate their beauty, the history of the handwritten letter and our complex and brilliant postal service than to give them their rightful, humble place on an envelope travelling from one heart to another? The mark of cancellation makes them even more beautiful to my eye, and the best compliment I can receive is when someone tells me they couldn't bear to throw the envelope away." ✣

NEW ZEALAND
INDIA POSTAGE
MORAVA
БЕЛАРУСЬ
POSTES
ISRAEL
SVERIGE
CANADA
LATVIJA
DEUTSCHE
DEMOKRATISCHE
ПОЧТА СССР
DEUTSCHE
POST
ESPAÑA
CORREOS
DANMARK
AUSTRALIA
INDIA
LIETUVA

"I design snail mail and decorate my envelopes using vintage stamps. Sometimes I curate by themes, sometimes I select by colours. The vintage feel of these stamps inspires me to create."

—Esméralda Jönsson

@lapaperlover
lapaperlover.com

POSTAGE STAMPS 381

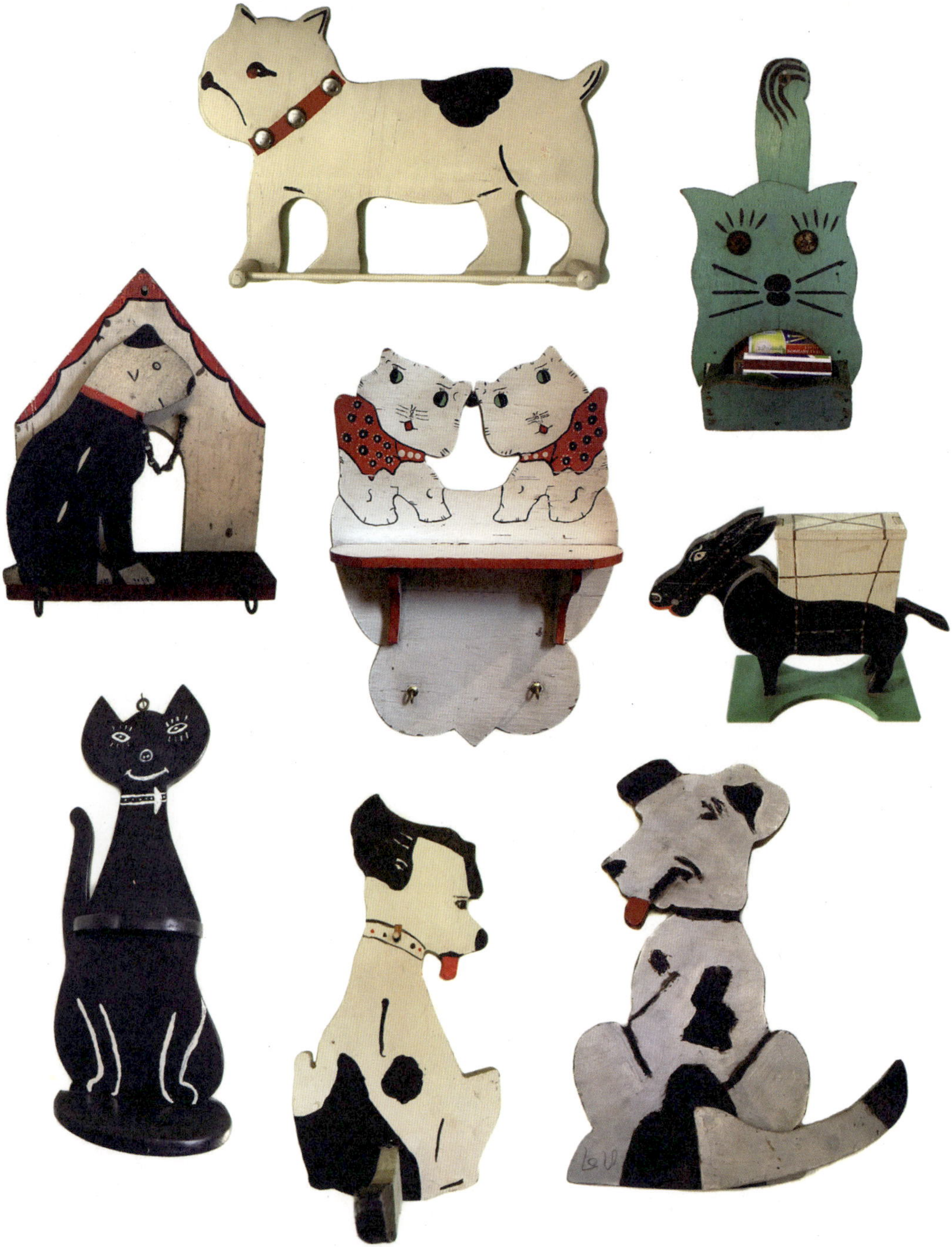

OBJECT OBSESSION

Shop Class Art

by
KRISTIN BICKAL

"If you need to hang up your potholders, you might as well use something delightful to do it!"

thesideshow.net

Kristin Bickal is a retired art director in Minneapolis, Minnesota, currently working as a teacher, designer and printmaker. "I can't quit looking for inspiration everywhere," she says. "I have been acquiring vintage furnishings for use in my home for several decades now, so must limit myself to collecting things that are both useful and interesting to me. These particular objects have both utility and naive charm, harkening to the tradition of outsider art. I'm not sure, but I theorize that they were assigned as projects in high school wood shop classes to train boys (since the girls were likely in home economics) on the use of the bandsaw or jigsaw in the 1930s, '40s and '50s perhaps. Maybe there were patterns in magazines like *Boys' Life*? They tend to be animals, mostly dogs, and are almost always painted in black, cream and red. The expressions are so charming! I love the ones that have moveable parts, like the dog whose tail swings out to form a hook or the very tricky donkey cigarette dispenser—you push the head down and it comes out the back end! Maybe these projects were an American Midwest thing, as that's where all these were found over a span of about 20 years. I don't see them that much anymore, but just found the bookends this weekend!" ✣

A. MAME & Cie TOURS.
MAME & Fils TOURS
MÉGARD & Cie ROUEN
A. MAME & Cie TOURS
FÉNELON

OBJECT OBSESSION

Chocolate Box Bindings

by

SHARON PATTISON

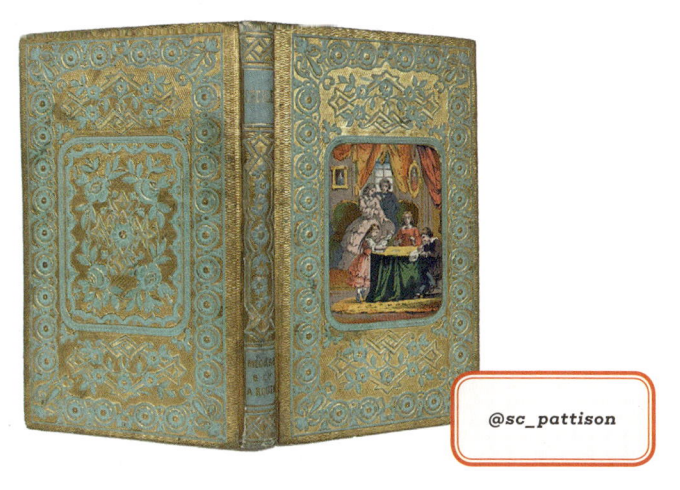

@sc_pattison

These delicious-looking books from France have an equally appealing name: "chocolate box bindings." French speakers with knowledge of bookbinding will know them as "cartonnages romantiques." These books, predominantly with text for children, were mass produced in France between 1840 and 1870.

Sharon Pattison first came across them two decades ago. "About 20 years ago, my husband and I were walking around New York and stopping in at several used bookshops. In one of the stores, I found a 19th-century French-language book with the most charming cover I had ever seen on a book. I don't speak French so couldn't read the book, but I was so taken with the cover that I just wanted to hold it and take it home with me anyway." Taken with the feel of the embossed paper covers, chromolithographs inset in cutout centres, patterns and gilding, she looked for more. "The price was quite reasonable, so I purchased it, and then purchased a couple of others we found in the other shops we visited that day, and thus my collection began."

Examples of books produced by industrialized bookbinding workshops in France with cheaper materials like cardboard and streamlined machine processes, cartonnages romantiques were made in the millions; more equivalent to inexpensive paperbacks of recent decades than high-quality handbound classics. "They are actually quite fragile," describes Sharon. "The embossed paper on the covers is easily damaged, so I am always excited when one of these delicate children's books from over 150 years ago has survived so that I can admire its beauty." ✽

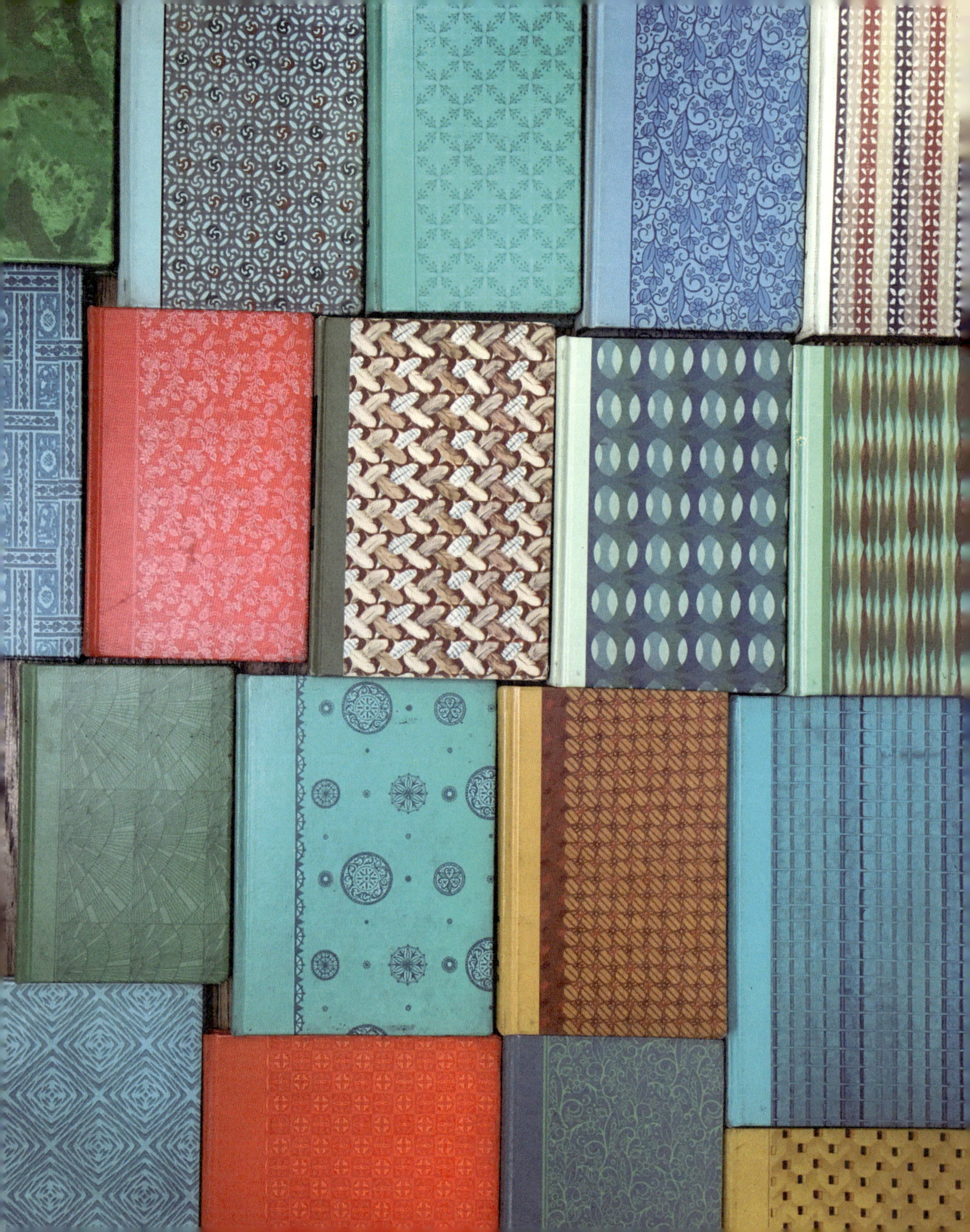

OBJECT OBSESSION

Old Books

by

LORI SIEBERT

@lorisiebertstudio

Old books are appealing for many reasons, not least of which is the pleasure of reading old literature and escaping into other worlds. But as visual creatives (and yes, we admit we judge a book by its cover!) we're sometimes simply smitten with how they look. Artist and designer Lori Siebert (see her paintings featured elsewhere in this book) was strolling through the stacks of her favourite used bookstore when a sliver of pattern caught her eye. "I grabbed this book from the kids' section and fell in love with the pattern and colour on the cover of the 1960-ish cover," she says. "As a graphic designer, I was swooning over the wonderful design. So, I began hunting for more. Each book that I found was wrapped in a pattern that was better than the last. I was totally and utterly obsessed. It was now a mission. While searching, my mind was concocting all of the things I might do with these gems. They have become an incredible source of inspiration. I felt like I won the lottery when I left that day with four huge bags full of these beautiful books." ✻

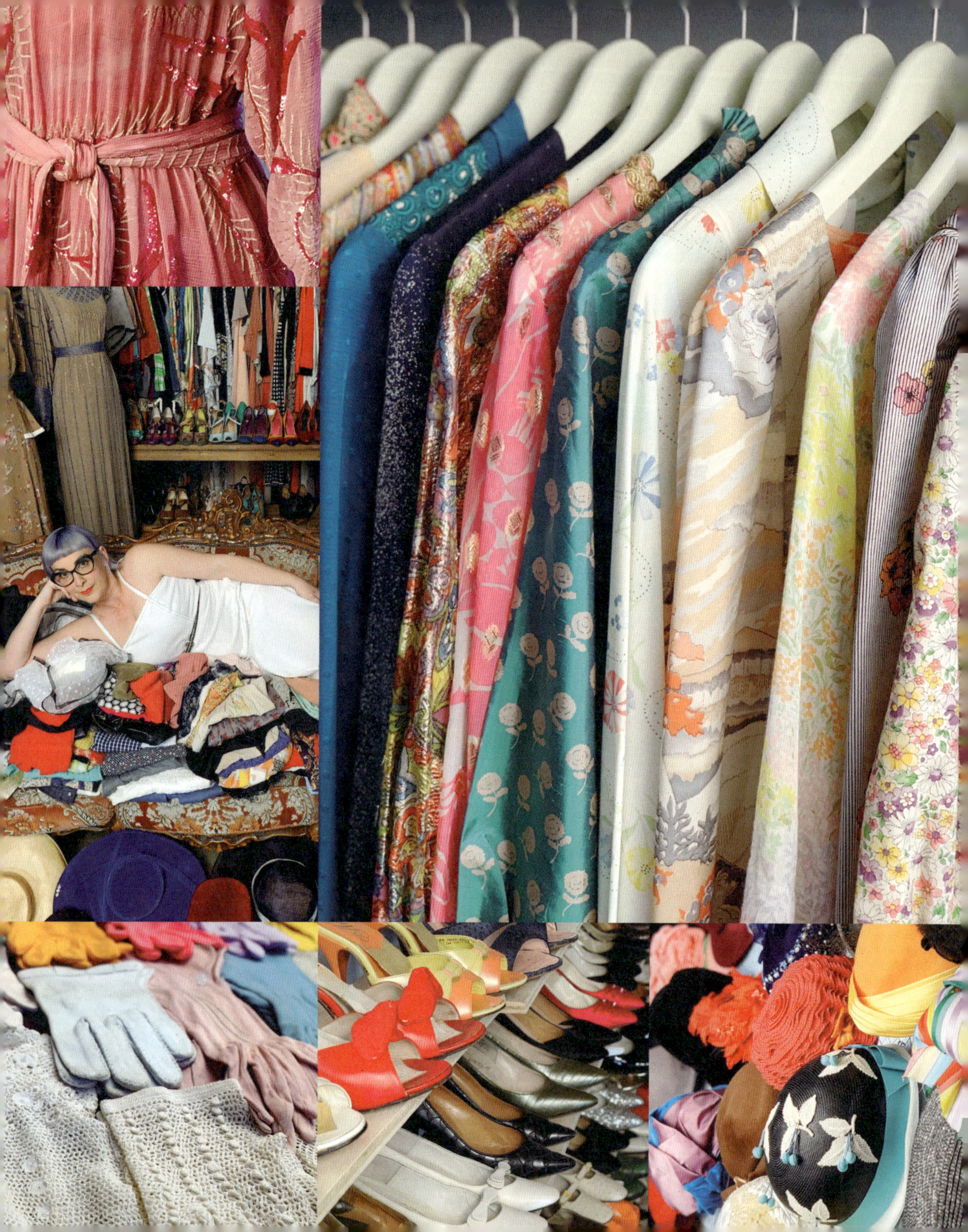

OBJECT OBSESSION

Vintage Clothing

by

KIKI STASH

"I've been a finder of old things my whole life."

stashonyork.com
@stashonyork

Kiki Stash's love for vintage clothing dates back to middle school when she spent the weekends at the Englishtown Flea Market in New Jersey assisting her parents in their menswear booth. Those clothes were new, but as Julia Posey, co-author of the book *111 Places in Los Angeles That You Must Not Miss*, describes, "Kiki was drawn to the vintage wear piled in heaps at the other booths and sold by the bag. Her middle school tastes tended toward psychedelic poly blends, and she still holds a soft spot for that today, but her collection now spans the decades with a rarefied eye that can tell you the rayon fibre in your WWII-era dress was used because silk was reserved for wartime parachutes."

"In college, I was a vintage-wearing art major working as a seamstress at a home goods store," describes Kiki in an interview in *Voyage LA*. "I sewed pillows for hours a day and made my own clothing on the side. After that, I started designing one-of-a-kind collections and working as a stylist, finding more and more vintage along the way."

At Stash on York, her appointment-only shop located in Los Angeles' Highland Park neighbourhood, Kiki can indulge in her passion for vintage fashion with flea market, yard sale and estate sale finds (and she kept her earlier teenage finds, too). With thousands of clothes in her collection spanning the 1920s through the post-1990s, Kiki is a creative director and stylist serving Los Angeles' wardrobe departments, costumers and starlets with clothing available for research, rental and sale. She also designs original couture and reconstructed vintage. ✼

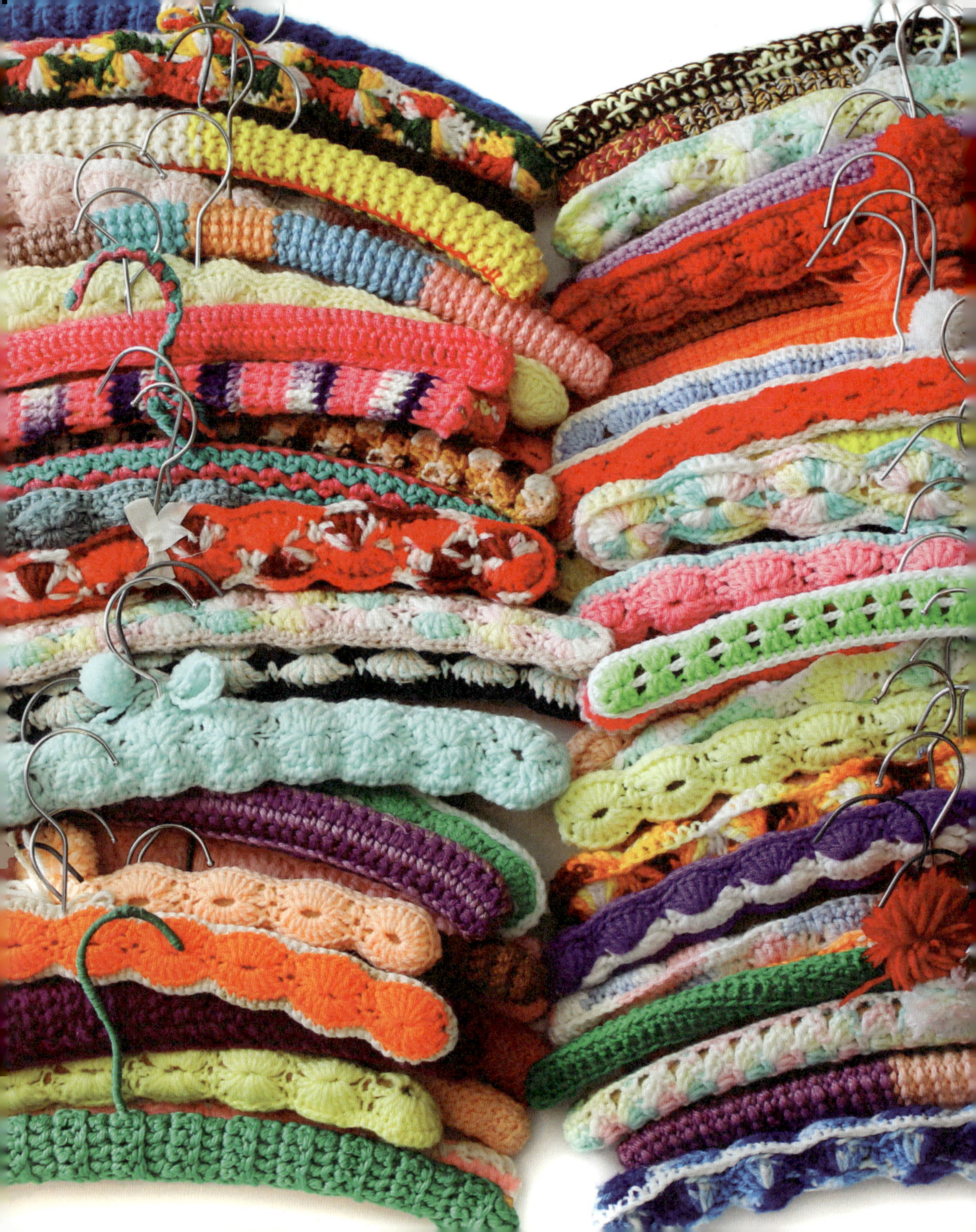

OBJECT OBSESSION

Crochet Hangers

by

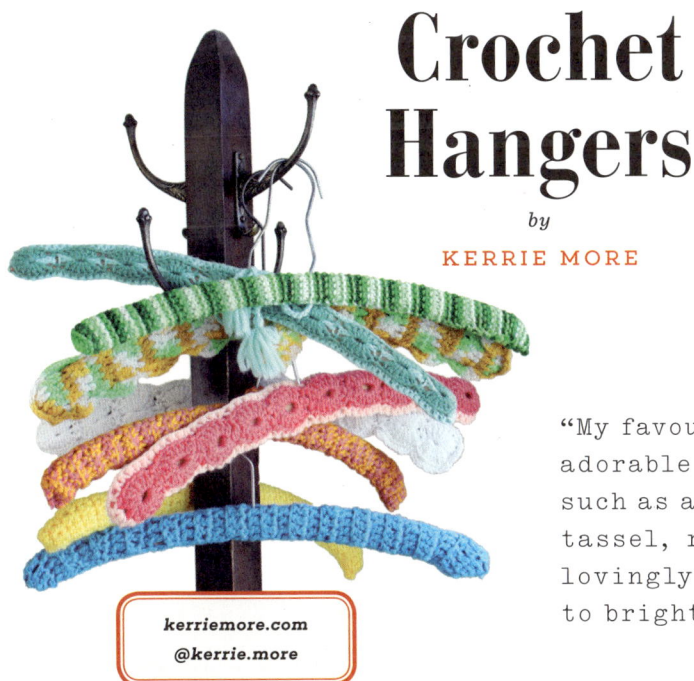

KERRIE MORE

kerriemore.com
@kerrie.more

"My favourites include adorable embellishments such as a pom-pom, bow, tassel, ribbon or flower lovingly chosen by its maker to brighten someone's day."

Kerrie More's great-aunt Helen was a lively character who lived on her own range and raised cattle. "She loved to ride horses—almost as much as she liked to make things!" recalls Kerrie. "One Christmas, I received a package in the mail from her. It contained a sweet collection of brightly coloured crocheted clothes hangers, handmade especially for me." Kerrie kept these cherished hangers, reserved for her most precious garments: prom dresses, graduation gowns and interview suits.

Stumbling upon a stash of crocheted hangers at a thrift store reignited her childhood memories of that earlier gift. "I started to pay attention and these vintage treasures seemed to find me. Over time, these one-of-a-kind treasures have transformed my closet into a cozy rainbow. Most are crocheted, some are knitted, many use soft, puffy yarn, while a few are stitched with thin, lacy thread. Their fun, funky hues, sometimes in unexpected combinations, evoke an earlier time."

"My vintage obsession is inherently practical, and almost every item in my closet has its own unique hanger. More often than not, I carefully select one to complement the garment it will hold. In doing so, I can't help but imagine the grandmother, mother, friend or aunt who chose the pattern and thoughtfully selected the perfect yarn to stitch it for a loved one. Without a doubt, my affinity for these colourful pieces of history is rooted in the joy of receiving that special gift from my aunt Helen so many years ago—and while my closet is full, there will always be room for one more." ✻

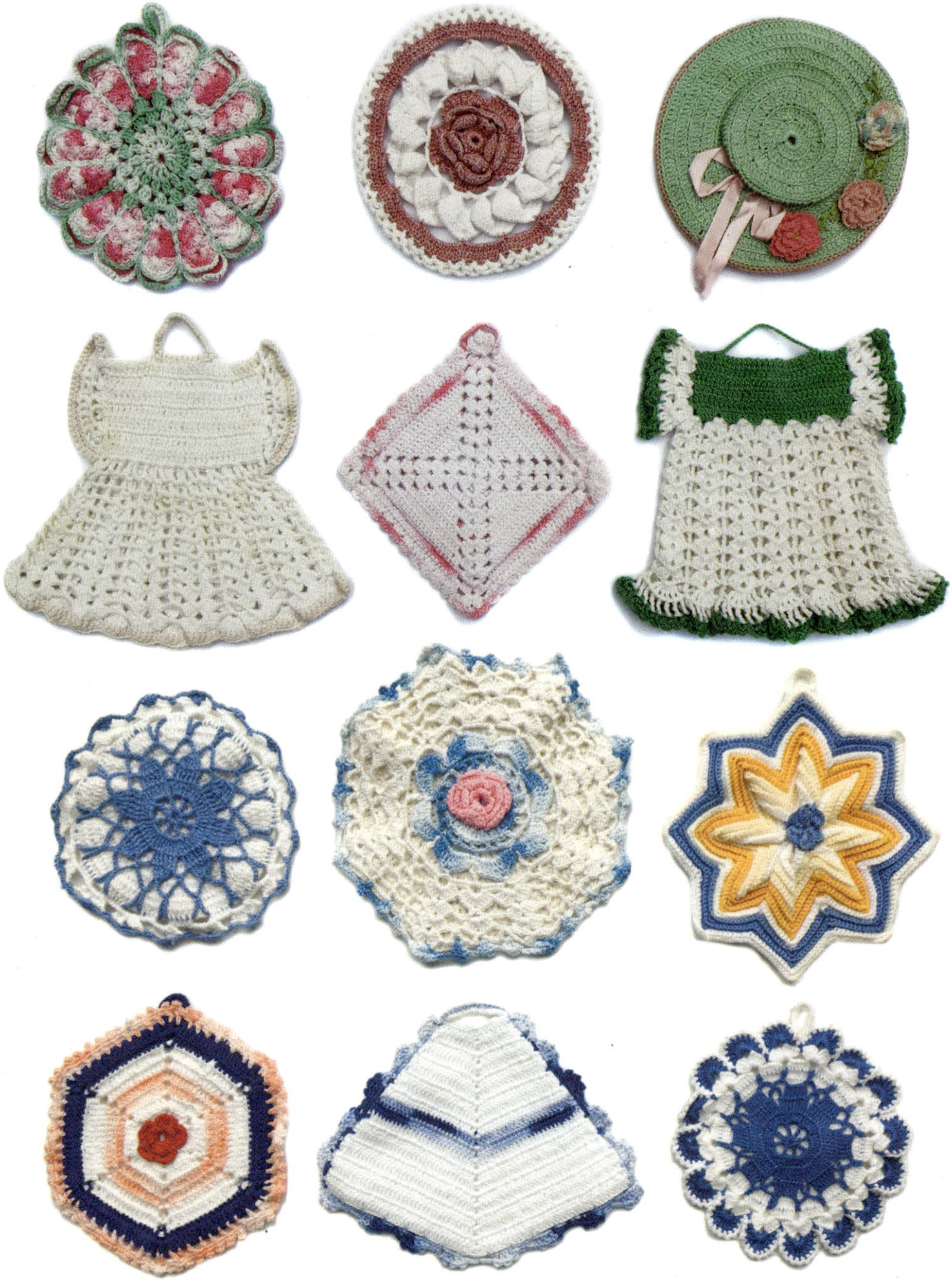

OBJECT OBSESSION

Crochet Potholders

by

NANCY MYERS

patchworkbreeze.blogspot.com
@patchworkbreeze

Crocheting a quick doily with leftover yarn from a sweater or afghan was a satisfying craft to do at the end of a long day of housework. "My paternal grandmother crocheted so many things in her life," says Nancy Myers. "But it was her crocheted doily hot pads in our family kitchen that I remember." After her grandmother passed away, eight-year-old Nancy received her grandmother's coveted crocheted dress-shaped hot pads. "Those hot pads travelled with me to college, when I moved for my first job and to my home as a newlywed." She has been actively collecting these doilies for a decade now. "I enjoy perusing vintage resale shops as I try to find more unique designs in good condition. And if I ever find a purple grape trivet crocheted over soda bottle caps, I will most definitely buy it because Grandma was famous for crocheting these!" ✽

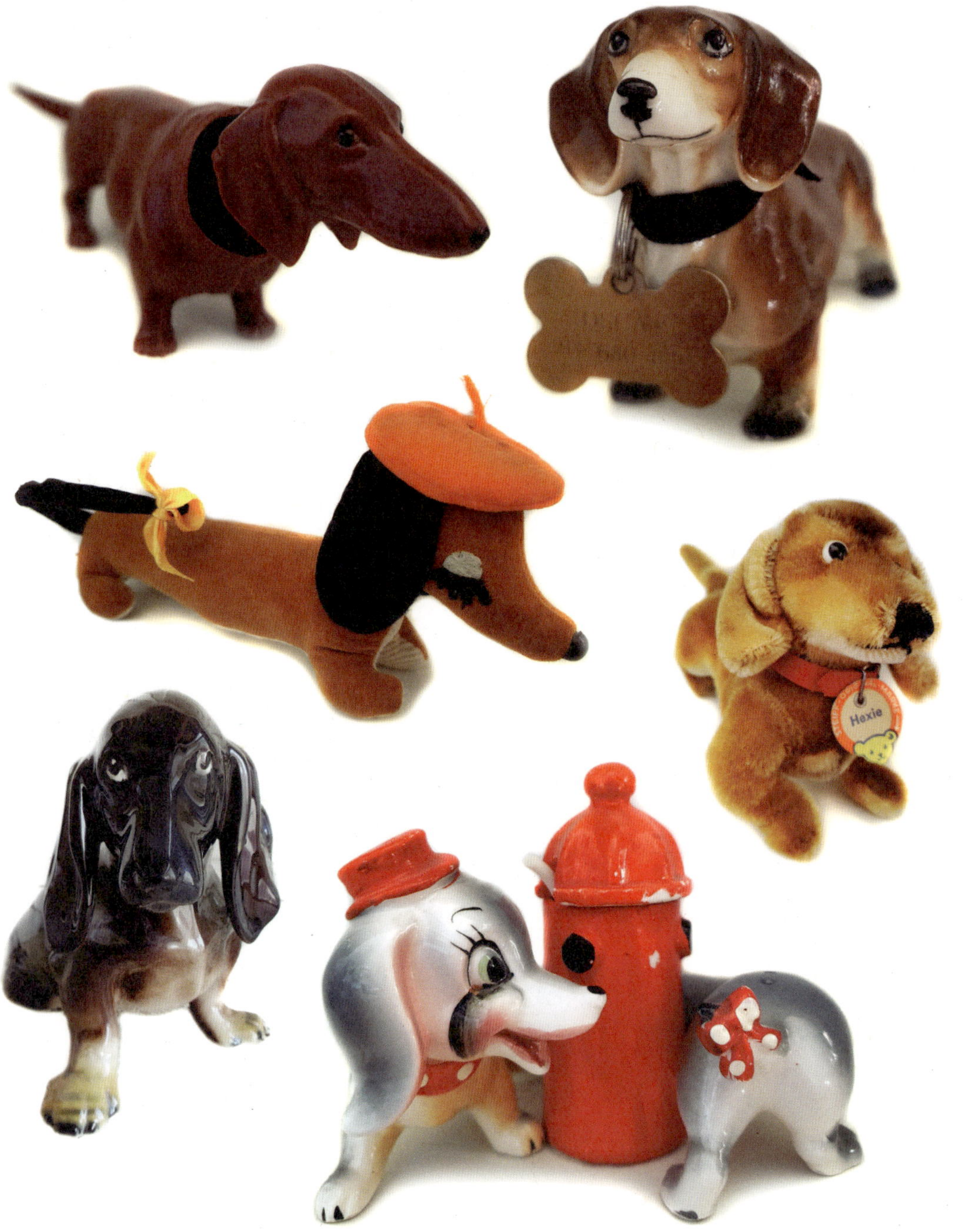
Hexie

OBJECT OBSESSION

Dachshunds!

by
JOANNA JEROME

@vintagebaby63

Very often, a collection starts with love. Love for a particular person, place or thing can extend to appreciation for objects that represent or evoke that special someone. For Joanna Jerome, her vintage obsession emerged from a love of all things dachshunds.

"I have had three doxies. Oscar, my first dachshund, lived to be 13 and I miss him every day. Jimmy Dean and Owen are my two boys and they are four years old. The joy they have brought to my life is immeasurable." Some eight years ago, Joanna began frequenting estate sales and started collecting figurines. "My collection has grown and continues to grow every time I see one that I don't have yet. Especially red ones, since they remind me so much of my dogs. I have now included other types of objects in my collection, anything that is a doxie or has a doxie on it or a doxie illustration in it. Books, toys, brooches, postcards, paint by numbers or art, anything is possible. I'm always on the hunt for more. These funny little fellows full of personality keep me on my toes, always! What better way to honour my love of the breed." ✽

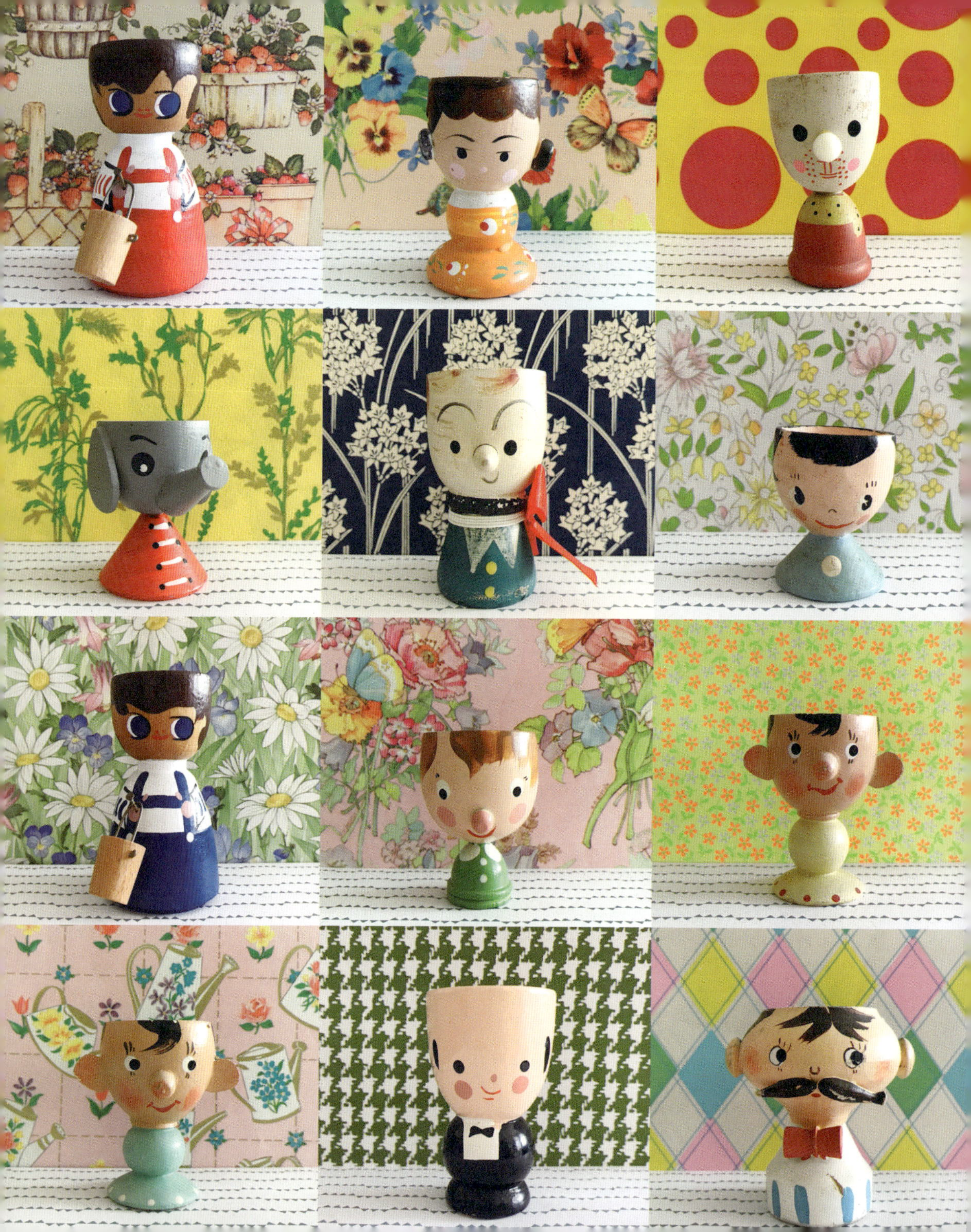

OBJECT OBSESSION

Anthropomorphic Egg Cups

by
SANDY MACHADO

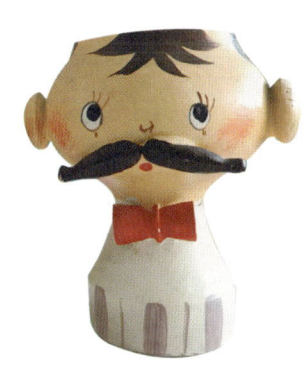

The simplest things can bring such pleasure! "Marie Kondo would probably disagree, but this collection brings me so much joy!" says collector and vintage paper ephemera seller Sandy Machado. "I have over 125 anthropomorphic wooden egg cups."

Why egg cups? "I love the texture, the faces and the character each little one has. I love that this little tool helped folks enjoy their breakfast meal and still are used to this day."

Sandy has taken their charm up a notch by photographing portraits of each little character against a background of vintage gift wrap. The contrasting patterns, motifs and colours add to their appeal. "I photographed them a few years ago for a Tumblr blog because I had intended on making a coffee table book but never got around to it." The little fellas have travelled, though: "They've been to Antiques Roadshow to be appraised! They loved the collection. So many of them are at least over 50 to 100 years old." ❖

eggcupsdoneup.tumblr.com
@bblvintage

EGG CUPS   397

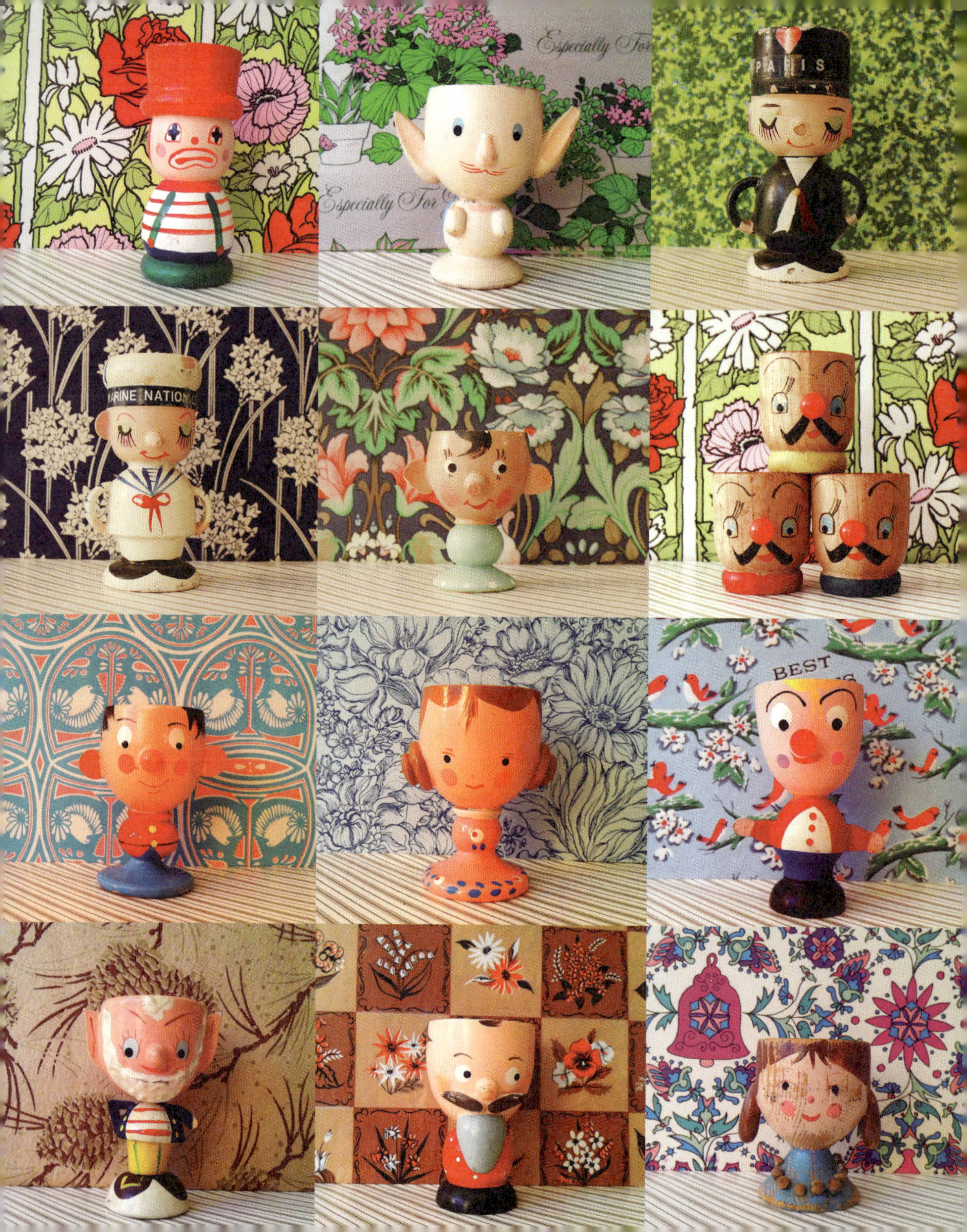
Especially For
Especially For
PARIS
BEST

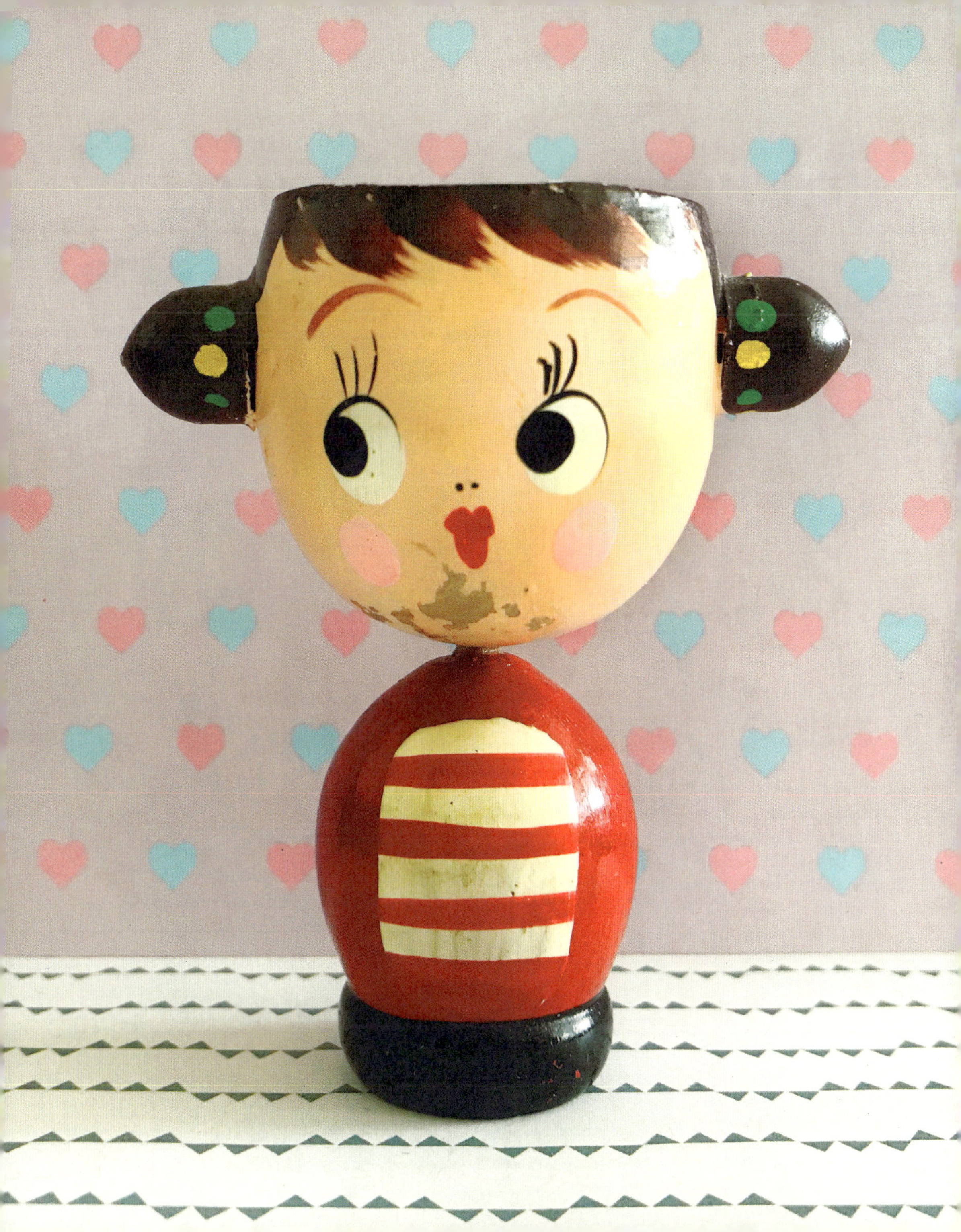

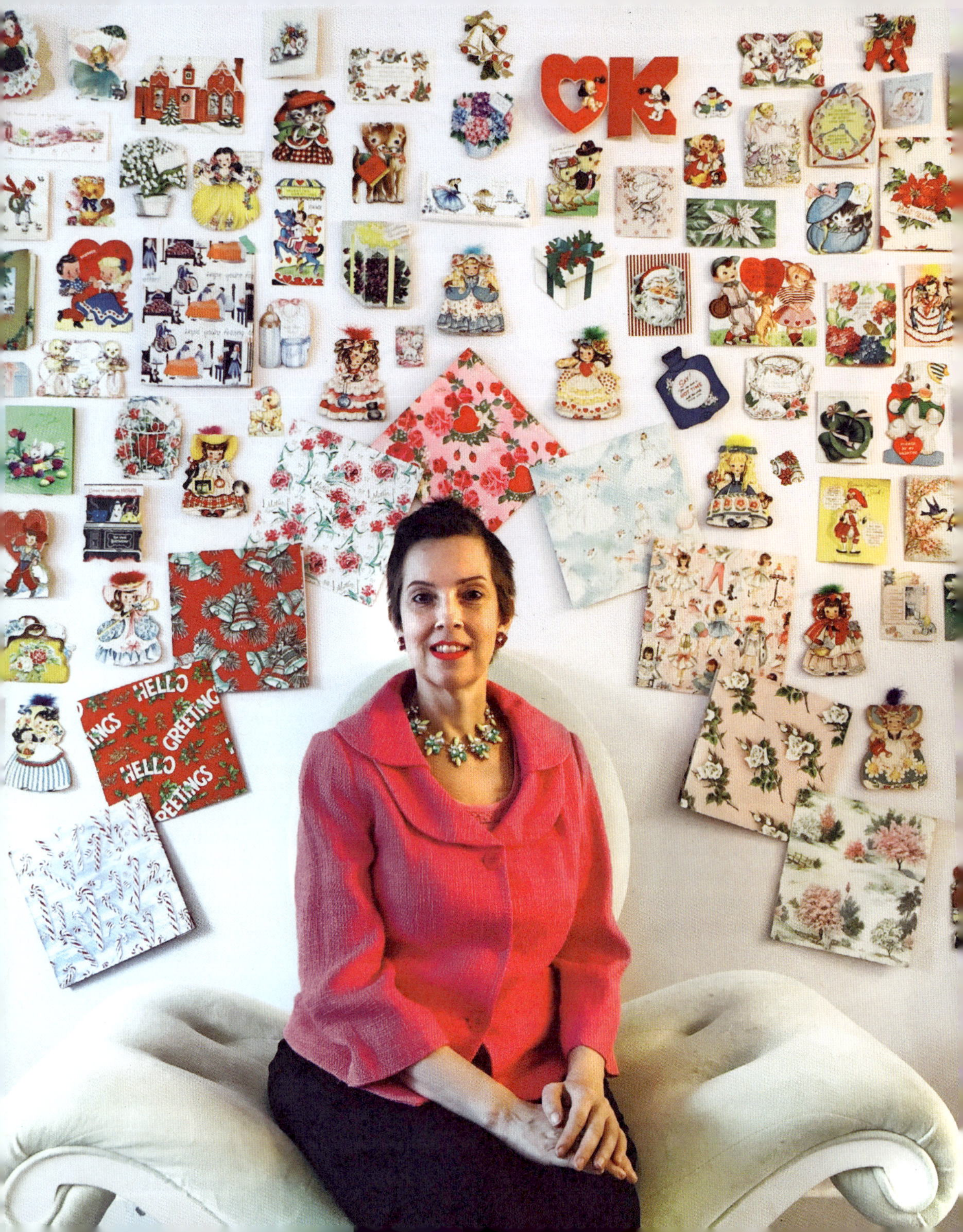
OK
HELLO
GREETINGS

OBJECT OBSESSION

Greetings & Gift Wrap

by

LISA ANDRADE

"I have always loved the beautiful illustrations, colourful designs and the decorative elements of mid-century gift items."

Decades ago, marking special occasions by sending a greeting card or wrapping a personal gift in decorative wrap was common politesse. "Growing up, my parents had a number of cards and items from the 1950s and 1960s that they had kept, and I was immediately drawn to the graphics and designs. Foils, glitter, satins, flocking and cut-out details were often used by manufacturers to make greeting cards that were really special," describes vintage gift stationery enthusiast Lisa Andrade. "Greeting cards were an important way for people at the time to send celebration messages and to show you were thinking of someone. This was an era when there was no Internet and long-distance calls were expensive and not commonplace. Greeting cards were treasured and often kept in scrapbooks or special boxes."

"Wrapping paper at this time also had colourful and fun designs, which reflected the optimism of the time. So many different designs were used then—like candles, bells and birthday cakes—that you don't see anymore on gift wrap. These items reflect an era of growing prosperity and optimism, when giving a gift or taking the time to share a greeting was an important thing."

Collecting these items is a nostalgic practice but a happy one; Lisa admires the creativity and beauty of these old illustrations. "Each is really a work of art and they bring joy to my eye! On a personal level, they remind me of my parents and older relatives and a period when things seemed simpler." ❉

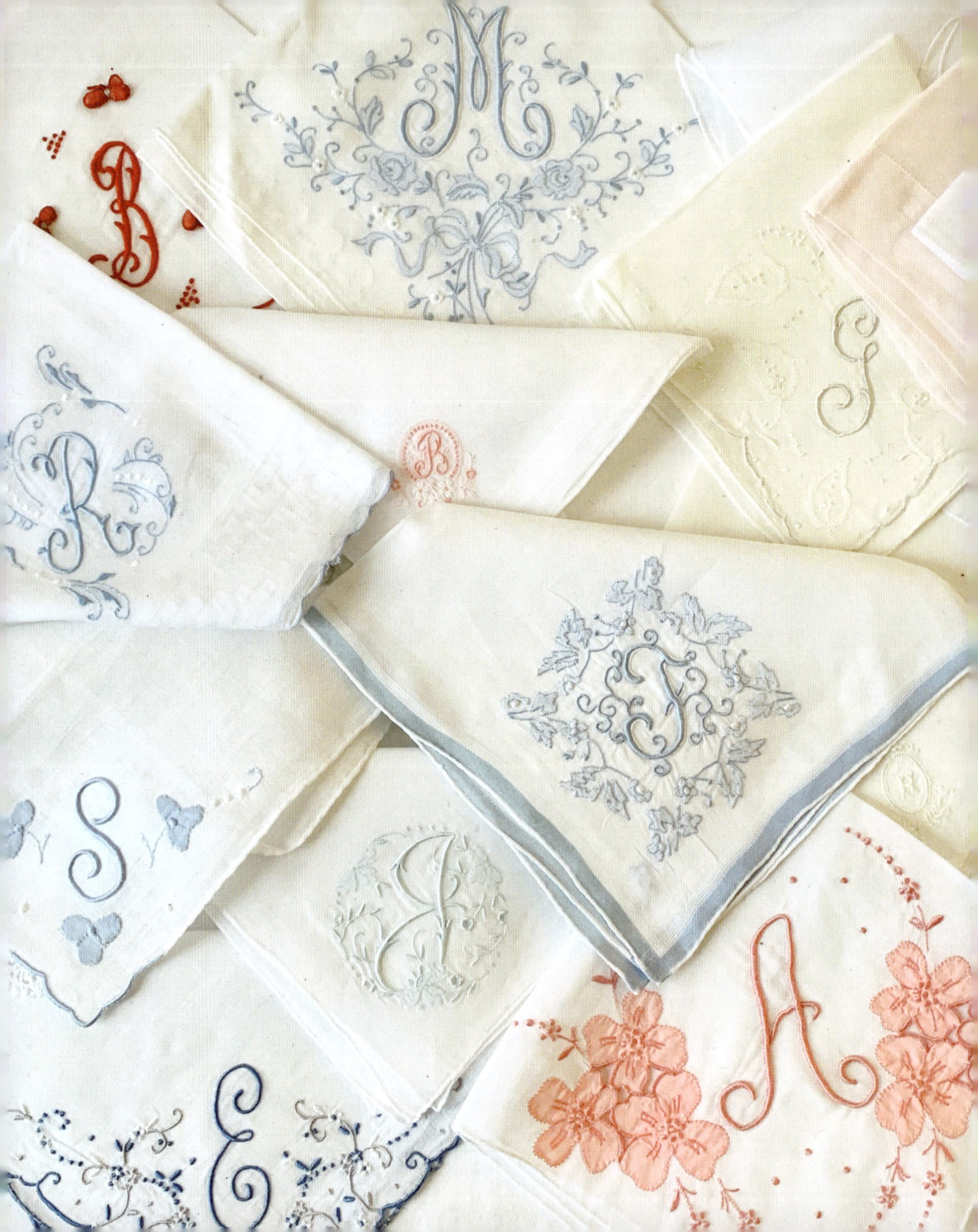

OBJECT OBSESSION

Handkerchiefs

by

BARB BROWN

Barb Brown first started collecting in the days when her young daughter was going to ballet class—browsing the nearby antique shop was a pleasant way to pass the time. In discovering vintage textiles, she says, "I immediately felt a sense of history and connection to those who owned them that energized and inspired me. Soon, uncovering vintage textiles and sewing notions—cuddly chenille bedspreads, textural barkcloth curtains, mother of pearl buttons and anything embroidered—became my driving force." One might assume that shopping for old blankets and hankies is a calm and soothing affair, but not so for those in pursuit of a great find! "I am ashamed to say," Barb confesses, "that once I nearly knocked an elderly woman out of the way at a rummage sale to get my hands on a stunning turkey red tablecloth!"

"Soon my little ballerina grew up and moved out," she says. It was time to downsize to an apartment, so she had some choices to make. "One of my earliest and lasting crushes is also one of the simplest: the vintage handkerchief. As light as a feather and generally sized at a petite 10 inches, my handkerchief collection stores easily and is very apartment friendly."

It's an easy collection to maintain. "And, I love to iron! The scent of spray starch and a hot iron throws me back to my childhood when I was kept busy in our home's 'ironing room,' ensuring my father's hankies were laundered just right. My tastes have expanded from those simple crisp white hankies to include stunning Madeira embroidered monograms, Irish linen, and delicate lace-edged and tatted fancies, as well as matching floral sets." ✻

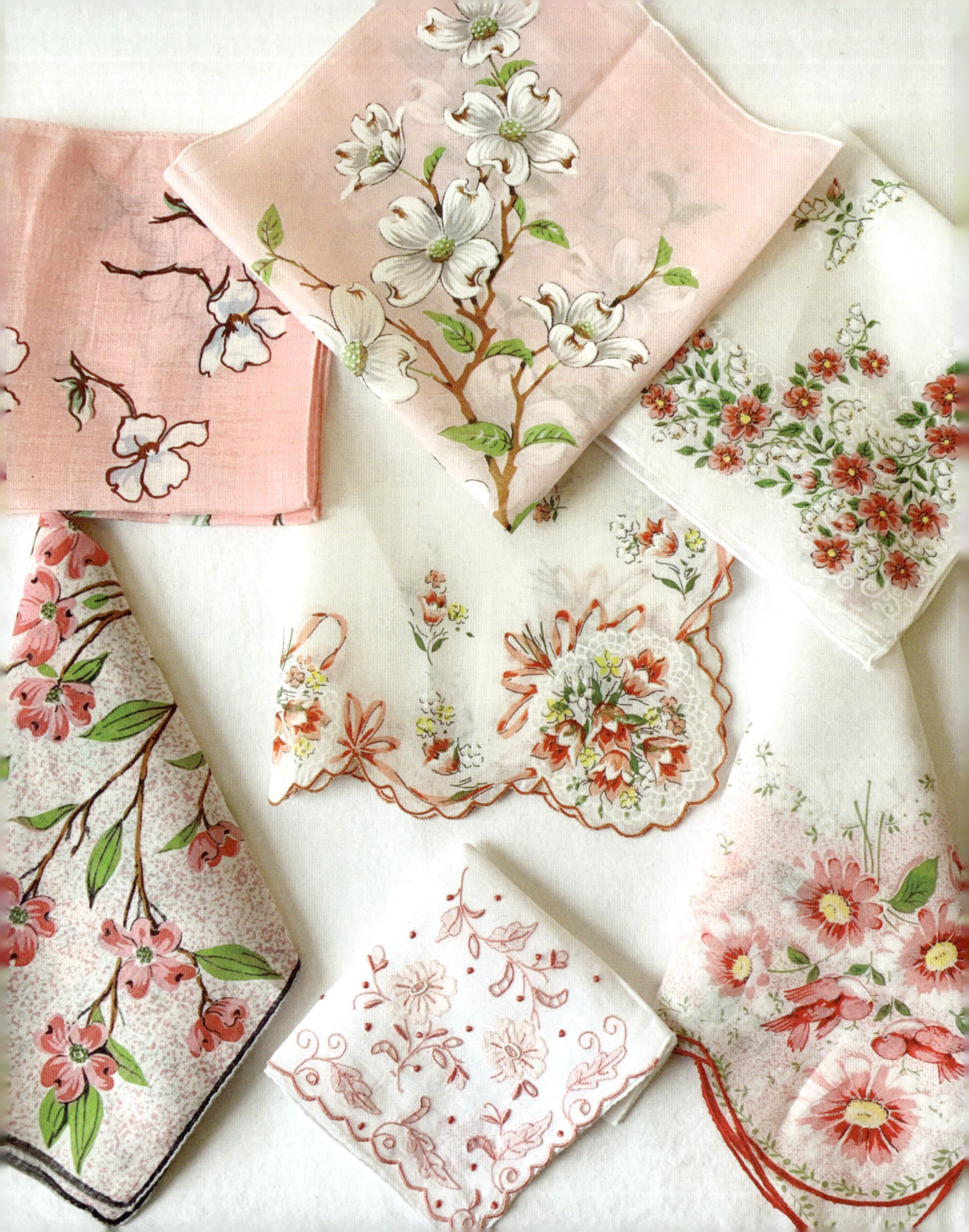

thevintagethread.wordpress.com
@thevintagethread

"I don't worry if the hankies are not perfect, as these cutters can be used to embellish and elevate a crafty home project as simple as a sachet or as lasting as a pillow in memory of a loved one."

CITY TAVERN
BLAZERS
THE DEVIL IN DESIGN
CREATIVE CURSING
CLASSIC AMERICAN QUILTS

OBJECT OBSESSION

Sewing Stuff

by

ERIKA MULVENNA

The ability to sew is often a skill passed on in families. For Erika Mulvenna, sewing runs in the family: "From my grandmother who sewed to 'make do and mend' to my mother who stitched clothes and toys for me as a child. I learned to use my mother's sewing machine at a young age and instantly fell in love with the entire process of sewing! I eventually earned a BFA, majoring in the fibre arts, and began collecting old sewing stuff during my college years."

Over the decades, Erika has gathered a collection of vintage sewing "stuff," including "everything from sewing tools to notions like needles, pins and tools." She collects irons, patterns, notions, tools, fabrics, sewing machines and more—lugging her growing collection across the state of Illinois. "Now that I've settled in our forever house, located in Chicago, my collection is lovingly displayed in my home studio."

"Some of my favourites include an old wire dress form that unsnaps to fit your body, a few toy sewing machines, old needle books, sewing books and notions. The old iron collection fits perfectly in the built-in shelves! The irons span over a century, from early 1800s flat irons to early turn-of-the-century electric models, and sleek 1930s to 1940s modern models."

"I'm constantly inspired by all of these vintage objects, which are a daily inspiration and reminder of the centuries-old tradition of women's craftiness, thriftiness and creativity in the art of home sewing." ✶

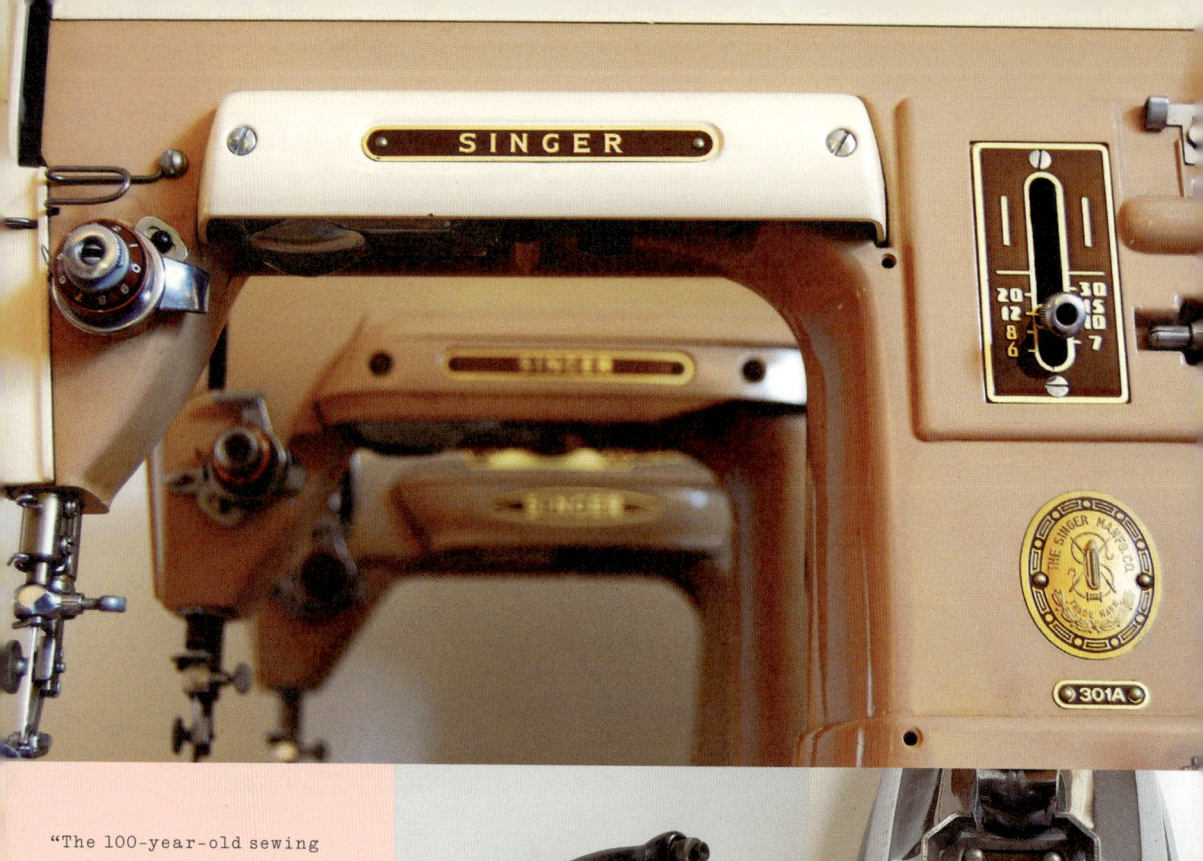

"The 100-year-old sewing machine on the bottom of my corner bookshelf belonged to an extended family member. It's well worn but still works. Another machine I hand-painted was saved from the landfill and survived a fire, and still sews like a dream."

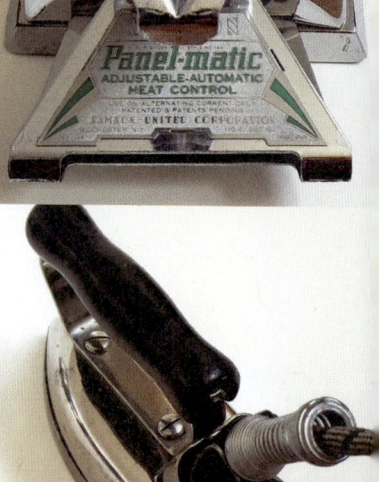

sewsitall.blogspot.com
@erika.mulvenna

"I love vintage picnic tins. Perfect for storage, I use loads of them for just that in my studio."

OBJECT OBSESSION

Picnic Tins

by

SUSAN BORGEN

tpartyantiques.com
@tpartyantiques

In Susan Borgen's vintage-decorated studio in Norwalk, Connecticut, every day is a picnic thanks to her medley of mid-century metal picnic tins. Featuring lithographed faux patterns, some look like they're woven and others have pretty plaid or florals. "My favourite one sports nursery rhyme characters, oak handles and a realistic basketweave pattern," she says.

The vaulted ceiling allows space for a 12-foot-long display shelf, the perfect spot for her collection. "I love the way these relics look when grouped together, forming a happy patchwork of colour and texture. All I have to do is look up and smile!"

"I have an eye for unearthing hidden gems at estate sales and flea markets," says Susan, who resells items in her Etsy shop. "I'm always on the hunt for vintage treasures to repurpose into something unique to share with my customers. I believe that there is magic in these items—they have a heart, a soul, a presence, good karma and stories to tell. These relics say, 'Look at me, use me, enjoy me; I have a long life left and I will make you happy.'" ❖

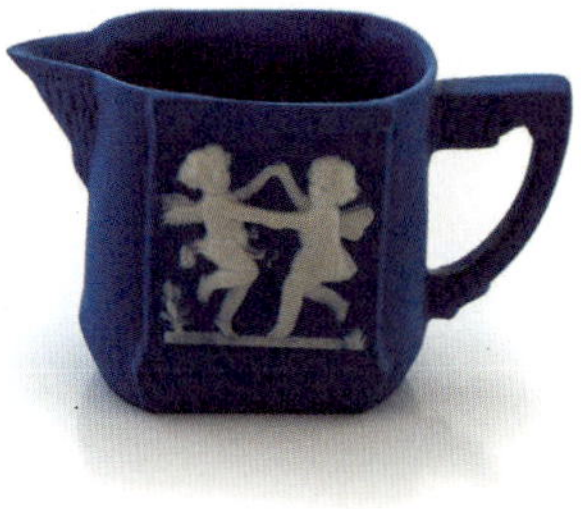
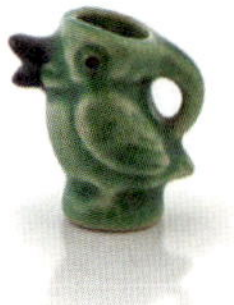
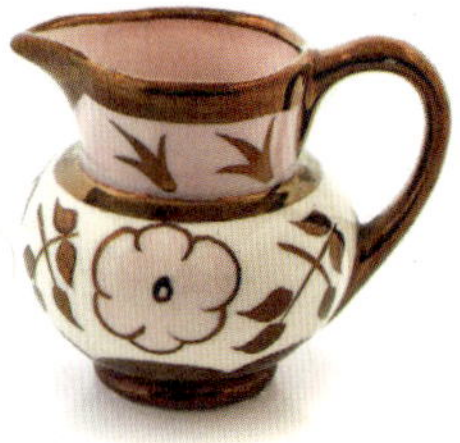
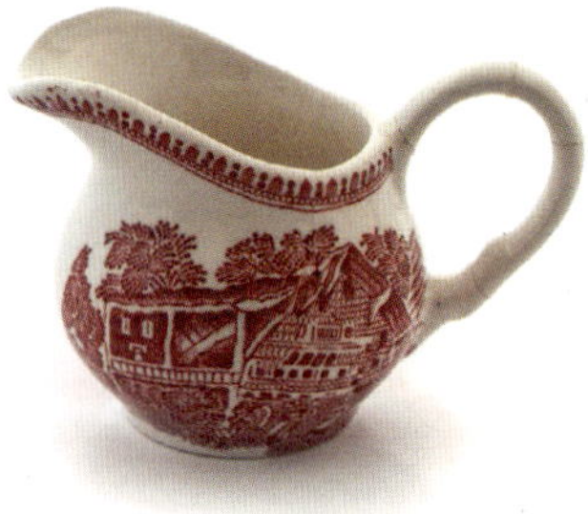
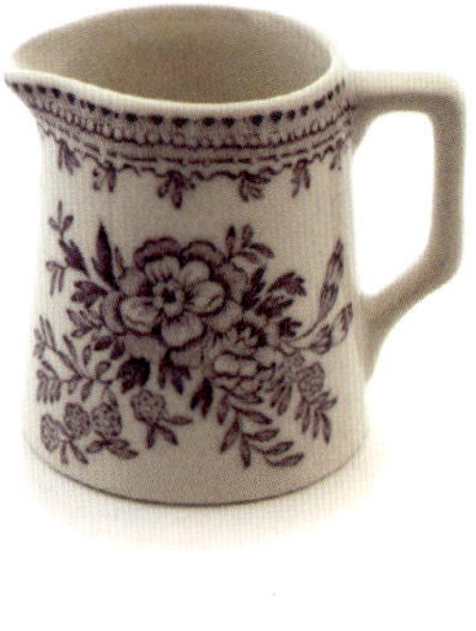
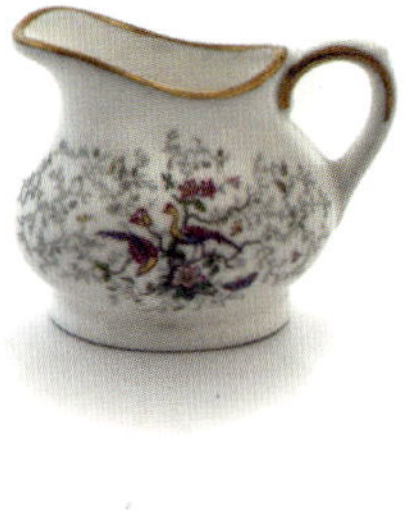

OBJECT OBSESSION

Stout Jugs & Creamers

by

CYNTHIA BOYD

The wonderful thing about collecting vintage items is that one can be as focussed or as broad as one prefers—and there's always more to discover in the world around us. Cynthia Boyd, from St. John's, Newfoundland, describes walking through an antique shop, a flea market or church jumble sale: "My eye will catch sight of a stout china creamer or pottery jug wedged in among other dishes, and I'm smitten." These tiny ceramics are just mere inches tall. "A tiny jug with an English country scene is a treasure, though I am more partial to one featuring a simple solid glaze of brown or green. A miniature creamer in look-alike Wedgwood blue began my collection 20 years ago, followed by an even tinier green jug in the shape of a chirping bird; both of these once belonged to long-lost doll's china tea sets. England's potteries such as Coalport, Burleigh and Aynsley, among others, have historically been recognized for producing china sets, but the finite detail characteristic of large pieces is also evident on the smallest of jugs and creamers. It is intriguing to discover how many of these were created as children's playthings, designed to teach them—by way of imitation—everyday traditions like taking tea in the afternoon. Others are truly a delightful distraction for women like me, whose children have grown but whose nesting habits are continually evolving." ❉

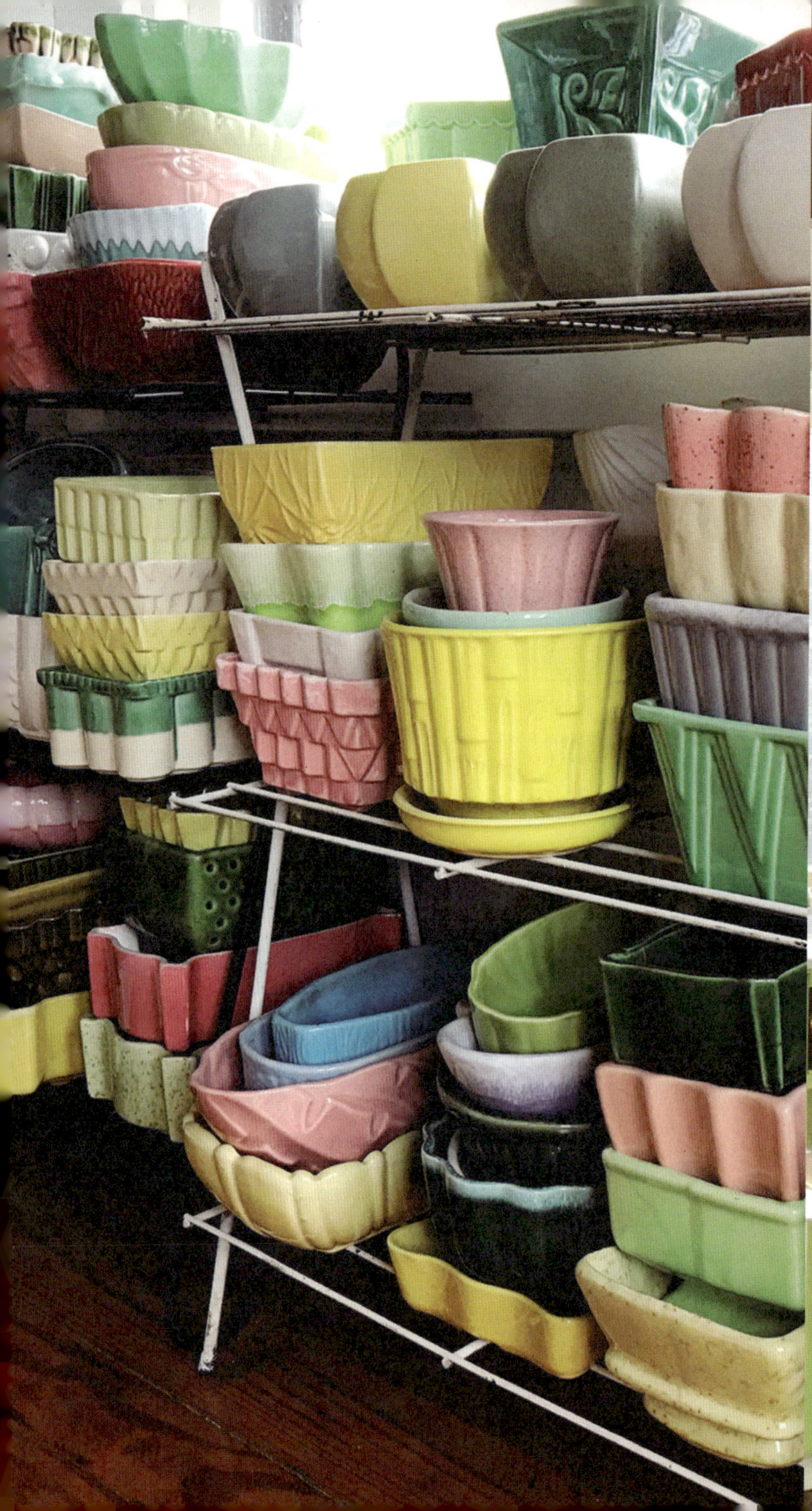
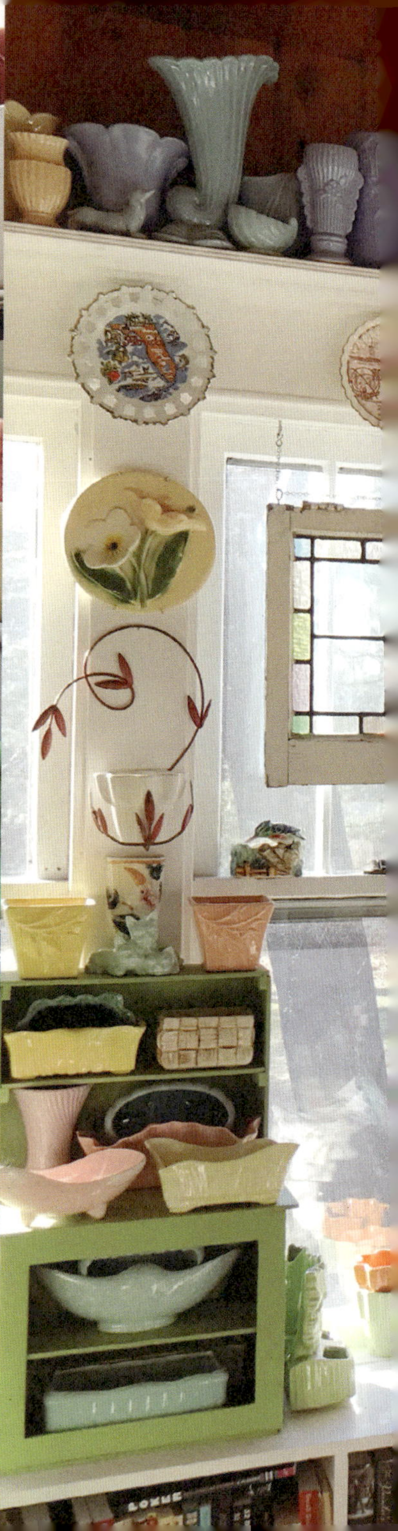

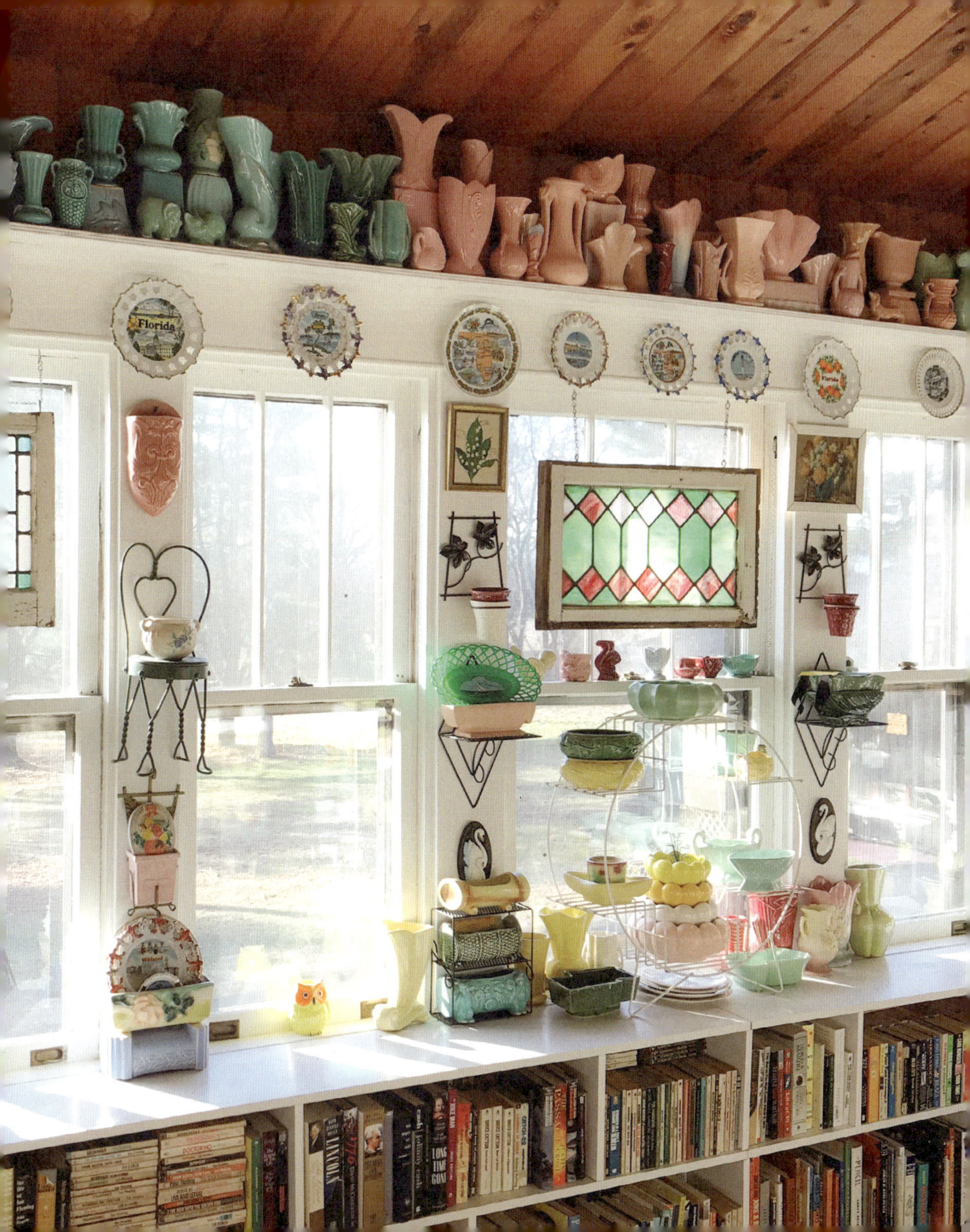
Florida
Florida

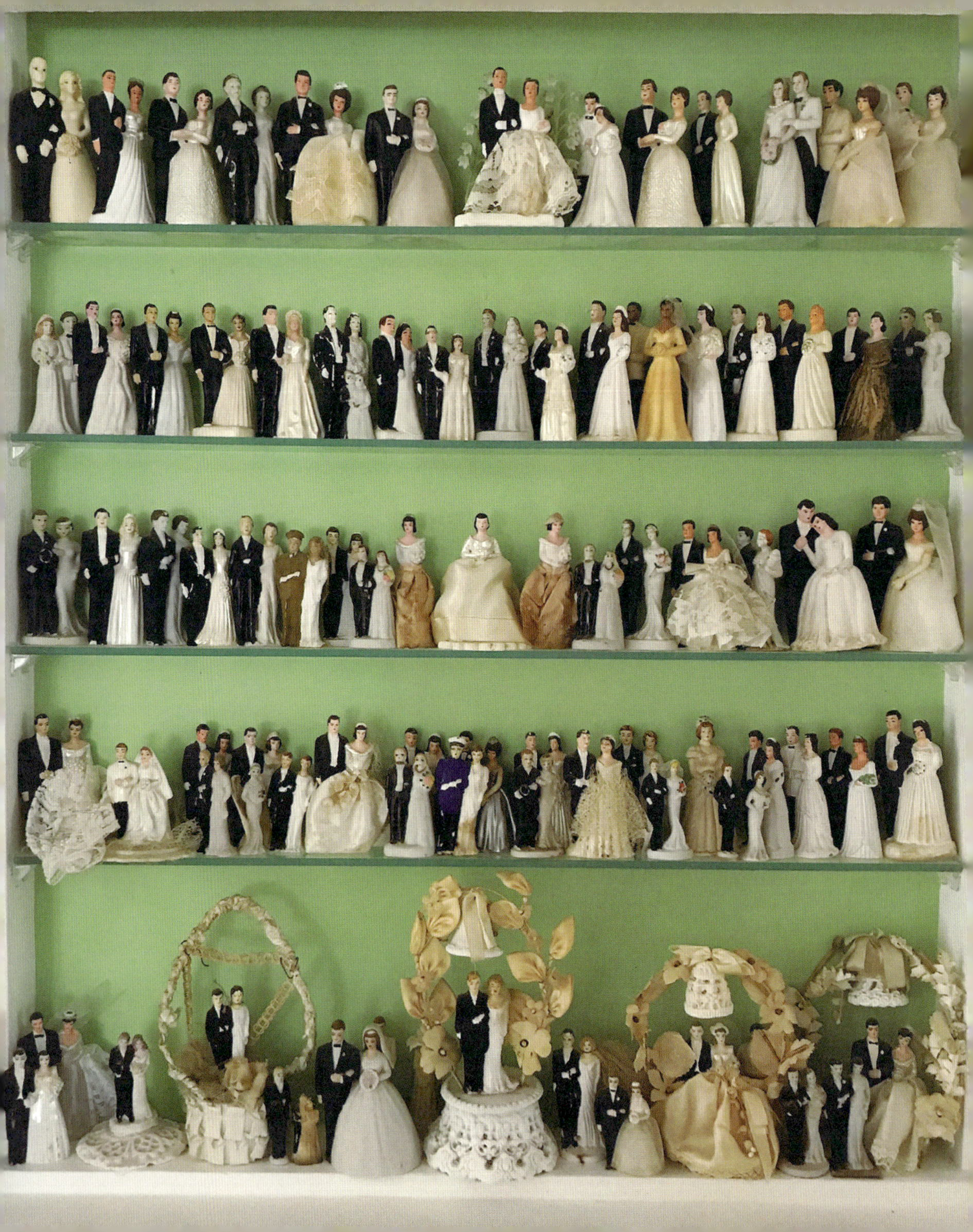

Second Presbyterian Church
La Rue
ELM LODGE
No 53
Thompson
BOWLES
Bickford's
Thompson
Thompson's
The Berghoff
Stickney's
Ford
Thompson's
The Berghoff
WHITE TOWER
Thompson's
Thompson's
Thompson's
Thompson's

STREATHAM HIGH ROAD, S.W.16.
DULWICH VILLAGE
ELECTRIC AVENUE
KENNINGTON OVAL SE11
BLACK PRINCE ROAD
BOROUGH OF ST PANCRAS EUSTON ROAD N.W.1
WATSON ST S.E.8
KENNINGTON ROAD
VAN GOGH WALK
CLAPHAM ROAD
DRAYCOTT PLACE
BRICK LANE E.1.
ALBERT EMBANKMENT
ALBERT SQUARE S.W.8
HIGH ST
AVE MARIA LANE EC4
CITY OF LONDON
IVERNA GARDENS, W.8.
STREATHAM HILL, S.W.2.
BOW STREET WC2
ASTORIA WALK S.W.9
MITCHAM LANE S.W.
GOWERS WALK, E.
THREADNEEDLE STREET EC2
KENNINGTON LANE.
LIBERTY STREET. SW.9
NOEL STREET
VOLTAIRE ROAD S.W.
LONG ACRE
LIVERPOOL ROAD N.
BOROUGH OF BATTERSEA PORTSLADE ROAD
LAMBETH WALK
NEWPORT STREET S.E.11
TABERNACLE STREET
NEBRASKA ST
Borough of St. Marylebone HARLEY STREET W.1.
FRYING PAN ALLEY E.1

OBJECT OBSESSION

Street Nameplates

by
GEORGE WRIGHT

atelierworks.co.uk/wayfinding
@londonstreetnameplates

At Atelier Works, a London-based design agency, George Wright was involved in a wayfinding and urban renewal project for the London Borough of Lambeth. "Unlike many cities, such as Paris or New York, where you will see a uniform set of street signs, London is different," describes George. "For over a century, each of the 30 London boroughs has been responsible for the installation of street nameplates in their neighbourhood. This has led to a huge and varied range of design types and styles; signs made from cast iron, vitreous enamel, pressed aluminium—even opaline glass and timber."

"I commissioned a graphic designer to revive the style of lettering found on original 1930s Lambeth enamel signs." That particular project led to the creation of a font, Northwood, to use in borough signage. It also began a personal collection when new nameplates meant that old ones were to be removed. "I discovered that all the old signs were going to be scrapped, made friends with the man coordinating the removals and so it began. Suddenly I was the proud owner of some gorgeous vintage signs, including Edwardian cast iron and 1930s vitreous enamel. Viewing them close up, I saw the lettering had been done by hand and began to appreciate the importance of proper letter spacing. These old signs are beautiful examples of skilled product design, something that's missing in many contemporary street signs. I started looking on auction sites and my collection grew. Current favourites include a glass Noel Street, the quirky lettering of Liberty Street and the subtle difference of each Kennington Lane 'N.'"

Through this collection, George met fellow graphic designer and photographer Alistair Hall, who shares George's enthusiasm for the rich array of street nameplates in London. Alistair's Instagram feed *@londonstreetnameplates* documents his new discoveries; he's also writing a book on the subject. ✼

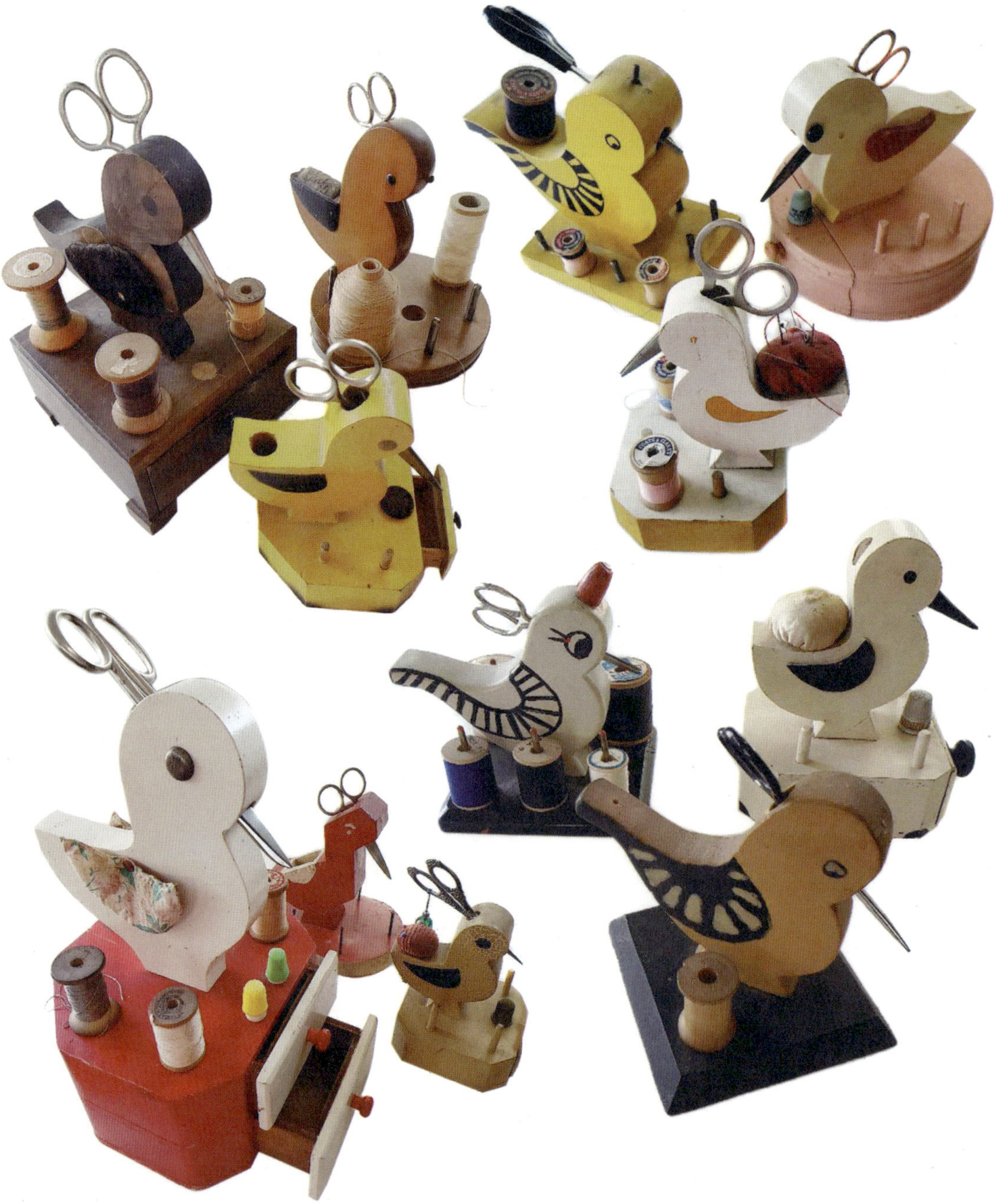

OBJECT OBSESSION

Sewing Ducks

by

NANCY JOHNSTON

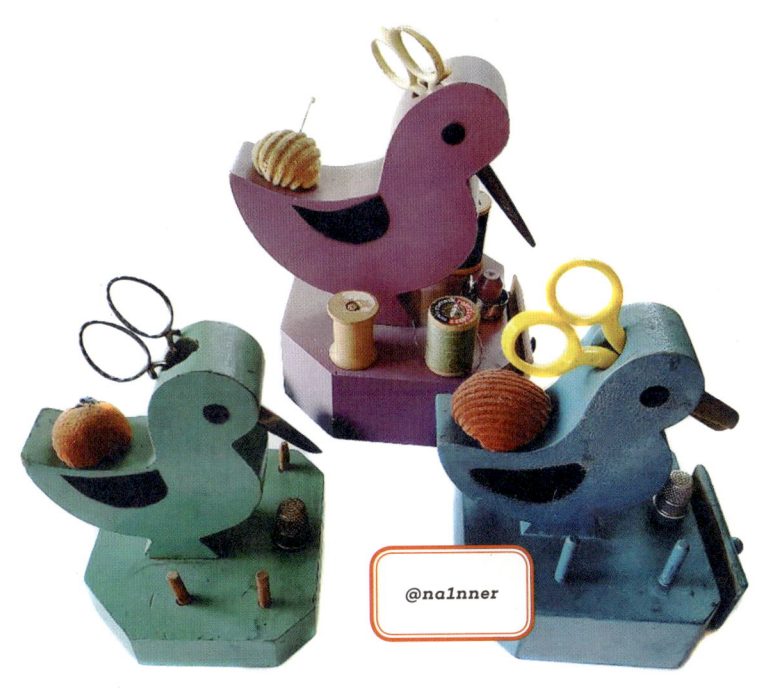

@na1nner

When we're sewing, sometimes we need to exercise our imagination against the tedium of mending, hemming or patchwork. What better companion than a wooden sewing duck! Scissor blades become its beak and other features hold spools of thread and tape measures. For Nancy Johnston of Lansing, Michigan, a fondness for these little birds dates back to her childhood in the 1950s and lazy days spent at her grandmother's house. "She had a little orange duck she kept by her rocking chair and mending basket," Nancy says. "On it was a couple of spools of thread; a small, ornate set of scissors; and a tiny silver thimble. I played with the duck as a very small toddler and was fascinated by its utility as I grew older. When I started seeing them now and then in an antique store, I heard them whisper to me. So adoption was mandatory, over and over!" Now she has quite a sweet family of ducklings. "They really are adorable on my shelves." ✣

Pikes Peak
ALTITUDE 14,110 FEET
Colorado
CHICAGO
O'HARE AIRPORT
JOHN HANCOCK CENTER
THE FIRST NAT'L BANK BUILDING
Washington
MOUNT RAINIER
STATE CAPITOL OLYMPIA
SEATTLE
APPLE
SALMON
GRAND COULEE DAM
SEATTLE WORLD'S FAIR
SPACE NEEDLE

OBJECT OBSESSION

Souvenir Plates

by
SNOWDEN FLOOD

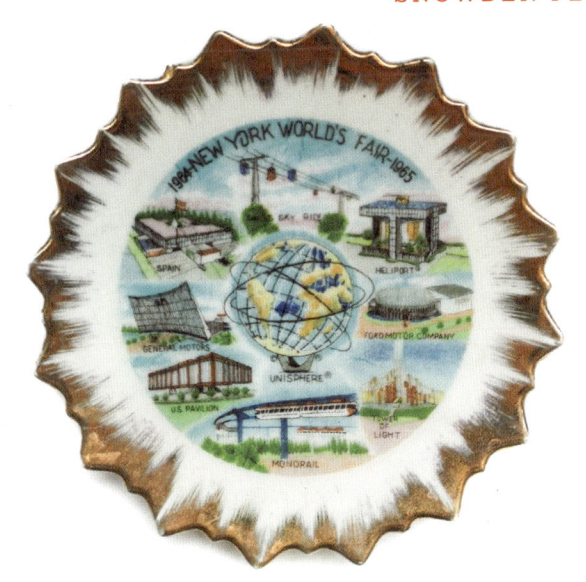

"When we visit or live somewhere we make a kind of connection with that place and it can become invested with a lot of meaning for us. So souvenirs and mementos are important, wonderful things that can bring back so many feelings and memories."

snowdenflood.com
@snowdenflood

Snowden Flood is a collector of collections—"I have many!" she says from her London home. One significant collection is her collection of American souvenir plates, since it had a big influence on her business. She designs and manufactures high-quality gifts and souvenirs, made in the United Kingdom, featuring British natural motifs and landmarks incorporated onto tableware and art prints.

"Growing up in the UK with American parents, to me objects from 'back home' had an almost mystical significance," she explains. "I particularly remember the excitement when their belongings were shipped over and finally unpacked, five years after they'd moved." She notes that this is perhaps how she grew to associate stories and memories with objects.

"As an adult, I moved to New York City and I often felt homesick for the UK. During my 10 years living in the States, I sometimes visited London and looked in vain for beautiful souvenirs to bring back from my trips. But I could never find anything I liked! They always seemed to be badly designed, of horrid quality and usually made so far away from the place that was selling them."

Moving back to London, Snowden set out to design her own souvenirs, working with local manufacturers. "The objects I made, inspired in part by this collection, resonated with people and sold all over the world." ✼

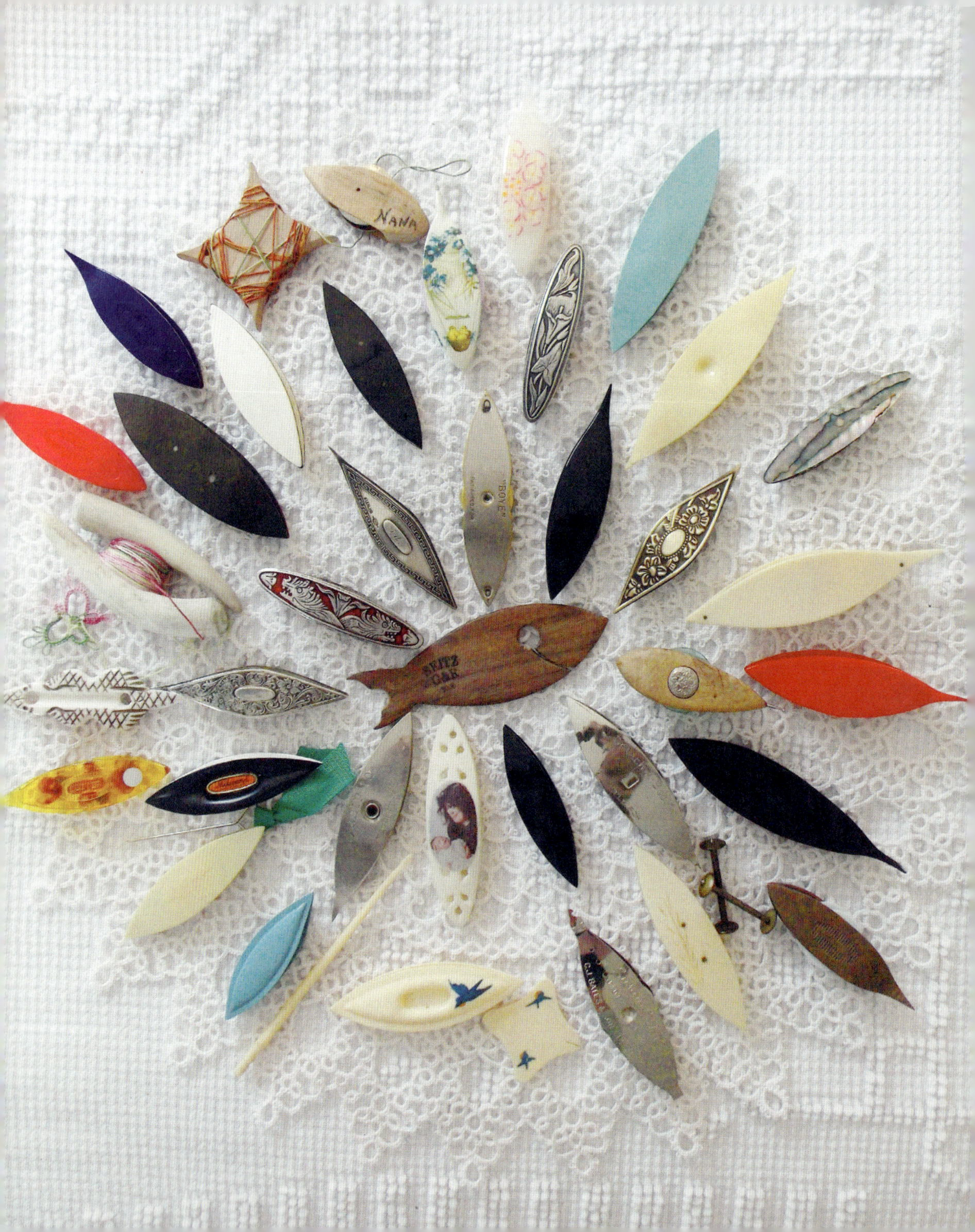
NANA
"BOYE"

OBJECT OBSESSION

Tatting Shuttles

by

DOROTHY A. COCHRAN

> "I always wonder who owned them previously and what project they made: a pair of baby booties for a special little one, an edging on a hanky, a doily or perhaps embellishment for a child's dress."

Dorothy A. Cochran of Bon Aqua, Tennessee, collects tatting shuttles. Tatting is a lacemaking technique that likely originated in the early 19th century. A shuttle is used to hold the wound thread and to move the thread through the necessary motions to create loops and knots. "Contrary to what some say," says Dorothy, "tatting is definitely not a dying art but alive and well today all around the world. There are tatting shuttle groups online for folks like myself and we love sharing our love of shuttles with our fellow tatters. Shuttle tatting does require a measurable amount of patience, I suppose, but I would recommend you give it a try and you just might find a new love in crafting. A project can take as little as one hour or as long as one year."

"Tatting shuttles can be over 100 years old and still perform as they did the day they were made. Shuttles are found in many different materials such as sterling silver, Gersilver (metal, but not really silver at all), bone, ivory, celluloid, resin, plastic, wood, abalone shell, mother of pearl, even rubber, and also in a wide array of colours. Some given away as company advertisements or sold for very little may today fetch hundreds because of their rarity. I love them all and each time I purchase one for my collection, I try to make at least one project with that shuttle before leaving it for display."

"A tatting shuttle can be bought today for as little as $2.50," advises Dorothy, "or if you are into collecting the rare, you might pay upwards of $1,000… so there's something for everyone, and this is one of the things I love about shuttles." ❖

Saturday's child works hard for a living

Eve Started
it all

A B C D E F G H I J K L M N O P Q R S T U V W X Y Z
BASSEREAU
DRY SHERRY
MARTINI
ROUYER
Van der Hum
VAT 69

Your move !
Wash up !

OBJECT OBSESSION

Tea Towels

by

CINDY FUNK

Chances are you've dried dishes with a printed dishtowel, but did you stop to admire its illustration and design? Cindy Funk of Decatur, Illinois, did notice this display of art and design—and has collected over a thousand tea towels in a large variety of subject matter, from animals, travel, cocktails, food, calendars and more.

"The variety of vintage printed tea towels is astounding," she says. "I'm still finding new designs after 15 years of collecting. I love them for elevating a utilitarian kitchen item to an art form. Their sense of nostalgia is what initially attracted me and their artistry fuelled my passion for them."

For folks who love colour and vintage graphics, Cindy's Etsy shop is the place to be. "I specialize in vintage linens from the mid-century with printed graphics in appealing patterns and colours. My shop is busy, bright and loaded with pattern. I have something for everyone, from the casual shopper who wants a nifty towel to brighten their kitchen to the serious collector who is looking for a rare textile to add to their stash. Hopefully you will have as much fun looking (and shopping) as I did hunting and gathering." ✤

"I'm partial to anything with appealing graphics that puts a smile on my face or strikes a nostalgic chord."

neatokeen.etsy.com
@neatokeen

TEA TOWELS 433

TELEVISION
SERVICE
FREEVIEW
CHANNEL 15
TV SCENES
TELEVISION
Plastic
TELEVISION
JERSEY

OBJECT OBSESSION

Tiny Toy Televisions

by

JANE HOUSHAM

janehousham.co.uk
@foundandchosen

Painter, collagist, author—Jane Housham has a universal rule: "If I find I've got three of something, I call that a new collection." Jane can name two factors that influence some collections to become more dominant than others: "Firstly, I need to find particular objects especially appealing, but secondly, there needs to be enough different exemplars of the object in the world to enable the collection to grow vigorously. When it comes to tiny televisions, these two circumstances have joyfully conspired to make possible a collection numbering hundreds."

"The television is an iconic object in popular culture and I love it for that. When TV was first invented in the early 20th century, a set was as exotic as a rocket ship and beyond the pockets of most. To own a television was a marker of affluence, and even in the 1950s, when televisions became more affordable and began to appear in ordinary homes, they were still objects of desire. Screens grew ever larger and there was always a bigger, better model to aspire to. Thus it was always pleasing to own little stand-in tellies; pencil sharpeners, cigarette lighters, jewellery boxes and so many other TV-shaped objects proliferated throughout the second half of the 20th century. The most modern doll houses had TVs, the best tourist resorts had TV-shaped souvenirs, and you could save for your new, bigger TV in a TV-shaped money box. In cahoots with David, my husband, I lovingly collect them all. The advent of television brought moving pictures into our living rooms and, later, the delight of collecting tiny TVs into my heart." ✤

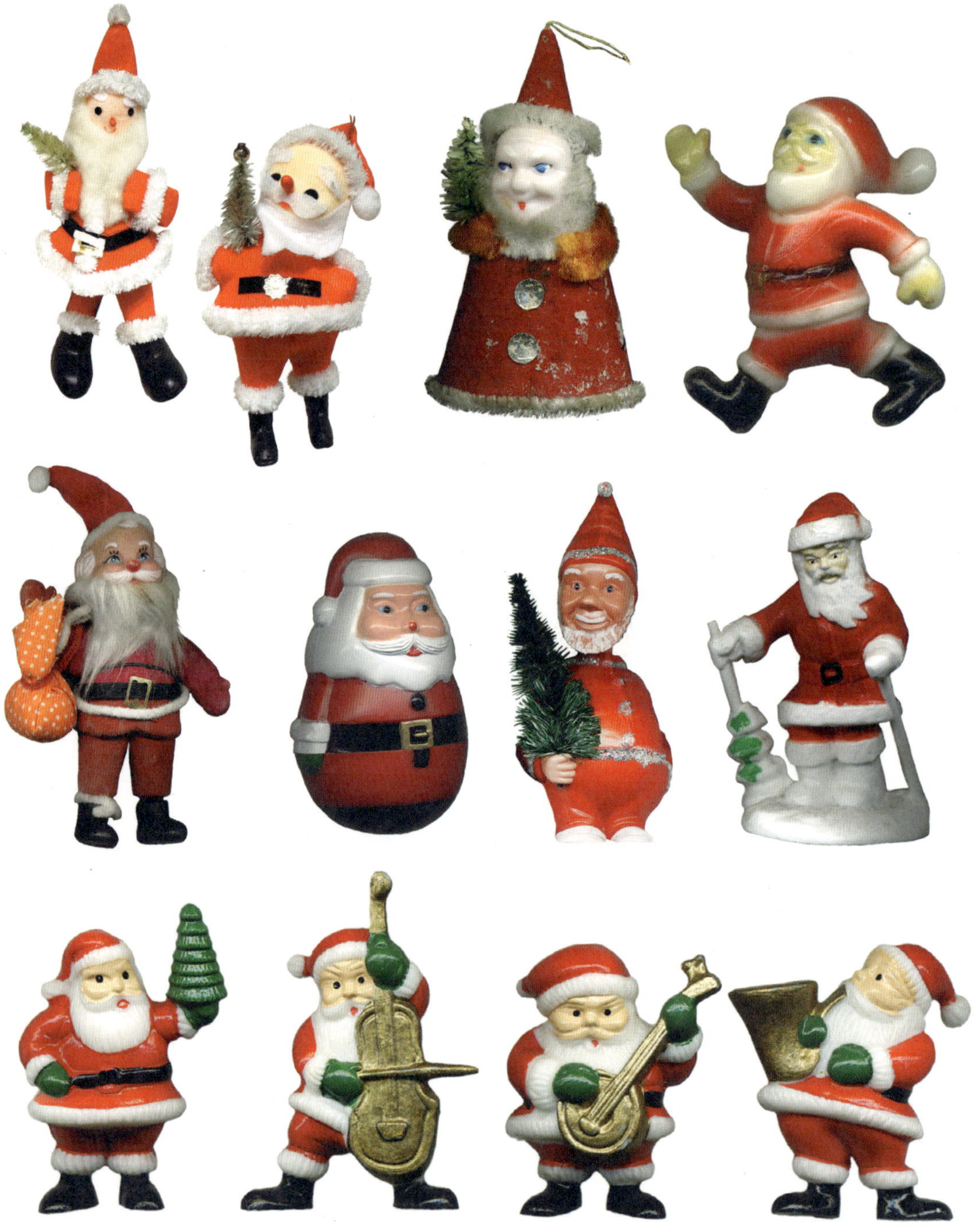

OBJECT OBSESSION

Santas

by
JEAN CAMERON

@jeanniecameron

Collecting seasonal decorations is a particularly nostalgic activity. For Jean Cameron, she attributes her infatuation with Santa Claus to her upbringing. "I think it must be because I grew up with English parents in a strange country, the Netherlands, where Christmas was hardly celebrated when I was small," she says. The Dutch typically celebrate Sinterklaas, St. Nicholas' Day, on December 6. On December 25, Jean and her family exchanged Christmas presents and filled pillowcases, set up Christmas trees and made Christmas pudding, mince pies and cake with Santa cake toppings. She started collecting Santas in her late teens and has since amassed around 300. "It makes me so happy when I find a really old one—I think only people who collect things will understand this. I only collect vintage ones now." ❉

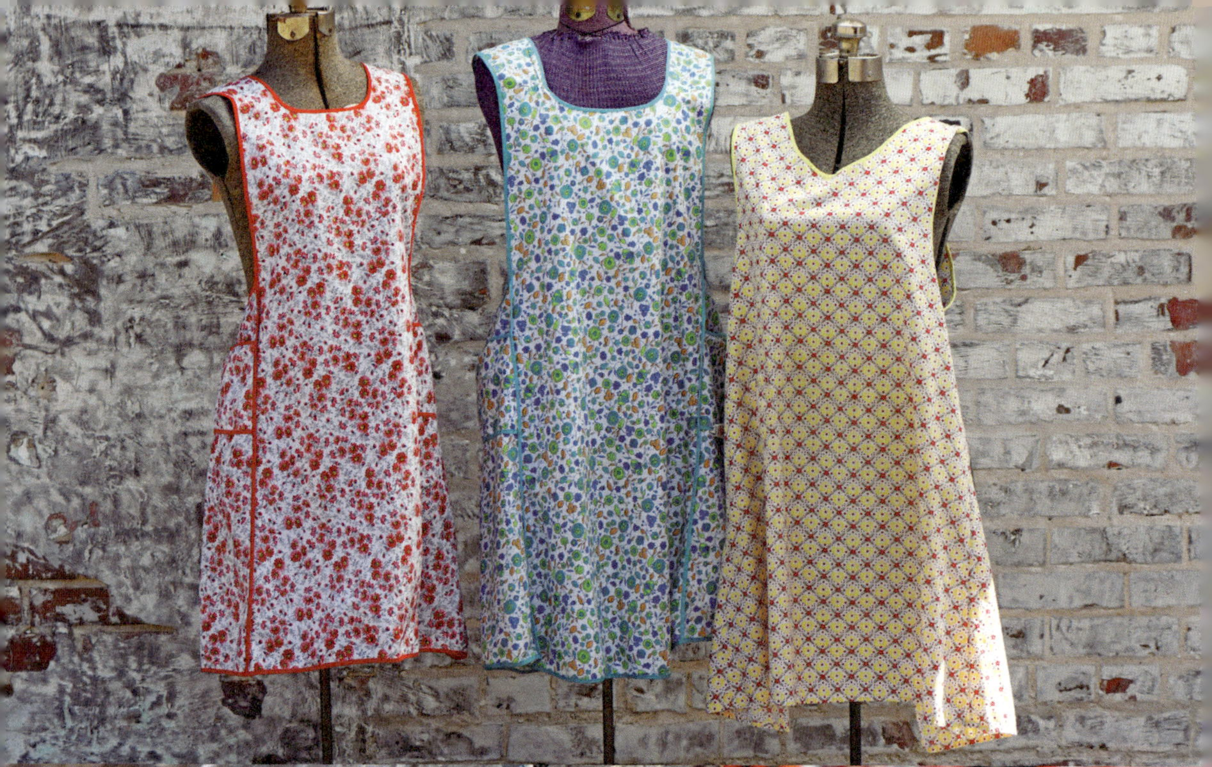

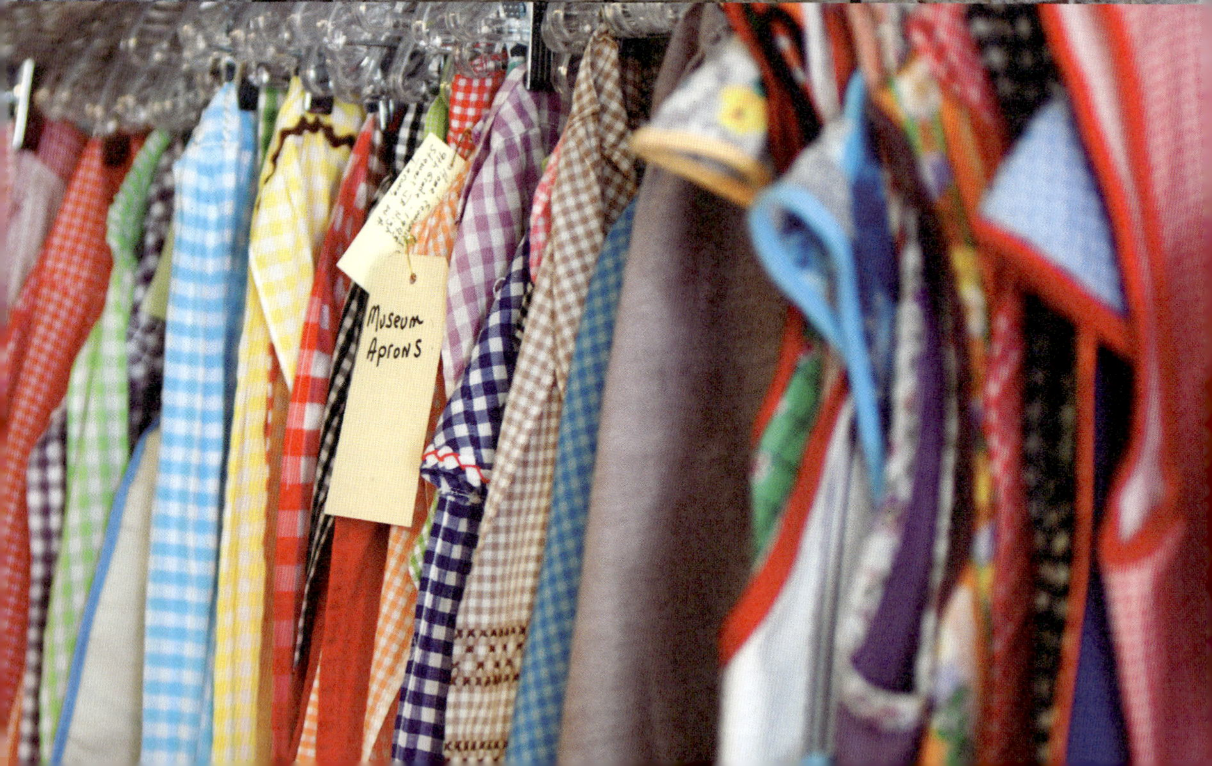
Museum
Aprons

OBJECT OBSESSION

Aprons

by

CAROLYN TERRY

"Humans have always needed aprons, in some form, since the beginning of history. The styles and materials have evolved with changes in fashion, social customs and the economy. Aprons of each generation offer a history lesson."

Despite serendipitously becoming the owner and curator of the world's first Apron Museum, located in Iuka, Mississippi, Carolyn Terry doesn't think of herself as an apron collector.

"At a young age, I explored museums and shops, allowing the sights and smells to absorb into my memory," she says. "Apron collecting began as a desire to hold onto these memories. Ultimately, the gathering of thoughts and impressions cultivated my appreciation for aprons—and the people who wear them." She likens each apron to a poem.

Her first apron was made by her Grandma Hester from Mississippi when Carolyn was seven or eight years old. "My sister received an identical one. Mine got stained with green paint, which was how I could tell it apart from my sister's, because hers was never stained."

Much later, at age 55, Carolyn moved to Iuka. "I discovered how aprons have the ability to engage people and spark conversation. This is when the collection expanded rapidly. A recurring idea expressed by collectors was that someone needed to open an apron museum. And thus a historic building we owned was converted into the first museum in the world dedicated to aprons."

"This particular museum is arranged to facilitate hands-on interaction with the exhibits. Some of the aprons are part of the permanent collection, including garments donated from all over the United States (and a few from other countries). The shop offers aprons for sale, including new and vintage. Visitors are allowed to try on different styles and remark at the patterns, fabrics and stitching. Aprons have changed in form and function through the years, and the museum features examples of various styles dating back several generations. Some displays are labelled by geographic region or other distinguishing characteristics. Visitors should come ready to see, feel and be inspired." ✣

PHOTOS BY KIM ROBERTS, HOUCK PORTRAITS, OPAL LOVELACE

APRONS 439

"Just as a poem is more than syllables arranged on a page, an apron is greater than the sum of its parts. Each garment is a lasting tribute to the person who wore it. Like the green stain on my grandma's apron, sometimes the flaws are what make something extra special, like souvenirs of a life well-lived. Show someone a collection of aprons, and it will spark conversations about people and places they love. This demure garment is textile poetry."

facebook.com/ApronMuseum

To hell with the diet!

VINTAGE APRONS FOR SALE

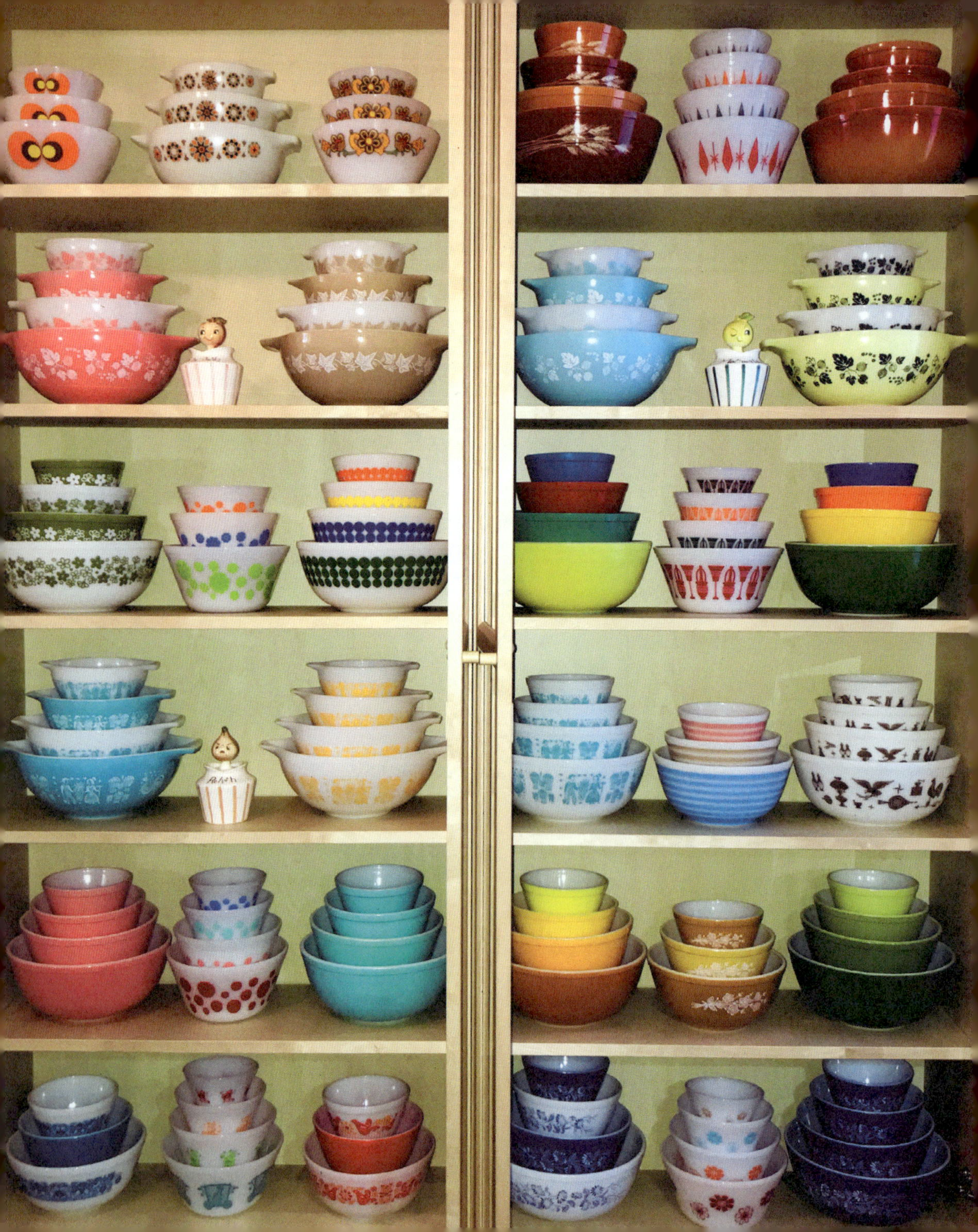

OBJECT OBSESSION

Pyrex

by

JACQUELINE GORING

@jagharp

Jacqueline Goring remembers the day: "It was December 2012, and I wandered up to this quirky store around the corner from me that sold electronics on one side and antiques on the other. I was looking around when I spotted the Pyrex White Daisy pattern. I can honestly say, it was love at first sight." She purchased the White Daisy divided dish, the White Daisy large oval casserole and a set of pink Gooseberry Cinderella bowls. "That was it," she says, "I was hooked and I started spending time researching vintage Pyrex online."

"Pyrex became an obsession, I learned about standard patterns, promotional patterns, rare patterns and other companies that held the patent for Pyrex such as JAJ Pyrex in England and Agee in Australia and New Zealand. The rabbit hole went deeper and I started collecting other companies such as Fire-King, Federal Glass, Hazel Atlas and Schott–Mainz Jenaer Glas. Being a Canadian, I was especially interested in the Pyrex that was briefly made at the Corning Glassworks of Canada plant in Leaside from 1946 to 1954. I love all the colours and designs, each one reflecting a different era from the 1940s to the 1980s."

While visiting her mother one day—and talking obsessively about vintage Pyrex, her mother looked at her and said, "Do you mean that set of coloured bowls?", referring to a classic set of multicoloured bowls. Jacqueline rushed over to the kitchen: "I realized that I had grown up with Pyrex, the largest yellow bowl was for potato salad and she used the smaller red bowl for her bean salad. The family set of multicoloured bowls had been bought and given to my grandmother by her aunt, then handed down to my mother and me." ❊

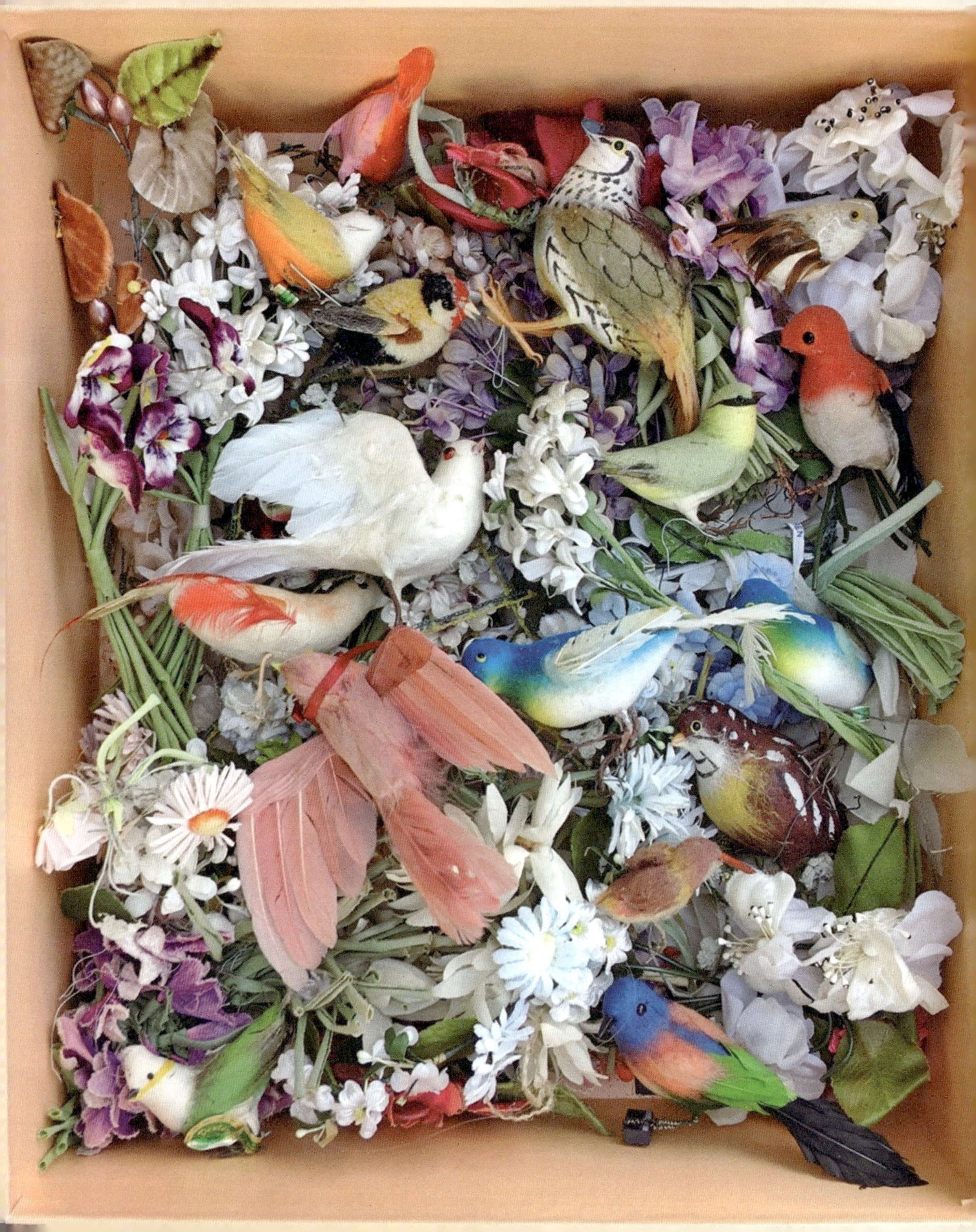

OBJECT OBSESSION

Millinery Florals & Birds

by
KATIE BAKER

@jkatiebaker

In days past, hats, bonetts and corsages used to complete a woman's attire. Milliners would fashion imaginative hats with florals, fruits and feathers—and, in the Victorian era, sometimes entire birds and taxidermied creatures. The plume trade was dire for many bird species, and protests for humane treatment emerged. Englishwomen Emily Williamson and Eliza Phillips co-founded a movement to end "murderous millinery" in 1891 with the foundation of what would become the Royal Society for the Protection of Birds.

Silk and synthetic flowers remained fashionable choices, and though millinery has become a specialized craft, the supplies and adornments of hatmaking are easy to find at flea markets and vintage sales.

Katie Baker, a lifelong sewer, has collected these artifacts of millinery, not for making hats but for the enjoyment of admiring their beauty. "I do use bits and pieces of them in my crafts sometimes, too. I love that they often have leaves and/or petals made of beautiful, worn velvet, and the birds have such personality." ✻

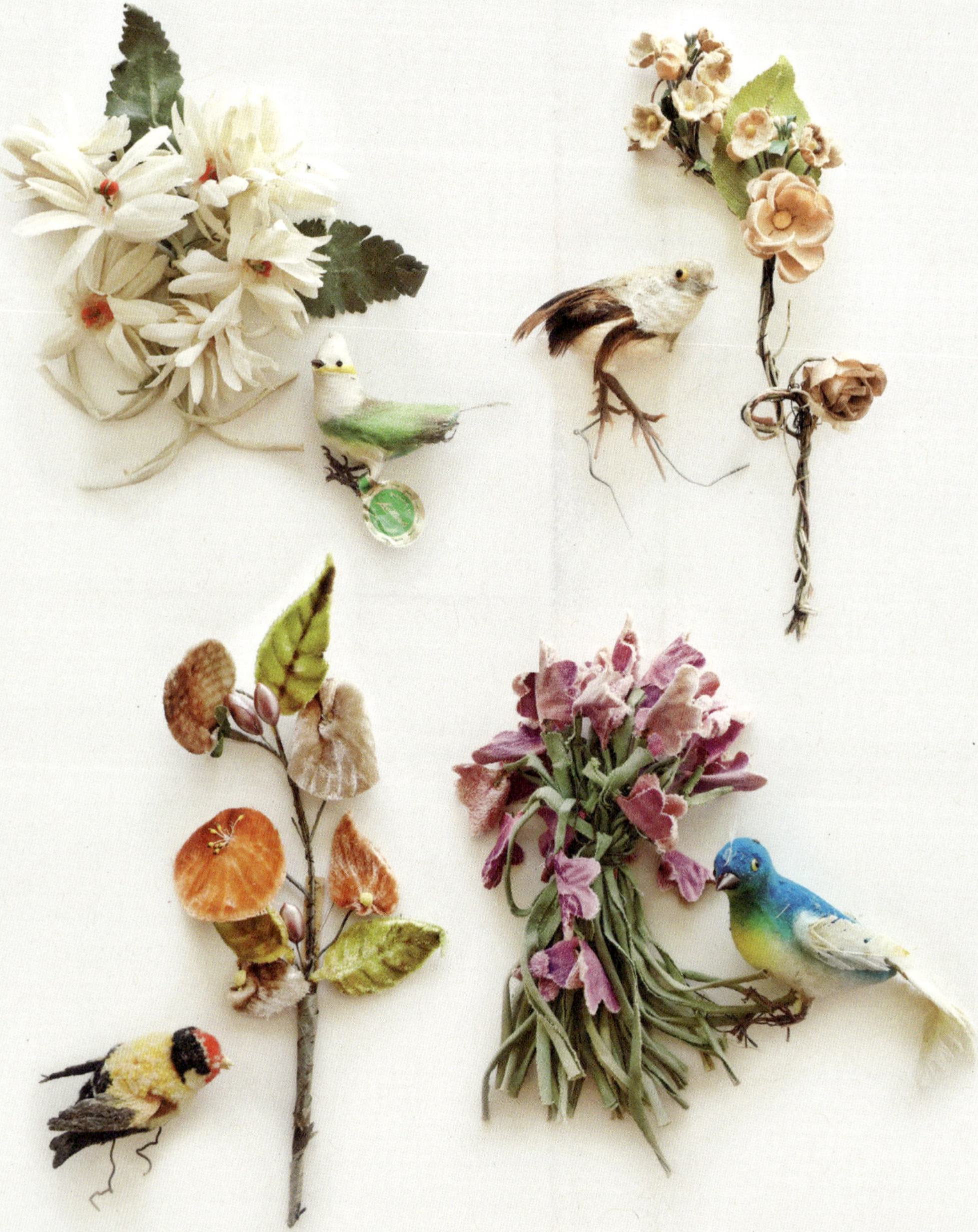

PHOTO BY KATIE BAKER